I0096011

HISTORY

OF

THE LUTHERAN CHURCH

IN

VIRGINIA AND EAST TENNESSEE

THE BIRTHPLACE OF LUTHERANISM IN VIRGINIA
Hebron Church (in the cluster of trees at left above) near Madison, Va.

HISTORY

OF

The Lutheran Church

IN

Virginia and East Tennessee

Edited by C. W. CASSELL, W. J. FINCK,
and ELON O. HENKEL

Published by the Authority of the Lutheran
Synod of Virginia

Clearfield Company
Baltimore, Maryland

Originally published by
Shenandoah Publishing House, Inc.
Strasburg, Virginia, 1930

Copyright © 1930
Shenandoah Publishing House, Inc.
Strasburg, Virginia

Reprinted for Clearfield Company by
Genealogical Publishing Company
Baltimore, Maryland
2009

ISBN 978-0-8063-5444-6

Made in the United States of America

Dedication

❧

"TO THE CHURCH IN THY HOUSE"
AND TO
THE CONGREGATIONS
OF
THE LUTHERAN SYNOD OF VIRGINIA
WE DEDICATE
THIS VOLUME

PREFACE

THE publication of this volume is the work of the Lutheran Synod of Virginia, through the Committee on Centennial and History. Following the organization of the Synod in 1922, the Rev. C. W. Cassell, of the former Virginia Synod, the Rev. L. A. Fox, D. D., of the former Southwestern Virginia Synod, and the Rev. F. M. Harr of the former Holston Synod, were constituted a committee to gather and put in book form the history of the three merging bodies. Dr. Fox having been removed by death in 1925, and in this same year the Virginia Conference of the former Tennessee Synod having become a part of the Lutheran Synod of Virginia, the committee was enlarged and charged with this two fold duty, namely, to provide for a fitting celebration of the centennial of the organization of the oldest of the three merging Synods, the former Virginia Synod in 1929, and to prepare and publish a history of the Synod as a memorial of the Centennial year. The Committee as it was constituted at the 1929 convention of Synod consists of the Rev. C. W. Cassell, Luray; the Rev. W. J. Finck, D. D., New Market; the Rev. W. P. Huddle, Staunton; the Rev. C. Brown Cox, D. D., Pulaski; the Rev. F. M. Harr, Crockett; the Rev. W. R. Brown, Rural Retreat; Prof. W. F. Morehead, Salem; Mr. Elon O. Henkel, New Market; and the Hon. O. V. Pence, Woodstock.

The Centennial Celebration was held at Woodstock, July 24-26, 1929, and is duly chronicled in Part I of this volume.

The general plan of the book is that proposed by the Chairman, and adopted by the Committee. Part I is wholly the work of Dr. W. J. Finck. Part II is the work of the Chairman of the Committee, except that the sketches of the congregations in East Tennessee were written by the Rev. F. M. Harr. Very much of the material for the sketches was furnished by the pastors and interested laymen, and several of them are published almost as they were written by those sending the data. Part III is the joint labor of Dr. Finck and the Chairman. Part IV was written by Mrs. W. F. Morehead, President of the Women's Missionary Society of The United Lutheran Church in America. Part V was prepared by the Chairman.

The Committee recognizes the incompleteness of the work. The want of time and space forbade including much that was greatly desired. We should like to have had longer and fuller congregational sketches. The brevity of many of them is due to our inability to secure the facts for the full story of their life. A number were constructed altogether from the data gleaned from the Minutes of Synod. Since the early Minutes do not, in very many cases, give the names of congregations, or group them in parishes, or note their admission into Synod, nor the building of churches, it is rather difficult to write even a brief history of a congregation from these records alone. We have faithfully used all material obtainable, and repeated efforts were made to secure that which is lacking. In a few cases original Church Records were provided.

The listing of the names of those who have belonged to the merging Synods and the Virginia Conference, presented many difficulties, since so very often the records do not show how and whence members were received, nor the manner of their removal. It must ever be borne in mind that each of these bodies lived and wrought during the Civil War. It is to their great credit that the records were preserved at all.

We should like to have had a series of biographical sketches, and pictures of the men, especially of the early leaders. This could not be, with the space and time at our disposal. The cuts of churches are those furnished by the congregations themselves, or they have been made from pictures sent us for that purpose. We have chosen to insert pictures of churches and institutions, rather than of pastors and other leaders.

The largest single source from which we have drawn the material is the Minutes of the Synods and of the Conference. Fortunately we had access to a complete file of each of these. Published accounts of Synodical and Congregational anniversaries, and published addresses delivered on such occasions have proved helpful. Histories of congregations, especially that of Hebron church in Madison County, by the Rev. W. P. Huddle, and histories of groups of congregations, such as that of the churches in Botetourt County, by the Rev. E. W. Leslie, have also proved of value. A scrap book of clippings of church news covering a period of about two-score years, belonging to one of the Committee, was brought into use. Histories of Synods in adjoining states, the historical works of Dr. J. W. Wayland, the writer of the beautiful Introduction to this volume, and the writings of other Virginia historians, have been used to an advantage. We are glad to record and express our grateful appreciation of the fine cooperation of the pastors, interested laymen, heads of institutions and Synodical authorities. Last, though not least, the ripe judgment of Mr. Elon O. Henkel, an experienced printer and publisher, has been of great value in the editing, and is hereby gratefully acknowledged.

We are not unmindful that in a work of this character there may be found errors and omissions. Such, if known, will be corrected in the copy belonging to the Synod, and kept for that purpose. It is our purpose to continue research work, and place the findings in the Archives of the Synod.

To us, this has been a labor of love, though it has been attended with great difficulties. There is no published history of either of these bodies, other than brief sketches or historical addresses, though it has long been desired. Efforts have been put forth heretofore at various times, but they have come to naught. We do not boast of success where others have failed, but we do wish to record our gratitude to the Heavenly Father who has used us as his agents in this Centennial year, to bring to realization the aspirations of the fathers, "A History of the Lutheran Church in Virginia and East Tennessee." If the possession and reading of this history will inspire the members of the Lutheran Synod of Virginia, those of today and those of tomorrow, to preach the Word and administer the Sacraments as faithfully as have their predecessors, the authors of this humble volume can rest assured that their labor has not been in vain.

C. W. CASSELL,
Chairman.

Luray, Virginia
Thanksgiving 1929

CONTENTS

PAGE

Preface _____ vii

Introduction by Dr. John W. Wayland _____ xv

Part I

History of Lutheranism in Virginia and East Tennessee xix

    Chapter I   The People _____ 1

    Chapter II The Pastors _____ 33

    Chapter III Organizations _____ 81

Part II

Historical Sketches of the Congregations of Synod ____153

Part III

History of the Educational Activities of Synod _____285

Part IV

Auxiliary Organizations of the Synod _____317

Part V

Tables _____341

LIST OF ILLUSTRATIONS

The Birthplace of Lutheranism in Virginia   *Frontispiece*

PAGE

Churches of Salem Congregation _____ 158

Mt. Hermon Lutheran Church, Newport, Va. _____ 161

Christ's Church, Staunton, Va. _____ 163

Grace Lutheran Church, Waynesboro, Va. _____ 164

Holy Trinity Lutheran Church, Lynchburg, Va. _____ 170

Gladesboro Lutheran Church _____ 171

Churches of Manassas Parish _____ 174

Grace Lutheran Church, Winchester, Va. _____ 176

Trinity Lutheran Church, Stephens City, Va. _____ 179

St. Paul's Lutheran Church, Fawcett's Gap, Va. _____ 180

First Evangelical Lutheran Church, Richmond, Va. _____ 185

Hebron Church, Madison, Va. _____ 186

Christ's Church, Radford, Va. _____ 192

First Lutheran Church, Norfolk, Va. _____ 194

Lutheran Churches of Page County, Va. _____196-197

College Church, Salem, Va. _____ 205

St. Mark's Lutheran Church, Roanoke, Va. _____ 206

Bethany Lutheran Church, Rockbridge County, Va. _____ 209

Rader's Church, Timberville, Va. _____ 215

Muhlenberg Church, Harrisonburg, Va. _____ 217

Churches of New Market Parish _____ 220

Churches of Forestville Parish _____ 222

Churches of Orkney Springs Parish _____ 227

Emanuel Lutheran Church, Woodstock, Va. _____ 230

Emanuel Lutheran Church, Woodstock, Va. (1803) _____ 231

Mt. Calvary Lutheran Church, near Woodstock, Va. _____ 232

St. Paul's Lutheran Church, Strasburg, Va. _____ 234

Holy Trinity Lutheran Church, Newport News, Va. _____ 241

xiii

St. Paul's Lutheran Church, Wythe County, Va. _____ 244

Grace Lutheran Church, Rural Retreat, Va. _____ 245

Churches of Kimberlin Parish _____ 249

Holy Trinity Church, Wytheville, Va. _____ 250

Old St. John's Lutheran Church, near Wytheville, Va. _____ 251

St. Peter's Lutheran Church, Shepherdstown, W. Va. _____ 255

St. James' Lutheran Church, Uvilla, W. Va. _____ 256

Immanuel Lutheran Church, Bluefield, W. Va. _____ 260

Immanuel Lutheran Church, Blountville, Tenn. _____ 262

Church of the Ascension, Chattanooga, Tenn. _____ 267

St. James' Lutheran Church, Greene County, Tenn. _____ 270

Solomon's Lutheran Church, Greene County, Tenn. _____ 271

Holy Trinity Lutheran Church, Kingsport, Tenn. _____ 274

St. John's Church, Knoxville, Tenn. _____ 277

Roanoke College, Salem, Va. _____ 290

Marion Junior College, Marion, Va. _____ 295

Lutheran Orphan Home, Salem, Va. _____ 305

INTRODUCTION

IT IS eminently fitting that a region so rich in Lutheran history as Virginia and East Tennessee should have its record preserved in a volume of authentic character and comprehensive scope. The Lutherans have been making history, creditable history, in this region for two hundred years. To tell the story fully one volume is not adequate. If honor due were to be fairly accorded and tasks achieved completely chronicled, many large volumes would be necessary.

It seems probable that Adam Miller, now recognized as the pioneer settler in the upper Shenandoah Valley, was a Lutheran. Hebron Church, in Madison County, Va., has been continuously used since 1740, and is, so far as known, the oldest church of the denomination in America. The Henkel Press at New Market, Shenandoah County, Va., founded in 1806, is said to be the oldest establishment of its kind and to have issued more theological works, truly Lutheran in character, in the English language, than any other printing house in the world. From this press in 1851 came a monumental work—an English translation of the Christian Book of Concord, or Symbolical Books of the Evangelical Lutheran Church, the splendid consummation of a task of seven devoted years on the part of translators and editors, printers and binders; and in 1890 the same press brought forth an octavo volume of 275 pages by the Rev. Socrates Henkel, D. D., "The History of the Evangelical Lutheran Tennessee Synod." Other books of like character too numerous to mention here have issued from this press from time to time.

One of the most prolific authors in American literature was a young Lutheran, Samuel Mosheim Smucker (1823-1863), born in New Market, Virginia. Charles Porterfield Krauth (1823-1883) was also a native son, born the same year as Smucker. The eminent Joseph A. Seiss, born in

Maryland, also in 1823, was for a short time a pastor in northern Virginia; and the distinguished John G. Morris (1803-1895) was a student for a time at New Market, and became a very prominent minister in the Lutheran Church in the North. The association of Peter Muhlenberg, preacher, soldier, and statesman, one of the eminent sons of the "Luther of America," with this part of the country, is too well known to need detailed rehearsal here. And "the time would fail me to tell of" Streit and Harr and Stoever and Carpenter and Flohr and Butler and Bennick and the Henkels and the Millers and the Stirewalts and the Smiths and the others who have been distinguished in founding and spreading the faith from colonial days to the present.

Among the men who have in years past made notable contributions to Lutheran history hereabouts was Rev. D. M. Gilbert, D. D. In 1876 he delivered a valuable historical discourse at Strasburg on the Lutheran Church in Virginia from 1776 to 1876. The next year at Winchester he spoke eloquently and instructively on "The Praises of the Lord in the Story of Our Fathers." And in 1884 he made another valuable contribution to church history in an address at Woodstock. All of these addresses were printed at the times delivered.

Numbers are always eloquent with many voices. The fact that the Lutherans have been numerous in northern Virginia and East Tennessee from colonial times is significant; but their upright conduct, conservative industry, and religious loyalty have meant even more to their neighbors and to the country at large. Their interest in education and their contributions to Christian culture through books, newspapers, church instruction, elementary week-day schools, academies, liberal arts colleges, and theological seminaries have been permanent and far-reaching. From the years of early settlement the schoolhouse and the church have risen together in every community, sometimes in the same building. Roanoke College at Salem, Va., and the Henkel Press at New Market, are two institutions in the field of education and literature that are outstanding, but many others, like Marion Junior College for young women, are worthy of recognition and have made contributions of high and lasting value.

In this book the various local churches receive individual treatment, which is fitting, as due to their merits, and which adds materially to the interest and value of the records herein preserved. The numerous pastors—the list is a long and honorable one—are made to speak again from an active and often heroic past. Not least, the devotion of the women and their vital services in home, church, school, and mission field are given places. The lists are long, but doubtless some who are worthy have been overlooked— without malice, without intention. But the rolls are all complete in the Lamb's Book of Life.

It is obviously appropriate that the Rev. W. J. Finck, a pastor at New Market, and the Rev. C. W. Cassell, a pastor at Luray, near the first Virginia home of Adam Miller, should be the editors and chief authors of this book. Dr. Finck, the well known author of "Lutheran Landmarks" and other scholarly works, does not need the associations of any particular locality for either inspiration or reputation, but it is a happy fact that he lives and works where so much of the history he herein records has been made. Mr. Cassell has also rendered notable service both in stimulating his associates in historical interest and in directing programs of historical research. His services in recent anniversary celebrations at Woodstock and elsewhere entitle him to the gratitude of all Lutherans and their friends. Both Dr. Finck and Mr. Cassell live and work within easy reach of old Hebron Church, whose site is encircled with fertility and beauty and whose ancient pipe organ has a tone that is still sweet and penetrating, undiminished by the years. And who shall forbid the chronicler to be also a dreamer and a seer? There must be a waking note and a vision, a sweetness to touch the soul now and then, unfailing from age to age, else how shall human hearts and hands be strong enough and patient enough to make history, or write it? or human nature kind enough to read it?

JOHN W. WAYLAND.

PART I

History of Lutheranism in Virginia and East Tennessee

CHAPTER I

THE PEOPLE

THE first representative of the land of the Church of the Reformation to enter the Colony of Virginia was John Lederer. No denomination, as far as known, has laid claim to him as a member, and as a consequence he is simply regarded as the first German that crossed the hills, valleys, and plains of Virginia and the Carolinas. He was in the employment of Sir William Berkeley, Governor of Virginia, and in the years 1669 and 1670 he explored the wide extent of territory as far south as the Santee River in South Carolina and as far west as the Alleghany Mountains in Virginia. His maps and journal show that he traversed the Valley of Virginia and touched points later covered by the towns of Strasburg and Front Royal.

Lederer opened a new world to the white man and though not followed immediately by immigrant trains, it was not long before the westward direction indicated by his reports was followed by eager explorers. Yet forty-six years passed before men were courageous enough to follow in his steps, then Governor Spottswood with his Knights of the Golden Horseshoe entered the Valley of Virginia and paved the way for future migrations into the western regions of the Colony of Virginia. This was one year before a little ship arrived in the waters of eastern Virginia bringing the first Lutheran settlers into the Colony, and no doubt in the mind of Gov. Spottswood there was suggested the possibility of following up his explorations to the west through new arrivals in his domain. When he learned that these German immigrants were in distress and unable to pay for their transportation, he entered into an agreement with them, according to which he advanced the money needed to pay their indebtedness to the shipmaster, and they on their part became his servants for the term of eight years. They proved to be hard and burdensome years, like those of

Jacob, full of many hardships and deprivations, and when they were over, all these Lutheran redemptioners, as they were called, freed from their enthralling service, migrated forty miles farther west, where they patented land on the banks of the Robinson River and White Oak Run, now in Madison County, Virginia. This was in the year 1725. When they arrived in 1717, there were twenty families with about eighty members. Among these we note the following names: Zerichias Fleshman, Henry Snyder, John and Michael Tanner, Matthias Blankenbeker, Nicholas Blankenbeker, Balthaser Blankenbeker, John Prial (Broyles), George Utz, Nicholas Yager, Christopher Zimmerman, Michael Smith, Jacob Crigler, Michael Clore, Michael Cook, George Mayer, George Woodroof, Matthias Beller, Michael Kaifer, William Zimmerman, Michael Holt, John Motz, John Harnsburger, George Scheible, and a few years later, Andrew Garr, John Michael Stoltz, Adam Garr, Andrew Kerker, Matthias Costler, George Lang, Mr. Wayman, Adam Wayland, and John Weaver. Many of these names are different from the original forms due to changes made by the clerk of court. Others assumed other forms later on, as for instance, Zimmerman became Carpenter. By 1725 there were at least forty families. Accessions were constantly received and the people multiplied and prospered, at one time one hundred and seventy-six attended communion in their newly built church. Soon the colony began to swarm and sent large numbers to different parts of Virginia, to Tennessee, Kentucky and the Northwest.

The news of the exploration of Gov. Spottswood and the arrival of German settlers in his colony, reached the ears of fellow-immigrants in Lancaster County, Pennsylvania, and one of them named Adam Müller made a long overland journey to investigate. Here among these Germans and the Knights of the Golden Horseshoe he learned of the way across the Blue Ridge, of the free lands there in unmeasured valleys, and of the desire on the part of the Governor to have his western possessions occupied. Returning home he entered upon an active canvass among his neighbors to go up with him and occupy these waiting fields. He met with success and in 1726 or 1727 he and a large party of Germans migrated to Virginia, taking the new Indian route by which they entered the Cumberland Valley north of the Potomac River and crossing that stream at some fordable point to the west of the present Harper's Ferry entered the Shenandoah Valley in Virginia. Indian trails already existed, and following the one running along the western side of the Blue Ridge and east of the Massanutten Mountains, they made a settlement on the South Fork of the Shenandoah on the banks of the Massanutten Creek. Among these settlers, mostly Mennonites, there were three Lutherans, Adam Müller, named above, Philip Lang and Matthias Selzer. Adam Müller, later written Miller, settled farther south and formed the nucleus of a large Lutheran settlement near Elkton. Many other Lutheran immigrants arrived, some coming from across the mountains, where Miller had first visited the colony, and peopled the country along the east side of the Massanutten Mountains; among them we should mention the Shulers, Kites, Kuntzes, George Printz, Wilhelm Pens, Balthaser Sauer, and many others.

Following these early Pennsylvania pioneers, many others came at the same time or later, not only from Pennsylvania, but also from Maryland, New Jersey, and New York. They did not seem to mind long distances and difficult traveling. They were attracted by the promise of running brooks and fertile fields. Forgetting all difficulties and bearing all hardships, they entered the Cumberland Valley in Pennsylvania or Maryland and crossed the Potomac at some suitable place as far west as Cumberland. South of the Potomac they followed one of the many streams emptying into the Potomac and draining the valleys between the mountain ranges. Thus it happened that Germans settled as many as five valleys as far west as Patterson's Creek, all opening into the north country on the Potomac River. The largest numbers naturally entered the eastern Valley drained by the two forks of the Shenandoah River and their tributaries. The first white settler was William Russell, who in 1728 took up land near Front Royal, followed by John and Isaac van Meter in 1730, and by Joist Hite (Justus Heid) in 1731. With the last named began the German immigrations, and with them the Lutherans began to arrive. Hite came from Strassburg, France, where many Germans lived and the Lutheran Reformation had met with much favor. Joist Hite brought a large family with him of his own, together with neighbors from York, Pennsylvania. Among them were his three sons-in-law, who with the others made a total of sixteen families. Hite settled five miles south of Winchester on the Great Indian trail, and his three sons-in-law, Jacob Christman, George Bauman (Bowman) and Paul Frohman (Froman), farther south, near the present site of Strasburg. Peter Stephan with others founded Stephansburg, which later became Stephens City. Adam Kern took up land on which Kernstown is now located.

Jacob Stauffer obtained a large grant of land as early as 1729 or 1730, made his home at the northern end of the Massanutten Mountains and founded Staufferstadt, later re-named Strasburg. So many Lutherans were among these early settlers that as early as 1747 they had a church building in Strasburg, erected in conjunction with the German Reformed. Among the many Lutherans we might mention Leonhard Baltheis, a friend and supporter of Paul Henkel, Jerome Baker, Martin Roller, Laurence Snapp, Henry Felkner, Adam, Henry and Amos Keister, Peter Philip Baker, and many others.

Winchester formed an interesting center for Lutheranism. As early as 1753 Lord Fairfax donated two half-acre lots to the Lutheran residents there and in 1764 they called a minister from Baltimore to grace the occasion of laying the corner stone for the stone church they had started to build. Between the time of the securing of the lot and the dedication of the finished church, a space of forty years with two wars intervened, each of eight years duration, so the people living there were not able to make much progress in their church work. The names of the earnest people, however, have been preserved to us through the thoughtfulness of the officiating minister called from

Baltimore. His name was Johann Caspar Kirchner, as he himself entered it upon the document deposited in the corner stone, with the names of "the Hearers and Founders of this Temple," "all and each members of the Evangelical Lutheran Church, at this time residing in this city of Winchester, to wit: Thomas Schmidt, Nicolaus Schrack, Christoph Heusckel (Heiskel), David Dieterich, Christoph Wetzel, Peter Helfenstein, George Michael Laubinger, Heinrich Becker (Baker), Jacob Braun, Stephen Fraenckel, Christoph Altrith (Aldrich, Eldridge), Tobias Otto, Eberhard Doring, Andreas Friedly, Christoph Heintz, Imanuel Buger (Bucher), Dewald Hiegel, Jacob Trautwein, Johann Sigmond Haenli, Johannes Lemley, Johannes Lentz, Christian Schumacher, Michael Roger, Michael Warnig, Christoph Lambert, Samuel Wendel, Michael Glück, Julius Spickert, Balthaser Po, Jacob Koppenhaber (Copenhaver), Heinrich Weller." The historian must be thankful for this array of certified Lutheran names; and their descendants, how proud they can be! There is another list of names, that we shall add to this, and though it is a military list, yet several of the names are names of Lutherans; we refer to the roll of "The Dutch Mess," that fought with much suffering under General Morgan in the Revolution; namely, Adam Kurtz, Adam Heiskell, Charles Grim, Jacob Sperry, Peter Lauck, and John Schultz. Five of these old soldiers are buried in Winchester. Their bravery, endurance and patriotism have not been forgotten.

Other names must be added as pillars of the Lutheran Church in Winchester.

John Tobias Otto, settled early in Winchester and signed the corner stone document of the Winchester Lutheran Church.

John Schultz was born in Pennsylvania in 1753 and settled in Winchester in 1766. He was one of the "Dutch Mess" under General Morgan in the Revolution. In 1788 he married Catharine Otto, daughter of John Tobias Otto.

John Adam Kurtz and his wife Anna Sybilla Utz left their home in Württemberg, Germany, in 1749, and in mid-ocean they had the happy but exciting experience of receiving an addition to their family, of a daughter, whom they named Anna Maria. Kurtz with his family settled in Winchester where he and his descendants became active members of the Lutheran Church, and established an undying name in his descendants.

Godfrey Miller was born in Saxony, Germany, in 1730. Leaving his parental home he emigrated from Germany after his confirmation in the Lutheran Church to America in 1763, first settling near Philadelphia, and then in Winchester. He married Anna Maria Kurtz mentioned above and reared a large family in the Lutheran Church.

Abraham Miller, his son, married Rebecca Schultz, daughter of John Schultz. Rebecca Miller, daughter of Godfrey, married Solomon Henkel of New Market. Anna Maria Miller, daughter of Abraham Miller, married Dr. S. P. C. Henkel of New Market, and her brother, Abraham Schultz Miller married Julia Virginia Henkel of New Market, Va.

Thomas and Edward Cooper were born and reared in Strasburg, and came to Winchester where they established themselves as successful business men and earnest workers in the church and generous supporters of all missionary operations.

The first names found in connection with the settlement of Woodstock are Jacob Miller and his son-in-law, Abraham Brubaker. This settlement was first named Millerstadt after Mr. Miller, and Mr. Brubaker gave the double lot of one acre to Burr Harrison, Taverner Beale, Joseph Pugh, Abraham Keller, Laurence Snapp, George Keller, John Tipton, Jacob Holtzman, Henry Nelson, Frederick Stover, Philip Hoffman and Henry Fravel, "for the use and purpose of building and supporting a church for public worship, a church yard and place of burial for the dead, and such other buildings as may be necessary for the purposes aforesaid." Seven of the names of this deed are the names of Germans representing the Lutheran Church; the others are English names representing the Church of England. The first names directly connected with the Lutheran Church are the two on the altar cloth bearing the date of

1767, Friederich Hengerer and Eva Margaretha Hengerer. The earliest names have been lost, as it is certain that the history of the congregation extends into the past to the time of the visitation of the Hebron pastors from 1748 to the coming of the first regular pastor in the person of Peter Muhlenberg in the summer or fall of 1772. What a pleasure it would afford the historian to record here the names of the faithful pioneers who worshiped in the Woodstock Lutheran Church in the early years of its history. For miles they came Sunday after Sunday seeking the ministrations of the Lutheran pastor. Traveling ministers preached here and always found people eager to hear the Gospel.

Many of the Bushongs were Lutherans, as is evidenced by the fact that the Rev. A. A. J. Bushong was a Lutheran minister. The history of the family is of interest. Jean Beauchamp, the original Huguenot name, arrived on the ship Brittania in charge of the Master Michael Franklin from Rotterdam, Holland, and qualified for entry into the port of Philadelphia, September 21, 1731. He first settled in Pennsylvania and lingered there with his growing family until he had become a naturalized citizen of his adopted country in 1739, the record of which is found in Lancaster, Pa. Some years after this event he and several of his sons moved to Virginia, and he took up large tracts of land along the Great Indian trail near Woodstock. The pastor mentioned above is supposed to be a descendant of Henry. His mother's name was Barbara Lohr Bushong. To preserve the proper French pronunciation the spelling of the name was early changed to Bushong, and Jean to John. Peter, another son, settled in the neighborhood of Timberville, and the many descendants in that community have helped to build up Rader's Lutheran Church, and furnished emigrants for Indiana and other western states.

In 1781 a family arrived in Pennsylvania that was destined to play an important part in the development of the Woodstock Lutheran Church, as well as the Lutheran Church in the Commonwealth of Virginia and the country at large in several of its branches. John Christopher

Schmucker left his native home in Germany with his family and settled first in Lehigh County, Pa., then after a year in Lancaster County, remaining here but another year, when once more he took up his family and possessions, started out for the Valley of Virginia, and settled on a tract west of Woodstock, never to be dissatisfied again. He was near enough to Woodstock to use the church for the spiritual education of his sons and daughters, which he did with much success, as three of his sons became Lutheran ministers. Let it suffice at this place to give these three names: John George, John Nicolas, and John Peter. The name John is a key to the spiritual inclination of father and sons.

East of Woodstock is Powell's Fort, early used as a hunting ground. In many ways it was a remarkable place in the estimation of the pioneers. After George Washington had surveyed it he never forgot its value as a place of retreat for the armies of the future. But he withstood the combined attack of the enemy at Yorktown, so it remained unused for military purposes. In course of a few years Lutheran settlers discovered its advantages for the cultivation of its fields, and the pasture of cattle. Its unfailing streams, fountains and springs were a boon not found everywhere. The ground was found to be fertile, and all kinds of fruit prospered abundantly. The first Lutheran settlers were John Bushong, Henry Cullers, Jacob Golladay, John Ritenour, Daniel Munch, Jacob Lichtlighter, John Lichtliter, Adam Lichtliter, and Henry Walther. They and their descendants, until they had pastors and churches of their own, used and supported the church in Woodstock. In a record of a class of persons confirmed in 1788, the following additional names are found: Hafer, Grebil, Frantz, Reitenauer, Hahn, Schmitt, Mordath, and Seibert. Other prominent names are Rinker, Kibler, Habron and Bowman. From these Lutheran families in Powell's Fort went forth in course of time three young men who became distinguished Lutheran ministers: Martin Walther, George E. Golladay, and William Spener Bowman.

Later names are also of interest. Henry Klein settled in Woodstock near the turn of the centuries, and after the

birth of his son John Philip in 1803, he moved to a farm
seven miles west of Woodstock. He was an ardent member
of the town church and reared his family in the fear of the
Lord, and his son John Philip became a minister of the
Gospel. The name of Jacob Ott is often mentioned in
the early records of the Woodstock Church as an officer and
as a delegate to various meetings. He came from Hagerstown, Md., and settled in Woodstock in 1793, becoming a
well established and successful business man in the town,
as well as an earnest church worker in those trying times.
His great granddaughter, Miss Maggie M. Stephenson,
married Dr. A. D. Henkel of Winchester, a loyal member
of Grace Lutheran Church of that city, and an ardent lover
of the history of his Church.

Among other old members of the Woodstock congregation we would mention Mrs. Mary Ware, one of the charter
members; John Dosh, who came from Strasburg, and his
son William, and in turn his son William L. Dosh, who
served the Sunday School as secretary for fifty-two years;
John Anderson, born in 1785, and his son Alexander
Anderson, born in 1809, whose son Robert Anderson served
as treasurer of the congregation for fifty-two years; Reuben
Kneisley who probably came from Strasburg, the father of
Lewis Kneisley and grandfather of J. Grove Kneisley;
and Milton Coffman, who was superintendent of the Sunday
School for fifty-two years.

Mr. Coffman's father was Obed Coffman, who spent his
early life in Toms Brook, and his father was George
Coffman, who was among the early members of Frieden's
Church, the forerunner of St. Matthew's and of St. Peter's,
Toms Brook. At Frieden's we find other names, like
David Hottel, John Snarr, George Swartz, Jacob Coffman,
Abraham Baker, and Philip Peer. On the records of St.
Matthew's Church similar names are found and also
William Coffman, Joel Borden, Mr. Barbe, Mr. Hamman,
and others.

On the records of St. Peter's, which begin with the year
1842, we find the names above repeating themselves, with

David Swartz, David Crabill, Ferdinand Schmucker and George Crabill given as the first elders and deacons.

West and southwest of Woodstock was a large Lutheran population extending from the river to the mountains, and in this territory congregations were organized as early as 1760, or even earlier, and to the present day they are found throughout the country only a few miles apart. As we see this stretch of fertile land it includes the church at Jerome, and takes in all the churches in the Orkney Springs district, the congregations about Hamburg, Pine Church, Solomon's and Rader's. The old settlers organized congregations and built churches often before they had pastors. Next to the Woodstock Church, Pine Church is one of the oldest, and Rader's dates back of its charter (1765) for a number of years. When Solomon's congregation was organized about 1793, its members came from Rader's and Pine Church, together with a number that had not as yet identified themselves with any congregation. To give a complete list of the early settlers that formed the many congregations in this large district under review is impossible. But we must note a few of them as we see them press into the back country over distressing roads, take up land which was cleared with much difficulty, and build their huts and cabins, and the sheds for their cattle and horses. With all their labor and privations they thought of the needs of their souls, came together for worship, and sent the children to the schoolmaster for instruction in secular and religious branches of knowledge. Here are a few of the names that are found on Lutheran rolls: George Miller, John Miller, Jacob Baughman, Adam and Jacob Barb, Christian Coffelt, Augustine Coffman, Emanuel Dellinger, Christian Funk-houser, Abraham Funkhouser, Peter Foltz, Abraham Hess, Andrew, John, George Henry, Michael and Christopher Lindamood, George and Leonard Lonas, Daniel Stickley. In the Zion Church neighborhood, we find the following names: John Painter (Bender), Peter Foltz, George Dellinger, Joseph Foltz, Jacob Helsley, Philip Helsley, George Coffelt, Jacob Keller, George P. Bender, Adam Bender, Jacob Frye, Moses Frye, and John Bowman.

Farther south we find the Lutheran settlers who made up the congregations of Pine, Solomon's and Rader's. Among the oldest of these settlers we name the following: Casper Branner, John Rausch, Baltzer Götz, Michael Nehs (Neese), and Andrew and Michael Zirkel. These were close neighbors and were settled on Holman's Creek and the drains of Mill Creek. They did not live far from the present location of Forestville. As the distance to Pine Church for many of them was very great, Solomon's Church was built between the years 1793 and 1795. Other names must be added out of justice to these loyal pioneers. Jacob Bönewitt, Nicolas Dusinger, Philip Tussing, Johannes Tusing, Michael and Conrad Bentz (Pence), Lewis Bauer (Bowers), Johannes Rubberd, Jacob Zerfass, Henry Frey, Christian Ehrhard (Arehart), Henry Fernsler, Peter Sommer, George Schäfer, Philip Herbein (Harpine), Henry Lutz, Jacob Olinger, John Roller, Adam Reider, Samuel Kerlin, Matthias Minnick, Andrew Trambauer, Philip Souder and others from Pennsylvania, and Ulrich Wittig from Germany.

George Painter (Bender), when he made settlement west of Edinburg on Stony Creek, selected a spot near two brooks rising in separate springs for his house and barn. He erected for his protection against the Indians a fort that has given the name of the Indian Fort Farm to his plantation, by which it is still known.

Two Hepner brothers came from Pennsylvania and were blessed with so many descendants that the community in which they settled formed a country village by the name of Hepners. Lonas Hollow was named in the same way. Michael Lohr after a short stay in Pennsylvania came with three of his sons to Virginia, first settling near Tenth Legion. His son George remained with him, while Philip moved to Madison County. The third son went to North Carolina. Michael Lohr now moved to a farm two miles north of Timberville where he reared a large family and manifested much interest first in Rader's Church and then in the organization of Mt. Zion, for which his son George gave a one-acre building lot.

The French and Indian War, and later the Revolution, caused much uneasiness and commotion among the Lutheran settlers. Some that had migrated as far south as North Carolina, returned to Virginia and sought refuge among the mountains of Hampshire, Hardy and Pendleton Counties. Others moved from one part of the Valley to another, especially after the Revolution, leaving the northern counties and settling in the southwest part of the state. As early as 1750 Justus Henkel had moved from Pennsylvania to North Carolina. Others were there speaking the same language and forming congenial neighbors, as a consequence the sons and daughters intermarried. This was the case of Justus Henkel, who was born in Germany and had come to this country with his father, the missionary pastor Anthony Jacob Henkel. His son Jacob married and reared a family. His wife was Barbara Dieter. The Indians becoming oppressive, the soil none too fertile, and malarial fever certain and incurable, the Henkels and the Dieters determined to seek more favorable homes in Virginia. Jacob and his young family seem to have left first and followed a course along the Piedmont into Maryland, then westward through Maryland, southward across the Potomac into one of the western valleys leading into the present Hardy County of West Virginia. What a long journey to be described in a few lines, but the journey itself took more than a year, as the family often stopped to labor for the means of sustenance. The hardships were many and the dangers were great. One of their little daughters lost her life through the Indians. Going back in our description to North Carolina and taking up the families of Justus Henkel and his neighbors, the Dieters, we see a larger caravan departing from the homes they had made in North Carolina, and following a different route as they laboriously travel northward. Leaving the Piedmont of North Carolina and entering the Valley of Virginia, they proceeded in a northeasterly direction until they reached Staunton where they secured the patents for the land they wished to occupy in the mountains to the west. Their directions led them to continue their course until they reached the present site of Harrisonburg, where they turned west and crossed one mountain after the other until they came to their particular cove in the mountains a mile wide and six miles long. Here they pitched their tents, and others came and filled the valley, all Germans, so that it was called Germany Valley. Ground was cleared, log cabins erected, and last of all, Fort Henkel was built for the protection of all the settlers. Among their neighbors was his son Jacob who was but a few miles away but separated by high mountains. These are two examples to show us how these mountains were filled up in the years as early as 1760. The valleys received our Lutheran people coming from the northern states and other parts of our own State. Near Jacob Henkel lived the Swiss family Nägley, that had moved there from New Jersey. Three sons of Mr. Dieter married three daughters of Justus Henkel. Large families were reared in the pure air of the Virginia mountains and many of the descendants became prominent in the State and Church. The sons of Justus Henkel aided in the establishment first of Rockingham County, and then of Pendleton. The sons of Jacob made their names illustrious by their active prominence in the Church, Paul and several of his brothers in the Lutheran Church, and Moses and his descendants in the Methodist and Methodist Protestant churches. Soon the valleys, filled with Henkels and Dieters, began to overflow into other counties and states. Many of the sons turned westward and labored in the ministry, in the work of education and publication in Tennessee, Ohio and other western states. Paul Henkel was the first to settle in the Shenandoah Valley, and practically all the descendants by the name of Henkel are the result of his moving into the Valley in 1784.

New Market was not originally settled by Germans. The names connected with its earliest history remind one of other nationalities. Peter Palsel laid out the town in March, 1785, but later sold the plat, then called Cross Roads, to Abraham Savage. John Sevier was also interested in the settlement of the town, but he desired to have it located farther north. It was incorporated by the Assembly

December 14, 1796, and the names of the trustees are with few exceptions other than German: William Byrd, Michael Shugart, John Oneil, Andrew Byrd, Isaac Gore, John Brock, and Jacob Steigle. The very name New Market is of English origin. It can be truthfully said that the coming of Paul Henkel to New Market in 1790, marks the beginning of the German and Lutheran character of the settlement. Henkel says in one of his notes that he and Lewis Zirkel went about looking for Lutheran people and there were none right in the settlement but towards the north and west, where the Zirkels had settled, they concluded it would be wise to locate a church, and they selected the site called Davidsburg. For years the worshipers for this church came from northwest and southeast directions. When Paul Henkel's family began to grow up and his sons Solomon and Ambrose settled in New Market and reared large families, and the Zirkels multiplied, the town began to have a Lutheran air about it, and with the establishment of the Henkel printery in 1806, the drug store, book shop and postoffice by Solomon Henkel, after 1793, and stores of merchandise by the younger Henkels and others, with numerous manufactories by new arrivals in the town, New Market became an important center for a territory extending far around. The sons of Solomon Henkel became experienced doctors and skillful surgeons and added to the importance of the town as a center of trade and usefulness. The death of Paul Henkel in 1825 increased the activity of those who felt that his work must be carried on and increased. Friends were won, new members gained, and many people from a distance were attracted to New Market by its educational, medical, industrial and religious advantages.

Before long there were so many Lutherans here in business and on farms that they began to swarm. Noah I. Henkel found available land east of the Blue Ridge in the neighborhood of Rochelle, Madison County, and gathered a group about him to migrate to the new possessions. Among those who joined the migration we note the following names: Noah I. Henkel, Samuel Tussing, Philip Lohr, Benjamin Lowry, Mary Kipps, Rebecca C. Sommers, Mary

M. Tussing, Dr. George A. Sommers, George W. Kipps, Daniel Lowry, Henry Kipps, Amanda Kipps Hale, Mary C. Lohr, Virginia Lohr Carpenter, A. Rebecca Lohr Carpenter, Mary M. Henkel, Catherine Lohr, and Mary Ann Kipps Estes. Others living in or near New Market migrated in other directions. The two sons of Col. S. T. Walker, who was killed in the Civil War at Chancellorsville, after they were reared in New Market, went to Woodstock, Luther Sommers Walker as clerk of court and Robert J. Walker to practice law. Both of these men were helpful members of the Woodstock Lutheran Church, and also made themselves useful in the general work of the Synod to which their congregation belonged.

In Page County there was considerable restlessness among the farmers, and a number of Lutheran people settled on farms east of the Blue Ridge, Julius Miller, David A. Griffeth, David Weaver, Adley Tutwiler, and John Miller bought farms near Catalpa and formed the nucleus of St. Luke's Church. William Sours moved to Elkwood and became a part of Trinity congregation. Nokesville and Manassas also received accessions but from different parts of the country. Isaac Wittig of Dovesville, now Bergton; Frank Rhodes from near Harrisonburg, and J. O. Bittle from Maryland, all settled near Nokesville and helped to build up Mt. Zion Church. Manassas received accessions from Reading, Pennsylvania, in the persons of Harrison D. Wenrich, David Young, and John Hettinger; Dovesville sent Suffary Whitmer and William R. May. Many other Lutheran people settled along the Southern railroad and built up the congregations in that section of the State.

The three Keiser brothers came from Pennsylvania and settled in Virginia, one in Rockingham County, one near Luray, and the third in Augusta County. John McCauley came from Scotland and settled near Salem. He married Miss Dingledine, a Lutheran, and their son William, became a prominent leader in Church and State. William gave his church three sons for the ministry, Ernest, John William, and Victor.

Special mention should be made of several families that gave a large Lutheran population to our State in the early years of our history, before we leave the lower Shenandoah Valley. First we shall enumerate the family of John Rausch.

Sailing up the Delaware in the closing months of the year 1736, the Perth Amboy from Rotterdam brought among its passengers one by the name of John Adam Rausch, who, however, in later years is known as John Rausch. After spending some years in eastern Pennsylvania, where no doubt he married, he moved to Virginia and settled on the drains of Mill Creek, near the village of Forestville, as mentioned above in these lines. After laboring with the usual privations perhaps for years he was able to patent a tract of four hundred acres. He reared a large family of eight sons and one daughter. Though living some distance from the church they were regular members of Pine Church and brought up their children with care in home and school. The names of the sons and their families are found on the Pine Church record. When Solomon's church was founded they became active supporters in the new congregation and one of the sons, Henry, and his wife deeded two acres of ground for the mere trifle of five shillings to the new congregation for church, school and burial purposes.

Faithful to the church, they were no less loyal to their country. Jacob saw active service in the war against the Indians in 1774, and all the sons as they reached the required age enlisted in the Army of the Revolution. Three of them are supposed to have been present at the Siege of Yorktown. When the war was over the sons settled down about the home again and followed their regular pursuits of farming. The father died in 1786, and was buried in the Pine Church graveyard. The mother lingered for ten years more continuing faithfully, as shown by the records, to receive her communion at the hands of her pastor. After her death the spirit of migration seized the sons one after the other, their names disappear from the communion records, and by 1800 all of them had migrated to the Ohio River near Point Pleasant, taking up lands on both sides of the river. Their Virginia pastor followed them and kept many of them and their children in the Lutheran Church. Their removal was a great loss to Pine and Solomon's congregations. Nearly all of their names appear in the Government census of 1790. Between 1770 and 1798, they were the life of the home church, helping also in the organization of the Davidsburg Church at New Market.

Another family that deserves to be mentioned is that of the Zirkles.

About the year 1725 Ludwig Zirkel (the name is now generally written Zirkle), left Germany and settled in Pennsylvania. Here he reared a family of five sons and two daughters. The five sons came to Virginia between 1760 and 1765 and settled on tracts of land lying east and west of New Market.

Michael and Andrew took up land on Holman's Creek not far from the present site of Forestville and attended services in Rader's Church and later assisted in the organization of Solomon's.

George Adam settled on the North Fork of the Shenandoah and consequently his descendants are known as the River branch. The family affiliated with Pine Church and in 1790 assisted in the organization of Davidsburg Church, now St. Matthew's of New Market.

Lewis and Peter selected land on Smith Creek, four miles southeast of New Market, and made a settlement, Lewis permanently, Peter soon taking up the march again and settling at the headwaters of the James River, where a numerous group of Zirkles now live. John, one of the sons of Lewis mentioned in this paragraph, migrated to Salem and many of his descendants are found there. Lewis and his children aided in the establishment of St. Matthew's Church, the father providing one-half acre of ground for the building and graveyard.

All these Zirkles have been throughout the generations industrious farmers, millers and tanners, and staunch Lutherans, populating our country far and wide with a large membership and a loyal citizenship.

It is necessary to make special mention also of the Koiner family. They settled near Waynesboro, Augusta County. Lutherans had settled to the north of them years before; in fact, they took up land in the southern end of the oldest Lutheran settlement west of the Blue Ridge. The eastern part of Shenandoah County, now Page County, filled up rapidly with Lutheran settlers. Conrad Bender lived here with many others. Settlers came across the Blue Ridge from the old Hebron colony; others came from Pennsylvania and Maryland, taking the eastern trail at Strasburg; farther south John Piedefish, William Bentz (Pence), with many others settled in the neighborhood occupied by the original Adam Miller near the Spottswood trail. To the north and west of them were found enough German settlers to form the villages of Keezletown, McGaheysville, and the Ermantraut neighborhood. McGaheysville is the location of one of the oldest of the Lutheran congregations west of the Blue Ridge, known by the name of The Peaked Mountain Church. Its records go back as far as 1750, and more will be read in these pages of its history. At this writing under its pastor, the Rev. H. E. H. Sloop, it has just celebrated the 125th anniversary of the building of the church now in use in McGaheysville. This congregation and St. Peter's were always visited by the early traveling ministers from the Hebron Church. Many names connected with these three points have been lost, others will be given later, a few remain to be mentioned at this place of our history: Leonhard Bender, Mr. Schramm, Jacob Küblinger, John Risch, Simon Jäger, Daniel Dingel, Peter and Henry Ermantraut.

The head of the American family was Michael Keinadt. The name was changed soon after his arrival in America to Koiner and other forms. His wife was Margaret Diller. Both came from Germany to Lancaster County about 1740 and were married in New Holland, Lancaster County, Pa., in 1749. They reared a large and influential family, all of them born in Pennsylvania, bearing the following names: George Adam, Conrad, George Michael, Elizabeth, Mary, Casper, Catharine, John, Martin, Jacob, Christian, Philip, and Frederick. All of these children came with the parents in 1789 to Virginia, except one son, Conrad, who remained in Pennsylvania. Casper was the first to come to Virginia, and he came in the spirit of adventure. He was most favorably impressed with the forests and streams and with the prospects for hunting, fishing and farming. He also fell in love with the Germans that were on the ground, especially the daughter of Jacob Barger, Sr. He soon induced his brother George Adam to come and investigate and the consequence was that in August, 1787, these two men with the help of their father bought several large farms and two years later the whole ancestral family arrived, bought more farms, lived and prospered with much success and happiness in the neighborhood of the land now covered by the city of Waynesboro and surrounding country. Some of the descendants according to the promptings of the times moved away to western states, but the great majority of them stayed on the original farms purchased, formed colonies within a few miles of the homestead, and finally when the second generation reached its end it found the mother and father and six sons laid away in the cemetery of the mother church. They were members of the Lutheran Church and built up one congregation after the other. The mother church was begun before their arrival, but the first comer, Casper, was there in time to aid the settlers in raising funds for the building of a log church. Daniel Keiser, Jacob Barger, Sr., Martin and Nicolas Bush, and the Messrs. Clemens, all Lutherans, were there to help. When the father arrived with his large caravan, he found that he had come in time to make himself useful in the exercise of his trade, for he was an iron worker, a chain maker, and at once proceeded to make by hand all the nails needed in the construction of the sanctuary. The children added to the membership of the church by wise marriages. Some of the daughters married sons of the many Scotch-Irish living in the neighborhood and brought them into the Lutheran Church. These clever Scotchmen studying the doctrines of the Lutheran Church and noting her many tender acts of love, learned to revere the Church they had

found through their wives and became staunch supporters
of Lutheranism. Thus the names of Baylor, McComb,
McClanahan, Campbell, McClelland, McConoughty,
McCron, McHenry, McKee, McReynalds, McCauley and
many others found their way to the Lutheran Church roll.
The sons sought Lutherans for their wives and therefore
intermarried with Lutheran families. Hence the name of
Henkel, Zirkle and others in the family names, like that of
Dr. Arthur Zirkle Koiner. Susan Koiner of the division
of Casper married Dr. Samuel Godfrey Henkel of New
Market; Margaret Koiner of the same division married
Siram P. Henkel of New Market. Many daughters
married Lutheran ministers; hence we find in the genealogy
the names of the following Lutheran pastors: J. M.
Schreckhise, James R. Keiser, John D. Shirey, J. E. Seneker,
Jacob Killian and J. E. Shenk. Ministers bearing the
Koiner name are also numerous: among them, the Rev.
Junius Samuel Koiner, and the Rev. J. I. Koiner. Miss
Effie Coyner, of the grand division of George Michael,
married William J. Showalter, the Assistant Editor of the
National Geographic Magazine, who has become an earnest
member of the Luther Place Memorial Church of Wash-
ington, D. C., and an active layman in the United Lutheran
Church. In his Virginia lineage are found on his mother's
side the Lutheran names of John Fultz, Peter Swope, and
Mr. Swank. His paternal ancestor, Daniel Showalter, who
settled in Rockingham County in 1788, was a Mennonite
minister.

To summarize the influence and the results of the settlement of these Lutheran families in this large community it
might be said that the large Scotch-Irish district was changed
in its character completely, so that what before had been
an English-speaking community of Presbyterians became
largely a German-speaking community of many Lutherans.
Their influence was not confined to a small territory, but it
spread out, reaching throughout the Valley to the southwest,
and taking in Bethlehem congregation fourteen miles to the
south, and Mt. Solon an equal distance or more to the
westward. Other names were added. Some of them

Scotch, others German or Swiss. Abraham Augy, James Collins, Samuel Trout, Jacob Harner, Lewis Croft, Thomas James, Michael Basil, and Mrs. Sarah Ramsey. Mr. Fied, who had first settled in Brock's Gap, moved with his family to the neighborhood of the Koiner Church. For many years the name has been written Freed. He was from Switzerland and had come to the Valley through Pennsylvania.

In the vicinity of Frieden's Church we find the name of Joseph Miller, the father of two Lutheran ministers, Peter and John I. Miller, and the grandfather of Dr. C. Armand Miller. At Mt. Solon we find many Lutheran names: Michael Reinhart, Michael Schuler, Johannes Bauman, Friedrich Hengerer, Jacob Gebert, August Argenbrecht, Jacob Bentz, Michael Hefner, Daniel Schäffer, Peter Auge, Johannes Roller, Wilhelm Orohrbach (Orebaugh), Wilhelm Kirchhof (Caricofe, or Kiracofe), Johannes Leinenweber, Johannes Stautemeier, Johannes Degen (Daggy), Heinrich Hoffert, Christian Staubus, Jacob Crum, Frederick Cupp, and Anthony Aylor.

Going westward from Staunton, we find a settlement of Germans at Churchville, among whom we notice these Lutheran names: Paul Sieg, Sr., David Cook, Lewis Haroff, Emanuel Rudibush, J. H. and Alexander Cupp. Turning south we find at Mt. Tabor George Shuey, Sr., George Dull, Peter Strouse, Jacob Beard, Mrs. Margaret Cale, Elijah Teaford, Philip Engleman, David Rusmiselle, David Summers, Jacob Bowman, Mr. Arehart, and William Alexander McComb.

In the county south of Augusta there were but few Lutherans as the land was taken up by the Scotch-Irish, and the Germans had to pass on through Rockbridge County over the Natural Bridge across the James River. In the neighborhood of Lexington, however, the following names might be noted: Henry Teaford, Elijah Teaford, George B. Shaner, John G. Houserman, John P. Cook, Charles P. Kirkpatrick, John H. Teaford, Thomas Teaford, Philip Engelman, and Mr. Obenchain.

Beginning with the James River in Botetourt County, Lutherans succeeded in securing farms, that the Scotch-Irish were willing to sell, or land that had not yet been patented. Peter Miller migrated through Frederick County and settled on the James River, where he built a mill. Many services were held in his house, and he proved to be a great help in the planting of the church in that community. Jacob Mayer, a Shenandoah County school teacher, had moved to the same county. Philip Spickert from Yorktown, Pa., had settled there to the great encouragement of the Lutheran pioneers. Other names are the following: Jacob Bierly and his son David, Peter Shaver, who had moved from Rockingham County, Philip Spiggle, Jacob and William H. Cronise, born in Frederick County, Md., bought farms in Botetourt County; Philip Feuerbach (Firebaugh), Daniel, Isaac and George W. Kessler; George W. Rader born in Woodstock, Va., when eight years of age was brought to this county by his parents for his permanent home; Jacob Miller, George Braun, Jacob Statler. On Glade Creek, were the following: Benjamin Kessler, Henry Spickert, Frederick Murray and John Hinderlicht.

On to Southwest Virginia

Passing through Montgomery County, the pilgrims of adventure reached Wythe County, the Shenandoah County of the southwest in the Lutheran Church. Everywhere the Lutheran settlers found neighbors of their own faith. Coming from other parts of the Valley, from Maryland, Pennsylvania and other northern states, from North Carolina, from Germany and Switzerland, with a few accessions from the Hessian prisoners released at Winchester and Charlottesville, the country filled up with Lutheran farmers and mechanics. The numbers grew more rapidly immediately after the close of the Revolutionary War. The majority were members of the Lutheran Church upon their arrival, or soon after affiliated with the Lutheran Church. They were attracted by the scripturalness of her doctrines, the tenderness of her love and the amiability of her daughters. They found permanent satisfaction in the church of their adoption, for there was much to believe, and human nature likes to believe. It is given unto men to believe. The growth of the Lutheran Church in southwest Virginia is a marvel, but yet it has its natural reasons and causes. Large accessions were gained from the Swiss, who are nationally members of the Reformed Church. Others came from the Scotch-Irish descendants. The language question was never a problem to any extent in southwest Virginia, as many of the ministers in the early days preached both German and English, and accommodated the English people with services in their own tongue. This was greatly appreciated by the inhabitants not understanding German.

At the same time the Lutheran Church lost many members in Virginia as well as in other parts of the country. She lost to the Presbyterians through marriage, to the Episcopalians through society, and to the Methodists through revivalism, but in spite of all, her gains were much greater than her losses. The loyalty of her members, born and adopted, has been remarkable, especially when the language question did not interfere with the use of their church.

Among the earliest names that we find in this great Lutheran country are some of members that settled here as early as 1776. The earliest settlements are three in number called later, St. John's, one mile north of Wythe Courthouse, St. Paul's ten or twelve miles west of the same place, and Kimberling some distance from these two. Among the names connected with these three points and scattered over the county and beyond are the following: John Schaeffer, whose father was a member of Pine Church, Shenandoah County, Henry Lambert, Martin Kümmerling (Kimberlin), Jacob Dobler, Casper Rother, Johannes Hercheröther, Jacob and Johannes Schnebely, Jacob Riede, Heinrich Happess, George Zerfass, Jacob Peiss, Michael, Christopher and Andreas Braun, Michael Kregger (Cregar), Michael Cassell, Heinrich and John Höttel (Hottel, Huddle), Thomas Kopenhäfer, Daniel Repass (Rabatz), Mr. Killinger, Mr. Spangler, Michael Wampler, Michael Steffey, Christopher Spracher, Henry Philippi, and Mr. Kagley.

Many other names should be added, but a few additional lines in regard to a few families mentioned must suffice. Other worthy names will appear in other parts of the history.

The story of Michael Cassell is interesting. He was the son of a supporter of the armies of Washington in Pennsylvania. After the war was over the son became restless because of the death of his mother and the arrival of a stepmother. His father noticing the young man's dissatisfaction suggested that he visit his uncle in southwest Virginia, and offered to provide him with the means for the journey, including a strong horse. Upon this Michael Cassell entered upon the pilgrimage, found all conditions favorable in the new land, married Miss Vogelsang (Birdsong), and became the father of a long line of descendants, not without well known ministers, as for instance the Rev. C. Willis Cassell, the editor of this historical volume, and his son Joseph B. Cassell, of New Brookland, S. C.

Daniel Repass came from Germany, or Switzerland, about 1750, lingered in Pennsylvania until the close of the Revolutionary War, and then migrated to southwest Virginia and settled near Wythe Courthouse. Here he became the progenitor of a very large and influential family, the members of which were and are mainly in the Lutheran Church, though the old father was a preacher in the German Reformed Church. He was no doubt from Switzerland as Paul Henkel who met him in 1887 calls him a Swiss. He had four sons, Samuel, Frederick, Daniel, Jr., and John. Samuel moved to Bland County and united with another church, but the other three brothers remained near Wytheville and helped in a large and material manner to build up the country. His son John had four children one of whom was Rufus who became the forefather of the large line of Lutheran ministers, not only by the name of Repass, but also by the name of Cassell, mentioned in the paragraph above, and by the name of Peery. The ministers bearing the name Brown were also linked to the families named, and will receive attention at the proper place. Mention of these faithful and successful ministers in the Lutheran ministry will be made in the next chapter of this history. The Scherers, five in number, came from North Carolina to Virginia but more as missionaries than as settlers. As, however, many of their descendants have made a permanent contribution in many ways to the Lutheran Church in southwest Virginia, it is but right to mention their coming as members of the Lutheran Church, reserving the notice of their missionary and educational labors for the proper place in other parts of this history. Jacob Scherer was the first to come as a traveling missionary, to be followed by his brother Daniel. When a few years later Jacob Scherer moved to Virginia with his family, it meant the arrival of three more valuable men added to Virginia's population and the membership of the Lutheran Church; Gideon, Simeon, and John Jacob. The last married and labored in southwest Virginia as a missionary and educator, becoming the father of a very useful family of children.

In Montgomery County early settlements were made on the New River. The Seventh Day Adventists from Ephrata, Pa., settled here as early as 1745. Lutherans followed soon after, and when the Moravian Missionary Schnell visited the community in 1749, he found a number of Lutherans among the settlers. Among the Lutheran names preserved we have the following: Adam Herrmann, Jacob Herrmann, Jacob Goldman, John Wahl, Michael Zerfass, John Philip Harless, Sr. and Jr., Heinrich Preisch, George Boscher, George Wilhelm, Johannes Zentmeyer, Samuel Obenschein, and Jacob Kessler.

In Floyd County, we find the old Zion Church with records in German dating back to 1793. The following names have been preserved: Johannes Mayer, George F. Pflüger, Jacob Ebberle, Daniel Welz, Christian Ebberle, Philip Stigelman, George Ebberle, Abraham. Pflüger, Heinrich Sauer, Samuel Ridinger, Heinrich Kronk, George Sauer, Michael Pflüger, Wilhelm Maichel, Jacob Maichel, Wilhelm Ruthrauf, Petrus Meigel, Johannes Weber, Johannes Maurer, Wilhelm Maichel, Jacob Theiss,

Christopher Schlosser, Johannes Kilterman, Johannes Ruthrauf, and Eli Cronk.

The Gladesboro Church in Carroll County was organized among the early settlers, of whom we mention the following: James Cassell, W. R. Kinzer, James L. Cassell, Thomas Cassell, David Cassell, Margaret Denton, Abraham Barr, W. L. Utt, L. G. Baily, Mr. Tobler, and J. W. Kinzer.

In Scott and Washington counties, we note the following Lutheran names: Isaac Shelley, James Flenor, Henry Flenor, Isaac Mumpower, Jacob Tranbarger, Michael Davoult, Henry Mottern, C. M. Scherretz, and Jacob Weisgerber.

On to Tennessee

We must follow the Lutheran pioneers in our narration for they did not stop in southwest Virginia, but continued their difficult journey throughout the southwest counties of the State, and pressed on into the eastern counties of Tennessee. It is certain that Lutheran settlers entered these counties while they were still a part of North Carolina. Many of them first settled in the Virginian counties and then took up lands on the Holston River in Tennessee. Naturally, the first Lutherans settled in the counties bordering on the southern Virginia boundary line, like Sullivan, then pressed on into the counties to the south, as Washington, Greene, Jefferson and Knox. Possibly some settlers came across the mountains from North Carolina, but it has not come to the knowledge of the writer that Lutherans came direct from the Lutheran colonies of western North Carolina. It is more likely that they first traveled to Virginia and from Virginia to Tennessee. However, the settlers in eastern Tennessee form a continuation of the great migration from Pennsylvania, southwest through the Valley, on, on, to the unoccupied lands of Tennessee. Some of the Virginia settlers did not have far to go to find homes in Sullivan County, Tenn. And when once in Sullivan County it was not hard to follow the promptings of the inborn wanderlust and continue the migration to the other counties named.

In giving a list of names of these Tennesseean pioneers we begin with Andreas Klein, who was totally blind, and Elias Wacker, living on the Cherokee River, who traveled over an untrodden country thirty miles to attend Lutheran services and to persuade the missionary to come to his distant home, baptize his children and preach the gospel to his neighbors, among them Mr. French and Mr. Keplinger. In Sullivan County lived the following Lutherans: Simon Haar (Harr), John Harr, William Hancher, who was born in Frederick County, Virginia, George Wolford, Jacob Droke, Leonhard Cain, George Rodeffer (Rodeheaver), Jacob Deck, Adam Miller, John Senaker, John Houser, Peter Harkins, Jacob Shaffer, Samuel Whiteman, Jacob Barb, Martin Roler, Benjamin Horn, George Barger, James Holt, Pemberton Hunt, Henry Herchelroth, (Harkleroad), Daniel Peters, James Booher, David Bushong, Samuel Vance, James Riley, and George Crumley. In Washington County lived the following: Conrad Keicher, Jacob Lideck, Philip Armentrout, Adam Probst, John Smith. In Greene County we find the following names: John Smith, John Froschauer (Freshour), David Parman, Frederick Gottschall (Cutshall), Immanuel Wilhoit, William Crum, Benjamin Farensworth, John Nehs (Neas), George Neas, Ambrose Oesterly (Easterly), John Bauer (Bower), Isaac Rader, William I. Lintz, John Ottinger, Jacob Ottinger, John Hauk, Adam Knipp, John Harmon, Isaac Bible, Frederick Schaeffer, John Cobble, John Smelser, John Bible, Jacob Harman, Henry Meyer, Andrew Bible, and Joseph Hauf (Huff). In Monroe County: John Moser, Jacob Clemmer, William Brakebill, Eusebius Summitt, Robert Boyd, John Kinser, John Mauer, and Jacob Barb. In Knox County: John and George Hauser, Solomon Spangler, Frederick Neibert (Newbert), John McCall, Daniel Booher, Joseph Miller, Henry Kinzel, Henry Lonas, Henry Mauck, Nicolas Gibbs, Henry Bauer (Bower), Henry Thomas and John Maurer. Also the following names: Joseph Nehs (Neas), Ezra Bible, and Adam Boyer.

Two brothers Martin and John Bucher came from Germany (perhaps Holland), in 1747, and settled in Lancaster County, Pa., as farmers. Later they came to southwest Virginia and settled in Wythe County. Even before this their name had been changed to Booher to accommodate the scribes in the courts. Each reared a large family. Martin's son John married John's daughter Mary. They soon moved to Sullivan County, Tenn., and when their son Daniel was of age he married and moved to Knox County, where he in turn reared a large family. Thus in three localities the Boohers had descendants. They multiplied rapidly and migrated in numbers to Indiana, where they and their kin helped to organize Lutheran churches in Boone and Montgomery counties, while still prospering in their ancestral homes in Tennessee and southwest Virginia, and giving the Church several ministers.

The Decks also have an interesting history. Adam Deck came from Saxony, Germany, and settled in western North Carolina. He had two sons, Michael and Jacob. Michael though born in North Carolina was reared in Washington County, Va., and there he married Miss Lydia Houser, who had come with the Pennsylvania immigrants to southwest Virginia, and reared a large family. Jacob grew up and settled in Sullivan County, Tennessee. Here four great families mingled and made the Lutheran Church prosper: The Decks, the Hanchers, the Harrs and the Senekers. Jacob's son Abraham had many children and among his sons three ministers, and a valuable layman, who labored for the advancement of the Lutheran Church in Tennessee and northern states: Rev. William Hancher Deck, Rev. Jacob Elias Deck, and Rev. John P. Deck, who is the father of Rev. Luther Bushong Deck, of Vancouver, Washington, and Mr. M. L. Deck, the supporter of the Chicago Seminary at Maywood, Illinois.

In 1856 a young man by the name of George H. Cox came to Knoxville, Tenn., taught school, served in the army during the war, and after the close of the war identified himself in a most noble way with the people. He made a serious study of religion, as a result of which he and his wife became earnest members of the Lutheran Church, exerting a wide influence for good among the people of eastern Tennessee.

On to the Towns and Cities

Lutherans have always been an agricultural people. They have always loved the soil and the Lord of the soil. Hence it follows that they have sought homes in the country and built their schoolhouses and churches in the country, sometimes at the cross roads and sometimes beyond the cross roads. The towns and cities in the meantime were occupied by others. The history of the Church in Virginia is a perfect example of these assertions. Winchester is possibly the only county seat in Virginia where the Lutheran congregation is as old as the city, and Strasburg, Woodstock and New Market are among the few towns in which the organization of a congregation is contemporaneous with the incorporation of the town, or older as in the case of Strasburg and Woodstock. It is a story of the love of the fireside in the country and a neglect of the populous settlements on the railroad and highways. Yet the time came when some of the church workers if not the lay members realized that something must be done for the diaspora in our towns and cities. As early as 1844 the newly-formed Synod of Western Virginia sent a representative to Richmond, the Capital City, to see whether the time had come to begin mission work there, and some encouragement was received by the visiting minister. Negotiations were opened with the Virginia Synod suggesting cooperation by the two synods in this important center. Yet many years passed before it was possible to rally the few Lutherans in the city around an organized congregation under the auspices of these two synods. Few of the people from the Valley had at that time begun to leave their home and gravitate toward populous centers, and when a movement was made it was usually not toward our Virginia centers but to the cities of the north, like Washington, Baltimore and Philadelphia. Germans arrived in Richmond direct from Germany, and perhaps a few of other nationalities, but they were not acquainted with our American operations in their behalf and often kept aloof, or even opposed efforts to organize a congregation of Lutherans.

But with the passing of time, the Valley began to pour out of its population a vast number of citizens, and they began to fill up the towns near at home and far away, and a large number of Lutheran people were among them, who flocked to Richmond and other cities of our Commonwealth. Their coming helped to solve the problem of city missions in Virginia. They were usually young men and women, unafraid and undaunted, free of prejudices, who spared no efforts to find the unchurched people, organize Sunday Schools, and provide the means for holding services and for building chapels and churches.

This is a picture of the pioneers of our Church in Virginia. Many have passed away without leaving their names. They belong to the company of the heroes of faith. There are many that have no memorial, who perished as though they had never been, but their righteousness has not been forgotten, and the honor of their deeds cannot be blotted out. They faced dangers and uncertainty, they suffered hardships and privations, they braved adversity and trials, but in patience and faith, they endured their sufferings until the day of better things dawned upon their heroic career. In their honor and to their memory we insert here the noble lines of Theodore O'Hara.

The Old Pioneers

A dirge for the brave old pioneer!
  Knight-errant of the wood!
Calmly beneath the green sod here
  He rests from field and flood;
The war whoop and the panther's screams
  No more his soul shall rouse,
For well the aged hunter dreams
  Beside his good old spouse.

A dirge for the brave old pioneer!
  Hushed now his rifle's peal;
The dews of many a vanished year
  Are on his rusted steel;
His horn and pouch lie mouldering
  Upon the cabin door,
The elk rests by the salted spring,
  Nor flees the fierce wild boar.

A dirge for the brave old pioneer!
  Old Druid of the West!
His offering was the fleet wild deer,
  His shrine the mountain's crest.
Within his wildwood temple's space
  An empire's towers nod,
Where erst, alone of all his race,
  He knelt to Nature's God.

A dirge for the brave old pioneer!
  Columbus of the land!
Who guided freedom's proud career
  Beyond the conquered strand;
And gave her pilgrim sons a home
  No monarch's step profanes,
Free as the chainless winds that roam
  Upon its boundless plains.

CHAPTER II

FORTH into this mass of unchurched people went the teachers of God. It is not recorded anywhere that any group of these pioneering settlers brought their teachers and pastors with them. It is true they brought their Bibles, Hymnbooks and Catechisms, but the living instructor was the head of the family, or a friendly neighbor, or old and young grew up without instruction, as was indeed often the case. And often for years these settlers heard no minister and their children remained unbaptized. Great was their joy if some day they heard the glad news that a pastor had come. Thankful they were, too, if they had one among them who could serve over the winter months as teacher, and in case of necessity bury their dead and baptize their children.

And when we ask the question, "Who were the first to come and minister unto these people?" then our answer must be the teachers that lived among them and often moved from one neighborhood to another. Often the neighbors met in one of the homes and the teacher would lead in the singing of some hymns they could find in their books, read from the Bible and also read a sermon. There were not many of the people that could lead in religious work of this kind, but it is evident that much of it was done, else the flocks would have been scattered much more than they were, but a desire for religious food and a willingness to receive what could be offered in their destitute condition preserved many a soul in those early days from spiritual starvation. We shall record here that it is our opinion that due justice will never be done to those who perhaps in very humble circumstances served among the people as teachers. Many of the preachers that were eminently successful in their work and shall find an honored place on these pages were first of all and perhaps for years simple teachers among these common people, working their farms over the summer for a living, and teaching school over the winter for humanity and love. Much remuneration they never did receive, and often little reward on earth. That they developed into pastors by their own aspirations, is not a reason why we should censure them, but rather a reason for acknowledging their earnestness and commending them for holding the souls of children and adults to the faith until the ordained minister finally arrived.

Several names we rejoice to be able to put on record here as forerunners in the spiritual work that was later taken up by the pastors. And if it is true, as we feel it is, that after the Revolution many of the Hessian soldiers that remained in our country, gave the people the benefit of their ordinary education of the schools of Germany, we say, "All honor to them!" They deserve the undying gratitude of the descendants of those they taught. Our only regret is that their names were buried with their bodies and we cannot memorialize them by name.

A few names that have been preserved shall be enumerated here on this page. First, the school master of Winchester, Antony Ludi, who was so fortunate as to have his name recorded on the Latin document in the corner stone of the church dedicated in 1764. We know not how long he served the congregation, nor how well he served, but his name was worth recording, together with a host of other worthies, and we honor him for his profession's sake. He was not the first one there, for Carl Friedrich Wildbahn had come from Pennsylvania two years before and served as teacher in the same congregation. He was a soldier and upon his earnest request he was released from service. He desired not to be a man of war but a man of peace, according to his name Friedrich (rich in peace). Later he became a faithful and successful minister in Pennsylvania.

The Ministerium of Pennsylvania sent two school teachers to the Hebron congregation in Madison County, John Schwarbach and Jacob Frank. They did excellent work there and proved to be not only good teachers but untiring missionaries.

Jacob Mayer and Peter Weber were two teachers in Shenandoah County; the latter was able to give instructions in Latin. John William Meyer migrated from one of the lower counties to Botetourt County and served there for many years.

If we had a complete record many more names could be mentioned. These are typical of a large class of helpful men who served their neighbors in secular and spiritual matters, and prepared the way for the formation and preservation of many congregations. A number of names given in succeeding paragraphs as ministers should be mentioned here as teachers, but it is not necessary to give their names twice, only let us remember that our Church owes much to a host of teachers whose names have long been forgotten. May they be found in the Lamb's Book of Life.

And now when we come to look for the shepherds that came to seek the scattered sheep in the territory we have described, we find a variety of classes of pastors and missionaries. First, there was the Mother Synod in Pennsylvania whose members had for years been leaving their home congregations and wandering to the southwest, as we have tried to describe, a true mother that could not forget her children, who was ever trying to find shepherds to seek the wandering sheep and to follow them through the trackless forests; then the second mother, the Ministerium of North Carolina, who after her organization in 1803, ever had in mind the many that were crossing the mountains and trying to care for them through traveling missionaries; then thirdly, it is surprising to note how many sons of her own territory became ministers of the Gospel, spending their days of usefulness in the home church, or, going beyond the borders of their own State, laboring in the vineyard of other states. Virginia has been a great producer of ministers, a generous giver as well as an abundant receiver. Then lastly, some pastors came direct from Germany, or from other states, without synodical intervention.

In speaking of these workers we shall follow as nearly as possible the order of time. This leads us to mention at the beginning

The First Lutheran Pastor In Virginia

John Caspar Stoever. He came direct from Germany
in company with his son, who bore the same name, arriving
in Philadelphia, September 11, 1728. They had come to
America with the sole intention of doing missionary work
among the Germans, but neither of them was ordained.
The son designated himself as a missionary and the father as
a student of theology. The younger Stoever remained in
eastern Pennsylvania and in the spring of 1733 he found an
opportunity to be ordained and accepted it. The father disappears from the records for a few years but he is supposed
to have traveled to North Carolina where even at that early
date there were a few Germans. Here he married, and in
1733 wandered up through Virginia to the settlement of the
Hebron Lutherans. He found that they had been without
a pastor for sixteen years, and that they were eager to call
him to minister to them as their shepherd. He was willing
to accept the offer they made him in the colony, and in order
that he might be able to perform all ministerial acts among
them and in their services, he yielded to their entreaty to go
to Pennsylvania and be ordained by the same minister that
had ordained his son. One of the members of the congregation, George Scheible, accompanied him and witnessed
the ceremony. The officiating minister was John Christian
Schulz.

For a year and a half the new pastor labored very
earnestly among the people. In the spring of 1734, his
family was brought from North Carolina at the expense of
the congregation. In the fall of that same year he and two
of his members, Michael Smith and Michael Holt, made a
tour to Europe and secured funds for a church, pastor's
farm, schoolhouse, books for himself and the congregation,
and an ordained minister for his assistant. About six
thousand dollars were collected, and the assistant pastor they
found was George Samuel Klug. But Pastor Stoever died
at sea on the way home early in the year 1739, and his body
was intrusted to the waters of the deep ocean. His life
was ended but his work continued. The person selected to

be his assistant became his successor. According to his will all affairs were arranged for the future welfare of the congregation. Pastor W. P. Huddle in his excellent History of the Hebron Lutheran Church gives the following estimate of his life and character: "Hebron Church was thus deprived of the services of this godly man, who had done so much for the Germans during the time he was with them as pastor and also while absent in Germany collecting the money with which the church was permanently established. To him the congregation will ever be deeply indebted."

It has been the fond hope of many that the first pastor of the Lutheran Church to minister to the Hebron people might be shown to be the Rev. Anthony Jacob Henkel, but the evidence has not been found. It is reasonable to suppose that some minister must have visited them in the years from 1717 to 1733, and Pastor Henkel came to America in the first of these two dates and settled in eastern Pennsylvania. His labors are known to have covered the territory from New Hanover to Philadelphia, and he could easily have learned of the existence of this little flock in the wilderness of Virginia. He was a man of education, piety and missionary zeal. He was ordained in Germany in 1692, just one hundred years before his famous great grandson Paul Henkel. He gave twenty-five years of earnest, self-denying service to his home church, and then with his large family, under great difficulties, crossed the ocean and cast in his lot with the children of the New World, serving them the rest of his days with much earnestness and self-denial. His many descendants, who have played so large and important a part in the history of Lutheranism in Virginia and in America, will rejoice if ever the discovery is made that Pastor Anthony Jacob Henkel visited the Lutheran people of the Hebron congregation and thus won the honor of having been the first Lutheran minister in the Old Dominion.

George Samuel Klug

began his work as pastor of the Hebron congregation in the spring of 1739. He was, therefore, on American soil two and one-half years before Muhlenberg. His first act was to hold a meeting with the returned collectors and make an entry in the collector's book to the effect that all accounts were correct and that the money had been paid to the congregation. A farm was bought and the work of building the church was begun at once and completed by 1740, as the figures show on the "great girder laid across the plates midway between the ends." He cared well for his people, providing school and church privileges for old and young. The school he established was the first German school in the South, and some think that this system of popular education was among the first of its kind in the province of Virginia.

Pastor Klug did not confine his pastoral labors to his own flock, but crossed the Blue Ridge to the west and visited the scattered Lutherans in the territory now embraced in the counties of Page, Rockingham, Shenandoah, and Frederick. The Moravian missionaries found evidences of his labors in the territory described between the years 1747 and 1755. Immediately west of the Blue Ridge he found Germans to whom he ministered, that later formed the present Mt. Calvary congregation; farther south it is certain that he collected a small congregation about the home of Adam Miller; very likely also the Peaked Mountain Church was begun in his day, as baptismal records are found bearing as early a date as the year 1750.

In material things Pastor Klug was well cared for. His congregation prospered and provided for his needs so that he was able to live in peace and comfort. He felt his loneliness and sought fellowship among his English brethren in the State Church, with whom he lived on good terms of friendship. His son received his education among his English neighbors, and went to Europe for ordination in the Church of England. Pastor Klug never applied for membership in the Ministerium of Pennsylvania, but he visited in 1749 the pastors in Philadelphia and seems to have been encouraged by the cordial reception given him by Brunnholtz and Muhlenberg. He continued his labors until his death in the spring of 1764. His people whom he had served for twenty-five years laid his body reverently in front of the chancel under the church.

Fortunately the congregation did not have to wait long for a teacher, who at least cared for the children and read a sermon at the Sunday services. The name of this teacher was John Schwarbach, of whom we hear for the first time in the minutes of the Ministerium of Pennsylvania in 1763. He was then a teacher near York, Pa., and desired to be licensed as a catechist that he might extend his usefulness to some outlying districts under the superivision of the pastor residing in York. This was granted by the Ministerium, and the next year or two he must have heard of the need of a pastor, or teacher, in Virginia. He traveled to the distant point to learn for himself what the needs were. As a consequence, he appeared at the meeting of the Ministerium in 1766 with three letters from congregations in Virginia, commending him for his services among them and earnestly requesting that he be licensed so that he might perform all ministerial acts in this distant field, separated by hundreds of miles from the homes of other Lutheran ministers. The members of the Ministerium considered the request carefully and sympathetically, examined the applicant thoroughly in questions of practice and doctrine, and granted him the license to perform all acts of a pastor.

He was a man of mature years when he took up this difficult work, but he labored abundantly in a way that is surprising. He prosecuted the work as it had been carried on by his predecessor, which included the three congregations uniting in the request for his services. The work in the home congregation continued to prosper. Across the mountains he served Mt. Calvary, St. Peter's, and Peaked Mountain, designated in the letter as the church on Fort Run. It was in the present town of McGaheysville. Some of these congregations were union churches, in which the German Reformed and the Lutherans were associated in the ownership and use of the church. We have the

record of such a union in the last named congregation.   It
is of interest in that it shows how these union congregations
managed their affairs so as to preserve peace and harmony.
Through the labors of Prof. W. J. Hinke, who translated a
large part of the early records of this congregation, and the
publication of the History of Rockingham County by Prof.
John W. Wayland, Ph. D., we wish to give our readers a
copy of the agreement adopted by the members of the
Lutheran and Reformed congregations with the names of
the signers.   In regard to the names it must be stated that
the writer is unable to classify them according to denominations.   Each reader must do that if he is able.   The names
are given as a list of accredited German settlers in that
community when it was still in Augusta County.

AGREEMENT

Between the Reformed and Lutheran Congregations Worshiping in the
Peaked Mountain Church, Augusta County, Va.,
Oct. 31, 1769

In the name of the Triune God and with the consent of the whole
congregation, we have commenced to build a new house of God, and it is
by the help of God, so far finished that the world may see it.

We have established it as a union church, in the use of which the
Lutherans and their descendants as well as the Reformed and their
descendants, shall have equal share.   But since it is necessary to keep in
repair the church and schoolhouse and support the minister and schoolmaster, therefore, we have drawn up this writing that each member sign
his name to the same and thereby certify that he will support the minister
and schoolmaster and help to keep in repair the church and the schoolhouse
as far as lies in his ability.

Should, however, one or another withdraw himself from such
Christian work (which we would not suppose a Christian would so),
we have unitedly concluded that such a one shall not be looked upon as a
member of our congregation, but he shall pay for the baptism of a child
2s. 6d., which shall go into the treasury of the church, for the confirmation of the child 5s., which shall be paid to the minister as his fee; and
further, should such a one come to the table of the Lord and partake of
the Holy Communion, he shall pay 5s., which shall go into the treasury
of church; and finally, if such a one desires burial in our graveyard, he
shall pay 5s., which shall also be paid into the treasury of the church.

In confirmation of which we have drawn up this document, and signed
it with our several signatures.

Done in Augusta County, at the Peaked Mountain and the Stony Creek churches, on October 31st, Anno Domini, 1769.

The present elders: George Mallo, Sr., John Hetrick, Nicholas Mildeberger, Frederick Ermentraut.

Philip Ermentraut, Henry Ermentraut, Daniel Kropf, Peter Müller, Sr., Adam Hetrich, Jacob Traut, Augustine Preisch, George Schillinger, Anthony Oehler, John Mann, Alwinus Boyer, Charles Risch, Henry Kohler, William Long, Jacob Bercke, Jacob Ergebrecht, John Reisch, Jacob E. Ergebrecht, John Mildeberger, John Hausman, George Mallo, Jr., Jacob Lingle, Peter Niclas, Jacob Kropf, Jacob Niclas, George Zimmermann, Christian Geiger, Augustine Preisch, Conrad Preisch, Jacob Kissling, Jacob Bens, Adam Herman, Michael Mallo, Christopher Hau, Peter Euler, William Michel, Jacob Risch, John Ermentraut, Conrad Lövenstein, John Schaefer, Christopher Ermentraut, Martin Schneider, John Bens.

It will be noticed that in this document with many names no names of ministers are given. This is the case in so many records of former times, when the names of the pastors would help to decide so many different problems. But in this case on the part of the Lutherans there can be no doubt as it is the time that John Schwarbach served in this field, and his name with that of the Reformed minister should be given in some way. No doubt the careful way the paper is drawn up shows the help of the pastors and the teachers. When members of union churches labored together in this careful manner there was no trouble as to the just division of the responsibility in the upkeep of the property and the support of the pastor and teacher.

Mr. Schwarbach extended his missionary journeys fifty, sixty, seventy and even a hundred miles from home. He went to Strasburg, Winchester, and west from Winchester into the valleys of Hampshire County. Journeying up this extended valley he came to the home of Jacob Henkel, Balthaser Nägley, the Dieters, Justus Henkel, and many more. On these missionary trips he was entertained in the home of Jacob Henkel, and no doubt in the home of Justus Henkel, and others likewise, but it happens that we have a record of it only in the home of Jacob Henkel. Jacob and his father Justus loved their Bible and their books of sermons, and when the pastor came the conversation would turn gradually to spiritual things. And the children would sit by and listen. The missionary gathered these people and their neighbors together into groups for preaching services, and they would sing under the leadership of the pastor, and he would pray and preach. He organized a congregation there and built a church for them, for there was a church there even after the war that the people called the Henkel's church. Paul Henkel tells us how he listened to the visiting pastor as he carried on a conversation with his father Jacob, and he learned to listen to the public sermons, attended catechetical instruction and in 1768 Paul Henkel was confirmed by Pastor Schwarbach. These missionaries received little pay for their labors, and made these wearisome journeys in the mountain valleys, and over the stony mountains, but they had their reward. This missionary's reward was that he confirmed a boy by the name of Paul Henkel that became a greater missionary than he was himself.

Ten years of labors such as these Schwarbach gave to Virginia and then he returned to Pennsylvania, old and feeble, where he lived a number of years in retirement. He united the Hebron congregation to the Ministerium of Pennsylvania, so that after he was gone there was some one to think of them and to try to provide them with ministers of the Word. So it follows that the officers of the Ministerium sent another school teacher, Jacob Frank from Philadelphia, a most capable man, licensed to do the same work that Pastor Schwarbach had done. He was sent for three years and for three years he stayed, 1775 to 1778, but oh! what precious years they were for the Hebron congregation. He labored in the home field only, giving all his time to church and school. The members responded nobly and unitedly. He was an excellent teacher, organizer, and singer. By his words and by his music he attracted the men, women, and children; yea, even the slaves crowded to the doors and galleries to hear his melodious voice and to join in the singing. He gave the congregation a constitution, which he brought with him from the Philadelphia church, and put the congregation upon a sound Lutheran basis set forth in a formal document. Up to this time its doctrinal principles had been unwritten. From its beginning it had been a pure Lutheran congregation, never a union church, but now that faith was expressed in positive Lutheran terms of the faith of the fathers and the Unaltered Augsburg Confession. This constitution which he brought with him was carried to southwest Virginia and later incorporated in a constitution recommended by the Synod to its congregations. Thus the good a man does, does not die with him but lives through others. Jacob Frank returned to Philadelphia, but the work he performed for the Hebron people still lives in the history of the Lutheran Church in the South.

In the Shenandoah Valley

All these years while these ministers were serving east of the Blue Ridge, the beautiful Shenandoah Valley had no resident pastor for the many people of the Lutheran faith until 1772.

There were a number of visiting ministers. The teacher, Carl Friedrich Wildbahn, returned a number of times to the land he had learned to know, and ministered to the needs of the people. On his visits he went farther south and preached to the people of Strasburg and other points. His entries in the church records written in a beautiful hand are noted at different places. He also encouraged others of the teachers and pastors in Pennsylvania to visit the scattered flocks of Virginia. Henry Möller before the War visited Madison County and the congregations in the Valley. He was pastor in Reading early in the War, and served for a time as chaplain of the soldiers in camp and on the battle-field. Among other visitors must be mentioned the name of Pastor John Christopher Hartwig, the founder of Hartwick Seminary in New York State. It is the oldest Lutheran educational institution in America, beginning operations in the training of ministers in 1797. He was the bachelor missionary of the Ministerium from 1746 to 1796, when he passed away, rich in years and desirous of perpetuating his work through his means that he left for the Church he loved and served. He refused to accept a call for a settled pastorate, but served as supply and visitor wherever he was sent, or found an open door. His territory extended from Albany, New York, to Woodstock, Virginia, and many were the blessed messages received from this consecrated and pious wandering spirit. Traces of his visits are found in many church records of congregations in the Valley. Pastor Göring of York was instructed to visit the congregations of the Valley of Virginia by the Ministerium and he reported that he had done so. Of this character there were others, as the Mother Synod was always concerned for the welfare of her members in Virginia.

And just as the Ministerium of Pennsylvania manifested this interest in the diaspora in northern Virginia, so the pastors that later entered into the formation of the Ministerium of North Carolina followed their members that crossed the mountains and settled in southwest Virginia and ministered to their spiritual needs. From the years 1773 to 1794, there were two Lutheran ministers in the piedmont of North Carolina. It is indeed probable that they followed their members across the mountains into southwest Virginia to look after their spiritual welfare. There are entries found on church records in this territory marking as early a time as 1776. Perhaps they were made by school teachers, but it is not at all unreasonable to suppose that the North Carolina pastors visited the people of southwest Virginia, baptized the children, held preaching services, and administered the Holy Communion. The older of the two pastors was Adolph Nussmann, who died in 1794, and Johann Gottfried Arends, who lived to aid in the organization of the Ministerium of North Carolina, though he had by this time become totally blind.

Coming back to the lower counties of Virginia, we enter upon the period of settled work, marked by the arrival of John Peter Gabriel Muhlenberg, whom we shall call according to his habit and desire simply Peter Muhlenberg. He was the oldest son of the Patriarch Muhlenberg and was born in Pennsylvania, October 1, 1746. He is so well known among us, as well as in history, that it is needless to undertake to give a biographical sketch here on these pages.

But he has done the Lutheran Church and his Country so much good that his life and works cannot be too deeply appreciated, and too much space cannot be given to him in this History.

He came to Woodstock in the summer or fall of 1772. He came with the knowledge and consent of the officers of the Ministerium of Pennsylvania. He had been prepared for the ministry by the famous provost of the Swedish Lutheran Church, Dr. Wrangel in Philadelphia, aided by his own father, and licensed to preach and catechise and to perform other ministerial acts under the supervision of his father. His first field was in New Jersey, where he faithfully performed his duties. His father was surprised that he succeeded so well, for Peter possessed many traits of his grandfather Conrad Weiser, that seemingly were no help for ministerial work, like hunting, fishing, horseback riding, and other out-of-doors activities. These proved to be suitable traits for his new field in the wilderness of Virginia, as Father Muhlenberg described our State.

Peter Muhlenberg was not sent to Virginia by the Ministerium. He was sought by the English people of the Valley, centering in Winchester, and representing the Parish of Beckford. They conceived the idea that it would be a good policy to secure a minister that could serve the Germans and at the same time perform all ministerial acts required by the members of the Church of England. There were not enough of the latter to justify the calling of a rector. But to perform the acts of the English people legally the minister had to have episcopal ordination. To receive this ordination it was necessary to go to England, as there was no bishop of the Church of England in America at the time. In developing this idea the English people inquired in New York for a suitable German preacher and there was recommended to them in rather superlative terms Pastor Peter Muhlenberg. The rectors of Philadelphia recommended him very highly, for they had known him for years, and his worthy father likewise. Objections prevailed nowhere and it was not long before Peter Muhlenberg was on the way across the ocean and on the twenty-fifth day of

April, 1772, he was ordained a priest by the Lord Bishop of London in the Chapel Royal within the Palace of St. James.

When Peter Muhlenberg received this episcopal ordination he did not renounce his Lutheran faith and his rights as a Lutheran minister, but added to these the right to serve as a rector according to the legal requirements of the Province of Virginia, which accepted only the acts of a member of the Church of England. Muhlenberg was a lifelong Lutheran, but for a few years, from 1772 to 1776, he exercised in addition the prerogatives of a priest of the Church of England. When he took up arms against the mother country his right to serve as a priest of the Church of England automatically came to an end.

Thus we see that both Kercheval and Bancroft are correct when they describe Peter Muhlenberg as a Lutheran minister. The footnote added in a later edition of Kercheval's history is a matter of ignorance. He came to Woodstock equipped in a double manner in two different ways. First he was doubly equipped in that he could serve both the members of the Lutheran Church and of the Church of England. Again, because he was fully able to preach both in the German and in the English language. He began his work with much earnestness, and showed his interest in religion, education and politics as the times demanded. There is reason to suppose that he served all parties to their entire satisfaction. No complaints are on record that he failed in the performance of any duties he owed either to the Germans or the English. Most of his work was connected with the Lutheran side of his call. He visited many neighboring congregations of Lutherans, and preached in schoolhouses when he had the opportunity. He was sent on a commission of investigation across the Blue Ridge to the Hebron Church, which shows at the same time that he still was regarded as a member by the Ministerium of Pennsylvania. Pine Church was then in existence and there can be no doubt that he held services for its members. There is evidence also that he preached in Strasburg and Winchester, and probably penetrated the mountains of Hampshire County. Everywhere he encouraged the people

in the care of their souls and the education of their children.
Then came the rumblings of war.

> "Out of the North the wild news came,
> Far flashing on its wings of flame,
> Swift as the boreal light which flies
> At midnight through the startled skies.
> And there was tumult in the air,
>   The fife's shrill note, the drum's loud beat,
> And through the wild land everywhere
>   The answered threat of hurrying feet;
> While the first oath of Freedom's gun
> Came on the blast at Lexington;
> And Concord roused, no longer tame,
> Forgot her old baptismal name,
> Made bare her patriotic arm of power,
> And swelled the discord of the hour."

Thus in martial strain the poet Thomas Buchanan Read
truly describes the feelings of the times into which Peter
Muhlenberg entered after he had been pastor at Woodstock
for two years. He could not resist the call of the country
for freedom against the wrongs inflicted upon them by
England. He was made chairman of the Committee of
safety in 1774, and a year later was elected the representative
of Dunmore County to the House of Burgesses meeting at
Williamsburg. In the fall of that year he was urged by
Washington and Patrick Henry to accept the appointment
as a colonel of the Continental Army, and on the twelfth of
January, 1776, he was duly elected to this position. His
acceptance, public demonstration, and successful call to arms
of his parishioners, are well known to all of us. As colonel
of the Eighth Virginia Regiment, known as the German
Regiment, he made a wonderful record, winning the praise
of his superiors, so that even Bancroft felt constrained to
make note of his achievements in his History of the United
States. In a year's time he was promoted to the position of
Brigadier General, and at the close of the war he was made
a Major General. He was in active service from the
beginning to the end of the War. But the Lutheran Church
lost an earnest and highly esteemed minister through his
retirement in 1783. He had entered the services of the

State and never returned to the ministry. He had laid aside his clerical gown, and in its place he assumed the toga of a statesman. In 1783, he sold his home in Woodstock to Matthias Zehring, and moved to Pennsylvania, near Philadelphia, where he resumed his membership in the German Lutheran congregation, and to the time of his death, October 1, 1807, remained an active layman. His last work as a Lutheran was connected with the organization of St. John's English Lutheran Church of Philadelphia, the first purely English Lutheran Church in the world. The following paragraph, which he wrote to the members of the Evangelical Lutheran Church in Philadelphia, in a letter bearing on the subject of allowing English services, will make a fitting close to this sketch and to the life of this worthy Lutheran and patriotic lover of liberty:

"Brethren, we have been born, baptized, and brought up in the Evangelical Lutheran Church. Many of us have vowed before God and the congregation, at our confirmation, to live and die by the doctrine of our church. In the doctrine of our church we have our joy, our brightest joy; we prize it the more highly since, in our opinion, it agrees most with the doctrine of the faithful and true witnesses of our Saviour Jesus Christ. We wish nothing more than that we and our children and our children's children and all our posterity may remain faithful to this doctrine."

Paul Henkel

Thirty years passed before a minister came to take up the work of Peter Muhlenberg in Woodstock, but before Yorktown had fallen a voice was heard in the forests of Hampshire County, and before Muhlenberg had moved away from Virginia in 1783, that voice was heard in Shenandoah County, and entered upon a ministry for the uplift and salvation of many people.

It was the voice of Paul Henkel. He had come from his home to preach to the German people that he heard lived on Stony Creek in Shenandoah County. He found them as elsewhere without a shepherd, and at once began to serve them, beginning in the home of Jacob and Peter Zink, who befriended him on this his first visit to this territory. They together with the school teacher Jacob

Mayer conducted him from place to place where appointments had been made, and sent messengers from house to house that each one might know of the appointed service in his neighborhood. His first sermon was preached on Monday, December 2, 1782; Wednesday, the fourth, he preached for the first time in "old Röder's Church;" on Thursday in a schoolhouse five miles from Woodstock; Friday in Lehman's schoolhouse not far from Woodstock, and on Sunday in Woodstock to a crowded house. This was on the eighth or fifteenth of December. His journal is not quite clear as to the date, but rather allows room for the suggestion that he spent two Sundays in Woodstock. From here he went to his friend Leonhard Baltheis (or Balthus), who befriended him until his death in 1810, and preached in the schoolhouse in Strasburg, and then continued north as far as Frederick, Maryland. The following spring, after Easter, he made another journey over the same territory, preaching the fifth Sunday after Easter in Rader's in the morning, in Pine Church at three in the afternoon, on Monday in Zion's, and on Tuesday in Woodstock. He made this journey for the purpose of getting letters of recommendation from various congregations, and he succeeded in securing a favorable letter together with a call from four congregations; namely, Rader's, Pine, Pine Hill near Winchester, and a congregation near Harpers Ferry. With these he appeared before the Ministerium in session at Yorktown, Pa., and on June 16, 1783, he was licensed to preach, catechise and baptize for one year under the supervision of Pastor Krug of Frederick.

He at once entered upon his work as pastor in the Shenandoah Valley, preaching once a month in each of the four congregations that had called him. His efforts were successful and his congregations were very enthusiastic over their new pastor. The next spring four delegates accompanied him to the meeting of the Ministerium, to request his ordination. The four earnest men willing to undertake the long and difficult journey to Lancaster, Pa., were the following: Andrew Zirkel of Rader's, Michael Nehs of Pine, Jacob Klein of Pine Hill, and Casper Sieber of

Harpers Ferry. The presence of the four delegates was noted in the minutes without giving their names, and the license of their pastor was renewed for another year. In 1787, we find the following entry in the minutes:

"Mr. Paul Henkel asked for a renewal of his license. It was unanimously granted, the license extended to all congregations in that section having no regular pastor, and hope was given him, that in time he should be ordained." This promise was fulfilled at the meeting held in Lancaster, Pa., when on the sixth day of June, 1792, he was ordained to the Gospel ministry.

His was a life of great activity and restless missionary zeal. A complete narration of his movements cannot be made without creating confusion in the mind of the reader. In 1783 he moved his family from Hampshire County to Shepherdstown on the Potomac, and in 1784 he changed his home again by moving to The Forest in the neighborhood of the present village of Forestville, Shenandoah County. In 1785 he began to make annual tours to North Carolina, on account of the destitute condition of the Lutheran people there, among whom were relatives of his who urged him to come and help them. The members of his four congregations were not very willing to spare their pastor for these journeys, which required three months, but he persuaded them that it was their Christian duty to allow him to go to the help of these people that lived without the benefit of the Gospel. While at home in his own field, he made extended trips to Hampshire County, where he catechized and confirmed his many relatives still living there; to Powell's Fort; to St. Peter's and St. Paul's in the southeastern corner of Shenandoah County; and to the Hebron congregation east of the Blue Ridge. On his way to North Carolina he stopped at many places to preach the Gospel and to baptize the children; thus Virginia throughout its length, and Tennessee in its eastern counties, received the benefit of his labors on these long journeys to North Carolina. Usually he was accompanied by candidates for the ministry, teachers, or relatives. On the tour of 1787, his wife went with him. They intrusted their three small children to relatives and sallied forth on horseback, stopping for the night wherever darkness overtook them. In a translation of Mr. Henkel's autobiography, which is written in German, we shall let the reader follow him in those parts of the journey, going and coming, which belong to the states of Virginia and Tennessee.

"I had not been at home long before I received letters from different people in North Carolina who earnestly urged me to visit them again, and as I without this urging had the inclination to do this, it was not hard to make me willing to undertake the journey. As my wife at that time was young and quite a good talker, she allowed herself to be persuaded to accompany me. It was in September that we started, though with many difficulties. During the previous summer I had traveled a great deal and had preached very often. Frequently I was overheated and became wet with perspiration. As a consequence a severe cold settled in my chest, resulting in an abscess, which gave me much trouble for a long time, and the more I preached the worse it became. But finally I was gradually restored and felt able to undertake the journey. Our son Ambrose was fourteen months old, so we took him across the mountains to Jacob Ruth, who had married my wife's oldest sister. As they had no children they were much attached to them, and took excellent care of our little baby boy. Thus these people also had to aid in the furtherance of the Gospel. The rest of our children we put into the care of my brother Benjamin and his wife.

"We rode through Pendleton County and a part of Botetourt County, crossing many streams, as the James River, Bull Pasture Creek and Cow Pasture Creek. I must relate here an experience that we had one evening as the darkness was overtaking us. We had ridden through a piece of woods and were to turn sharp to the left over a hill, but I did not notice the turn and we kept on along the level through the valley, when the path came to an end. We turned face about to make another effort, when we heard the clatter of hoofs coming toward us, and the noise of a man falling from a horse, while it was evident that we heard the sound of a horse rapidly riding away. My wife was greatly alarmed. As the fallen rider heard us talk he called us to him and told us of his trouble. He and the man that had ridden off were due the next morning at ten o'clock at the county courthouse to appear as witnesses in a suit, but they had lingered over the cups in a tavern so that both were drunk and he himself was unable to sit on the horse. He begged me to help him on his horse, saying he must ride all night, or pay a heavy fine in the morning. I helped him upon his beast, he directed us over the mountain, advised us to stop at the next house, and started off on his long journey. We followed his directions and found the house, where we stayed over night. The next day we journeyed to Jacob Mayer on the James River. Mr. Mayer was the man who helped me in 1782 when I made my first visit to Röder's Church. Here we remained from Friday to Monday. I preached in Mayer's home. On Monday we rode down the stream and came to Peter Miller. Here we stayed a week. I instructed the children and adults. The following Sunday I was to confirm the class and administer the communion, but I was compelled to postpone these ministrations until my return.

"We rode away from here and continued our journey without stopping to hold services until we reached the German congregation at Reedy Creek. We were received with much friendliness. The old Mr. Dobler received us into his home. He and his whole household entertained us with the greatest hospitality. The large class that I had instructed and confirmed the year before assembled immediately and I reviewed the whole course with them. I also preached several times in the church and at other places in the regions about, both German and English. I also had my difficulties on this visit. The old Mr. Repass, a Swiss, was also here and Andrew Loretz, who also came from Switzerland. (These were two Reformed ministers.) * * * Loretz was seeking congregations. He gave instructions to a number, and. as he could not restrain his feelings, he was not able to hide his pride, and as he had a great desire to be considered as the one who was the head and master, he spoke against Pastor Willy and against me in the presence of those who he thought were his trusted friends. But as others heard his words he was soon betrayed. A storm of ill feeling arose in consequence of his unkind remarks, and I was unable to allay the storm and restore peace and confidence.

"My wife and I rode to the German neighborhood on the Holston River, and I preached there in the congregations. A German, Elias Wacker by name, living thirty miles away from the congregations on the Holston heard of me and came to me and begged me to come to the region where he lived. My wife remained with my uncle, Adam Büffel. I rode on as far as the Catawba River, there I found good lodging with an Englishman by the name of Dougens, who had moved from the neighborhood of Shepherdstown on the Potomac. The next morning I started off early and on the way I was met by Mr. Wacker who lives on the Cherokee Creek. We ate breakfast and then journeyed on to the home of a German by the name of Frentch, where Mr. Keplinger now lives. Here I preached and baptized several children, two for Mr. Wacker. At that time the neighborhood was sparsely settled by white people. I had planned to meet my wife that same evening at the home of Andrew Greer, who lived on the Catawba. The few Germans made up sufficient money to hire a man to conduct me to that place. I found her there together with the man that had accompanied her. The next morning we rode up the stream and found lodging with poor people that cared for us the best they could. The householder's wife confessed to my wife that she would like to have her child baptized. So before leaving the next morning I baptized the child.

"The same day we crossed the Stone Mountain into North Carolina."

* * *

"On our return the friends in North Carolina sent two young men to accompany us for two days. We also had in our company the wife of our uncle Anthony Henkel and her son. The old aunt traveled all the way to New Holland, Pennsylvania. When we came to Botetourt County and to our old friend Peter Miller, we remained there for some time. I continued the catechetical instruction with those whom I instructed on my journey southward, holding the meetings in Fincastle. While here we lodged most of the time with Philip Spickert, who had come from Yorktown, Pa. I continued the instructions for eight days, and then confirmed the class, and gave them the Lord's Supper. This was the first time services of confirmation and communion were held in this place.

"Our old aunt and her son had gone on ahead to our home. My wife and I journeyed from here again across the mountains through Pendleton County until we reached the home of Jacob Ruth, where we had left our little Ambrose. I preached several times in this neighborhood and then we rode to our home. It was now the beginning of December in the year 1787.

"Die Reis ist nun vollendet,
Daran viel Müh gewendet.
Was war denn damit ausgericht?
Das weiss Gott, ich weiss es nicht;
Das zeigt sich erst in jenem Leben,
Da wird die Sach sich selbst ergeben."

This narration will give our readers an idea of the work Paul Henkel performed on his journeys to North Carolina. There was always some variation, according to circumstances and traveling companions. Usually the course lay along the Indian trail north through Lexington and Staunton. Often messengers would precede him and make appointments at various points along the route, as for instance Kieselstadt and other places. Now let us multiply the service of usefulness performed on each trip by fifteen, and we must marvel at the sum total. We read much of the evidence of his labors in southwest Virginia in local records. We can consider all these acts recorded as the fruits of his labors beginning with the first journey in 1785 and continuing with some interruptions until 1823, when age and affliction ended his itinerant work.

Now to return in our account to the days he lived in the Forest, we must record that in 1789 he bought a building lot in the new town of New Market, with a plat of ground near the town for pasturage. In the spring of the next year his house was ready for occupancy and he moved to New Market in the year 1790. While New Market remained the center of his operations for the rest of his life, he moved a number of times to other points to facilitate the prosecution of his missionary operations. In the fall, October, 1794, he moved to Staunton, returning to New Market just three years later. While living here he was pastor of Koiner's Church near Waynesboro, and served many other points near and far, continuing also his trips to the southwest and to North Carolina. In 1800 he moved with his large family to North Carolina and spent five years in active service there, doing an immense amount of good in those distressing times of revivalism. As a defense against the enemies of the church he succeeded in organizing the Synod and Ministerium of North Carolina, and before leaving the State saw his son Philip ordained as a minister of the Gospel.

Upon his return to New Market, he took up his work again, and once more became pastor of the Davidsburg Church, now called St. Matthews. It was now 1806, and the date is an important one as it marks the time of his appointment as a traveling missionary by the Ministerium of Pennsylvania. His first tour was planned in answer to the call coming from former parishioners and relatives living on the Ohio River, both on the Virginia side at Point Pleasant, Mason County, and on the northern shore of the river in the new State of Ohio. Twice he moved to Point Pleasant with his family, and eventually assisted in the organization of the Joint Synod of Ohio in 1818, and left two sons to labor in the territory of this venerable Synod.

Upon his second return to New Market from Point Pleasant in 1816, he gave himself largely to the work of composition and publication, without, however, relaxing his missionary activity. He wrote prose and poetry, in German and English, hymnbooks, catechisms and homilies. He used every form of ministerial usefulness. His home was a school for ministerial candidates. His knowledge and office were at the service of everyone. He trained his brothers and his sons for the ministry. Of his brothers John, Joseph, Benjamin and Isaac were Lutheran preachers. Of his sons, he gave Philip and David to the Tennessee Synod; Andrew and Charles to the Joint Synod of Ohio; and Ambrose to the work in Virginia in connection with the Tennessee Synod.

He was stricken one hundred and twenty miles away from his home on a journey arranged by the Tennessee Synod to meet an appointment in Kentucky. Fortunately his wife was traveling with him at the time. His left side was completely paralyzed, affecting even his speech. The misfortune was so great that they were compelled to return home, where he gradually improved in his ability to walk and to talk. He was thankful that his ability to write was not impaired as his right side was spared; his speech gradually improved so much that he could perform the ordinary ministerial acts, and even preach occasionally. The last time he attended a meeting of his synod was in 1824, in Koiner's Church, when his son Ambrose was ordained. He made a report to the meeting of Synod in 1825, of twenty infant and five adult baptisms, and ten confirmed. His last ministerial work was done in New Market, where he preached to a number of Lutherans in the schoolhouse and in homes, which eventually led to the organization of Emmanuel Lutheran Church. He died November 27, 1825, at the age of seventy years, eleven months, and twelve days, full of years and honor. His name and his work will never be forgotten in the history of the Church he loved so deeply and served so faithfully. True is the testimony engraved on the tablet of his tomb in Emmanuel cemetery in New Market:

His Zeal for the promulgation of the Gospel
of Christ Jesus was exemplary, and
his labors were many and dif-
ficult. He is now with
Christ and no evil
can befall him.

Christian Streit

gave the last twenty-seven years of his useful life to the Lutheran Church in Virginia. Not only were they years of ordinary service, but they were years laden with a rich heritage, marked ability, careful training and varied and helpful experience.

He was a gift from the North sent by the Ministerium of Pennsylvania. He was born June 7, 1749, in New Jersey, twenty-five or thirty miles east of Phillipsburg and Easton. His father, John Leonhard Streit, was an officer in one of the German congregations on the Raritan, earnest, faithful, and loyal. His grandfather was Christian Streit, and is supposed to have come from Switzerland. John Leonhard Streit loved his church so deeply that in the year 1753 he made a journey of seventy miles to bring the Patriarch Muhlenberg to his home church for a two weeks' series of services. Muhlenberg speaks very highly of this home of hospitality and spirituality, in which the little son Christian was born. His parents and grandparents watched over him very carefully, and when he was old enough they sent him to Philadelphia to be educated in the Academy and College of Philadelphia, which a few years later became the University of Pennsylvania. He was graduated with distinction in 1768, and three years later received his master's degree. While pursuing his classical course, the home of Pastor Muhlenberg in Philadelphia was open to him, and under him and the learned and affable Dr. Wrangel he studied theology. Two others were associated with him as students for the ministry at the same time under the same distinguished instructors, namely, Peter Muhlenberg and Daniel Kuhn. These three students while they were studying preached in the neighboring Lutheran churches in English for Dr. Wrangel, and in German for Pastor Muhlenberg. Their services were much appreciated. The Swedes were hungry for English preaching, and their Swedish pastors realized that the request could no longer be denied. On the minutes of the Ministerium they are first mentioned as students in 1768, and a year later they were licensed as candidates for the ministry. In 1770

Christian Streit in company with two sons of the Patriarch Muhlenberg was ordained to the Christian ministry.

Streit's first charge was Easton, where he served a congregation for about eight years. When the Revolution broke out, no doubt upon the recommendation of his friend Peter Muhlenberg, Pastor Streit was appointed Chaplain of the Eighth Virginia Regiment. Complete records of his services in the army have not been found by the writer. Personal inquiry at the War Department, Washington, received the following official reply: "The records show that Christian Streit served as chaplain of the Eighth Regiment, commanded by Colonel Abraham Bowman, Revolutionary War. He was appointed August 1, 1776, and his name is last borne on a muster roll for July, 1777, dated August 5, 1777, but neither the place of his birth, the names of his parents, nor the date and manner of the termination of his service are shown."

While we cannot follow Streit in his movements in the army on these pages, it is nevertheless necessary that we mention the events in his life which helped in the development of the worker that came to the help of the Lutheran Church in Virginia. When Washington and his men retired to Valley Forge for the winter 1777-1778, Pastor Streit was urged to go to Charleston, S. C. It is not known to the writer whether he was requested to go as chaplain, or whether the congregation at Charleston called him. This much, however, is known, that at this time the unique Southern city was living in full enjoyment of peace, and the German congregation there desired English preaching in addition to the regular German services. Pastor Streit was there when later the British came and laid siege to the city. The whole Virginia line was sent to Charleston in defense of the besieged community, and Streit evidently became chaplain of the Ninth Virginia regiment, as he was mentioned as holding this position by General Muhlenberg, who surely would be in a position to know.

When Charleston fell, he was taken prisoner by the British with the whole Virginia line and all the American soldiers in the city. When he was set free by exchange of prisoners, he took his wife and child and made his way to the home of the Patriarch Muhlenberg who for safety had moved to The Trappe, thirty miles inland from Philadelphia. This was in 1782. Muhlenberg recommended him to New Holland where he served three years. July 19, 1785, he arrived in Winchester and took up the work that meant so much for the Lutheran people of Winchester and the surrounding country.

He not only served the Winchester congregation and the people of Winchester, but he took up much of the work that had been without care and attention since the removal of General Muhlenberg from Woodstock, especially the old and important church at Strasburg, and other points, radiating in usefulness in many directions, and far into the mountain valleys that opened into the level territory about Winchester. He preached at the beginning of his residence in Winchester mostly in German, but gradually he used the English language more and more, as the work of transition progressed.

In considering the many-sided usefulness of Christian Streit we shall mention first his mechanical skill. It is not a requisite of a minister but in Streit's case it proved to be a very helpful acquisition. When he reached Winchester he found four walls with a roof over them. He set to work at once with his own hands making doors and windows, furniture and whatever was needed to complete the sanctuary, thus leading the way for volunteer carpenters to do this work that had been neglected for so many years. At another time when an organ was needed at one of his preaching points he set to work and built one to serve the purpose for many years. Thus many a table and altar, reading desk and pulpit needed in the church were made by his skill for the use of the little churches scattered throughout the vicinity.

He was a born teacher. His catechetical work was continuous among young and old, in German and English, according to the needs of the place where he labored. His home was a seminary for theological students. William Carpenter of the Old Hebron congregation spent a whole year in his house preparing for the work of a teacher and preacher. Paul Henkel stopped with him often for a day or more to augment his knowledge of Latin and Greek. Streit's education was well adapted to all work of this kind, because it was of the highest that could be gotten at that time. He was no doubt the best educated man in the Valley during his residence in Winchester. He gave his parishioners and his friends the full benefit of his erudition. He and Dr. Hill for years conducted an advanced school for girls, that gained a wide reputation in Virginia and Maryland for culture and efficiency. His pupils delighted to dwell on the gentleness and amiability of his temper. His aim was to build spiritual character as well as to develop the intelligence.

But he was above all a preacher. To this great calling he gave his thought and energy. His life was a life of faith and love, hope and zeal; to this he added the grandeur of a magnanimous spirit, and delivered his message with the eloquence of beauty. The melody of music adorned his life in the sanctuary and in the home. He loved and appreciated the harmony of sweet sounds; he could sing and play, and added greatly to his usefulness in the school and church by freely availing himself of his ability and genius. We shall quote a few words from Charles Philip Krauth in order to give us a fuller account of his work as preacher in the Valley of Virginia:

"As a minister of Jesus Christ, I have ample means of learning that he was regarded not only by his own churches, and he had many, but by all that knew him, as most conscientiously and faithfully devoted to his work. * * * Devoted to the Lutheran Church and extending his labors over a wide field, he secured the confidence of the most intelligent as well as the least intelligent portion of the Church. The common people heard him gladly. He preached—a rare thing in that day and not very common now—equally well in the German and English languages. His labors were greatly instrumental in building up the churches in Winchester and the adjoining region.

"Though naturally inclined to be sad and often greatly depressed, he finished his course with joy. All who know him bore testimony to his exalted worth. Often have I heard the members of his charge speak of him with the greatest affection, of the great grief his removal produced, the apprehension felt by them that his place could never be supplied.

His sermons were carefully treasured long after he had departed, and one especially of uncommon power was spoken of in one of his churches, * * * 'The voice said, Cry. And he said, "What shall I cry? All flesh is grass, and all the goodliness thereof is as the flower of the field: The grass withereth, the flower fadeth, but the word of our God shall stand forever!' (Isa. 40:6,8.) On this text he preached a most melting sermon, which was not forgotten after many years, and the fruits of which, we may believe, will be manifest in another sphere."

We shall also quote a few lines from one of the successors of Christian Streit, Charles Porterfield Krauth, from his sermon which he preached upon the burning of the old sanctuary on the night of September 27, 1854, on the text, "Our holy and our beautiful house, where our fathers praised thee, is burned up with fire." Isa. 64:11.

"But our church is hallowed not only by the ashes on which its shadows fall; it is hallowed by the ashes it contains. Within it lie the remains of him who is entitled to the name of its first pastor; who, though preceded by transient supplies, may be regarded as the father of our church in this place. * * * This venerable man, who so long, so faithfully, and so successfully labored in his ministrations of love, entered on his toils in this place July 19, 1785. He commenced at once to preach both in German and English and to act as the untitled but true bishop of all our congregations in this portion of the Valley of Virginia. At the first two communions which he held in Winchester, the number added by confirmation was sixty-five, more than doubling the membership. He at once took steps for completing the church. Our congregation was worshiping at the time of his coming in the log church on the hill. But they soon had the happiness of occupying a house of worship of their own. Fort twenty-seven years they enjoyed the faithful preaching, the spotless example, and the untiring pastoral attentions of one of the most unpretending and good men with whom a church has ever been blessed."

This in brief is the life of the man that made history for Lutheranism in Virginia until his death, March 10, 1812. Besides Winchester, Stone's Chapel, Newtown, Strasburg, Old Furnace, Pine Hills, Capon, and Warm Springs (Pembroke Springs), heard his sermons and were influenced by his words and example. When he passed away his members reverently laid his body in a grave in front of the pulpit, where it rested until after the church was consumed by fire, when they exhumed it and buried it in the family lot at the side of the remaining wall of the revered sanctuary, marked

by a suitable monument, which bears an inscription ending
with the following words of Scripture:

I HAVE FOUGHT A GOOD FIGHT

I HAVE FINISHED MY COURSE

I HAVE KEPT THE FAITH

We still feel the eloquence of this good man's life.
His many nameless, unrecorded acts of kindness and love—
they form the best portion of his biography.

"The dead are like the stars by day,
Unseen by mortal eye,
And yet triumphant hold their way
In glory through the sky."

William Carpenter

helped to make civil and ecclesiastical history in the State of
Virginia. He was the first minister sent out by the Old
Hebron congregation and gave a total of forty-six years to
the ministry, twenty-six of which he spent in his own congregation, and twenty in the daughter congregation of Old
Hebron in Boone County, Kentucky. He was born May 20,
1762, and confirmed by Pastor Frank in 1778. Immediately upon his confirmation though only sixteen years of age
he entered the Continental army and served under Gen.
Peter Muhlenberg until the end of the war. He was
present with his father at the surrender of Cornwallis at
Yorktown. His army service was one of privation, as he
records in his diary the following words: "Soldiers endure
great hardships, frequently subsisting two or three days
without their rations, and then receiving only a meager
allowance of corn meal, which they hastily mix with a little
water and after covering it with oak leaves lay it on a bed
of warm coals until it is baked, and then partake of this
homely meal with the greatest of zest."

Carpenter is a descendant of one of the oldest families
in the Hebron settlement, coming from the original Zimmermann family. In his own day the name was translated
to Carpenter. He early received the inspiration to become
a soldier of the cross as he had been a soldier of the sword,

and he availed himself of the opportunities offered by the home of the nearest pastor, Christian Streit, and the encouragement of Paul Henkel, who began to come to Old Hebron in the fall of 1784. In 1786, he went to Streit and studied the rudiments of secular and religious knowledge and in 1787 he was licensed as a catechist by the Ministerium of Pennsylvania. In 1791 he was ordained to the Gospel ministry as a pastor with full authority. He served the congregation faithfully in German and with the help of Paul Henkel introduced the English language, but not without considerable difficulty.

His thirty years of service were a great factor in the history of Virginia Lutheranism. His whole life spent in his own State would have added still more glory to his name and to his Church, but he felt called to follow his former parishioners, who had now been without a pastor for seven years. While in Virginia he labored not for himself but for his Master whom he loved and whom he served often with much affliction. It was a potent trio of Lutheran ministers that labored together for many years, Henkel, Streit and Carpenter. They thought much of each other and cooperated with much fondness and satisfaction in their Virginia "wilderness" of trackless forests and fertile fields.

Pastor W. P. Huddle gives the following summary of his character and labors: "He was a man of great simplicity, integrity, and force of character, of blameless life, and of ardent devotion his whole lifelong. The old church records are silent witnesses to the zeal and fidelity with which he discharged the duties of his holy office and to the visible fruits of his labors. The harvest of souls gathered during his protracted ministry in Madison County was large. During sixteen of the thirty years of which he was pastor of the church, he baptized 865 persons besides numerous confirmations. * * * Here (in Boone County, Ky.) he labored faithfully for twenty years longer, till the summons from the Master came February 18, 1833. His remains were laid to rest on his farm near Florence. The modest inscription on his tombstone simply tells his name, date of death, and age." His life forms a vital part of the

history of Lutheranism in Virginia, and to his memory we
make this mention of his labors and inscribe the following
words written by Bayard Taylor as our testimonial of
appreciation upon these pages:

> "Courage and Truth, the children we beget,
> Unmixed of baser earth, shall be eternal,
> A finer spirit in the blood shall give
> The token of the lives wherein we live—
> Unselfish force, unconscious nobleness
> That in the shocks of fortune stand unshaken—
> The hopes that in their very being bless,
> The aspirations that to deeds awaken!"

John David Young

came from Germany in the fall of 1789, with recommenda-
tions from certain Lutheran authorities in Saxony, which
is a strong Lutheran country, and presented himself to the
president of the Ministerium, who gave him a license ad
interim, by virtue of which he at once went to work in
Manheim, Pa.   When the Ministerium met the following
year his license was continued and in 1791 he was ordained
in company with William Carpenter to the ministry.   Even
before his ordination in 1790 he began to labor in the State
of Virginia, in Martinsburg and Shepherdstown.   This
brought him into close relation with our Virginia ministers
Streit and Carpenter, with whom he cooperated harmoniously, both being conversant with the German tongue, and
thus able to enjoy conversations with the brother in the
ministry.   He was advanced in years beyond the others
when he arrived in Virginia and labored as a consequence but
a comparatively short time in this field, until his death in
1804.   Yet as he gave his last years of life to the service of
the ministry in our State, and united with the others in their
efforts to provide for the growing needs of the Church, we
desire to mention him on these pages.   Dr. Wentz says,
"His labors were abundantly blessed and he added to the
church during his short ministry no less than one hundred
and forty-three members.   He it was who drew up the first
constitution and form of government for the congregation.
It shows great prudence and splendid judgment."

While these four distinguished ministers were laboring in the lower Shenandoah Valley, and adjoining states and territories, other pastors and teachers were growing up into the ministry, born on Virginia soil and sons of the Lutheran Church itself. They were not as strong and prominent as the ones mentioned, but faithful and energetic, and members of the Ministerium. The first that shall be mentioned of these native pastors is William Forster (Wilhelm Förster). He was first licensed in 1798, and after continuing his services to the satisfaction of the Ministerium for several years he was ordained by the Ministerium June 16, 1802. He labored continuously in eastern Shenandoah, in the part which is now Page County. In 1805, he began to make missionary journeys to the State of Ohio, and in 1807, he moved to the northwestern part of that State and became the first settled Lutheran pastor in Ohio. Here he continued his work most vigorously till his death, which occurred in 1815.

John Foltz was a pastor of much usefulness in Rockingham County. As early as 1786 he came to Paul Henkel for instructions in writing and secular branches, and was impressed with the feeling that he should be a teacher and preacher. For practice and experience he spent much time with Mr. Henkel and accompained him on his trip to North Carolina in 1786. He appeared before the Ministerium for the first time in May, 1796, and was licensed to serve as a candidate for St. Peter's, Röder's, Powell's Fort, and Brock's Gap. He was ordained June 16, 1802, and spent his ministerial life ending in 1810 in various congregations in Rockingham and Shenandoah counties. He was pastor also of the Davidsburg congregation, New Market, while Paul Henkel was in North Carolina. He spent a life of usefulness and efficiency, serving also as pastor of Koiner's church from 1800 to his death.

Adolph Spindler was also a son of Virginia and one of the early pastors that served the church faithfully in a time when pastors were few in number. His name is always connected with Augusta County. He was licensed by the

Ministerium May 24, 1796 for St. John's, the Hone Meeting House and Frieden's. He was ordained June 7, 1803. He was the last pastor to preach in the German language only in the Union Church near Middlebrook, which was divided in 1738 into St. John's Reformed and Mt. Tabor Lutheran Church. Even during his life an assistant was elected to give the people sermons in the language they understood better than German. But harmony continued and he was pastor of the Lutheran congregation in the union church until his death in 1837. His body lies buried in the cemetery near St. John's Reformed church. But a year after his death the separation took place and Mt. Tabor church was built. His widow who outlived him by several years is buried in Mt. Tabor cemetery.

The Schmuckers

On his preaching tours in Shenandoah County, Paul Henkel found a wonderful family of German immigrants, living just west of Woodstock by the name of Schmucker. The son John George attracted Henkel's attention first of all and the result was that he found a student who was eager to learn theology. For a year he sat at the feet of his pastor Paul Henkel and studied the branches of learning that would help him to become a minister. In 1790 he went to Philadelphia to the German pastors there and continued his studies. In 1792 the Ministerium licensed him, and on the tenth day of June, 1800, ordained him to the Lutheran ministry. After spending fifty-eight years in the work of his Church in Maryland and Pennsylvania he passed away October 7, 1854. He was born in Germany but reared in Virginia. His son Samuel Simon, after graduating in Princeton, the college and seminary of the Presbyterian Church, gave five years of his life to the work of the Lutheran Church in Virginia, as pastor of the Lutheran Church at New Market, and as teacher of six candidates of theology: John Philip Cline, John G. Morris, John Reck, George Schmucker, Samuel K. Hoshour, and H. D. Kyle. Two of these were natives of Virginia; namely, John P. Cline and George Schmucker.

Two brothers of John George Schmucker also enlisted in the army of the Lord, giving their services to the Lutheran Church in Virginia. John Nicholas Schmucker had already married when he felt the pressure of the call to enter the ministry, but the call came to him in such strong terms that he could not resist. He was largely self-educated and began to make himself of use in his own congregation in Woodstock before being called by the Ministerium. This is the reason he is considered the pastor of the congregation in Woodstock beginning with 1806, whereas he was not licensed by the Ministerium until 1812. No doubt he assisted the pastorless congregation long before the year 1806. He was a retiring man, not much for publicity, but exceedingly helpful, wise, and unwearying in his far-flung labors. Born in Germany September 24, 1779, he died advanced in years in 1855. His son George also became a minister and labored in the valleys of northern Virginia, especially in Pendleton and Hardy Counties, in connection with the Virginia, Tennessee and Ohio synods.

The second brother of John George Schmucker, the third son of John Christopher Schmucker, was John Peter Schmucker, who was born soon after the arrival of the family in America in 1781, and began his life as a minister with his licensure by the North Carolina Ministerium, October 19, 1813, and was ordained by the same body May 30, 1820. He evidently never changed his synodical membership, but is known to have labored in Virginia all his lifetime.

The Henkels

Mention has been made of the five sons of Paul Henkel, who as ministers served the Lutheran Church in various parts of the Union; it remains to speak briefly of the four brothers of the same Paul Henkel, who as Lutheran ministers served the Church in various counties of Virginia, and while we have but few records of their activities we know that two of the four were held in such high esteem by the people they served that their mortal bodies found a last resting place before the pulpit from which they had preached. Benjamin labored mostly in Rockingham County and is buried under the chancel of St. Michael's Church of that county. We give the words of Dr. Wayland in his History of Rockingham County (1912): "St. Michael's, three miles south of Bridgewater, organized as Lutheran, or as Lutheran and Reformed, in 1764; house had dirt floor; Rev. Benjamin Henkel (Lutheran) said to have been buried under the chancel, about 1794; in 1830 the old log house was remodeled; in 1876 it was torn down and the present brick church was built." Isaac Henkel also labored in Rockingham County. We have no details of his work. The same must be said of Joseph Henkel. John labored efficiently in Shenandoah County. He was called to North Carolina in 1803, but before preparations for his departure for the distant field were completed he passed away and his body was buried under the pulpit of Zion Lutheran Church near Hamburg, Shenandoah County.

The Stirewalts

Among the ministers that spent many years in active service in the lower Shenandoah Valley are the Stirewalts. They first settled in North Carolina through Captain John Stirewalt, who left Pennsylvania before the end of the eighteenth century and established a home in the State of his adoption. He was an ardent lover of the faith and confessions of the Lutheran Church and brought up two sons for the ministry. John N. Stirewalt spent most of his time in North Carolina but had become acquainted with the Valley of Virginia, and had bought a farm near New Market, to which he intended to move. Death, however, interfered with his plans, but his widow moved with her three sons and one daughter to the farm near New Market, and educated the three boys for the ministry. Paul J. Stirewalt was educated in the University of Virginia, after which he studied theology and was ordained in 1855 by the Tennessee Synod. He spent his ministerial life in Ohio and Indiana. The second son, Julius L. Stirewalt, studied at Capital University, Columbus, Ohio, and was ordained in 1858, and labored in Indiana. The third son, Quintus

Spener Stirewalt, was prevented by ill health from entering the ministry.

The second son of Capt. John Stirewalt to become a minister was Jacob Stirewalt, who though born in North Carolina early came to Virginia, bought a home in New Market, and a farm near by, and spent all his ministerial life covering thirty-two years in the lower counties of Virginia. His was an active life. He was a constant worker in the Synod and Conference, and served congregations in Shenandoah, Page, and Rockingham Counties. He also made missionary trips into the neighboring counties of West Virginia. He reared a large family and two of his sons entered the ministry.

John N. Stirewalt was ordained in 1871, and continued in the service for thirty-seven years. He began early to take up the lines laid down by his father, but later concentrated his efforts upon the congregations in Page County, and became the first resident Lutheran minister of this county. He spent one year in Indiana. His son Arthur J. Stirewalt entered the foreign service in Japan.

Jerome Paul Stirewalt was the second son of Jacob Stirewalt to enter the ministry of the Lutheran Church. He was born April 11, 1850 in New Market, and ordained in 1873. His has been an energetic life in the ministry reaching distant points in Shenandoah, Page and Rockingham Counties, extending his labors into Prince William County, serving congregations, organizing missions, and in every possible way furthering the work to which he had been called. His two sons are Prof. William J. Stirewalt, A. M., New Market, and Prof. Martin L. Stirewalt, D. D., Maywood, Illinois.   * * * * *

We cannot leave this part of the territory of the Lutheran Church in Virginia, without making mention of the ministers sent from the North to labor for a while in our State as pastors of congregations and helping to build up the vineyard of the Lord in Virginia before leaving for fields of activity elsewhere in the Church and becoming famous as leaders on account of the superior services which they

rendered. The congregations that were fortunate enough
to have these noble men as their pastors are mainly Winchester, Martinsburg, Shepherdstown, Harrisonburg and Staunton. Among these we mention Charles Philip Krauth,
Charles Porterfield Krauth, Beale M. Schmucker, Joseph A.
Seiss, Daniel J. Hauer, Abraham Reck, Samuel Sprecher,
Lewis F. Eichelberger, and David M. Gilbert.

On to Southwest Virginia

In the territory of our State beginning with Botetourt
County we have found that Paul Henkel was among the
first of the known missionaries and pastors to serve the
scattered Germans of our Church. His labors were
seconded by the efforts of the school teachers, among whom
we must mention for Botetourt County John William
Meyer. He does not seem to have been related to others
of this name, but he began to apply for licensure early in
the century. In 1806 and 1807 he appealed to the Special
Virginia Conference for encouragement and licensure but
the members did not know him sufficiently to do more than
put him off with a promise; in 1809 the Ministerium gave
him a license as catechist under the oversight of Paul Henkel
for one year. In 1812 the North Carolina Synod licensed
him as a candidate, and renewed his license for several years,
but in 1817 refused to renew it, as reports proving him to be
unworthy had reached the Synod. He continued his labors
in Botetourt County until about 1816, when he accepted an
offer to labor in North Carolina. All these years mentioned
he continued to preach and teach, baptize and confirm,
whether he had the authority or not, causing much confusion
in the Church, but there were no regular ministers to do the
work, consequently, much of it was done after the manner
of Mr. Meyer. In 1811 the first ordered missionary
journey of the North Carolina Synod was made through its
active traveling preacher, Robert Johnson Miller, and he
endeavored to remove these irregularities. In this work he
was very helpful. He was an Englishman who had come
to America just at the outbreak of the Revolution and after
its end settled in North Carolina. As he was not able to

preach German he was free to make these missionary trips
for his Synod. On this trip and the one made two years
later in company with Jacob Scherer he turned the attention
of the shepherdless congregations in southwest Virginia to
North Carolina, and through his influence many congregations united with this Synod, others were organized under
the authority of the Synod, and the ministers were induced
to study and apply for licensure in a regular way. With
the help coming from the Ministerium of Pennsylvania in
the North, and from the Synod of North Carolina from the
South, the Church in Virginia enjoyed a twofold helpfulness
from which it greatly prospered. It accounts for the large
Lutheran population in southwest Virginia and for the many
ministers that came from the various congregations of this
territory and gave our Church pastors to fill the many
vacancies in our State and beyond. Among these names are
the following: Scherer, Brown, Cassell, Repass, Kegley,
Greever, Philippi, Cronk, Huddle, Peery, Spiggle, Oney,
Wetzel, Bonham, .Copenhaver, Huffard, Utz, and many
others.

The Scherers

Among the most important workers and missionaries
sent by the North Carolina Synod were the Scherers. The
family settled in North Carolina about 1764. The ship
Richard and Mary brought the first of the family to the
American shores in 1752. His name was Jacob Daniel and
he was a journeyman tailor. His bride, Hannah Sophia
Dick, followed him to America and they were married in
Pennsylvania about 1757. He became prominent in his
North Carolinian home and his name was entered upon the
census register of 1790. His son Frederick served honorably in the Revolution. It is to be noted of the descendants
that they were universally teachers, and many of them
became preachers, and these two characteristics have
remained with the members of the family to this day, in
regard to both sons and daughters, for they have been
eminent in the work of education and missions.

We are interested in this narration in two sons of
Frederick mentioned above, Jacob and Daniel. According

to the native bent of mind these two men taught school in their early manhood, and Jacob early expressed his desire to Paul Henkel that he might become a preacher, also. He received the encouragement that he deserved and in 1810 he was licensed by the North Carolina Synod. He was so active and earnest in his work as candidate that he had to wait but two years for his ordination which took place, October 18, 1812. His first work in the line of education that we wish to note here is the training for the ministry he gave his younger brother Daniel, who in turn was licensed by his Synod in 1816 and ordained June 18, 1821. Jacob was soon attracted by the call coming unceasingly from southwest Virginia. He was ready therefore in 1813, to join, at the direction of Synod, Robert J. Miller to make a missionary journey through Virginia to points in the Northwest Territory, for relatives of his family, and many neighbors had left home and emigrated to Virginia and Ohio. The pilgrimage was a most fruitful one. The two. missionaries were well mated for they found that everywhere there was a demand for preaching in both English and German. Scherer delivered the German sermon and Miller followed with the English. Services were held wherever a house, barn, or church could be found; children were baptized; congregations formed; names of young and old desiring instruction for confirmation enrolled; teachers appointed and where communicant members could be grouped together communion was administered. The two traveled north through the Virginia counties to the Upper Tract in Pendleton County and there they separated, Scherer going north and westward to Ohio, and Miller east and southward on the eastern side of the Blue Ridge to his home. To give the results of a trip like this in Virginia and Ohio let us notice Scherer's totals that he gives at the end of his report to his synod: Time, three months less three days; distance, 1617 miles; sermons, fifty; baptism of infants, seventy-two; organized congregations, thirteen, with 1175 members; number enrolled for catechetical instruction, two hundred and fifteen; compensation received $76.70; expenses, $34.85.

From this time on Jacob Scherer frequently visited in southwest Virginia, and in 1829 or 1830 his love for his Virginia mission field constrained him to move with his family to the State, and there he labored abundantly until about 1853 when he followed his son to Texas, where ten more years in teaching and preaching were given to the extension of the Kingdom of Christ, and there in that distant State his body lies buried, far from home but not far from heaven. He gave three sons to labor in the vineyard in Virginia, Gideon, Simeon, and John Jacob. Gideon remained in our State for twelve years, but in 1852 or 1853 he moved to Texas and there established Colorado College in Colorado County, to which he gave his means and talents, his body and soul until his death in 1861. There he was buried a martyr to the cause of education and the preaching of the Gospel. Simeon labored in Virginia until 1851, when he returned to the ancestral field of labor in North Carolina and served the Church prominently and efficiently until his death in 1876. He is the father of our beloved Secretary of the United Lutheran Church in America, the Rev. Melanchthon G. G. Scherer, D. D. John Jacob is a true son of Virginia, born near Rural Retreat, February 7, 1830. He was educated in the Virginia Collegiate Institute at Middlebrook and Salem, and graduated in Pennsylvania College, Gettysburg, Pa., in 1852. Immediately upon his return from Gettysburg he went with his brother Gideon to Texas, and there he labored in teaching and preaching until he had laid away both father and brother, when upon the urgent request of his brethren in Virginia he returned to his native State to organize Marion Junior College for young women, which was done in 1873, the school being chartered in August, 1874. Of the abundance of his labors in education, administration, and preaching we cannot here speak. Everywhere his usefulness is cheerfully acknowledged, and undying honors were showered upon him. He is the father of John Jacob Junior, Katherine Scherer Cronk, Laura Scherer Copenhaver, and Miss May Scherer, and through his children, he being dead yet speaketh, and his labors do follow him.

Jacob's younger brother Daniel, whom he had helped to educate, was filled with the same zeal for the work in the vineyard of the Lord. Though he had his assigned work in North Carolina he came as early as 1816, bringing his family with him, that he might preach and teach in the waste places of southwest Virginia. He did not finally give up his work in North Carolina until about 1828, when he moved to Virginia, and reported faithfully to his synod. He did a wonderful work in those years when the ministers were few and some of them were returning to their northern homes, or passing away, having completed their work on earth. But he soon grew restless. The missionary spirit within him gave him no peace, for the settlers were calling from Illinois, "Come over and help us." Before 1832 he was in that distant state; by 1834 he had organized a flourishing congregation, with many preaching places, and by 1836 his mother synod had to dismiss him in order that he might unite with The Synod of the West, organized a year before. And he became the Patriarch of the Lutheran Church in the State of Illinois.

After the Mother Synod of the South had given up these workers for the vineyard in Virginia and beyond, she seemed to say, "It is enough!" Of her outstretched hand of blessing the palm rightly rested over the Church in her own State, but the fingers reached out over distant parts of the wide field to Virginia, Texas, Ohio and Illinois.

* * * * *

There were other teachers and preachers in southwest Virginia in the early years of our history. Three are linked closely together, Leonhard Willy, John George Butler, and George Daniel Flohr. Paul Henkel met the first one of the three as early as 1787 in the neighborhood of Wythe Courthouse. Nothing is known of him as to his origin, education or authority, except that he is supposed to be of Swiss nationality. He probably served as a school teacher and naturally grew into the ministry by the call of circumstances. He served a number of congregations and acquitted himself well in his work, laying the foundation of true Lutheranism in a call that he drew up for four congregations that desired to call him as pastor. This call formed the basis of the constitution for these congregations and its sound Lutheran character speaks well of the man who was the author. After a few years his name disappears and no one knows whither he went. His congregations were taken over by George Daniel Flohr who labored faithfully in this field for twenty-seven years, laying down his work in 1826. The names of the four congregations are the following: St. Paul's, St. John's, Kimberlin, and St. Mark's. All of these are in Wythe County, except the last which is in Smythe County. Jacob Scherer served these congregations from 1827 to 1837.

Pastor Flohr came from Germany and had intended to become a doctor, but peculiar experiences in Paris led him to a change of mind and in 1795, or a year or two later, he reached the Hebron congregation and taught school and studied theology under Pastor Carpenter. In 1799 the Ministerium of Pennsylvania licensed him as a candidate and in 1803 ordained him as a minister of the Gospel. While serving as a teacher he found the constitution which Candidate Frank had brought from Philadelphia and given to the congregation in Madison County. Of this he made a careful copy and in turn proposed it to his congregations in southwest Virginia. From here it found its way into the model constitution recommended by the synod to its members, and thus the work of the Patriarch Muhlenberg for sound doctrine extended even to the vineyard in southwest Virginia.

Pastor Flohr was a man of commanding and dignified personal appearance, an excellent scholar and theologian, and above all a pious, devoted minister, a genuine Lutheran, fully accepting the doctrines and usages of his Church. Some of his sermons were collected and printed in a good sized volume with a sketch of his interesting life. His body lies buried in the cemetery of St. John's Church, where he served so long and faithfully.

While Willy and Flohr served in Wythe County as a center, John George Butler made Botetourt County his headquarters. Butler was a Philadelphia boy, a member of the German Zion's congregation there, and Dr. Helmuth was his pastor. He was born in 1754, and served in the Revolution. He received his first encouragement and instruction from his pastor, who saw in the young man much that might be of benefit in the Lord's vineyard. After his licensure by the Ministerium of Pennsylvania he gave nine years of great activity and self-denial to the work in Botetourt County. With all the energies of an ardent soul, he constantly prosecuted missionary operations into districts lying far beyond, often making appointments a year in advance. The Ministerium sent him as traveling missionary throughout all the neighboring counties and far into eastern Tennessee. In 1805 he left this important field and took up work in Maryland. He had gone to Pennsylvania for his ordination and no doubt he saw the wide open field on the way, and entered the open door presented to him. To his end in 1816, he labored unceasingly without the least regard to bodily limitations, crossing the mountains, and preaching in counties far, far from home.

After his departure the field suffered much from neglect and from the work of worthless teachers, until Daniel Scherer settled in Botetourt County and served the church for three or four years. His labors in Botetourt were prosecuted with his usual zeal and earnestness. He was well liked both as a man and as a preacher. He gave to the church a permanence and stability which it had not hitherto enjoyed. He is represented as being of gentle, solemn bearing; one of those saintly men whose goodness stamps itself upon the countenance. He was a medium sized man, straight and spare, an excellent preacher and singer.

Some time after Daniel Scherer left, Martin Walther became the pastor in Botetourt County. Walther was a Virginian, born in Powell's Fort, and received his first instructions from Paul Henkel. In 1815 the Ministerium licensed him as a catechist under the supervision of his former teacher. Accepting work in southwest Virginia, to which he gave all the remaining days of his life, he received his license as a candidate from the North Carolina Synod, and was ordained by the same body in 1821. He extended the charge into Montgomery County, and spared himself no labor in reaching his distant preaching places. He took an interest in the general work of the Church, attended the meetings of his Synod, and arranged for synodical meetings in his congregations wherever possible. Toward the close of his life Daniel J. Hauer shared the work in Botetourt County with him. Walther reached the end of his earthly pilgrimage about 1834.

Daniel J. Hauer was born in Frederick, Md., March 3, 1806. He was educated near his home in the classical branches and instructed in theology by his pastor, the Rev. D. F. Schaeffer; he was licensed by the Synod of North Carolina in 1826, and ordained by the same synod May 6, 1829, in St. John's Church, Wythe County, Va., in those days when this synod still extended its arms of care over southwest Virginia. He was first a missionary in Virginia sent out by the Synod of Maryland and Virginia and then took up work in North Carolina from which he was called to southwest Virginia in 1828, operating in Roanoke, Montgomery, Floyd and Botetourt Counties, and frequently extending his tours into Greenbriar, Pendleton and Hardy Counties. In August 1832, Hauer accepted a call to Lovettsville, Loudoun Co., on the Potomac, where he labored faithfully and successfully until 1845, when he moved to Maryland, and later to Hanover, Pa., where he rounded out a useful life in the ministry at the age of over ninety-five years. He died November 27, 1901.

Three other names are found in the early history of the Lutheran Church in southwest Virginia, names of pastors who contributed in different ways to the upbuilding of the kingdom in this territory. A confirmation certificate has been preserved which gives names of people living on the New River that united in organizing what was later called St. Peter's Church, near Blacksburg, Va. The minister gives his name in full as Peter M. Brugell, D. D., western Virginia, in Montgomery County, first day of June, 1788. We have no further knowledge of this preacher, but his name is here given so as to help future historians to complete his record. The second is better known as he appears on the records of the history of the Lutheran Church in South Carolina. He gives his name in full as Wolfgang Friedrich Augustine Daser, signed to a constitution which he had St. Peter's Church adopt in 1796. He signed himself as pastor for the time being, but his entries in the records show that he served the congregation until June, 1800. His history in connection with the church in South Carolina is given in Bernheim's German Settlements in the Carolinas, pages 212 to 224, 277 to 279. As he came from Germany in 1769, he was well advanced in years, and may not have lived long after 1800. No facts of his life are known to the writer after the date given, 1800.

The Rev. John Stanger preached in St. Peter's about 1800. The records at Christiansburg show that he performed marriages in 1790, 1799 and 1800. Mr. Stanger lived in Wythe County and served churches in the county, and at one time was a member of the Virginia Assembly. We have no further knowledge of his life or work. His name is not found on any of our old synodical rolls of ministers.

Pastors in Eastern Tennessee

The first workers in Tennessee were three school teachers, Charles Z. H. Schmidt, Jacob Zink and Adam Miller. When these men began their labors in this territory is hard to say, but it is certain that they were on the field with the organization of the first congregations in 1795, earlier or later, and that they supplemented the work of the traveling ministers as they came from Pennsylvania, Virginia, or North Carolina. Jacob Zink may have been one of the first, as it is evident that he and others of his family came from Virginia long before the close of the eighteenth century. How much he accomplished and how far he went in his ministrations we are left without information. He was united in family relations, and evidently in his work, with Adam Miller. The two were licensed together by the North Carolina Synod, October 18, 1814, and also ordained together July 19, 1820. The third one, Pastor Schmidt, was evidently older in years than they and it is certain that he was far more advanced in his ministrations, as in 1811 he appeared before the North Carolina Synod as the pastor of nine congregations which were received into the synod in this year. He was ordained by this synod, April 6, 1812. His congregations were located in Sullivan, Washington, Green, Knox and Blount Counties. He has the distinction of doing the most of his ministerial work before his ordination as he passed away two years afterwards, and left a large unoccupied field upon his death. But the appeals of these shepherdless flocks made to the synod soon brought other laborers, among whom the chief one is Philip Henkel, who had been occupied since 1800 in Lincoln County, N. C. He found the need so great that he soon moved to the new state, and spent the rest of his days in active service in eastern Tennessee. In 1816 he found a young English Presbyterian, Joseph E. Bell, whom he encouraged to make use of his education and talents as a teacher and minister. He was received by the North Carolina Synod as a catechist in 1816. With these forces at work the numbers of the believers increased and in 1817, three new congregations were received by the synod. In addition to the missionary labors of these four men in the ministry, Henkel and Bell began a classical and theological seminary on their own responsibility. It was established in Greene County, under the supervision of these two men, who undertook to impart instruction in theology, German, English, Greek and Latin. The synod rejoiced over this new venture in faith and was filled with much hope for a bright future. But the times and the conditions were against the noble undertaking, and in a few years nothing more was heard of it. It was too far away, the ministers did not cooperate substantially, and Mr. Bell returned to the Presbyterian Church. Though this educational venture failed, the missionary operations prospered and the Church grew.

Other laborers were added to the ranks. Deacon George Easterly was ordained as a pastor in 1822; Christian Moretz and Jacob Costner were ordained as deacons. Costner labored many years as a deacon, but Moretz was ordained as pastor after serving two years as deacon, filling a long life with self-sacrificing labors for the extension of the kingdom in Tennessee and many distant states. Other pastors were ordained for work in the State of Tennessee: William Hancher, Abel J. Brown, George H. Cox, J. K. Hancher, James C. Barb, J. M. Wagner, J. M. Schaeffer, W. G. Wolford, F. M. Harr, W. C. Davis, H. G. Davis, W. C. Schaeffer.

The Rev. William Hancher was affectionately known among the people as Father Hancher. Born in Frederick County, Va., he came to Sullivan County, Tenn., when a young man, and was ordained by the Tennessee Synod in 1836. At the time of his ordination he was perhaps the only minister in eastern Tennessee who understood the English language only and preached exclusively in that language. In the difficult period of transition he not only saved the old members of the church but also brought into it most of their children, and many others who were outside of the church. To his labors we are largely indebted for the firm hold of Lutheranism in Sullivan County and for its prosperity in later years.

His son, James K. Hancher, was a preacher of unusual ability, eloquent, interesting and sometimes dramatic. He gave his long life to east Tennessee and is regarded as one of the strongest men that has lived in that territory.

Abel J. Brown was considered one of the strongest men in the Southern Church. He was ordained by the Tennessee Synod in 1836, and became a staunch defender of the conservative Lutheran faith. He was a scholar and theologian of the first rank, the peer of any man in the Southern Church in his day. He exerted no little influence in bringing the Lutheran Church in this country to its present confessional basis. He lived to see his high ideals realized in the organization of the United Synod in the South in 1886. He was a painstaking and faithful pastor, spending the last thirty-six years of his long ministry in one charge consisting of Immanuel's and Buehler's congregations in Sullivan County.

Eastern Tennessee was unfortunate in that it could not hold all the ministers it produced. Many of its strong men went out from its congregations into neighboring states and filled responsible positions with great credit to themselves and to the church they served. We mention J. H. Turner, for many years connected with Lutherville Female Seminary; M. L. Wagner holding prominent positions in the Missouri Synod both as pastor and educator; J. P. Deck, well known in the General Council as pastor of St. Michael's, Germantown, Philadelphia, Pa., and Binghamton, N. Y., the father of the Rev. Luther Bushong Deck, of Vancouver, Washington; J. L. Murphy, prominent in our Church in the Middle West; George H. Cox, for many years a beloved veteran in the North Carolina Synod; J. B. Fox, a leading minister in South Carolina; A. D. R. Hancher, General Secretary of the Board of Home Missions, now known as the Board of American Missions; and James C. Barb, located at Whitestown, Indiana, one of the leading ministers in the Indiana Synod.

CHAPTER III

ORGANIZATIONS

I T IS the object of this part of our History to show how the people, gathered in their congregations, with their pastors, united to form during a hundred years and more the various conferential and synodical bodies that have existed in the territory of Virginia and eastern Tennessee. It is not a short story, as many are the organizations that must be mentioned to make the narration complete.

The first that claims our interest is the formation of the Special Conferences of the Ministerium of Pennsylvania. In the Constitution of the Ministerium in force in 1781, we read the following paragraph:

Last of all, the ministers dwelling close together in one county or district (shall) confer in regard to special meetings or conferences to be appointed, concerning which the details may be determined in due time by resolutions of Synod. Whenever a special matter has been referred to a conference of that kind, such conference must be positively determined upon, and with the knowledge of all the others.

1783. The present congregations are divided into districts, and it is most earnestly recommended to all the brethren, that they renew and maintain Special Conferences.

1792. Special meetings are to be held by pastors of the Ministerium, living contiguous to each other, as often as circumstances may require, and each congregation under the care of such minister may send a delegate to said meeting, having seat and vote. * * *

The objects of such meetings are to promote the welfare of the respective congregations and of the German schools within the district; to examine, decide and determine the business and occurrences in their congregations that are brought before them; provided, however, that each party enjoys the right of appeal to Synod and Ministerium from the decisions of the conference.

A special meeting is not permitted under any pretence whatever to enter upon business belonging to the Ministerium, as set forth in Chapter III and VII. * * *

The acts of the meeting are to be transmitted by the chairman to the President of the Ministerium to be laid by him before the next Synodical or Ministerial meeting.

1801. A new arrangement of districts centering about: 1. Philadelphia, 2. Easton, 3. Lancaster, 4. Yorktown, 5. Baltimore, 6. Western District, 7. Virginia.

The Special Conference in Virginia

Under these rules and regulations the first district to organize was the Virginia District. Only two Lutheran organizations of pastors and congregations had been formed before the date of the formation of the Virginia Conference, 1793: The Mother Synod, 1748, and the Ministerium of New York, 1786. The date 1793 is therefore one of historic significance, of which we in Virginia can be justly proud.

There were four sons of the Ministerium at work in Virginia at that time, faithful and tried. Paul Henkel had been on the field the longest and had the most experience no doubt in synodical work. Christian Streit came next in time of service, and exceeded the others in the varied nature of his work in the ministry, having served the Lord both in freedom and in prison. William Carpenter was a born son of Virginia, hardened for the toils of a soldier of the cross by his experience in the camp of the Revolutionary army, and trained for the ministry by Christian Streit, to whom he looked as to a spiritual father. John David Young, was, it seems, the oldest in years but the youngest in service in America, as he had come over the waters from Germany but a few years before and had been ordained but recently. These four noble sons of the Ministerium met and formed the first Special Conference. We shall allow Dr. David M. Gilbert to give us an account of their first meeting and of the subsequent meetings for five or six years, as he has had access indirectly to the protocol which we have of their meetings.

1793, January 6th, 7th, the first Special Conference meeting of Lutheran ministers in Virginia was held at Winchester. The ministers present were Christian Streit, Winchester; John David Young, Martinsburg; Paul Henkel, New Market; and William Carpenter, Madison. The record opens thus: "We four ministers of the Evangelical Lutheran Church, living and serving congregations in the State of Virginia, being present in Winchester, on the sixth of January, 1793, began our Conference on this Epiphany Sunday by holding religious services."

Rev. Paul Henkel preached in the morning from John 7:38, on 1. The nature; 2. The fruits of saving faith.

Rev. William Carpenter preached in the afternoon from Romans 8:2, on the contrast between the law of sin and death, and the law of the Spirit of life.

Monday, January 7th, the first business session was held. Christian Streit was elected president, and John David Young, secretary. Lay delegates were present from the church councils of Winchester, Martinsburg, Shepherdstown, Stone Church, Newtown, Strasburg, and Woodstock; but their names are not given.

The members of the convention resolved that a Conference meeting should be held annually on the first Sunday in October; that they would not separate themselves from the Ministerium of Pennsylvania, nor take any action that would come in conflict with its regulations; that lay delegates regularly chosen and presenting themselves properly accredited, one from each congregation having a pastor, or desiring to procure one, regularly connected with the Synod, should be received into the Conference with the privilege of participating in all its business. * * * It was further resolved, that the Conference should always make "the devising of ways and means for the improvement of our young people and children in knowledge and piety a prominent aim;" and that "the proceedings of this Conference shall be made known to the congregations, and if approved by them they shall be laid before the Synod for examination and endorsement of these several resolutions."

The Conference was closed on Monday evening by a solemn and impressive public service in the church; Rev. John D. Young preached from the first Psalm, on "The blessedness of the man who walks in the way of faith and piety," after which the president expressed in a most feeling manner his thanks to his brethren and dismissed the congregation with the benediction.

1793, October 6th and 7th, XIX Trinity Sunday, the second convention of the Conference was held in Strasburg, Shenandoah County. Four ministers, Streit, Young, Henkel and Carpenter, met in the church two hours before the service. The officers of the former convention were re-elected.

It was resolved, that as Jehovah had during this remarkable year stretched forth his hand in judgment over Europe and also in this country, an unheard of mortality having taken place in Philadelphia, especially during August, September and October, the XXII Sunday after Trinity should be set apart as a day of humiliation and fasting in all our churches in the State of Virginia.

At 10 o'clock a. m., Rev. John D. Young preached from I Cor. 4:6; and in the afternoon Rev. William Carpenter from Gen. 19:17. * * *

1794, October 12th, 13th, XVII Trinity Sunday, Conference assembled at Martinsburg. The ministers present: Pastors Streit, Henkel, and Samuel Mau of Kentucky. Pastor Carpenter was asbent. Lay delegates were enrolled from Martinsburg, Shepherdstown, Winchester and Staunton.

On Sunday morning Rev. Paul Henkel preached from Isaiah 59:26, after which the Communion was administered. In the afternoon, Rev. Samuel Mau preached from the text John 12:35-37.

On Monday morning Pastor Streit preached from II Cor. 6:10. In the afternoon Conference held a business session in the schoolhouse.

1795, October 5th, Conference met in Staunton, Christian Streit, Paul Henkel and William Carpenter being present. Lay delegates enrolled: Jacob Rausch, Madison; Caspar Deiner, South River Church; Johannes Mess, Thurmis Church; Johannes Rohr, Rohr's Church; Johannes Rausch, Peaked Mountain Church; Simon Jäger, Kieselstadt; and Moses Henkel, South Branch, Pendleton County.

Christian Streit presided and in the absence of Pastor Young, Victor George Charles Stock, a theological student, perhaps a licentiate, acted as secretary.

1796, October 3d, 4th, the fifth convention was held at Madison. There were present, Pastors Henkel and Carpenter of the ordained ministers; V. G. C. Stock, Adolph Spindler and John Foltz, licentiates; and Messrs. John Risch, Gotwald Schirmer, Jacob Zanger, and John Jäger, lay delegates.

Pastors Streit and Young could not reach the place of meeting on account of high waters, and in their absence, Paul Henkel acted as president, and V. G. C. Stock as secretary.

1797, October 1st, 2d, XVI Trinity Sunday, Conference met in Woodstock. Ministers present: Streit, Henkel, Carpenter, Young, Stock and Foltz. Lay delegates: Nicholas Strear, Col. Risch, Mr. Capp, George Christler, Mr. Roller, J. Nees, and George Prinz. Pastor Streit addressed the brethren, and Rev. John David Young preached from 2 Cor. 5:19,20. Business sessions were held in the schoolhouse.

1798, October 7th, 8th, XVIII Trinity Sunday, Conference met in Shepherdstown. On Sunday Pastor Streit preached from Psalm 96:9.

On Monday morning at the organization for business there were present of ordained ministers: Christian Streit, William Carpenter, Paul Henkel, John David Young, and John George Schmucker, of Hagerstown, who was received as an advisory member. Licentiates: John Foltz, William Forster, and George Daniel Flohr, of Wythe County. Officers: Streit and Young. When the Conference adjourned it was to meet in convention at Winchester on the first Sunday in October, 1799.

Here the review of the written protocol of these meetings ends. Dr. Gilbert in his summary has given us the chief items of interest, which we have reproduced with a few omissions and variations. Following the reports made by the president to the Ministerium as found in the translated minutes of that body, we find that the members of the Ministerium were much impressed with the earnestness and fidelity of these fellow laborers in Virginia, and their reports and minutes were read with much interest. We find in the minutes for the meeting of 1793 the following references to the protocol of the first Virginia Conference:

A letter from Rev. Christian Streit was read, in which he excused his absence with satisfactory reasons, and gave a pleasing report of a Special Conference held in Virginia, the Protocol of which was referred to the Ministerial Meeting. * * *

A protocol of a Special Conference held in Virginia was read and listened to with pleasure.

It is evident from the published minutes of the Ministerium that the Virginia Conference was the most regular and faithful of all of the conferences. In the minutes for 1807, the following item is found:

The Virginia District sent its printed transactions. They were read, and it was unanimously resolved that these transactions be honorably mentioned in the Protocol, and the brethren be requested to continue their praiseworthy efforts.

It is to be regretted that we have no minutes of meetings succeeding the one held in 1798 in Martinsburg. We know, however, from the reports made to the Ministerium that meetings were held in 1802, 1803, and 1804. Much as we desire to have information in regard to these meetings, no data are given in the minutes of the Ministerium except that mention is made of the fact that the protocol for 1802 and 1804 was printed. We have in our possession the printed minutes in German for 1805 and the following years except 1814, but it is of interest to read that the minutes were printed previous to the year 1805. The explanation is that the members of the Virginia Conference made use of the German printing establishment of John Gruber in Hagerstown, Md., and had their minutes printed.

In the following paragraphs we shall give a hurried review of the meetings held in the year 1805, and the succeeding years, of which the German minutes are before us as we write.

1805, October 6 and 7, the Special Conference was held in the unfinished church in Woodstock. Only the first preaching service was held in the new house of worship, all the other sermons were delivered in the Reformed Church. Twice during the convention appeals were made for offerings to assist in completing the church. The business sessions were held in the schoolhouse. The following pastors were present: Christian Streit, William Carpenter, Paul Henkel, John Foltz, and Adolph Spindler. William Forster and John G. Butler had been sent out as traveling missionaries and therefore were absent. George Daniel Flohr sent a letter of excuse. The roll of lay delegates was as follows: Dr. Solomon Henkel of New Market, Jacob Rausch of Madison County, Balthaser Sauer of the Hawksbill congregation, John Roller of Röder's and Jacob Nees of Solomon's.

Christian Streit was elected president and Paul Henkel secretary. Many important items of business engaged the attention of the Conference and it is of interest to note the prominent part played by the lay delegates. William Carpenter proposed that an address or admonition be annually added to the minutes for the benefit of the congregations. Dr. Solomon Henkel proposed that the twenty-one doctrinal articles of the Augsburg Confession be added as an appendix to the minutes. Both of these proposals were adopted and carried out. Paul Henkel added an instructive introduction to the Augsburg Confession. Dr. Solomon Henkel offered to provide for the cost of the minutes, including the admonition and the articles of the Augsburg Confession. The last was reprinted from the Nuremberg Bible, which was about the only place where the people could find a copy of the Unaltered Augsburg Confession. Shepherdless congregations in Pendleton County appealed for services and Paul Henkel was asked to make a journey to that part of the State as soon as possible. Upon a motion made by Jacob Rausch it was decided that in the future all lay delegates must bring to the Conference a certificate of their appointment signed by the elders and deacons. Balthaser Sauer proposed, and it was adopted, that the teachers in each congregation conduct catechetical instructions either before or after the sermon. John Roller moved, seconded by Jacob Nees, that the practice of lining out the hymns be done away with as speedily as possible. Adopted. Zions congregation through its deacon George Foltz requested that they be supplied with services. Paul Henkel was instructed to visit them until other arrangements could be made. Röder's church was selected for the next meeting, with the object in view of dedicating the new church.

1806, October 5 and 6, according to previous appointment, the Conference was held in the new Röder's Church to dedicate the church for the Lutherans and Reformed. Sunday, the 5th, was set aside for the services of dedication. Paul Henkel represented the Lutheran congregation and Pastor John Braun the Reformed. After the sermon in German by the Reformed minister on the text, Psalm 95:5, "Holiness becometh thine house forever," Paul Henkel preached in English on the words, Psalm 84:1,2, "How amiable are thy tabernacles, O Lord of hosts!" A very large and attentive audience was present for the dedicatory services.

Monday morning the Conference organized for its business session. Three ministers were present: Paul Henkel, Adolph Spindler, and John Foltz. Christian Streit was absent on account of sickness; likewise, Pastor Carpenter. Lay delegates present were Andrew Zirkle of Solomon's, John Bauman of Röder's and Lawrence Spiegel of New Market. Paul Henkel was chosen president and Adolph Spindler secretary.

At the suggestion of Lawrence Spiegel an address of thanksgiving for the Lord's blessing, especially for the abundant rains of the recent past, was made before the sermon of the first public service. George Prinz and Friedrich Sauer testified to the faithful services rendered the Hawksbill congregation by Pastor Forster for several years. A letter was received from Daniel Maus, an elder of one of the Pendleton congregations, pleading for services for the vacant congregations of that county. In answer Pastor Foltz with the consent of the elders of his congregations, who were present, was instructed to make four visits in that county, and Pastors Spindler and Henkel promised to make at least one visit each during the year.

A request for a recommendation from John William Meyer of Botetourt County was received, but the Conference not knowing him could do nothing except to promise to investigate his work during the coming year. George Prinz requested that in case of a death in a congregation, with no minister within reach, it be allowed that a school teacher, or a lay reader, perform the service; this was granted by the Conference. Daniel Dinkel requested the appointment of a committee to investigate the causes for the restlessness in the Frieden's congregation in Rockingham County. The following committee was appointed: Pastors Streit and Henkel, Messrs. Andrew Zirkle, John Roller, William Pens and Lawrence Spiegel. Time, the first Sunday in the new year. It was decided that the address to be appended to the minutes this year shall be on the subject of church attendance. New Market was selected for the place of the next convention and the dedication of the church as the object.

This year's minutes are the first to come from the Henkel press of New Market. Some claim that this was the first work done by the newly established printery. It marks the beginning of a long history in the field of religious publications.

1807, October 3, 4, 5. This meeting of the Special Conference was remarkable for the large number of visiting ministers. No doubt the

Davidsburg Church in New Market was considered as an important center, and the invitation for the dedication of the sanctuary was accepted with gladness by the many who were interested in this field through their knowledge of the labors of Paul Henkel. From Hagerstown, Md., came John George Schmucker; from Huntingdon, Pa., came Friedrich Haas, a candidate of the Ministerium; and from North Carolina, Philip Henkel and Louis Marckert. Of the members there were present Paul Henkel, William Carpenter and John Foltz. Henkel was chosen president and Carpenter secretary. Aaron Crigler from Madison County, Jacob Nees from Solomon's, and Lawrence Spiegel of the local church were the lay delegates enrolled.

The services began on Saturday evening when Philip Henkel preached a preparatory sermon. The Communion sermon was preached on Sunday morning by Pastor Schmucker on the text Isa. 55:1. This was followed by the administration of the Holy Communion.

In the afternoon Pastor Marckert preached in German and in the evening Philip Henkel followed with a sermon in English. These services constituted the act of dedication, as no mention is made of this special service in the minutes. Probably the prayer of dedication preceded the morning service, but as Paul Henkel was pastor of the congregation all reference to him and his acts were suppressed in the minutes.

On Monday morning the Conference met in the schoolhouse for its business session. Letters of excuse were first heard from Pastors Streit, Flohr and Butler. The last had moved to Fort Cumberland, Md., and was no longer a member, but still he sent his excuse out of regard for the brethren. First a testimony was considered which had come from several congregations on Jackson River, Botetourt County, served by John William Meyer. The members present gave the matter a thorough consideration, and concluded to send the congregations a letter of encouragement, promising if reports during the coming year were favorable that they would receive their pastor at the next convention.

Aaron Crigler proposed that inasmuch as it had been agreed the previous year that school teachers or other suitable officer in the congregation should perform funeral services in the absence of the pastor, an order for burial should be appended to the minutes in place of the usual address or admonition. This was agreed to, and Pastor Schmucker suggested that the Conference should consider a form which he saw in the possession of Dr. Solomon Henkel. This was done and it was agreed that after the president and secretary had revised it, it should be published as directed for the benefit of school teachers and others. (It appears in full with hymns in this year's minutes, covering fourteen pages.)

Jacob Nees urged that no funeral be ever allowed to interfere with the holding of a communion service, but that the funeral service should be postponed, or be conducted by a teacher.

Dr. Solomon Henkel again offered to provide for the printing and distribution of the minutes, of which two hundred copies were to be issued. It was decided to hold the next convention in the pastorate of George Daniel Flohr in Wythe County. The convention was closed with a sermon in the evening by Candidate Haas, on the text, James 4:2, "Ye have not, because ye ask not."

1808, October 2,3. The place of the meeting is not Wythe County, but Winchester. No explanation is made why the meeting place was changed. Pastors present were Christian Streit, Paul Henkel, and John Foltz. Absent were Carpenter, Flohr, and Spindler. The delegates were Solomon Henkel, Heinrich Hahn of Strasburg, and Abraham Lauck of Winchester. Paul Henkel was elected president and Christian Streit secretary.

On Sunday Paul Henkel preached both in the morning and in the evening. The business on Monday was transacted in the schoolhouse. Dr. Solomon Henkel moved that in each congregation a lay reader be appointed to hold services on Sunday in the absence of a pastor, and to instruct the youth in the Catechism. Adopted. Upon motion of Abraham Lauck it was decided that the minister should hold private meetings with his members as often as possible and edify them with religious exercises and with instructions in the Word of God. Pastor Henkel moved that all regular ministers of the North Carolina Synod be received as members of the Virginia Conference if agreeable to the North Carolina Synod. Pastor Streit moved that on account of the unsettled condition of the country at this time the eighteenth day of next month be set aside as a day of repentance and prayer. Adopted.

Dr. Solomon Henkel moved that for the next convention each minister prepare a list of the congregations served by him, with the location of each one and the names of the elders, deacons, and lay readers, together with the name of the nearest post office. Adopted.

It was decided that the subject of the admonition to be printed with the minutes of this convention be, The Usefulness and Necessity of the Lay Reader. Henkel and Streit were directed to prepare the paper.

Solomon's church was selected as the next meeting place.

1809, October 1, 2, in Solomon's Church as appointed. Ministers present were Christian Streit, Adolph Spindler, and John Carl Rebenack of Martinsburg, who had come as an ordained minister from Germany in 1804, and served the Martinsburg congregation 1808 to 1814. As a visiting minister John Nicolas Schmucker of Woodstock was present. The enrolled lay delegates were George Bauer of Solomon's, John Bender (Painter) of Zion's, John Roller of Röder's, Jacob Rausch of Jäger's Church, Mason County, and Solomon Henkel of New Market. Pastor Streit was elected chairman and Solomon Henkel secretary. The business sessions were held in the schoolhouse. The excuses of the absentees were first heard. Carpenter and Foltz were absent on account of sickness. Pastor Flohr sent no excuse. Paul Henkel was away on a missionary journey to North Carolina. Dr. Solomon Henkel suggested a plan, which had for its object the supplying of pastorless fields with occasional services. Final conclusions were reserved for the next Special Conference. Dr. Henkel also suggested an order of services to be conducted by lay readers, consisting of prayer, singing, instruction of the young, reading of a portion of the Bible, or a sermon. Pastor Streit urged all the ministers to visit their members faithfully in their homes. Upon the request of John Nicolas Schmucker, the Conference decided to give him a recommendation to the Ministerium of Pennsylvania for reception into the Ministerium as a candidate.

In reference to the resolution of the previous year, a call was made for the register of congregations, and they were handed in to the secretary, who tabulated them with much labor and care and printed the complete register as an appendix to the minutes. The table is as large as three pages in width and one and a half in length, and was folded in as a part of the bound copy of minutes. This table is considered so valuable as a record of the strength of the Lutheran Church in Virginia in the year 1809, that it is reproduced here in a rearrangement. No names of ministers are given in this table, so it is well to remember the names of the ministers then in service in the State. John Carl Rebenack was at Martinsburg, Christian Streit at Winchester, John Nicolas Schmucker at Woodstock, Paul Henkel at New Market, John Foltz in Rockingham County, Adolph Spindler in Augusta County, William Carpenter in Madison County, and George Daniel Flohr in Wythe County.

The Register of Churches, Elders, Deacons and Lay Readers in Virginia

Berkeley County

Martinsburg Church—Officers: Jacob Bischof, Valentine Oehl, Jacob Schmal, Peter Schnaudigel, John Fischer, Jacob Beisel, Peter Riel, Adam Young.

Smithfield Church—Officers: Henry Seibert, Nicolas Scholl, Jacob Boltz, Valentine Knop.

Jefferson County

Shepherdstown Church—Officers: Philip Schott, John Matter, Adam Link, N. N. Lechleiter, G. Gausle, M. Burket, Philip Kraft, G. Weis.

Frederick County

Winchester Church—Officers: Philip Huber, Peter Lauck, John Heist, John Reile, Abraham Lauck, John Linn.

Penbrook Church, near Winchester—Officers: John Kiefer, Henry Beile.

Stephens City Church—Officers: Jacob Leonard, Anton Klein.

Shenandoah County

Strasburg Church—Officers: Henry Hahn, Philip Peter Becker.

Woodstock Church—Officers: Samuel Rotenhäffer, Michael Haas, Jacob Schmucker.

Powell's Fort Church—Officers: Jacob Lechleiter, Henry Walther, Adam Lechleiter, Henry Borner, Martin Walther.

Solomon's Church—Officers: G. Bauer, Louis Bauer, Jacob Zerfass, Bernhard Götz.

William's Church (Steinberger)—Officer: John Nauman.

Hawksbill Church, near Luray—Officers: George Printz, Friedrich Sauer, John Schenk.

Davidsburg Church (New Market)—Officers: Louis Zirkel, Solomon Henkel, Lawrence Spiegel, Henry Ruppert.

Zion's Church, near Woodstock—Officers: Jacob Höltzle, George Foltz, John and Philip Bender.

Madison County

Culpeper Church (Hebron)—Officers: Matthias Haus, Christopher Zimmerman (Carpenter), Aaron Crigler, Samuel Carpenter, Jr., Cornelius Carpenter, Daniel Utz, Moses Weber.

Rockingham County

St. Peter's Church—Officers: William Bens, Michael Reinhart, Michael Schuler.

St. Paul's Church—Officer: Jacob Foltz.

Röder's Church—Officers: John Roller, John Bauman.

Peaked Mountain Church—Officer: John Risch.

Frieden's Church—Officers: Jacob Schenk, Henry Kessel, John Erman, Philip Keller.

Ermantraut's Church—Officers: Peter Ermantraut, Henry Ermantraut.

Augusta County

St. John's Church, near Middlebrook—Officers: Friedrich Henger, Jacob Gebert, Peter Egel, George Frenckerer.

Brown's Church, near Staunton—Officer: August Argenbrecht.

Emmanuel's Church—Officers: John Perst, Henry Herman, Mr. Heise, Mr. Kirchhof, John Herman, Daniel Schäfer.

Salem Church—Officers: Matthias Link, Peter Link.

Jenings Branch Church—Officers: Louis Schmidt, Mr. Schierman.

Keiner's Church (Koiner's)—Officers: Casper Keiner, George Keiner.

Rockbridge County

Samuel's Church, near Brownsburg—Officer: Friedrich Mohler.

Botetourt County

Roanoke Church, near Salem—Officers: George Braun, Jacob Stattler.

Mill Creek Church, near Fincastle—Officers: Samuel Ovenschein, Michael Gohn, Jr.

James River Church, near Fincastle—Officers: Nicholas Young, Jacob Young.

Jackson River Church, near Fincastle—Officers: John Brunnerer, Christian Fuchs.

Montgomery County

Price's Church—Officers: George Zerfass, Jacob Price.

Little River Church—Officers: George Eberly, Henry Krank, John Sendmeier.

Wythe County

St. John's Church at Eavansham—Officers: Casper Röther, John Hercheröther, Christopher Braun, Christian Geckle.

Kimmerling's Church—Officers: John Kimmerling, Henry Happes.

Schneble's Church—Officers: John Schneble, John Schneider.

Elk Creek Church—Officer: John Riede.

Cripple Creek Church—Officer: Christophel Sprecher.

Greenbrier County

Louisburg Church—Officers: Martin Scheuerer, Samuel Fleischmann.

Pendleton County

Brobst Church, near Franklin—Officers: Christian Ruhlman, George Brobst, Christian Ruhlman, Jr.

Wildfang's Church, near Franklin—Officers: Friedrich Grummet, John Simon.

Upper Tract Church, near Franklin—Officers: Jacob Miller, Henry Mallo.

North Fork Church, near Franklin—Officers: Daniel Maus, George Negley.

Hardy County

Mill Creek Church, near Moorefield—Officer: Nicodemus Bergdoll.

Hampshire County

Great Capon Church, near Romney—Officers: John Schweitzer, Philip Klein, Mr. Sechrist.

Patterson's Creek, near Frankford—Officers: Jacob Blaum, Peter Umstadt.

Mason County

Jäger's Church, near Point Pleasant—Officers: Daniel Rausch, G. Schweitzer.

Before adjourning, the Conference in 1809 agreed to hold its next annual convention in Woodstock. No minutes and no records of this convention have been found. Likewise, it must be here recorded that no account either in the form of minutes or references of any kind has been found for meetings in the following years of 1811, 1812, 1813, 1814, and 1816. It is more than likely that meetings were held in some of these years, though some we know were omitted, as the country was again in the throes of war, and many changes had taken place in the ranks of the ministers. Paul Henkel had moved to Point Pleasant, far away on the Ohio. Several of the ministers had passed away. John David Young died in 1804, John Foltz in 1810, Christian Streit in 1812. John George Butler moved to Maryland in 1806, William Forster to Ohio in 1807, and William Carpenter to Kentucky in 1813. Thus with the depleted ranks in troublesome war times it was with difficulty that the pastors assembled for their annual meetings. There may be minutes of some meetings in existence. It is to be hoped that if any minutes of the years mentioned, together with the years 1799 to 1804, are found at any time, they will be sent to the archives of our Synod. The review of the remaining minutes will now be resumed.

1815, March 19 and 20, in Solomon's Church. The pastors present were the following: Paul Henkel, John Peter Schmucker, pastor of Solomon's Church, Andrew Henkel of Point Pleasant, Martin Walther of Powell's Fort, and Daniel Scherer of North Carolina. It will be noticed that only one name remains of the old membership. Lay delegates: John Bauman of Röder's; Jacob Nees, Bernhard Götz, John Rubbert, and George Maurer of Solomon's; Jacob Foltz of St. Paul's; Solomon Henkel of New Market. Paul Henkel was elected president and J. P. Schmucker secretary. At the Sunday services Paul Henkel preached on the epistle for Palm Sunday and Martin Walther on Hosea 2:19,20. The first matter discussed Monday morning at the business session was the upholding of the German schools. This was becoming a serious matter in all Lutheran congregations in Virginia. On the one hand German must be maintained for the Germans and English introduced for those who could not understand the German tongue.

The resolution of the Woodstock convention (1805) in reference to lining out hymns was again brought up for discussion and it was urged that the resolution be enforced as rapidly as possible and good hymn books in both English and German introduced for the use of the members.

In compliance with the recommendation of the President of the United States setting aside the second Thursday of April as a day of repentance and thanksgiving, it was unanimously decided to urge all congregations to observe the day.

A number of copies of an address to the Christian people of the Lutheran Church were received from the Ministerium of Pennsylvania. A vote of thanks was passed for this gift, and the members of the Conference were urged to distribute them with care.

Upon the request of Andrew Henkel it was decided to send Paul Henkel or J. P. Schmucker to Mason County to administer the communion to the congregation there. Martin Walther was instructed to visit Pendleton and Hardy counties and try to arrange for services in the congregations of that needy field. It was decided to hold the next annual convention in the Hawksbill congregation, beginning the second Sunday in May, 1816.

1815, September 24, 25, in Woodstock. This convention bears the nature of a special meeting, though no mention of this is made in the printed minutes. Four sermons were preached in the church on Sunday, three in German and one in English, by Paul Henkel, J. Peter Schmucker, Andrew Henkel and Pastor Reck, who preached the English sermon. On Monday morning the following roll was formed: Pastors, Paul Henkel, Friedrich Haas, Abraham Reck of Winchester, J. Nicolas Schmucker, J. Peter Schmucker, Martin Walther, and Andrew Henkel of Zanesville, Ohio; lay delegates, Friedrich Bisch of Röder's, Jacob Ott of Woodstock, Michael Haas, Jacob Scheets, and Jacob Schmucker, also of Woodstock, and Dr. Solomon Henkel. Paul Henkel was elected president and Friedrich Haas secretary.

The morning business meeting was interrupted by a misunderstanding among the people, who began to assemble with the idea that a religious service had been appointed. When the matter was brought to the attention of the assembled Conference it was deemed wise to yield to the expectation of the people and hold the expected service. The bell was rung, a large gathering filled the church, and Martin Walther preached on the text Isa. 52:7, "Hearken unto me, ye that know righteousness."

Business was resumed at two o'clock in the afternoon. It was recommended that upon communion occasions, several of the neighboring pastors unite and hold several services for the edification of the people. It was decided that according to a resolution of 1805, the pastors of the Conference try to supply the vacant congregations, and that during their absence pastors living near by perform the ministerial acts for the absent pastor. Action was taken to improve the singing in the congregations, and all pastors were urged to do their utmost to introduce hymn books among their people and to teach them to sing. Pastors were urged once more to carry out the resolutions of the preceding convention in reference to the maintenance of German schools. It was also decided to send a copy of the printed minutes to the officers of the North Carolina Synod, in order that they might see that a number of their members had attended the Virginia Conference, cooperated heartily with the others, and that their attendance and cooperation are deeply appreciated.

Before separating the members of the Conference both lay and clerical contributed liberally for the publication and distribution of the minutes. It was arranged that the next convention of the Conference be held in Strasburg, beginning the second Sunday in September, 1816. At the request of Andrew Henkel, Friedrick Haas consented to visit the congregations in Monongahela County.

1817, September 14, 15, 16, in Madison County Church. The following pastors were present: George Henry Riemenschneider of Augusta County, Michael Meyerhöffer, pastor of the local church, Abraham Reck, J. Nicolas Schmucker, and J. Peter Schmucker. On Sunday three sermons were given to the assembled congregation. Pastors Riemenschneider and J. Nicolas Schmucker preached in German and Pastor Reck in English. Before the time arrived for the Monday session heavy rains set in, and but a small audience gathered for the meeting. Pastor Reck was kept away by the rainstorm. Pastor J. P. Schmucker preached in German and Pastor Meyerhöffer in English. On Tuesday morning the Conference was able to hold its business session. The following lay delegates presented their credentials: John Risch of the Peaked Mountain Church, Anton Klein of Newtown, near Winchester, Adam Küster of Strasburg, Jacob Ott of Woodstock, Friedrich Bisch of Röder's, Friedrich Sauer of Hawksbill, George Zirkle of Solomon's, Aaron Krigler, Daniel Utz, Samuel Carpenter, Joshua Zimmermann, and Michael Haus, of Madison County.

Among the ministers there were two new members, Pastors Riemenschneider and Meyerhöffer. Riemenschneider came from Germany, a student of Göttingen, and first appears on the minutes of the Ministerium of Pennsylvania in 1806, when he applied to be received as a student of theology. He was licensed in 1808 and assigned to a field in Pennsylvania, and ordained in 1815. He appeared in Rockingham County, Virginia, about 1810 and spent a long life in a useful ministry in the State, chiefly in Rockingham, Augusta and Pendleton Counties. Meyerhöffer was born in Frederick, Md., in 1794, received his early training in his home town, and his instructions in theology under his pastor, the Rev. D. F. Schaeffer. He was licensed by the Ministerium of Pennsylvania in 1815, and ordained by the same body in 1818. In response to a call made to the Ministerium for a successor to Carpenter in the Hebron congregation, Meyerhöffer came to Virginia in 1815, and after six years of successful work in this congregation he changed the center of his activities to Rockingham County. He spent the rest of his days in Virginia, ministering not only in the county mentioned, but also in Augusta, Rockbridge and Pendleton Counties. He died April 18, 1833.

The first business transacted was the election of Pastor Riemenschneider as president and Pastor Reck as secretary. Many matters of a spiritual nature were considered. The use of the Lord's Prayer at every public service was unanimously approved. The Rev. J. Nicòlas Schmucker sought advice in regard to the securing of a constitution for congregations, and it was suggested to him that perhaps from the North Carolina Synod he might receive the desired model, which could be adopted by his congregation by a majority vote. It was also decided that when parents choose sponsors for the baptism of their children they should also stand before the minister and answer the questions with the sponsors. Congregations were urged to use care in the election of elders and deacons so that only worthy men be elected. Jacob Crigler, a student of theology under Peter Schmucker, was permitted by vote to hold exhortations in his teacher's congregations, and under his supervision to visit the South Branch congregations and edify them with exhortations. By resolution Pastor N. Schmucker was requested to visit the congregation in Brock's Gap as often as he could make it possible.

The Peaked Mountain Church was selected as the place for the next meeting of the Conference, beginning on the first Sunday in October, 1818. With a sermon in German by Pastor N. Schmucker, and an admonition in English by Pastor Reck, the Conference adjourned.

It was the last one of which we have minutes, or a record. The minutes of the 1818 convention, and of subsequent meetings, if held, are still hidden in desks, drawers, and closets of Virginia homes and churches; if found let them be sent to the archives of Synod.

* * * * *

This Special Conference did not develop into a synodical organization, but its existence extended into a time of expansion marked by the formation of many different church bodies. In the same year in which the Special Conference had arranged to meet in Peaked Mountain Church, 1818, the Western Conference in Ohio, in spite of discouragement and protest from the Mother Synod, changed into a full-fledged Synod, and one of the members of the Virginia Conference was the first secretary of that body. Two years later, a number of ministers separated from the North Carolina Synod and July 19, 1820, organized the Tennessee Synod with six ministers, one from North Carolina, four from Tennessee, and one from Virginia. Three months later, October 11, 1820, eleven ministers, six from Maryland and five from Virginia, met in Winchester and organized the sixth Synod on the roll of the Lutheran Church in America. Eleven days later delegates of four of the six Synods in America met in Hagerstown, Md., and organized the General Synod of the Evangelical Lutheran Church in the United States. This was the culmination of this era of expansion, and for a period of five years there were no more Synods organized.

The Evangelical Lutheran Synod of Maryland and Virginia

It is not surprising that the ministers laboring in Virginia and Maryland, separated only by the Potomac, should feel the breezes stirring about in the Lord's vineyard in Virginia during these times of centralizing forces. When the subject was broached on the floor of the Ministerium, to the surprise of many no doubt, approval was voiced and the movement was given an impetus that was most encouraging to the members living in the territory designated above. When the call was issued for the gathering of the ministers and lay delegates the response was unanimous in Maryland, and in Virginia extended as far south as the James River; south of that line seemed to be considered the territory of the North Carolina Synod. On the opening day the following ministers and lay delegates were enrolled: From Maryland, Daniel Kurtz, John Grob, David F. Schaeffer, Benjamin Kurtz, John Keyler, and Michael Wachter; from Virginia, Martin Sackman, Loudoun City, Abraham Reck, Winchester, Michael Meyerhöffer, Madison, Charles Philip Krauth, Shepherdstown, and J. Nicolas Schmucker, Woodstock. Lay Delegates from Maryland, Frederick Löhr, Abraham Reck, and George Shryock; from Virginia, John Baker, Winchester, Frederick Kiefer, Loudoun City, Jacob Bishop, Shepherdstown, and Jacob Ott, Woodstock.

Daniel Kurtz was elected president, David F. Schaeffer secretary, and Pastor Reck, treasurer. Mr. Martin Kibler and Samuel Hersche applied for admission into the new Synod, and were told to continue their studies and return to the next meeting for examination. It was resolved that all members who had been ordained as deacons by the Ministerium of Pennsylvania should become by this action pastors in the Evangelical Lutheran Church.

The following is of interest as an indication of the spirit and foresight of the members of this Synod:

Resolved, That the propriety of a religious publication, devoted to the interests of our Church, be and the same is hereby recommended to the serious consideration of the next annual meeting of this Synod.

The second convention was held in Frederick, Md., beginning the first Sunday in September, 1821. The officers of the preceding year were reelected. Six new members were added, including S. S. Schmucker of New Market, Virginia, and Frederick Haas of Woodstock. The Synod entered upon a career of great enterprise and usefulness. It steadily grew in numbers and activity. In 1822, George H. Riemenschneider became a member; in 1823, George Daniel Flohr, and in 1826, S. K. Houshour, of New Market.

The Synod was during its early career the life and savior of the General Synod, and through its first hundred years the chief source of the strength of the General Synod was found in the Maryland Synod. "Of the first thirteen conventions of that body ten were held on the territory of the Maryland Synod. Of the first eight presidents of that body six were members of the Maryland Synod. And throughout the hundred years of the history of the General Synod more than one-third of her presiding officers were elected from among the delegates of the Maryland Synod." These lines are quoted from the History of the Maryland Synod by Dr. A. R. Wentz.

The interest of the Virginia Lutherans continued in the new Synod for nine years. It was found that the territory of the workers in Virginia was so large, and so distinctly separated from the interests of the men living on the Potomac and beyond, that it was not long before the pastors laboring on this soil began to long for a union of their own that their forces might if possible be united into one Synod. At the time under consideration, three or four organizations had members on the territory. The long journeys and the protracted absences from home made necessary in order to attend a convention of these distant Synods were detrimental to the home work. A call was therefore issued and sent to all the Lutheran ministers residing in Virginia, "for the purpose of taking into consideration the expediency of forming a separate and distinct Synod."

The Evangelical Lutheran Synod of Virginia

The pastors operating in the State of Virginia and entering into union with the ministers living north of the Potomac to form the Synod of Maryland and Virginia in 1820, soon realized that their State was but partially included. Of the five pastors who attended the convention not one lived south of a line drawn east and west through Madison and Shenandoah Counties. The feeling grew on them year by year that the interests of their portion of the vineyard did not receive the attention of the new Synod that its importance deserved. It was a Synod looking northward from the Potomac and not southward. Moved by sentiments of this kind and prompted by the interests of their work in the whole of Virginia, a number of pastors called a special meeting to consider these matters. We shall let the minutes of the first and second conventions which are lying before us in the bound volume of English minutes tell the story:

PROCEEDINGS

OF THE

EVANGELICAL LUTHERAN CONFERENCE

HELD AT WOODSTOCK, VIRGINIA

AUGUST 10TH AND 11TH, 1829.

The brethren who assembled themselves at Woodstock, Virginia, on the 10th day of August, 1829, for the purpose of taking into consideration the expediency of forming a separate and distinct Synod, consisting of the Ministers resident in Virginia, were the following, viz.:—

Ministers

Rev. Nicolas Schmucker, Woodstock.
Rev. Martin Walter, Botetourt County.
Rev. Michael Meyerhoeffer, Rockingham County.
Rev. John Kehler, Madison County.
Rev. Jacob Medtart, Martinsburg, Berkeley County.
Rev. John P. Cline, New Market, Shenandoah County.
Rev. Daniel J. Hauer, Botetourt County.
Rev. Lewis Eichelberger, Frederick County.

Lay Delegates

Jacob Ott, Woodstock.

Lawrence Pitman, Mount Jackson.

The business of the Synod was introduced by the singing of a hymn and a prayer by the Rev. N. Schmucker.

The brethren then proceeded to the election of Officers to officiate during the present session, the result of which was as follows, viz.:

Rev. Nicolas Schmucker, President.

Rev. John Kehler, Secretary.

1. Resolved, That a committee of three be appointed for the purpose of framing a preamble and resolutions expressive of the views and object of this Conference.

On motion, the Conference adjourned until 3 o'clock, P. M.

AFTERNOON SESSION

Monday, half past 3 o'clock, P. M.

The session was opened by singing and prayer.

The committee appointed to draft a preamble and resolutions of the views of the Conference, handed in the following report:

We, who are now assembled together in the providence of God, feel it important to take into consideration some measures for the welfare of our Church in Virginia. We are, moreover, urged to this on account of various difficulties on the one hand, which we, the ministers and our Church, have been labouring under; and the advantages, on the other hand, that might result by adopting some plan more favorable to the interest of our Church. The distance we have frequently to travel to our Synodical meetings being so great, necessarily requiring too long an absence from our congregations, that their interests are thereby sometimes neglected.

We further feel the importance of diffusing ecclesiastical knowledge among our people, and especially of informing them relative to the nature of the government of our Church, and its peculiar circumstances and wants in our section of the country. And inasmuch as our difficulties are of a peculiar character, and as frequent meetings and public preaching would have considerable tendency to enlighten our members on ecclesiastical subjects, and also to enlist their influence and support more immediately in the Church in our own State, and inasmuch as it would concentrate our own exertions and means within our section of country, and as provision is made in the Constitution of the General Synod, Art. 3, Sec. 3, for the formation of New Synods, when the situation of our Church requires them, and as the number of our ordained Ministers is above that specified by the said Constitution, and as we feel it necessary for the welfare of our Church, to organize a Synod in Virginia, Therefore,

1. *Resolved,* That this Conference, after such deliberations as the importance of the subject requires, hereby unanimously form themselves into a Synod, separate from the Synods to which we have heretofore belonged.

2. *Resolved,* That this Synod shall be called The Evangelical Lutheran Synod of Virginia.

3. *Resolved,* That this Synod entertains the highest regard for their brethren of the neighboring Synods, and that nothing has induced us to separate from them but a desire to promote more effectually the interests of our Church.

4. *Resolved,* That it shall be the duty of every member of this Synod to collect materials for the formation of a Constitution, adapted to the peculiar circumstances of our Church in Virginia, and be submitted for adoption at its next session.

5. *Resolved,* That a copy of the proceedings of this Synod be presented to the Synods of Maryland and North Carolina, with a hope that they will meet their approbation.

6. *Resolved,* That the same be presented to the General Synod.

7. *Resolved,* That every member of this Synod exert himself not only in his own congregations, but in the Church generally, and particularly for the promotion of our periodicals, and our Seminary at Gettysburg.

8. *Resolved,* That the basis of the Constitution of this body be the Holy Scriptures, the Divinity of Christ, as taught therein, and the Unaltered Augsburg Confession.

9. *Resolved,* That our Synod hold its next session in the Union Church, Rockingham County, Va., on the 2d Sunday in October, 1830.

10. *Resolved,* That the Secretary of this Synod present a copy of our proceedings to the editor of the "Intelligencer," requesting him to publish the same.

MINUTES
of the
EVANGELICAL LUTHERAN SYNOD OF VIRGINIA

Held at the Union Church, Rockingham County, on the

10th, 11th, 12th, and 13th of October, 1830

The Ministers and Lay Delegates composing the Evangelical Lutheran Synod of Virginia convened at Union Church, Rockingham County, on the 2d Sunday in October, 1830.

A large concourse of persons having assembled at the church, the Synodical Discourse was delivered by the Rev. President N. Schmucker, in the German language from John 10:27. And at the same time Divine service was performed at a stand erected in the woods, where the

Rev. Secretary J. Kehler preached in English, after which the Sacrament of the Lord's Supper was administered in the church, and the Ministers and Lay Delegates, together with members of the church, united in the celebration of this blessed ordinance.

In the afternoon the Rev. Mr. Reimensnyder preached in· the church in the German language on I Cor. 11:28, and the Rev. Mr. Eichelberger officiated at the stand in the English; text, Isaiah 65:13, 14.

On Saturday previous, the Rev. N. Schmucker preached a preparatory discourse (in German) from I Cor. 11:28, 29, 30, 31. And the Rev.˙ D. J. Hauer in English from Joshua 3:5.

Monday, October 11, 8 o'clock, A. M.

The Synodical Session was opened by singing a Hymn and an Address to the Throne of Grace. The names of the Clergy were called—the following were present:

Names	Places of Residence
Rev. Geo. H. Reimensnyder	Pendleton County·
Rev. Nicolas Schmucker	Woodstock
Rev. Martin Walter	Fincastle, Botetourt County
Rev. Michael Meyerhoeffer	Rockingham County
Rev. John Kehler	Madison County
Rev. Jacob Medtart	Shepherdstown
Rev. John P. Cline	New Market
Rev. Daniel J. Hauer	Salem, Botetourt County
Rev. David Eyster	Martinsburg
Rev. Lewis Eichelberger	Winchester

The following Lay Delegates presented their credentials and were admitted as members of the Synod:

Mr. Henry Skyles	Pendleton County
Mr. Adam Kister	Woodstock
Mr. George Ott	Woodstock
Mr. Philip Firebaugh	Fincastle
Mr. John Bentz	Rockingham County
Mr. Moses Weaver	Madison County
Mr. Michael Miller	Botetourt County
Mr. Henry Cronk	Botetourt County
Mr. John Zirkel	New Market

* * * The Synod then proceeded to the election of officers for the ensuing year, when the following brethren were chosen:

Rev. Michael Meyerhoeffer, President.
Rev. John Kehler, Secretary.
Rev. Daniel J. Hauer, Treasurer.

The Communications addressed to the Synod were then handed in and given to two committees for examination and report. * * *

The Synod adjourned to half past 1 o'clock, P. M.

During the recess the Rev. Jacob Medtart preached; text, Ezekiel 18:32.

AFTERNOON SESSION

Monday, half past 1 o'clock P. M.

The session was commenced with prayer by brother Hauer.

Resolved, That a committee of four Ministers and four Lay Delegates be appointed to draft a Constitution for the government of this Synod, and that they report tomorrow morning. The committee consisted of the Rev. Messrs. Schmucker, Reimensnyder, Medtart, and Cline, from amongst the Clergy, the Messrs. Kister, Miller, Bentz and Weaver, from amongst the Laity.

The session closed with Prayer by brother Eichelberger.

Tuesday, October 12th, 8 o'clock, A. M.

The Synod was constituted by singing a Hymn, and Prayer by brother Walter.

The committee appointed to draft a Constitution report: That, considering the undertaking of the greatest importance, they recommend that they be discharged, and that another committee be appointed, whose duty it shall be to prepare and present a Constitution at the next annual session for adoption.

The Synod adjourned until after public service; Prayer by brother Eyster. During the intermission brother Cline preached; text, Jeremiah 23:58.

AFTERNOON SESSION

Tuesday, half past 1 o'clock, P. M.

According to adjournment, the Synod convened at the church. The session was introduced by a Prayer from brother Medtart.

The committee No. 1, on Communications, report as follows:

That letter A contains a petition from the Church Council at Strasburg, praying that not only their Pastor N. Schmucker, but the brethren constituting the Evangelical Lutheran Synod of Virginia, may not attach themselves to the General Synod.

Letter B is of a similar import from Frieden's Church, Shenandoah County.

Letter C is a communication from Emanuel's Church, Woodstock, and Zion's Church, Shenandoah County, in which they express their entire satisfaction with their present Pastor N. Schmucker, and pray that this body may not unite with the General Synod.

The committee recommend that said letters be read before the Synod.

On motion made and recorded, it was

Resolved, That this Synod do hereby withdraw from all connection with the Evangelical Lutheran General Synod.

It was moved and seconded, That the further organization of this Synod be indefinitely postponed.

The vote being taken it was found that the majority were opposed to this indefinite postponement.

The Synod adjourned until Wednesday morning; Prayer by the Rev. brother Hauer.

Wednesday, October 13, 8 o'clock, A. M.

The Synod was constituted by singing, and Prayer by brother Reimensnyder.

The Rev. Messrs. Reimensnyder, Meyerhoeffer, Walter, Hauer, and Cline were present, together with their Lay Delegates. (To this number of ministers must be added the name of Schmucker, as he remained with the Synod.) The Rev. Messrs. Medtart, Eichelberger, Kehler and Eyster had withdrawn.

On motion made and seconded, it was

Resolved, That this Synod adopt the Constitution of the Synod of East Pennsylvania, and that it remain open for amendment until next Synod. (The Ministerium of Pennsylvania must be intended, as the East Pennsylvania Synod was not organized until 1842.)

*   *   *   *   *   *

We omit the rest of the paragraphs of the minutes for this session. As the secretary was among the number of those who withdrew, the minutes are signed by Daniel J. Hauer, Secretary *pro tem.*

After fixing the time and place for the next convention, and arranging for a Special Conference to be held in Strasburg, Shenandoah County, on Festum Trinitatis, 1831, the synodical session was brought to a close, and the pastors held a ministerial meeting in which they examined two candidates, Mr. John P. Dagey, who was licensed for one year, and a son of Pastor Riemenschneider, John Junius by name, who was encouraged to continue his studies under his father. With the year 1832 the name of the elder Riemenschneider disappears from the roll of Synod, but in 1838 the name of the son is entered upon the roll as having been received by a certificate of dismissal from the Ohio Synod. He was an active member of the Synod until the fall of 1841, when he accepted work in Maryland, and united with the Synod of that state. He was present at the meeting of the Virginia Synod in 1842, and participated in the services and in the transaction of business. Just before

moving away from Virginia, his son Junius B. was born,
February 24, 1842, who became the pastor of great fame of
St. James' Church, New York City.

It will be noted from the minutes reproduced on these
pages that the troubles of the young Synod began very
early in its career, even with its second convention in 1830,
when four active ministers withdrew summarily because the
Synod had decided to withdraw from the General Synod.
The question that arose to disturb the peace of the young
Synod was one that had become a debatable question among
the laity. The New York and the Pennsylvania Minister-
iums had to face the same question brought to an issue by the
lay membership of their congregations. Strange as it may
seem the originators of the idea and plan of a General Synod
had to withdraw after the organization had been formed,
and the General Synod was left in a very perilous condition
and but few thought that it could survive the loss caused by
the withdrawal of the synods named. By the organization
of new synods the General Synod was kept alive until it
prospered. The Virginia Synod in the following year gave
its reasons for the step it took, but in 1839 it returned to the
ranks of the general body largely through the encouragement of the Winchester pastor, Lewis F. Eichelberger, who
returned to the Virginia Synod with his congregations, and
reported that such changes had been made in the constitution
of the General Synod as would remove the objectionable
features of former years, and justify the Virginia Synod in
returning to its membership. This was done and no further
dissatisfaction manifested itself even among the laity.

But other troubles arose and continued to retard the
progress of the Synod, the chief one of which seems to have
been the constant loss of its ministers on account of insufficient support. Without the benefit of a farm, or some
occupation, it was impossible for the pastor to support
himself and his family, and consequently there was an
unceasing restlessness among the ministers, many of them
seeking and finding positions in the North and leaving their
fields in a destitute condition. The number of members of

the Synod became so small that with the other difficulties of the territory it was impossible to hold conventions in the years 1836 and 1837, and even in 1838 some were in doubt, but the president Thomas Miller made bold to make the effort and he succeeded in getting four ministers and two lay delegates to report for a meeting in Madison County, May 19, 1838. When the Synod met in Zion's Church, near Waynesborough, Augusta Co., Va., in 1835, five ordained ministers and three licentiates were present. In 1838, only two of the eight were present, Thomas Miller and Samuel Oswald; three others had been received during the interim by the president, John B. Davis by ordination, G. F. Staehlin by letter from the Ministerium of Pennsylvania, and David F. Bittle by licensure; two old members were absent at this convention, Nicolas Schmucker and Samuel Sayford; and five were received at this meeting: Dr. J. Hamilton, Wardensville, Lewis Eichelberger, Winchester, Isaac Baker, Wardensville, Theophilus Stork, Winchester, and John Junius Reimensnyder, Staunton. This gave the Synod an enrollment of twelve ministers, and as can be readily understood infused the Synod with new life and energy. Some of these men were men of influence and power and wielded a wonderful potency in furthering the work of the Synod in Virginia. Stork was the son of the pioneer Stork in North Carolina, and though he did not stay long in Winchester he succeeded in doing a substantial work while there. D. F. Bittle became the great educator in the State, serving as the first president of Roanoke College for twenty-three years, 1853 to 1876.

The officers of Synod elected at this meeting were John B. Davis, president, Theopilus Stork, secretary, and Thomas Miller, treasurer. From this time the conventions followed in regular succession without any interruption, even during the war and the career of the Synod for the most part was one of steadily increasing prosperity. The convention of 1839 was marked by the decision to return to the General Synod, and the organization of a Foreign Missionary Society; and that of 1840 by the dedication of the new Mt.

Tabor Church, of which the Rev. D. F. Bittle was the pastor. The sermon on this occasion was preached by the Rev. Lewis Eichelberger from Luke 23:33. The consecration is thus described in the minutes under date of May 17, 1840:

The beautiful edifice, which had been recently built, was then solemnly consecrated to the worship of the true God, by the Rev. Charles Philip Krauth, D. D., who accompanied the usual mode of dedication with a short but peculiarly pertinent and eloquent address. And as he most happily adverted to the name, Mt. Tabor, and expressed his prayer, that scenes similar to those which transpired on that Mount might be witnessed within the consecrated walls, every heart responded, Amen. After which the Lord's Supper was administered to many that thronged around the sacred board.

In 1842 two special conferences were provided for, one in the northern and one in the southern part of the territory of the Synod, with the western branch of the Shenandoah as the dividing line. Joseph A. Seiss was examined and licensed to serve in Rockingham County, with Harrisonburg as his center. Plans were laid for the worthy celebration of the centennial celebration of Lutheranism in America, 1742-1842.

The convention of 1843, beginning May 6th, and held in Woodstock, was made memorable by the reception of the licentiates C. C. Baughman and Anders Rudolph Rude. Both of these men were licensed by the Maryland Synod and came to Virginia in response to the urgent call of its president. Baughman took up his residence in Staunton, and Mr. Rude began his labors in Shenandoah County, living first in the neighborhood of Woodstock, and then at the foot of Rude's Hill, where he had his home for twenty years. He was born in Copenhagen, Denmark, October 5, 1813. In 1863 he moved to Columbia, S. C., where he spent twenty years in various activities as editor and teacher, preacher and lecturer.

In 1844, May 15th, Joseph A. Seiss was ordained. In the spring of that year he had moved from Harrisonburg to Martinsburg. Four new churches were reported at this convention, two ready for dedication, and two that had recently been dedicated.

In 1847, John P. Cline, after an absence of twelve years, returned to the Synod from Maryland and took up the work of the New Market pastorate. Joseph A. Seiss removed from the bounds of the Synod, going to Cumberland, Md.

In 1860, David M. Gilbert, licensed by the West Pennsylvania Synod in 1859, was ordained by the Virginia Synod. He had taken up the missionary work at Staunton, and remained there until 1863 when he went to the Church of the Ascension in Savannah, Georgia, returning to Staunton in 1871, and in 1873 assumed the duties of the Winchester congregation, remaining there until he moved to Pennsylvania in 1887. He spent all but the last eighteen years of his fruitful ministry in the South. To him we owe much of the success of the Southern Church, as well as of the Synod of Virginia, as he was a wise and faithful pilot during the distressful days of the war and the trying times of the formation of the United Synod in the South, of which he was the first president. To him also we are indebted for his excellent and painstaking historical papers, on the history of Muhlenberg's ministry, of the Winchester congregation and of the Virginia Synod. He died in Harrisburg, Pa., October 16, 1905.

These passing years were years of activity and expansion. The Synod was always interested in the education of ministers, though in the early years the young men desiring an education had to go to institutions beyond her bounds. It has never been the good fortune of the Synod to have an institution of learning on her territory, except for the space of five years, when the Virginia Classical Institute was located near Middlebrook. But even under these conditions she heartily cooperated with the schools that were needed for the advancement of her work.

The Virginia Classical Institute was the fruit of the labors of C. C. Baughman, encouraged and assisted by D. F. Bittle. Its beginning was made in the year 1842, in connection with the missionary labors of Mr. Bittle at Middlebrook. The school prospered from the start, and arrangements were made to board students, the outcome of which was that two log buildings were erected for the school. Students came from southwestern Virginia to augment the numbers from the immediate neighborhood. In 1847 the school was moved to Salem, the name changed to the Virginia Collegiate Institute, and in 1853 a charter was applied for and the institute became Roanoke College. Again the Virginia Synod was without an institution of learning upon its territory, but it heartily cooperated with the school, and rejoiced when its former member D. F. Bittle became its first president.

In regard to the education of its daughters the history of the Synod is different, as in later years several institutions for the education of women were maintained on its territory, but gradually these gave way to the larger schools conducted at other places. The noble efforts of our educators should not be overlooked, as each school has to its credit the doing of a great deal of seen and unseen good.

In Foreign Missions little could be done because no work had been begun by American Lutherans before 1842, but even as early as 1839 an effort was made in the Virginia Synod to take offerings for this cause. Then followed a season of years during which the Southern Lutheran Church endeavored to unite with the General Synod in assisting in sending out missionaries to India. Many societies were organized in different congregations for this purpose. Then the Southern Lutherans desired to support a missionary of their own. After this was tried for a few years it proved unsatisfactory, and the conclusion was reached that no successful and satisfactory work could be done until the Southern Church had a field of its own, and acting on this principle the United Lutheran Synod in the South established its mission field in Japan, and the date 1892, when James A. B. Scherer and Rufus B. Peery were sent to Japan, men in whom all Lutherans of Virginia were deeply interested, marks the beginning of a new and illustrious period in southern foreign mission work. The congregations of the Virginia Synod cooperated most heartily in this work and members of the church, like the Coopers of

Winchester, became substantial supporters. The Synod gave in the course of years the following missionaries to the new field in Japan: L. S. G. Miller, Frisby D. Smith, and C. W. Hepner.

In Home Missions there was a continuous activity, interrupted only by the war period. Harrisonburg and Staunton are both referred to in the 1842 minutes. Though the work had its great difficulties, yet in two years time Staunton was trying to buy a lot. The young missionary Seiss reported that the prospects at Harrisonburg were good. The formal organization did not take place till 1850. The following are among the earliest members and workers: Miss Phoebe Shipp, Mrs. Sallie Kisling, Miss Sarah Ott, Anthony Hockman, Aaron Wilson, and William Boaker. At Staunton the missionary was C. C. Baughman, and upon urgent request the president of Synod appointed the following board of trustees so that the lot could be purchased and the work of building proceed without legal delays: James Points, Chesley Kenney, C. C. Baughman, Paul Sieg, George Shuey, and Robert H. Holland. In a few years the congregation was ready for organization. The following were among the charter members: Abraham Venable, Miss Bell Graves, Miss Carrie Pickering, Miss Elvira Davis, George Baylor, Miss Mary Sue Baylor, Miss Amanda Baylor, Henry Wehn, Frank Prufer, David Bucher, Alexander Grove, William Wilson, and John Bucher. After Missionary Baughman moved to Salem with the Institute, the Rev. J. B. Davis took up the work in Staunton, and on the 30th day of November, 1856, he was able to lead his people in the dedication of the house of worship. The congregation was organized in 1853.

Richmond furnishes one of the most interesting items of home missionary operations. It is the story of many beginnings, many disappointments, but also of wonderful results, expected and unexpected. The part played by the Virginia Synod in this mission work begins with its acceptance of the request of the Southwestern Virginia Synod to cooperate. Harmoniously the two synods planned and labored together in this distant and difficult field. For a time the Virginia Synod seems to have had sole control, as a minister was attracted by the field who came from the Maryland Synod having been licensed by the Synod in 1851. He was a student of Gettysburg Seminary, having come from Prussia in 1849, where he had studied theology and missions under the great Missionary Gossner. He was a man of such active mentality, that he is reported to have preached an English sermon at the convention of his Synod. He was received and ordained by the Virginia Synod in 1852 and sent to Richmond. His reports were excellent. He spent his first and second years largely in collecting funds for a lot and building, and June 4, 1854, he dedicated a house of worship for his congregation of seventy communicants, called Bethlehem. His name was John Samuel William Schmogrow, styled in the minutes, William Schmogrow. He resigned June 1, 1855, and moved to Ohio. A few efforts were made to supply the vacancy, but it was but a partial success. When the President of Synod, one day in 1856, opened his mail he found there to his surprise an official communication informing him that the congregation on February 7, 1856, had severed its connection with the Virginia Synod and united with the Missouri Synod. When the convention of Synod was held and the Missionary Society met in annual session it closed its report with these striking and generous words: "As this congregation has united with the Missouri Synod, no further appropriations have been asked for. May the Lord favor this new relation."

For years no reference is found in the minutes to Richmond and mission work there. The war came on and passed slowly away, and then the thought once more arose, that even if there were a prosperous German Lutheran Church in Richmond, there might be room for English missionary operations, and the president was instructed to make inquiries of the German pastors there, and favorable replies came from two sources, from these very German pastors and from the Southwestern Virginia Synod, request-

ing the cooperation of the Virginia Synod in the support of
Jacob G. Neiffer, who was ordained by the old friend of
Virginia Lutheranism, the Ministerium of Pennsylvania,
in 1868, and sent to Virginia to do missionary work with the
promise of support to the extent of $250 annually. The
Southwestern Virginia Synod had promised an equal amount,
and the Virginia Synod immediately took a similar step.
Neiffer organized St. Mark's English Evangelical Lutheran
Church soon after his arrival, and the Southwestern Virginia
Synod transferred it officially to the Virginia Synod, so that
there might be no doubt of the proper enrollment of the
new congregation. Its organization late in 1868, or early
in 1869, is crowned with a number of noble workers standing
faithfully at the side of the missionary. His first delegate
to Synod was David G. Yuenling, and the first officers given
in the records of the first Church Council meeting held with
their pastor dated March 11, 1869, were the following:
Elders E. Rex, William Meyer, Theodore Krohne;
Deacons August Polig, George Gaesdorf, David Yuenling,
and Henry Boschen; Elder George Fulk and Deacons Julius
Ide and Lewis Bromm were added June 10th of the same
year. The charter members—a noble band—will be given
in connection with the history of the congregation. This
mission was later merged with another one carried on in the
city and the two became The First Church of Richmond.

With the establishment of the English mission in
Richmond, the Virginia Synod received a new vision of the
future. And as the Lutheran people from the Valley, as
well as from Pennsylvania and Maryland poured into the
cities, English mission work, became much more encouraging.
The Synod realized that its youth lay in its missions and
that it renewed its strength in its youth. New life entered
the missions in Richmond, Norfolk, Newport News, and
Portsmouth, as the newcomers came in one by one and by
groups and added their strength to the forces of those
already at work. The Valley of Virginia, conservative in
all things, slowly added its contribution to the Lutheran
forces slowly gathering about missionary centers. Mr.

Murphy and E. H. Ritenour came from the neighborhood of Strasburg to Richmond; Jacob Umlauf began to "walk about" the walls of Zion; J. Luther Kibler left his home near Woodstock and settled in Newport News, doing excellent work for the mission, and at the same time studying the history of his Church; A. J. Hamman, also from the Valley of Virginia, assisted nobly in the early days of Newport News, together with H. W. Frondt from Germany, Mr. Oscar Dahl from Sweden, and William T. Stauffer from Pennsylvania. The last has served as Elder for twenty-one years, and over, and in other capacities for many years as is well known, a sufficiency in himself, but extending back in his lineage to the Mayflower in two lines, and to the strongholds of Lutheranism in Pennsylvania through his mother to Dr. S. K. Brobst, of Allentown, Pa. Many others from abroad and from the homeland should be mentioned, in all these seaport cities, but it is sufficient to state that as a result of the faithfulness and service of men like these and a thousand others in 1894 a congregation was organized in Norfolk, one in Newport News in 1898, and one in Portsmouth in 1908. This is a remarkable record and speaks strongly for the activity of the Virginia Synod in her home mission work and the many agencies of support available, and of the loyalty and patience of a numerous constituency that was formed from all tongues of the globe and welded into active and prosperous English missions that in turn developed into helpful congregations. It is but an indication of the drift of the things of the kingdom that the pastor at Portsmouth is a son of the congregation of Newport News.

All these years the internal work of development was going on in Synod and congregation. Progress that cannot be recorded is in evidence on all sides. The response of the Lutheran Church in Virginia to the trial of a paid president was in the nature of salaried superintendent of the Synod. The services rendered by the faithful men who occupied this position beginning with Dr. E. C. Cronk, a noble son of Virginia, followed by George H. Rhodes, Charles M. Teufel and R. Homer Anderson, have proved to the satisfaction

of all, before the Merger ·and since that time, that no
mistake was made in the designation of the office or the
selection of occupants, and the results of the labors of these
men while hidden from sight are nevertheless decidedly
positive for good.

Swiftly onward moved the Synod toward the day of
amalgamation. The Synod of Virginia for years studied
the problem of the Lutheran forces in operation in the
Commonwealth of Virginia. It never has been difficult in
past years to count at least ten. To reduce this number has
been its hope, and it had the joy, too, of seeing its hope
realized, when the mutual efforts of its own body and that
of the Southwestern Virginia Synod were harmonious
throughout, without encountering any insurmountable
difficulties. As in other states the Merger of 1918 removed
all constitutional difficulties, and helped still further by the
adoption of the Declaration of Principles at its second
convention held in Washington.

When the time approached the brethren were all ready,
with their congregations, to form the new Synod. They
entered the new relation numbering thirty-nine ministers
and fifty-eight congregations. The union was formed
March 17, 1922.

The Evangelical Lutheran Synod and Ministerium of Southwest Virginia

At the thirty-seventh convention of the North Carolina
Synod held in St. Michael's Church, Iredell County, N. C.,
October 3, 1840, a petition was presented by the ministers
and lay delegates in southwest Virginia, asking permission
to form their congregations into a separate Synod. The
petition was signed by the pastors Jacob Scherer and Elijah
Hawkins, the licentiates John J. Greever and Gideon
Scherer, and the lay delegates Michael Brown of Wythe
County, John Groseclose of Smythe County, and Stephen
Sprecher of Burke's Garden. The Synod in a generous
spirit granted the request, and the persons named agreed to
meet in St. John's Church, Wythe County, Va., on the 20th

day of September, 1841, in order to make the preliminary arrangements for the contemplated union. This was done; a committee was appointed to draft a constitution and the congregations were requested to elect lay delegates for the first meeting to be held in May, 1842, in Zion Church, Floyd County, Va.

In the printed minutes of this first convention the secretary begins his protocol with the following paragraphs:

Pursuant with a resolution adopted at a convention held in Wythe County, on the 20th of September last, the ministers residing in western Virginia, with their lay delegates assembled in Zion Church, Floyd County, Virginia, on Saturday, the 21st of May, 1842. A sermon was preached by Rev. E. Hawkins from Ps. 119:33-40. At 2 o'clock, P. M., Rev. S. Sayford being called to the chair, opened the session by singing and prayer, after which the names of the ministers present were registered; the representatives elected by their churches were called on for the certificates of their appointment, and also registered as follows:

Ministers

Rev. Jacob Scherer _____ Rural Retreat, Wythe Co., Va.
Rev. Samuel Sayford _____ Floyd Court House, Va.
Rev. Elijah Hawkins _____ Pleasant Hill, Smythe Co., Va.
Rev. John J. Greever _____
Rev. Gideon Scherer _____ Amsterdam, Botetourt Co., Va.
Rev. Stephen Rhudy _____ Burke's Garden, Tazewell Co., Va.

Lay Delegates

Mr. John Copenhaver _____ From Jacob Scherer's Congregation
Mr. Philip Sowers _____ From Samuel Sayford's Congregation
Mr. John Groseclose _____ From E. Hawkins' Congregation
Mr. Joseph Brown _____ From J. J. Greever's Congregation
Mr. John H. Hartman ___ From Gideon Scherer's Congregation

Fifteen congregations which previously had been members of the North Carolina Synod united to form the new Synod. Their names and county location are as follows: In Wythe County, Zion, St. Paul's, St. Peter's, Kimmerling, St. John's, Bethel, and Sharon; in Tazewell County, Burke's Garden; in Botetourt County, Union and Cop's; in Roanoke, Zion and Glade Creek; in Floyd County, Zion; in Smythe County, Pleasant Hill and Chilhowie. At the first convention two more applied for admission and were gladly received.

At the afternoon session on Saturday, the Constitution proposed by the committee was considered, amended and adopted. It is printed in full as an appendix to the minutes. It is the constitution proposed by the General Synod. The adoption of this basis of government paved the way to membership in the General Synod, and the necessary action was taken to consummate this course by the election of a delegate to the next convention. It remained a loyal member up to the time of the outbreak of the Civil War, when it withdrew and participated in the formation of the General Synod in the South.

Sunday was a day of successful services with throngs in attendance so large that the meetings had to be held in the grove, where seats had been prepared for the accommodation of the immense multitude. On Monday morning the organization was completed by the election of the following officers: President, Rev. Jacob Scherer; secretary, Rev. Elijah Hawkins; treasurer, Mr. Joseph Brown.

Much business was transacted at this first convention. Fraternal delegates were elected to attend the meetings of the Virginia and North Carolina Synods. Efforts were made to provide services for vacant congregations. Eight hundred copies of the minutes were ordered printed. Burke's Garden was selected as the place for the next convention, and the time fixed for the meeting was the first Sunday in June, 1843.

Of the six ministers forming the Synod, two were ordained at this convention, Pastors Greever and Gideon Scherer, and Stephen Rhudy was licensed to serve for one year. Greever and Scherer had been licensed two years before by the North Carolina Synod. Greever and Rhudy were sons of southwest Virginia. Rhudy had just returned from Gettysburg Seminary where he completed the theological course. He engaged in missionary labors in Tazewell and Bland counties, was ordained by his own Synod in 1846, and lived beyond the Jubilee celebration of the Synod he helped to organize. He died June 9, 1894.

Pastor Elijah Hawkins was from South Carolina. He was a member of the first class that matriculated in the Southern Lutheran Seminary in 1834, and was graduated in 1836. The seminary was then at Lexington, S. C. He came north to Virginia and was ordained by the North Carolina Synod in Zion's Church, May 16, 1838. He spent his active ministry in the Southwest Virginia Synod. He was a useful and beloved member.

Samuel Sayford came to the Southwest Virginia Synod from the Virginia Synod. He was born in Harrisburg, Pa., February .16, 1806. He studied theology in the Gettysburg Seminary and completed his course in 1835. Coming to Virginia and taking up work, he was ordained by the Virginia Synod in 1835. He was pastor in Botetourt, Roanoke, and Floyd counties until the year 1848, when he notified his Synod that he would move to Delaware County, Indiana, in response to a call to that distant field. Here he labored usefully and faithfully, building among others a church for Lutheran settlers from Pennsylvania and Virginia at Ovid, Madison County, Indiana, that is still the home of a flourishing congregation. He died in Indiana, November 18, 1865.

The name this new Synod adopted at its organization was The Evangelical Lutheran Synod and Ministerium of Western Virginia and Adjacent Parts. In 1867 the name was changed to The Evangelical Lutheran Synod and Ministerium of Southwestern Virginia. In 1855 the boundary between the Virginia Synod and its own territory was fixed by making the James River the dividing line as far as Covington.

The Synod from its birth enjoyed a healthy growth. At the second convention held in Burke's Garden, beginning June 3, 1843, one minister and one new congregation were received into membership. The minister was James Andrew Brown, a Virginian, the son of Christopher Brown of Wythe County. He was born December 22, 1815, completed the theological course in Gettysburg Seminary in 1842, and before leaving Pennsylvania was licensed by the West

Pennsylvania Synod. Two years later he was ordained by his home Synod at its third convention in Union Church, Botetourt County, May 29, 1844. He spent forty years in active service as pastor of the Wytheville charge, consisting of three or four congregations. He was a very active and energetic preacher, passing away at the age of eighty-five, March 4, 1900.

In 1845, the name of Solomon Schaeffer was added to the roll of ministers, and in 1848, the names of Simeon Scherer and Henry J. Bowers. The names of the original six charter members continued to head the list for years. There was no death in the ranks until 1860, and the first withdrawal was that of Samuel Sayford. In 1845 the communicant membership was reported to be 1414, an increase of 370 over the previous year.

John C. Repass was licensed in 1854, and ordained in 1856. Year by year others were received and increased the usefulness of the Synod. Interests that projected themselves far into the future had their origin in the deliberations and resolutions of these early days. These interests are defined in the terms of home and foreign missions, education and works of mercy.

When the Synod was organized it inherited from the North Carolina Synod an Auxiliary Society of the "Parent Mission and Education Society" which had its center in Wythe County. The Society was invited to hold its meetings at the same time the Synod met, that the cooperation might be the more complete. In 1849 the Society with its double object was divided into two societies, bearing the respective names, each with its own constitution. In 1854 the two were again united under the first name and continued in this form until 1878 when the Mission and Education Society was merged into the Synod and its business became a part of the regular synodical work.

As early as 1847 at the suggestion of Mrs. James A. Brown members of the Synod united to assist in the support of the Rev. Walter Gunn, Lutheran Missionary to India, 1844 to 1851.

The home mission work was begun with the organization of the Synod, when several of the members of the new Synod visited Tennessee to look after the interests of the Synod. In 1844 a committee consisting of James A. Brown and Gideon Scherer was sent to Richmond to inquire into the prospects of establishing a Lutheran mission. The committee brought in a favorable report the following year and the Virginia Synod was asked to join in the effort to establish an English Lutheran Church in the Capital of the Commonwealth.

In 1853 the Synod received the new congregation of Salem, Va., the fruit of the establishment of Roanoke College in that fortunate town. When Stephen A. Repass became pastor in 1869, upon his ordination by the Ministerium of Pennsylvania, he soon noted the growing neighboring town of Roanoke, and in 1870 organized a congregation which built its first church in 1873 on ground donated by the Hon. John Trout. Here the Trouts, Terrys, the Howberts and others from churches in outlying districts, joined hand in hand, grew and prospered in spite of panic and disappointment and in later years organized two daughter congregations in growing residential sections, in Virginia Heights in 1916, and in Villa Heights in 1922.

The work of city missions was vigorously prosecuted through the agency of self-denying pastors and energetic missionaries. Graham, Pulaski and Radford were established soon after Salem and Roanoke were cared for. Then followed Bluefield, Bristol, Lynchburg, Marion, and Wytheville, some developing as missions, others as parts of existing charges, but in either case adding to the strength and prestige of the Synod and Church. To the Southwestern Virginia Synod, too, belongs the credit of beginning and maintaining, through its son Kenneth Killinger, the only Lutheran mountain mission field in the State.

Few Synods have an educational history as wonderful as that of the Southwestern Synod. From its inception the Virginia Classical Institute near Middlebrook, Augusta County, received the encouragement of the Synod and

Simeon Scherer was sent to it as the first student from southwest Virginia. When this institution was removed to Salem in 1847 and renamed The Virginia Classical Institute, and in 1853 chartered as Roanoke College, the Synod had a promising college upon its own territory, and received a benefit in the education of ministers that cannot be overestimated. Of thirty-three ministers on its roll in 1892, according to the calculations of Dr. J. J. Scherer, Sr., twenty-three received their collegiate training within the walls of Roanoke College. Its officers and instructors, many of them brought from other parts of our church, have been a help and inspiration to the Synod. This was true to a still greater extent while the Southern Lutheran Seminary, largely under the care and supervision of Dr. S. A. Repass, was in operation in Salem.

The Synod was also interested in the education of her daughters, and encouraged their education from early years. In 1854 the establishment of a college for women was brought about in Wytheville, and carried on, not without many difficulties, for many years. Its friends sacrificed time, talent and money for the success of this school, but the education of the young women of the Lutheran Church did not meet with success until Marion Junior College was begun in 1873, and chartered in 1874, under the presidency of Rev. J. J. Scherer, Sr. For a few years Elizabeth College was also located on the territory of this wonderfully fortunate Synod.

Nor should it be overlooked that the orphanage of the southern Lutheran Church, now established so favorably in Salem, had its beginning within the bounds of the Synod of Southwestern Virginia, and that its cradle stood in the home of one of its ministers, the Rev. W. S. McClanahan. The local encouragement and support were always sufficient, even in the days of its trying infancy in the South View Home, to hold it in spite of calls that came from other states in the South with tempting offers.

Thus the Synod grew in faith and numbers, and when the first fifty years were over it was considered but proper that the happy event should be celebrated in a fitting manner. From the historical address delivered by Dr. Scherer on that occasion (1892), we glean the following facts: Ninety-eight names of ministers were entered upon the roll of the Synod during these fifty years. Of the original six charter members and the members of the second convention, only two were living in 1892, the Rev. Stephen Rhudy and the Rev. James A. Brown, both in retirement. Of the whole number (98), forty-two were sons of the congregations of the Synod. During the fifty years fifty-two ministers were transferred to other Lutheran bodies, in which some of the leading pastors and educators received their education and pastoral training within the bounds of the Synod of Southwestern Virginia. Seven of the ministers enrolled in 1892 never labored outside of southwestern Virginia. "The story of their self-sacrifice which they endured in many cases rather than leave, would, if known, command the sympathy of all who admire devotion to duty."

The Synod has given two of her enrolled members to the foreign mission field in Japan: Rev. Rufus Benton Peery and the Rev. Charles Lafayette Brown, besides also educating the pioneer missionary to Japan, James A. B. Scherer, who was sent in the spring of 1892. Dr. Nellie Cassell went from southwest Virginia to India as a Medical Missionary.

In 1886, the Synod of Southwestern Virginia joined forces with the other Synods in the South and formed The United Synod in the South, planting itself unanimously upon the conservative platform adopted by the United Synod, and later upon the Basis of Union of the United Lutheran Church in America, of which the Synod became a loyal and devoted member in 1918, through the merging of the three general bodies. In 1922, the Synod participated in the local merger, first with the Holston Synod, and then with the Synod of Virginia, consummated March 17, 1922, under the name of THE LUTHERAN SYNOD OF VIRGINIA. The Synod entered the Merger with twenty-eight ministers and sixty-two congregations.

The Virginia Conference of the Tennessee Synod

Of the early ministers laboring on the soil of Virginia there was only one who did not affiliate with the various synods formed in the State. He was active in conference meetings, but in regard to his synodical relations he adhered to his first loves, the Ministerium of Pennsylvania, then the Synod of North Carolina, later the Synod of Ohio, and lastly the Tennessee Synod. He does not seem to have been dismissed from any of these but by some principle we do not understand now, he remained a member of each one, but here with these four he rested, and each one upon his death felt that a venerable member had been removed from their ranks. This fourfold relationship never interfered with any local unions until the ministers in Virginia and Maryland organized their Synod. Paul Henkel was this man of many Synods. As he exerted a wide influence he had a large following which went with him into the Tennessee Synod in 1820. Before his death his son Ambrose took up his work in Virginia, and gradually others followed, who persevered in their adherence to the Tennessee Synod.

The congregations served by Paul Henkel, his son and other adherents of the Tennessee Synod, looked to this Synod for their pastors, and as a consequence pastors arrived from time to time from North Carolina and located in the Valley of Virginia. Jacob Stirewalt was among those who arrived soon after his ordination as deacon in 1837, and about the same time Jacob Killian accepted the work in Koiner's Church, Augusta County, and served the congregation from his ordination in 1837 to his death in 1871. Socrates Henkel arrived from North Carolina as a young man and was ordained in Koiner's Church at a called meeting of the Tennessee Synod, April 7, 1850. He spent his long life of activity and usefulness in Virginia. Joel Swartz came from Ohio and took up work in Tennessee congregations near Woodstock, for which purpose he was ordained at a special service by authority of the Tennessee Synod in 1855.

These were the men who were laboring in Virginia as members of the Tennessee Synod when the Synod at its meeting in Emmanuel Church, New Market, in September, 1855, recommended "that the members of this Synod who reside near enough to each other for that purpose, hold some annual meeting, according to their own appointment, where they may transact such matters as would not seem to call for the united advice of Synod." It was suggested that a meeting of this kind might be called a "Special Conference." It seems that it was understood that one of the acts that these conferences might perform was the examination and ordination of candidates for the ministry. The ministers living in the Valley of Virginia very promptly acted on this recommendation and formed a Special Conference. The minutes of its transactions covering a space of seventy years are before us in two volumes, partly written by hand and partly preserved in scrapbook fashion from printed reports. Both books are well preserved. The first five protocols are in the fine, regular script of John H. Hunton. The minutes for the sixth meeting are missing. The first page of the protocol of the first meeting follows:

MINUTES

OF .

THE FIRST SESSION OF THE VIRGINIA SPECIAL CONFERENCE OF THE EVANGELICAL LUTHERAN TENNESSEE SYNOD, HELD IN McGAHEYSVILLE, ROCKINGHAM COUNTY, VA.

In pursuance with previous appointment, the following ministers and lay delegates met at McGaheysville, Rockingham Co., Va., on the 17th of May, 1856.

Ministers

Rev. Ambrose Henkel ___ New Market, Shenandoah Co., Va.
Rev. Henry Wetzel _____ Mt. Solon, Augusta Co., Va.
Rev. Jacob Killian _____ Waynesboro, Augusta Co., Va.
Rev. Socrates Henkel _____ New Market, Shenandoah Co., Va.
Rev. Joel Swartz _____ Woodstock, Shenandoah, Co., Va.
Rev. Julius L. Stirewalt _ West Germantown, Wayne Co., Ind.

Lay Delegates

Mr. D. Sluss _____ St. Jacob's, Rockingham Co., Va.
Mr. P. Miller _____ McGaheysville, Rockingham Co., Va.
Mr. J. Hostler _____ Ermantrout's, Rockingham Co., Va.
Mr. G. A. Orebaugh _____ St. Paul's, Augusta Co., Va.
Mr. F. Barger _____ Koiner's, Augusta Co., Va.
Mr. G. Sheetz _____ Mt. Calvary, Shenandoah Co., Va.

Mr. I. S. Hockman _____ Frieden's, Shenandoah Co., Va.
Mr. J. H. Hunton _____ Emmanuel's, Shenandoah Co., Va.

The hour for worship having arrived, the exercises were opened, and Rev. Joel Swartz preached a sermon. He was then followed by Rev. Jacob Killian.

After a short intermission, the ministers and lay delegates reassembled in the church for the transaction of business.

On motion, Rev. A. Henkel was appointed Chairman pro tem., and Rev. S. Henkel, Secretary.

An election was now held for permanent officers, which resulted in favor of Rev. H. Wetzel, President, and Rev. S. Henkel, Secretary.

The name of the Rev. Jacob Stirewalt does not appear in the roll given. It is evident that he could not be present at this convention. His name appears on the roll for the third convention. The Rev. Henry Wetzel was the son of George Wetzel of southwest Virginia. He was ordained by the Tennessee Synod in September, 1841.

Among the transactions of the conference was the appointment of a committee to propose subjects for discussion. It gives us an idea of the times when we report that the two subjects proposed were the destitution of our Church in Virginia and the necessity of sustaining ministers and supporting pious young men in their efforts to prepare themselves for the ministry; and the second, "The Subject of the 'Definite Synodical Platform.'"

The second convention was held in St. Paul's Church, Augusta County, beginning Saturday, August 29, 1857. Two names are missing from the roll, Pastors Joel Swartz and Julius L. Stirewalt. The former had accepted work in Ohio, and the latter had been dismissed to one of the district Synods of Ohio, as his field of labor was across the line in Indiana. A new name appears, that of Martin Sondhaus, who was a Prussian and had come to America as a young man. He was in Gettysburg College and Seminary 1840 to 1844. In the latter year he was licensed by the West Pennsylvania Synod and in 1850 ordained by the Ministerium of Pennsylvania. He had visited the Valley of Virginia while a student at Gettysburg, and in 1855 he presented his letter of dismissal to the Tennessee Synod and was received as a member, serving congregations in Brock's Gap, Pendleton and Hardy Counties. He was a useful and energetic man, preaching both in German and English. He moved to Ohio in 1859 and was dismissed to the District Synod of that State.

To the roll of the third convention held in Rader's Church, in May, 1858, three new names were added: Jacob Stirewalt, John H. Hunton, and George Schmucker. The last was the son of John Nicolas Schmucker, for many years the pastor of the Woodstock congregation. George Schmucker labored in Pendleton and Hardy Counties with much self-sacrifice demanded by the difficulties of his widely scattered field. He was earnest and conservative. Two names are also added to the list as students of theology, Spener Stirewalt and Henry Miller. As lay delegates seventeen names appear on the record, making a total membership of twenty-five. Among the new names we notice the following: Daniel Sibert of St. David's, Moses Tussing of Mt. Zion (near New Market), Jonathan Shutters of Solomon's, Nicholas Miller of Peaked Mountain, Siram Henkel of Rader's, Josiah Souders of Phanuel's, Martin Coyner of Bethlehem's, Abraham Link of Zion's Church, Hardy Co., Jacob Shank of Mt. Calvary, Page County.

An interesting feature of the convention was the reception of George Schmucker upon his unqualified asseveration that he accepted "as his confession the entire body of the Symbolical Books of the Evangelical Lutheran Church," and the ordination of John H. Hunton, a young man who had endeared himself to all the brethren by his studious habits and his careful and irreproachable bearing among them. Mr. Hunton took up the work relinquished by Joel Swartz near Woodstock.

At the fourth convention the roll of ministers remained unchanged. Twenty lay delegates were present. The Rev. Thomas Miller of the Virginia Synod was received as an advisory member. The fifth convention was held in Mt. Calvary Church, Page County, in May, 1860, with the same roll of ministers. This was followed by the regular convention in 1861, but of which the minutes were not recorded. The years of the Civil War interfered with the regular meetings and the seventh convention was held in Rader's Church in October, 1865. The name of John H. Hunton is missing; he had accepted a call to Canada. Two new names are found on the roll: The Rev. Thomas Miller who had accepted the congregations near Woodstock, and the Rev. James E. Seneker, who had come from North Carolina and accepted work centering about Waynesboro. Two students had been lost through the war, Mr. Henry Miller and Mr. Martin Luther Wetzel. John S. Bennick, who had come from North Carolina just before the war and had been received as a student of theology, served throughout the war and returned to take up his studies again. He was licensed to preach in 1865. William H. Swaney, a teacher in New Market, was also licensed at this convention. John P. Cline, of the Virginia Synod, John H. Hunton of Canada, and Julius L. Stirewalt, of the Joint Synod of Ohio, were received as advisory members.

Thus far it is noticed that progress and harmony express the characteristics of the Conference. Now in a most innocent manner a firebrand is cast into the otherwise calm proceedings. The committee on general business reported as the first item for consideration the following: "First, we suggest to Conference the propriety and expediency of organizing a Synod within the geographical limits of this Conference." In response to this suggestion Conference adopted the following resolution: "Resolved, That a convention of this Conference convene in McGaheysville Church, Rockingham County, Va., on Saturday before the third Sunday of May, 1866, to form this Conference into a Synod." This convention ended with the recorded protest of Socrates Henkel against the action of the Conference in convening the Conference for the purpose of forming a Synod, as the proceeding was considered irregular by him. When the convention met in McGaheysville in May, 1866, it was evident that much interest had been created, and that no doubt a division of sentiment had arisen. The attendance was large. Ten ministers were on the roll and a large lay delegation was present. The outcome of the proceedings were, that a special meeting should be held in Solomon's Church in November of this same year; that a committee of two should in person or by letter make due request of the Synod for their approval or disapproval of the contemplated step; that a committee should draft a constitution to present at the special meeting for the new Synod.

When the time arrived, all the ministers and a full delegation of lay members were present in Solomon's Church in November, 1866. This time was chosen so that an answer could be received from the Tennessee Synod, which met that year in October, in Davidson County, N. C. One visitor was present, the Rev. Irenaeus Conder, of North Carolina. The committee appointed to ask the advice of the Synod reported that a favorable response had been received, couched in these words:

> Be it resolved, That we unanimously approve the measure proposed by our brethren in Virginia, and advise them as soon as possible to organize a Synod with such constitution and other regulations as may not be inconsistent with the Word of God and the Symbolical Writings of the Evangelical Lutheran Church, and promise as soon as we have been officially informed that this has been done the president will give them an honorable dismission from this Synod, with a distinct understanding, however, that a regular correspondence be maintained by the interchange of delegates or by the formation of some central organization.

The committee on the proposed constitution reported and the report was adopted item by item. It remained only to consummate the action of the Conference to change into a Synod, and this was done by two resolutions that were adopted: First,

> Resolved, That we form and constitute ourselves into an Evangelical Lutheran Synod under the name and title Evangelical Lutheran Concordia Synod of Virginia; and second,

> Resolved, That when this Synod adjourns it adjourn to meet at Koiner's Church, Augusta County, Va., on Saturday before the second Sunday in October, 1867.

When the time came, only three ministers reported for the meeting of the new Synod, Pastors Wetzel, Schmucker and Seneker, with their lay delegates. Deep chagrin and disappointment seized the three earnest men, and they hardly knew what to do. Wetzel was in favor of giving up the effort to form a Synod, but the other two overruled him and the Concordia Synod was formed. It was too weak to live. It became a district conference of the Joint Synod of Ohio. Ten of the eleven congregations following their pastor, Henry Wetzel, returned to the Tennessee Synod. Wetzel himself upon his insistent pleading was received into the fold again in 1884. The large, historic Koiner congregation finally passed from the Joint Synod of Ohio into the Missouri Synod. Neither Schmucker nor Seneker ever returned to the Tennessee Synod, but it is recorded of them that in their last days they expressed a desire to be enrolled again in the Synod in which they had spent so many active days and years.

The rest of the ministers of the Virginia Conference having the president and secretary in their number, and the records in their possession, issued a call for a meeting of the original Virginia Conference to be held in Rader's Church, October 17, 1868. All the ministers except the three mentioned appeared in response to the call, together with the Rev. I. Conder, who early in the year, 1867, had moved to Virginia from North Carolina to accept a call as teacher and pastor. Fourteen lay delegates were present. On Tuesday, the 20th, the ordination of John Silvanus Bennick and William H. Swaney took place.

After this unfortunate experience was passed, the Conference took a new start, as it were, and continued year by year to maintain a steady interest in beneficiary education and missions. Its growth within its limits was constant, though never great. The roll of ministers had its losses and its gains. The first to drop out of the ranks was the much beloved veteran, Jacob Stirewalt, who passed away August 17, 1869. His place was taken a few years later by his son John N. Stirewalt, who was ordained in 1871 by the Conference. In 1873, December 9th, his second son, J. Paul, was ordained by the Conference. The faithful patriarch of the Conference, Ambrose Henkel, passed away January 6, 1870, and the veteran Jacob Killian followed

July 5, 1871. The last of the charter members to pass away was Dr. Socrates Henkel, who died June 20, 1901.

Among the ministers who were received as members of the Virginia Conference we mention the following: Luther A. Fox, J. W. Hausenfluck, A. L. Crouse, J. I. Miller, P. C. Wike, J. S. Koiner, R. H. Cline, J. K. Efird, A. R. Beck, A. L. Boliek, F. C. Oberly, E. H. Kohn, M. L. Pence, M. Grossman, J. L. Deaton, E. L. Wessinger, M. A. Ashby, A. J. Stirewalt, W. L. Darr, D. L. Miller, O. W. Aderholdt, Enoch Hite, P. L. Snapp, J. S. Wessinger, W. J. Finck, C. K. Rhodes, Lester L. Huffman, E. Z. Pence, F. M. Speagle, V. L. Fulmer, H. D. Chapman, C. I. Morgan, and L. L. Lohr.

Throughout its long history the Conference never forgot the importance of educating its young men for the ministry. Several students of theology were always under way, either in the homes of its ministers, or in schools near home or far away. The Polytechnic Institute of New Market served as the source of education in the classics for many a young man. After Lenoir College was established the students usually pursued their classical course in that institution of the Church. As a consequence of the close attention paid to beneficiary education many of the ministers whose names are mentioned above were sons of the Conference, in whom the Conference felt a just pride. Two of these accepted work in the foreign mission field of Japan, the Rev. A. J. Stirewalt, D. D. and the Rev. M. M. Kipps, of the Mt. Nebo congregation.

A striking characteristic of the Conference was its activity in its local home mission field. Besides maintaining the congregations belonging to its membership, it organized through its missionary pastors congregation after congregation, as can be inferred from the following list of congregations organized after 1870: St. John's, near Timberville, Morning Star and Grace, Page County, St. Mark's, Luray, Mt. Nebo, Morning Star and Powder Springs in Shenandoah County, Bethel of Brock's Gap, Bethel of Manassas, St. James, Rileyville, St. Paul's, Hupp,

Trinity, St. Luke's and Mt. Zion, all three of the Manassas charge.

As with other ecclesiastical bodies in Virginia, the Virginia Conference did not escape the agitation of Mergers. It was not actively concerned in the Merger of 1918, as it moved with its own Synod, but scarcely had this passed when the merger of the Tennessee Synod and the North Carolina Synod came to the front and produced much interest. It was the sentiment of the members of the Virginia Conference that they would adhere to the Mother Synod and make whatever movements should be made as a part of the complete body. In this also the members of the South Carolina Conference concurred. When the act of merging was consummated in 1921, the Virginia Conference of the Tennessee Synod automatically became the Virginia Conference of the United Evangelical Lutheran Synod of North Carolina. Under this title it continued its existence for four years. It seemed a long time for some, and two congregations asked for their dismissal to unite with the Lutheran Synod of Virginia before further action on the part of the Virginia Conference was taken. The South Carolina Conference united with the Synod of South Carolina in November, 1922. Negotiations, however, were soon under way between the Lutheran Synod of Virginia and a committee of Virginia Conference men appointed by the United Synod of North Carolina. The members of this committee were M. L. Pence, C. I. Morgan and Elon O. Henkel. The corresponding merger committee of the Lutheran Synod of Virginia was composed of C. W. Cassell, C. F. Steck, Sr., and John W. Shuey. Their negotiations were successful and in November, 1924, the United Synod of North Carolina was asked to grant a letter of dismissal to each of the pastors and congregations in Virginia in order that they might unite with the Lutheran Synod of Virginia. The complete roll of the Virginia Conference consisted of nine active pastors and two retired ministers, and thirty-three congregations. Of the thirty-three congregations all but one were transferred as requested; this one, Beth Eden, of Page County, retained its membership for legal reasons in the United Synod of North Carolina. Of the ministers two had entered upon work in other states, and two more, though present at the merger meeting, had accepted calls to other fields beyond the bounds of the Conference. Thus the Conference, which prided itself in running for long spaces of time without vacancies, at the time of the Merger was far from being in a perfect condition.

The last meeting of the Virginia Conference was held in Christ Church, Staunton, immediately preceding the time of the meeting of the Lutheran Synod of Virginia. Final action was taken in all things requiring attention before adjournment *sine die.* A president was elected in the person of the Rev. A. L. Boliek, who by action of the Synod became the president of the Conference that was to come forth from the Merger. The treasurer, C. S. Kerlin, rendered his last report and was instructed to hold the funds in trust for the treasurer of the new Conference.

The reception into the Lutheran Synod of Virginia followed immediately after this meeting. Seats had been reserved and before a large congregation the members of the Virginia Conference were received into unity with the Synod assembled for its annual session. Words of special greeting and appreciation were spoken to the incoming Conference in behalf of the Synod by the Rev. J. A. Huffard, D. D. The aged pastors of the Conference were presented to the Synod, the Rev. I. Conder in person, and the Rev. J. P. Stirewalt *in absentia.* The other members were cordially greeted, A. L. Boliek, C. I. Morgan, W. J. Finck, in person, and W. L. Darr and H. D. Chapman *in absentia.* Pastors L. L. Lohr and F. M. Speagle were received as advisory members. The lay delegates present were the following: Charles E. Koontz, John W. Foltz, J. L. Hoak, Walter S. Daggy, George R. Golladay, E. M. Minnick, Luther A. Lohr, I. P. Wittig, George M. Harpine, John Moomaw, and William Moomaw. The treasurer, Charles S. Kerlin, was also present. Many delegates and two of the pastors were kept away by the severity of the winter's cold and snowstorm. The date of the Merger meeting' was January 27, 1925. A few weeks later, the Rev. L. L. Lohr was received by letter.

The following enabling acts were adopted by the Synod upon the reception of the new members:

> *Resolved,* That the congregations herein received be and hereby are constituted as a conference which shall be known as the New Market Conference of the Lutheran Synod of Virginia.

> *Resolved,* That the officers of the Virginia Conference of the United Evangelical Lutheran Synod of North Carolina and of the Sunday School Convention of said Conference and all the officers and committees of these organizations be and are hereby appointed to serve according to the intent of their election and appointment, in the New Market Conference and its Sunday School Convention, till their successors are elected at the regular annual meeting of these organizations.

Immediately after the Merger meeting the members of the former Virginia Conference were called together as the New Market Conference of the Lutheran Synod of Virginia. The Pastors L. L. Lohr and F. M. Speagle were received as advisory members and Mr. Speagle was requested to write the minutes for the meeting and have them published in the Conference paper, The Lutheran Messenger. Upon motion of the Rev. C. I. Morgan, it was

> *Resolved,* That we accept the trust, bequests, property, organizations and appointments bestowed upon us by the Virginia Conference of the United Evangelical Lutheran Synod of North Carolina and by the Lutheran Synod of Virginia.

The Conference thereupon adjourned to meet at the call of the president.

During the four years of the existence of the New Market Conference its work has continued to develop in peace and harmony. All the appointments inherited from the former Virginia Conference, like the Sunday School Association, have been successfully continued. Other agencies of usefulness in church activities have been inaugurated, like the Women's Missionary Society of the Conference and the intensive work of the Luther League in the congregations, together with the beginnings of a Conference Luther League. Mt. Calvary and St. Stephen's congregations, for better parish arrangements, have been transferred to the Winchester Conference, and the Luray parish consisting of St. Mark's, Luray, and Bethlehem, near Luray, with their pastor, the Rev. C. W. Cassell, have been received as an integral part of the New Market Conference. All the vacancies existing at the time of the Merger have been filled and for two years every parish in the Conference has had its resident pastor. The following ministers have come into the Conference since the Merger in 1925: Luther F. Miller from Maryland, Manassas, Va.; Henry E. H. Sloop from North Carolina, Rockingham, Va.; Dewey W. Zipperer, from Georgia, Forestville charge; Russell P. Knoebel, from Pennsylvania, Orkney Springs, Va.; Arthur W. Ballentine, from South Carolina, Timberville, Va.

Thus, as in the early days so in these last days, pastors have come from all points of the compass to bring the Gospel to the people of the Dominion and Commonwealth of Virginia!

The Evangelical Lutheran Holston Synod
of East Tennessee

For some years prior to 1860 there was considerable restlessness among the Lutheran ministers and congregations of eastern Tennessee. For forty years they had been a part of the Tennessee Synod. The Synod bore the name of the territory covered by the congregations served by these pastors; the doctrinal standard of the Tennessee Synod was satisfactory to them, and they rejoiced that the principles of their Synod were strictly and distinctively Lutheran, but the geographical distances that had to be covered to attend an annual convention, the intervening mountains, and the length of time it took to make effective the actions of their Synod, convinced the workers in Tennessee more and more that a separate and independent Synod was demanded in the interests of their territory and the prosecution of the work of their Church. The special conference no longer satisfied their needs, as that still left the members amenable to the Synod. That the geographical disadvantages were great can be seen from the fact that when the Tennessee Synod met in Augusta County, Va., in 1859, not a single minister or lay delegate was present from the State of Tennessee.

Dr. Abel J. Brown in his anniversary discourse in 1886, says: "The Lutheran churches and ministers in East Tennessee remained in connection with the Tennessee Synod till 1860. They then petitioned the Synod for an honorable dismission for the purpose of organizing a new Lutheran Synod in East Tennessee, and their petition was granted in very complimentary terms.

"The withdrawal of the East Tennessee Lutherans from the Tennessee Synod was not a step taken hastily and rashly, but after long, deliberate and prayerful reflection. Nor was it taken because of dissatisfaction with the doctrinal position of the Synod, or because of any personal difficulties with any of its members, or for the accomplishment of any selfish or sinister ends; but solely because it was believed that the best interests of the Lutheran Church in East Tennessee imperatively demanded the formation of an independent Synod within its limits. Amongst the reasons assigned by the petitioners for the step which they proposed, were the inconvenience and expensiveness of attending the annual conventions of the Synod when it met in another State, which was three years in every four; the loss to the people of whatever advantages might result from a meeting of the Synod in the midst of them annually; the slowness of the process by which any measure for the good of the Church could be introduced, because the Synod was scattered over so vast an extent of territory, that it was difficult to get as full a meeting of the Synod as was necessary for the adoption of any important measure; and because all business transacted by the Synod could be just as well transacted by the new Synod contemplated, as could be in the Tennessee Synod."

It was a new experience for the Tennessee Synod to receive a petition of this character entailing the loss of a very respectable portion of its membership, but it received the request in a fraternal spirit and with unanimous generosity adopted the following:

Whereas our ministerial brethren in the State of Tennessee * * * with their congregations have asked an honorable dismission from this body with a view to the formation of a new Synod in their own State, and

Whereas they give us the assurance, that in taking this step, they have no other object in view than the welfare of our beloved Lutheran Zion, and the more extensive dissemination of the time-honored and Heaven-blessed doctrines of our Church; therefore, be it

Resolved, That whilst we are sincerely sorry to sever the ties which have bound them to us as a part of our Synod, we feel it to be our duty to grant their request, with the fervent prayer that the smiles and rich blessings of the Great Head of the Church may rest upon them, and that all their efforts to extend the Redeemer's Kingdom may be crowned with abundant success.

This action was taken September 22, 1860, and in accordance with the permission granted in this request, the ministers and the delegates in eastern Tennessee met in Zion's Church, Sullivan County, Tenn., on the 29th day of December, 1860, and remained in session until the second day of January, 1861, on which day the convention unanimously

Resolved, That we now organize ourselves into a Synod, to be known by the name of

THE EVANGELICAL LUTHERAN HOLSTON SYNOD

The new Synod embraced ten ministers, as follows: William Hancher, Abel J. Brown, Jacob M. Schaeffer, James K. Hancher, Jacob B. Emmert, James Fleenor, Adam Fleenor, John A. Seneker, Jacob Cloniger, and James C. Barb. The name of Henry D. Giesler was added to the roll by ordination at the first convention.

The history of the Holston Synod falls into three periods.

The First Period

1861-1886

Organized at the beginning of the Civil War, the new Synod had difficulty in meeting in regular time year by year. In 1861, no further meetings were held. At the next convention of the Synod in October, 1862, the committee appointed to draft a constitution reported. Their report was adopted and the constitution was ordered to be printed in connection with the minutes of the Synod for examination by the congregations. It was approved by the congregations but inasmuch as the attendance in 1863 was small, and no convention was held in 1864, final action was not taken until September, 1865, when the constitution was ratified by the Synod in session in Immanuel Church, Sullivan County, Tenn.

The history of the confessional development of the Synod is of interest as it has features connected with it not found in the history of other Synods in the South. Its confessional basis underwent more changes than that of other Synods because it was in its history connected with more general bodies than any other Synod. Just before leaving the Tennessee Synod it participated in the adoption of the complete, threefold confessional basis of the Holy Scriptures, the Ecumenical Creeds and the Symbolical Books. Soon after the War, it unlike any other southern Synod united with the General Synod North (1867-1873), but in a few years it was attracted by the General Council which had adopted the original full, threefold doctrinal basis obtaining in the Holston Synod at the time of leaving the Tennessee Synod. In this connection (1874-1886) and on this basis the Holston Synod remained until it asked to be dismissed in 1886, in order that it might unite with the United Synod in the South, in the organization of which the Holston Synod joined hands with all the other Synods in the South. The condition of this last union was that it should be done without in the least compromising the standard of Lutheranism prevailing in the Holston Synod. This was accomplished without difficulty, as three of the southern Synods had already made the full confessional basis of the Evangelical Lutheran Church a part of their constitution: The Tennessee Synod, 1860, the North Carolina Synod, 1869, and the Holston Synod, 1873.

Considering the external growth and development of the Holston Synod, it must be recorded that it gave itself during its early and later years to the accomplishment of the

purposes for which it had been organized.   It set itself about
the elevation of the standard of education among its ministers
and laymen, the promotion of the cause of education, and
the enlargement of the liberality of its membership for all
works of benevolence, education and missions.   In numbers
it could not grow fast as it was limited in its territory, and
the parishes barely supported the pastors and missionaries.
Many fields had to be neglected on account of lack of men
and means.   But the members made an earnest effort to
fulfill the high mission of the Synod in domestic and
foreign missions, in education by fostering an educational
institution called the Mosheim Academy, and by planning
for the establishment of missions in cities like Bristol,
Blountville, Greeneville, Morristown, Knoxville, Kingsport
and Chattanooga.

When twenty-five years of its history were past it had
to be acknowledged that in number and style of its churches,
in the increase of its numerical strength in the ministry and
laity as seen in its statistical reports, its growth had not been
very rapid, still its progress had been considerable and
highly encouraging.   It was organized with sixteen congregations; in 1886, the number was twenty-seven.   In 1861,
it had very few houses of worship that were even comfortable to say nothing of elegance; many of them were old
log structures, while some congregations worshiped in small
schoolhouses.   In 1886, there were but few congregations
in its bounds that had not a neat and comfortable church in
which to worship; some were substantial brick buildings, set
off with well proportioned steeples, furnished with bells.

The number of ministers had grown from ten to fifteen,
but seventeen names had been added to the roll during these
twenty-five years.   Among these we note the following:
Joseph E. Bell, Jacob M. Wagner, M. L. Thornburg,
Jacob M. Schaeffer, James M. Turner, Andrew Rader,
Luther M. Wagner, John P. Deck, James C. Barb, George
H. Cox, Junius B. Fox, J. H. Summit, A. C. Gearhart, John
B. Rogers, John G. Schaidt, and George Bushong Hancher.
Seven pastors had died during this first period.

Three of the organizers were still living at the time of the silver anniversary, James K. Hancher, Abel J. Brown, and Jacob Cloniger. Pastors Hancher and Brown took a prominent part in the celebration, and Dr. Brown was himself honored at the time by his brethren, as the year 1886 was the fiftieth anniversary of his ordination, and the other members of the Synod presented him with a testimonial engrossed on parchment and expressed in the following language:

To Our Senior Pastor and President of the Evangelical Lutheran Holston Synod, the Rev. Abel J. Brown, Doctor of Divinity

At the Fiftieth Anniversary of his Ordination to the Holy Office of the Gospel Ministry, and the Twenty-fifth Annual Convention of our Synod, which he helped to organize and of which he has ever been a faithful and zealous member, we his brethren and friends present this token of our affection and esteem, praying God and our Lord Jesus Christ for His richest blessing upon him.

Given this fourteenth day of August, 1886, at Immanuel Church, Sullivan County, Tennessee.

THE SYNOD.

The Second Period

1886-1911

When the Holston Synod entered the second period of its history in 1886, its leaders were still at the helm, but soon they were called away. Two years after the anniversary three 'dismissals to other Synods were granted to three of the pastors, and two others were inactive on account of age and ill health. In 1894 Abel J. Brown to the great sorrow of the Synod was reported among the departed; soon after Pastor Hancher, the old pillar of the Synod, Jacob Cloniger, and a recent addition, one of the youngest of the pastors, all three laid down the tools of service and departed. Many ministers came and stayed but a few years. This restlessness continued for a number of years causing great

IN VIRGINIA AND EAST TENNESSEE   139

distress among the congregations, and destitution of spiritual attention throughout the Synod.

The troubles in the educational field were distressing. Mosheim Institute, which was bought by the Synod in 1872, at times brought much satisfaction to the members of Synod, but in general more sorrow and chagrin. It had its days of prosperity when everybody could rejoice over the good work it was doing with its hundred and seventy-five young men and women who were attending its sessions. Then it would suffer from lack of financial support and the teachers would become desperate on account of unpaid salaries. At times it would be closed because teachers could not be found to carry on the work. Before the close of the last period Prof. A. C. Gearhart came from the west and put new life into the noble undertaking. In 1897, Prof. J. B. Greever arrived from southwest Virginia, and the school entered into a new estate of promise. The name was changed to The Holston Synodical College, a new location was bought and new buildings erected. But the Synod became financially involved in the enterprise, lawsuits followed and in 1901, the Synod allowed the college buildings and grounds to be sold by the Court, through which on account of the loss of the suit all that they had invested in this promising enterprise of education was lost, but when the lawyers were paid, the cause of the trouble was at an end, and nothing more is found in the minutes except the settlement of the final disputes with those at the head of the institution. But the ill feeling and divisions among the people continued for years and interfered with the prosperity of the Synod in other branches of Church work.

This period is also marked with defections on the part of ministers and congregations that caused the Synod heavy loss in membership and much pain and discouragement. The German congregations, two in number, withdrew without any ceremony and united with the Missouri Synod; several ministers split their congregations on account of differences in practice and morals, dividing their congregations and causing sad havoc among the weak flocks that they had tried to serve. The old congregations could not be properly cared for with religious services, catechization was neglected, salaries remained unpaid, the missions did not prosper because both men and means were lacking and the mission fields were neglected. In 1903, the mission in Bristol could not be prevented from accepting the aid of the Southwest Virginia Synod and joining the helpful Synod; in 1904. Buehler's congregation formed a charge with the Bristol mission and likewise joined the Southwest Virginia Synod.

These were sad years for the faithful in the Holston Synod. Discouragement and hopelessness had taken hold of many hearts. But before this second period neared its end relief came to the faithful brethren. In various ways this help came to them, but it began with the arrival of faithful pastors to take up the neglected work in East Tennessee, and to man the missions in the important cities. James C. Barb returned from Indiana to his native State in 1895. Two sturdy sons of the State were ordained: Francis Marion Harr in 1891; Anthony D. R. Hancher in 1892; these native workers were followed by a succession of pastors from without, a few of whom we shall mention: Michael M. Kinard, Henry E. H. Sloop, W. C. Schaeffer, Sr., William H. Roof, and Walter C. Davis. All these men helped to bring about a new era in the Synod. The change began before Dr. Kinard left in 1907, and Pastor Sloop while president organized the pastors into two conferences and set them into active motion. Two that worked together side by side during these cloudy times were: W. H. Roof and W. C. Davis, chiefly the former as president and the latter as secretary. Of the eleven years Mr. Roof spent in the Synod he served eight years as president. He spoke in the most hopeful manner in his reports from year to year. "The field is very important. The possibilities are great for our Lutheran Church. The opportunities and privileges are still ours. The development of the field will necessarily be slow. But if we go forth gradually in the strength of the Lord, with unity of spirit, unity of purpose, and unity of action 'our labors will not be in vain in the Lord.'" Again he writes: "Ten years ago (1906) we had only four pastors in regular service in our Synod. We now have eight pastors,

and our work is developing gradually in all directions.
The growth is not as rapid as many of us would like to see,
but if we continue to work, watch and pray, God will give
the increase in due time. To my mind, the outlook for the
future of our Synod is much brighter than it has been since
I have been a member."

The success of the missionary operations helped to cheer
up conditions for the Synod. Knoxville was the first of the
important mission points that yielded to the efforts of the
Synod. The United Synod Mission Board took a hand in
furthering the interests of the English Lutherans in Knoxville. Its secretary labored here for a number of years and
in 1889 organized St. John's English Lutheran Church. A
number of strong men followed the secretary as missionaries
and added much strength to the personnel of the Synod.
In 1913 the congregation dedicated a beautiful stone
memorial church in memory of James A. Henson, the
erection of which was made possible by the generosity of his
widow, Mrs. Martha Henson.

Dr. W. C. Schaeffer, Sr., took up the two missions,
Morristown and Greeneville in 1907, and gave the work in
both places a start that helped them in spite of many troubles
and delays on to the way of success. A few years later Dr.
Schaeffer pushed into Chattanooga and in the fall of 1913,
organized the Church of the Ascension in that important
center, and his son, H. Brent Schaeffer, became pastor upon
his graduation from the Southern Seminary in May, 1915,
followed by his ordination by the Holston Synod. One
other mission point runs into the next period with Chattanooga and that is Kingsport, which has been one of the most
remarkable mission points of modern times, culminating in
the call of James A. Huffard just at the time of the Merger
in 1922.

Thus this period of history was at its end entirely
different from its condition at its beginning, full of light
and encouragement. The president suggested that the time
be duly celebrated, as had been the close of the first quarter
of a century, but the members of the Synod were not as yet

filled with enthusiasm over their past history, and they let the first half century come to an end without stopping to celebrate, or to look into the future for inspiration. But a loving Providence silently drew a curtain over the past, and allowed the actors on the stage to stand only in front of that curtain, to be filled with the light of the future.

With 1911, it can be truthfully stated that the discouraging troubles were over, and the Synod moved forward with more success. Many leaders of the Church from without came to the meetings and aided in the difficult work of East Tennessee. Among these must be mentioned Robert C. Holland, John A. Morehead, Robert S. Patterson. John J. Scherer, Sr., Paul Sieg, John T. Crabtree, and others, the representatives of the various causes of the United Synod South and of the educational and eleemosynary institutions located on the southern territory. Their addresses and appeals inspired the Holston Synod with new life and a holy ambition to do much for the Kingdom, and stirred up the laity to a liberality and generosity before unknown.

The Third Period
1911-1922

New life and new growth mark the course of the Holston Synod during this brief period, ending with the larger life and growth of the Merger.

The vacancies are filled; the short pastorates are lengthened; for the first time in many years all parishes are reported supplied with pastors in 1914, and the discouraged congregations of the past delight in the new day that has dawned upon them and arise to face the task of missions, education and benevolence with their leaders. The prosperity of their missions at Knoxville and Chattanooga encouraged them, and they responded gladly to the call to enter earnestly the field opening up to them in Kingsport. This is the great missionary enterprise of this period. The city had a phenomenal growth. In 1918, the population amounted to nine thousand. Lutheran people from Wytheville and many points in Virginia and other states had come to the prosperous city. Services were begun in August, 1915, by the Rev. W. G. Cobb, Jr., a neighboring pastor, and in the spring of 1917, he effected the organization of the Holy Trinity Evangelical Lutheran Church, with about twenty charter members. In May, 1918, Henry Grady Davis, a son of the Holston Synod, took charge as the first settled pastor. He found a willing people ready for action. A fine and suitable lot was soon bought by the combined contribution of the Mission Board of the United Synod South, the Holston Synod and the congregation. Mission and Synod were traveling in a bright and promising day.

The Synodical Women's Missionary Society added much to the activity and progress of the Synod during this period. It was first recommended by the retiring president, H. E. H. Sloop, in 1907, and on July 31, 1908, the called meeting was held at which the following were elected the officers: President, Mrs. W. C. Schaeffer; Vice President, Miss Louie Bible; Recording Secretary, Miss Dora E. Kinser; Corresponding Secretary, Miss Mattie Akard. The first regular meeting was held the next day and was called The Woman's Conference of the Holston Synod. The Synod was in session at the same time and aided in the program. The Rev. E. C. Cronk was present and made an interesting and inspiring address. The following year Mrs. Catherine Scherer Cronk was present and assisted in the exercises of the convention. The interest of the Synodical Society reached far afield and led to the organization of many congregational societies, that helped in the furtherance of all the causes of the United Synod South and brought new life into the synodical and congregational activities.

The progress that the Synod was making during these years brought back repeatedly the question, Whether it would not be to the advantage of the Holston Synod to unite its forces with those of some adjoining Synod? It was an old question. As early as 1878 the president of the Synod suggested that it might be well to consider a union with the Southwest Virginia Synod. Nothing was done as in a few years the plan of forming a union among all the Synods of the South agitated the minds of all. But after this union was successfully consummated the question arose again in 1894, but other matters intervened and nothing of a practical nature was undertaken. Still the question persisted. The territory covered by the Holston Synod was an extension geographically of Southwest Virginia; the people were of the same extraction and history, coming mainly by migration from Pennsylvania; their work and the causes in which the two Synods were interested were the same. Union would result in strengthening both Synods in the performance of their responsibilities.

Thus it happened that before the two larger Synods of Virginia, The Evangelical Lutheran Synod of Virginia and The Southwestern Virginia Synod, had agreed to merge, the Holston Synod and Southwestern Virginia Synod were ready to unite their interests and their forces into one Synod. However, that History might have a clear record, on the seventeenth day of March, 1922, in St. Mark's Church, Roanoke, Virginia, the three Synods met and entered their names separately to form the roll of the merged Synod styled

The Lutheran Synod of Virginia,

and on September 6, 1922, they held in the same church the second session of the Merger Convention and completed the necessary work of this convention.

The Holston Synod entered the Merger convention with eight ministers and twenty-four congregations.

Roll of the Three Synods Forming the Lutheran Synod of Virginia

The Evangelical Lutheran Synod and Ministerium of Virginia

Ministers

Rev. R. Homer Anderson _____ Strasburg, Va.
Rev. R. C. Cline _____ Stephens City, Va.
Rev. C. W. Cassell _____ Mt. Sidney, Va.
Rev. Norman E. Cooper _____ Rio, W. Va.
Rev. W. A. Craun _____ Maywood, Ill.
Rev. E. C. Cronk, D. D. _____ Richmond, Va.

Rev. J. B. Derrick _____ Augusta, Ga.
Rev. D. S. Fox _____ Waynesboro, Va.
Rev. D. W. Files _____ Wardensville, W. Va.
Rev. L. W. Gross _____ Woodstock, Va.
Rev. A. D. R. Hancher _____ Richmond, Va.
Rev. W. P. Huddle _____ Churchville, Va.
Rev. J. A. Huffard, D. D. _____ Kingsport, Tenn.
Rev. G. S. C. Hasskarl, Ph. D. _____ Jeffersonville, N. Y.
Rev. Charles W. Hepner _____ Omuta, Japan
Rev. D. Hunda _____ Saga, Japan
Rev. S. W. Kuhns _____ Woodstock, Va.
Rev. T. O. Keister, D. D. _____ Staunton, Va.
Rev. A. A. Kelly _____ Winchester, Va.
Rev. J. W. Link _____ New Market, Va.
Rev. E. W. Leslie _____ Salem, Va.
Rev. C. A. Marks _____ Waynesboro, Va.
Rev. J. A. Morehead, D. D. _____ Salem, Va.
Rev. E. R. McCauley, D. D. _____ Norfolk, Va.
Rev. J. A. L. Miller _____ Bridgewater, Va.
Rev. L. S. G. Miller _____ Hakata, Japan
Rev. Grover Morgan _____ Madison, Va.
Rev. W. B. Oney _____ Staunton, Va.
Rev. James Oosterling _____ Norfolk, Va.
Rev. P. H. Pearson _____ Newport News, Va.
Rev. Asa Richard _____ Lovettsville, Va.
Rev. E. L. Ritchie _____ Waynesboro, Va.
Rev. W. W. J. Ritchie _____ Churchville, Va.
Rev. Paul L. Royer _____ Mt. Jackson, Va.
Rev. H. E. H. Sloop _____ Bloom, Va.
Rev. J. W. Shuey _____ Lexington, Va.
Rev. J. J. Scherer, Jr., D. D. _____ Richmond, Va.
Rev. P. L. Snapp _____ Middlebrook, Va.
Rev. K. Y. Umberger _____ Waynesboro, Va.
Rev. I. D. Worman _____ Shepherdstown, W. Va.
Rev. N. Yamanouchi _____ Tokyo, Japan

Lay Delegates

L. L. Alpine _____ Lexington, Va.
S. B. Harper _____ Stuarts Draft, Va.
G. V. Link _____ Staunton, Va.
M. S. Glaize _____ Albin, Va.
D. B. Foltz _____ Harrisonburg, Va.
W. H. Crigler _____ Madison, Va.
George R. Geary _____ Mt. Jackson, Va.
W. A. McComb _____ Staunton, Va.
C. N. Hoover _____ New Market, Va.
L. L. Arehart _____ Fairfield, Va.

W. T. Stauffer _____ Newport News, Va.
W. A. Burchard _____ Norfolk, Va.
L. A. Coleman _____ Portsmouth, Va.
A. D. Smith _____ Richmond, Va.
C. L. Gowl _____ Harrisonburg, Va.
N. I. Kagey _____ Weyers Cave, Va.
S. B. Hepner _____ Woodstock, Va.
H. L. Snyder _____ Shepherdstown, W. Va.
J. O. Snyder _____ Staunton, Va.
C. W. Snapp _____ Opequon, Va.
Harry S. Crabill _____ Toms Brook, Va.
E. L. Keiser _____ Waynesboro, Va.
A. L. Henkel _____ Winchester, Va.
G. M. Grove _____ Fishersville, Va.

The Evangelical Lutheran Synod and Ministerium of Southwestern Virginia

Ministers

Rev. S. C. Ballentine _____ Damascus, Va.
Rev. H. E. Bailey _____ Eggleston, Va.
Rev. O. F. Blackwelder _____ Roanoke, Va.
Rev. James A. Boord _____ Salem, Va.
Rev. W. R. Brown _____ Rural Retreat, Va.
Rev. E. A. Byers _____ Salem, Va.
Rev. W. G. Cobb _____ Pulaski, Va.
Rev. E. H. Copenhaver _____ Marion, Va.
Rev. C. Brown Cox _____ Marion, Va.
Rev. B. W. Cronk _____ Pembroke, Va.
Rev. L. A. Fox, D. D. _____ Salem, Va.
Rev. C. W. Hunton _____ Salem, Va.
Rev. J. A. C. Hurt _____ Wytheville, Va.
Rev. J. M. Killian _____ Lockland, O.
Rev. J. M. McCauley _____ Salem, Va.
Rev. T. C. Parker _____ Blacksburg, Va.
Rev. C. J. Rice _____ Wytheville, Va.
Rev. J. H. Richard _____ Rural Retreat, Va.
Rev. P. E. Shealy _____ Rural Retreat, Va.
Rev. J. L. Sieber _____ Roanoke, Va.
Rev. Paul Sieg _____ Salem, Va.
Rev. J. L. Smith _____ Bristol, Tenn.
Rev. G. W. Spiggle _____ Wytheville, Va.
Rev. C. F. Steck, Jr. _____ Bluefield, Va.
Rev. J. M. Tise _____ Floyd, Va.
Rev. A. F. Tobler _____ Crockett, Va.
Rev. J. D. Utt _____ Nace, Va.
Rev. H. P. Wyrick _____ Blacksburg, Va.

Lay Delegates

C. A. Crabtree _____ Ceres, Va.
O. V. Hefner _____ Bluefield, W. Va.
J. Edgar Harr _____ Bristol, Tenn.
A. S. Greever _____ Burkes Garden, Va.
S. D. Steffy _____ Cripple Creek, Va.
Dr. E. W. Peery _____ Lynchburg, Va.
J. A. Groseclose _____ Marion, Va.
Prof. H. Gudheim _____ Blacksburg, Va.
William Kenzie _____ Newport, Va.
R. E. Fry _____ Pulaski, Va.
G. W. Stoudemire _____ Salem, Va.
J. S. Etter _____ Rural Retreat, Va.
Frank Walters _____ Salem, Va.
H. D. Derrick _____ Roanoke, Va.
J. H. Marsteller _____ Roanoke, Va.
E. B. Bonham _____ Chilhowie, Va.
H. C. Buchanan _____ Wytheville, Va.
W. R. Huffard _____ Wytheville, Va.

THE EVANGELICAL LUTHERAN HOLSTON SYNOD

Ministers

Rev. F. M. Harr _____ Knoxville, Tenn
Rev. J. D. Graichen _____ Morristown, Tenn.
Rev. B. S. Brown, Jr. _____ Parrottsville, Tenn.
Rev. E. B. Smith _____ Greeneville, Tenn.
Rev. J. C. Miller _____ Mosheim, Tenn.
Rev. George H. Rhodes _____ Knoxville, Tenn.
Rev. W. H. Roof _____ Blountville, Tenn.
Rev. C. L. Miller _____ Chattanooga, Tenn.

Lay Delegates

W. C. Ailshie _____ Mosheim, Tenn.
J. H. Wilhoit _____ Greeneville, Tenn.
Houston Wolford _____ Blountville, Tenn.
A. P. Harkins _____ Parrottsville, Tenn.
W. J. Probst _____ Telford, Tenn.
J. A. Booher _____ Knoxville, Tenn.
C. H. Barger _____ Blountville, Tenn.
J. M. Laudy _____ Bristol, Tenn.
Matthias Ottinger _____ Parrottsville, Tenn.
J. W. Littleford _____ Bristol, Tenn
A. Lee Harr _____ Midway, Tenn.
Frank Crum _____ Greeneville, Tenn.
J. W. Airheart _____ Madisonville, Tenn.
A. H. Neas _____ Greeneville, Tenn.
J. M. Lichtenwanger _____ Knoxville, Tenn.

J. H. Childs _____ Bristol, Tenn.
E. H. Kinzer _____ Madisonville, Tenn.
Elmer Houser _____ Knoxville, Tenn.

During the period of the history of the Lutheran Synod of Virginia from the time of the merger in 1922 to the Centennial Celebration in 1929, the following ministers were received into the membership of the Synod:

Rev. Charles J. Smith, D. D. _____ Salem, Va.
Rev. George S. Bearden _____ Toms Brook, Va.
Rev. H. E. Beatty _____ Harrisonburg, Va.
Rev. C. E. Kepley _____ Radford, Va.
Rev. P. A. Atkins _____ Portsmouth, Va.
Rev. E. L. Baker _____ Burkes Garden, Va.
Rev. C. F. Steck, D. D. _____ Waynesboro, Va.
Rev. E. O. Graham _____ Stephens City, Va.
Rev. George S. Bowden _____ Strasburg, Va.
Rev. Joseph S. Kleckner _____ Salem, Va.
Rev. V. Y. Boozer, D. D. _____ Madison, Va.
Rev. L. R. Haus _____ Mt. Sidney, Va.
Rev. C. L. Hunt _____ Mosheim, Tenn.
Rev. F. J. Lottich _____ Wytheville, Va.
Rev. J. A. Shealy _____ Greeneville, Tenn.
Rev. P. E. Seidler _____ Damascus, Va.
Rev. Irenaeus Conder _____ McGaheysville, Va.
Rev. J. P. Stirewalt, D. D. _____ New Market, Va.
Rev. W. J. Finck, D. D. _____ New Market, Va.
Rev. W. L. Darr _____ Edinburg, Va.
Rev. A. L. Boliek _____ Shenandoah, Va.
Rev. C. I. Morgan _____ Luray, Va.
Rev. H. D. Chapman _____ Rockingham, Va.
Rev. R. R. Sowers _____ Irmo, S. C.
Rev. Russell D. Snyder _____ Shepherdstown, W. Va.
Rev. S. L. Nease _____ Willis, Va.
Rev. F. V. Christ _____ Norfolk, Va.
Rev. Charles M. Teufel _____ Newport News, Va.
Rev. John P. Derrick _____ Radford, Va.
Rev. Turner Ashby Graves _____ New Market, Va.
Rev. W. C. Huddle _____ Greeneville, Tenn.
Rev. L. L. Lohr, D. D. _____ Timberville, Va.
Rev. Luther F. Miller _____ Manassas, Va.
Rev. C. A. Freed, D. D. _____ Winchester, Va.
Rev. F. C. Longaker, Ph. D. _____ Salem, Va.
Rev. Frank H. Miller _____ Rural Retreat, Va.
Rev. Harry A. Jackson _____ Newport, Va.

Rev. Dewey W. Zipperer _____ Mt. Jackson, Va.
Rev. James M. Lotz _____ Roanoke, Va.
Rev. L. W. Strickler _____ Norfolk, Va.
Rev. H. E. Henning _____ Bristol, Tenn.
Rev. Paul Sieg _____ Salem, Va.
Rev. Theodore G. Shuey _____ Swoope, Va.
Rev. B. D. Castor _____ Parrottsville, Tenn.
Rev. R. T. Troutman _____ Salem, Va.
Rev. J. Ira Coiner _____ Portsmouth, Va.
Rev. George A. Stoudemayer _____ Wardensville, W. Va.
Rev. B. A. Barringer _____ Rural Retreat, Va.
Rev. M. J. Kluttz _____ Waynesboro, Va.
Rev. Russell P. Knoebel _____ Orkney Springs, Va.
Rev. J. W. Groth _____ Middlebrook, Va.
Rev. C. M. Coffelt _____ Harrisonburg, Va.
Rev. B. S. Dasher _____ Greeneville, Tenn.
Rev. W. C. Buck _____ Blacksburg, Va.
Rev. R. S. Poffenbarger _____ New Market, Va.
Rev. A. W. Ballentine _____ Timberville, Va.
Rev. P. J. Bame _____ Newport News, Va.
Rev. J. Edward Lowe, Jr. _____ Hanover, Pa.
Rev. Lester A. Wertz _____ Midway, Tenn.
Rev. Herman E. Knies _____ Roanoke, Va.
Rev. A. K. Yount _____ Danville, Va.
Rev. Snyder Alleman _____ Stephens City, Va.
Rev. C. K. Rhodes _____ Madison, Va.
Rev. 'Raymond L. Markley _____ Lynchburg, Va.
Rev. J. P. Miller, D. D. _____ Wytheville, Va.
Rev. Walter W. Simon _____ Shepherdstown, W. Va.
Rev. Albert J. Shumate _____ Churchville, Va.
Rev. Alfred J. Shumate _____ Middlebrook, Va.
Rev. Harmon E. Poff _____ Radford, Va.
Rev. Malcolm L. Minnick _____ Knoxville, Tenn.

The anniversary was celebrated in Emanuel Evangelical Lutheran Church, Woodstock, where the Evangelical Lutheran Synod was organized on the eleventh of August, 1829. The date of the celebration was July 23-25, 1929, beginning with an exalted service Tuesday evening, at which the President of Roanoke College, the Rev. Charles J. Smith, D. D., a lineal descendant of Christian Streit, preached the historical sermon. Wednesday morning an opportunity was given to review the past by having first an introductory address by the synodical representative, the Rev. C. Brown Cox, D. D., followed by a number of speakers who formed in each case a connecting link with the past, among whom were the Rev. Asa Richard, of Lovettsville, Va., the oldest member of the Synod; the Rev. F. M. Harr, of Crockett, Va., who represented the Holston Synod as its oldest member; the Rev. W. B. Oney, of Staunton, who spoke for Southwest Virginia; Mr. Milton Coffman, of Woodstock, whose faithful career in the Church goes back to the semi-centennial of the Synod celebrated in 1879; and Mr. Elon O. Henkel, the veteran printer and editor of New Market, whose life and labors connect the history under review with the constructive activity of the Tennessee Synod in Virginia.

These addresses were followed on the program by the historical address assigned to the Rev. J. A. Morehead, D.D., President of the Lutheran World Conference, but as it was impossible for him to return from the convention in Copenhagen, Denmark, in time to fill his appointment, his place was taken by the writer, who gave a short review of the history of the Lutheran Church in Virginia and East Tennessee, basing his address on the words of Psalm 126:3, "The Lord hath done great things for us, whereof we are glad."

In the afternoon the representatives of the three synods directly interested in the organization of Lutheranism in Virginia were heard. The Ministerium of Pennsylvania sent the Rev. Russell D. Snyder, formerly of Shepherdstown, W. Va., but more recently of Philadelphia, Pa. The United Evangelical Lutheran Synod of North Carolina sent its president, the Rev. J. L. Morgan, D. D., of Salisbury, N. C. The Synod of Maryland sent the Hon. Harry Tennyson Domer, Litt. D., of Washington, D. C. The greetings and congratulations of these three worthy representatives were received with much interest and deeply appreciated by all present.

In the evening the speaker was the Rev. Walter H. Greever, D. D., of Columbia, S. C., who in a masterly manner portrayed the prospects of the future of Lutheranism in the South and in America.

The third day, Thursday, the climax of the celebration was reached in a large open-air mass meeting held on the extensive grounds of the Shenandoah Caverns, near Mt. Jackson, Va. Two thousand people joined in the festive exercises and listened to the speakers of the day, the Rev. J. L. Morgan, D. D., and Prof. J. C. Kinard, of Newberry, S. C.

Dr. Morgan in his powerful address enumerated the elements of strength in the faith and Confessions of the Lutheran Church, and urged with cogent reasoning an unwavering fidelity to the truth believed, confessed and taught by the fathers of old.

Prof. Kinard stressed the dangers of hurry and speed in the course of life and of the Church, and enunciated the principles of true success that will lead to a secure future in life and faith.

* * * * *

History goes on, however, and the celebration, great as it was, marked but a station, not a terminal.

> Onward, onward, ever onward,
> Moves the mighty Church of God.

PART II

Historical Sketches of the Congregations of Synod

CONGREGATIONAL SKETCHES

N THE following chapter are brief sketches of the congregations of Synod. An earnest effort has been made to collect and record the main facts as to the origin of the congregations, their present strength, the church buildings, and the pastors. The data for the sketches having been gathered from various sources, preference is given to the statements in the Minutes of Synod. In giving the names of those entering the ministry, the congregation in which one was reared and confirmed, is given, rather than that to which he belonged at the time of ordination. For the sake of uniform appearance, dates are printed in a similar form and academic titles of pastors are used only as they appear in the Minutes. The word "parish" being the accepted designation of the Synod for a pastoral district, or charge, or pastorate, it is used throughout these sketches.

AUGUSTA COUNTY

There are sixteen Lutheran congregations in the county—two of these, Trinity, near Crimora, and Bethany, in Waynesboro, belong to the Missouri Synod. Trinity (Koiner's Church), is the oldest Lutheran congregation in the County.

MT. TABOR PARISH

Mt. Tabor—Of the fourteen Virginia Synod congregations, Mt. Tabor is the oldest. It began as early as 1785, but by whom it was organized, and who first administered to the Lutheran people here, is not known. St. John's, Lutheran and Reformed, three miles south of Mt. Tabor, was its first home, and the Rev. Adolph Spindle the first regular pastor. Mt. Tabor Church was completed in 1839, Messrs. Geo. Shuey, Sr., Geo. Dull, Peter Strouse, and Jacob Beard having been the building committee. The church now standing was built in 1888. The congregation has given an unusually large number of her sons to the Gospel ministry, whose names are noted at the end of the sketches of the congregations of the county. In 1842 Pastor D. F. Bittle began teaching some young men in a log building, two miles northwest of the church, which school was known as Virginia Institute. It was moved to Salem, Virginia, in 1847 and became Roanoke College in 1853.

The present membership is 192; that of the Sunday School is 180 and the church property is valued at $7000. Adjoining the church is a large cemetery, well laid off and well kept, for which the congregation is indebted largely to W. A. McComb, a prominent member of the congregation and frequent delegate to Synod. The parsonage, built of money given by Mrs. Margaret Cale, was sold in 1921, and relocated at Middlebrook. It is valued at $5000.

Below is given the list of pastors of Mt. Tabor church.

A. Spindle, 1785-1820	Geo. A. Lee, M. D., 1883-1884
M. Meyerhoeffer, 1823-1832	G. W. Spiggle, 1885-1894
A. Babb, 1833-1837	C. N. A. Yonce, 1894-1896
D. F. Bittle, 1837-1844	C. A. Marks, 1896-1899
A. P. Ludden, 1845-1850	E. A. Repass, 1900-1904
J. B. Davis, 1850-1851	J. H. Wyse, 1904-1908
X. J. Richardson, 1852-1860	J. F. Bruch, 1909-1912
J. D. Shirey, 1860-1867	D. W. Files, 1913-1918
A. A. J. Bushong, 1867-1879	P. L. Snapp, 1921-1926
L. L. Smith, 1880-1882	Theo. G. Shuey, 1926-

CHURCHVILLE PARISH

St. Peter's, at Churchville, originally Lutheran and Reformed, possesses the record of an infant baptism in 1790. In 1805, a lot was conveyed to Jacob Eccord and Jeremiah Runkle, trustees, but possibly a church was built thereon earlier than this date. In 1834, at a meeting of the German churches, the Lutheran officers elected were Paul Sieg and David Cook, elders; Lewis Haroff and Emanuel Rudibush, deacons. The church, a brick structure, was of early date as is evident from the interior arrangement. In 1921, a new church was built, also of brick, Gothic in style, and with churchly appointments. The present membership of St. Peter's is 122, with a Sunday school of 109. The church property is valued at $12,000.

The names of the ministers rendering the first pastoral service are not known, but were most likely those who served the other early churches in the county. The following list is the fullest and most accurate that can be made from the data at hand.

D. F. Bittle, 1837-1845	B. S. Brown, 1891-1892
P. Shickel, 1845-1850	H. E. Bailey, 1892-1894
J. B. Davis, 1850-1856	Neighboring Lutheran Pastors
J. M. Shreckhise, 1856-1859	P. Miller, 1896-1898
J. B. Davis, 1860-1865	Geo. E. Shuey, 1899-1903
W. S. McClanahan ⎫	W. W. J. Ritchie, 1905-1914
J. I. Miller ⎬ (Supply)	J. M. Tise, 1914-1920
M. R. Minnich ⎭	W. P. Huddle, 1921-1928
J. M. Hedrick, 1877-1882	A. J. Shumate ⎫
C. Beard, 1882-1889	P. Sieg ⎬ (Supply)
J. Willis (supply)	A. J. Shumate, 1929-

Pleasant View, a daughter of Salem congregation, was organized by the Rev. C. Beard on July 26, 1879. Of the sixteen charter members, twelve were of the name "Houff." Before this, a union Sunday school was conducted in a schoolhouse where the church now stands, four miles north of Staunton, on the Spring Hill pike. The church, a concrete structure, was erected in 1879, and was dedicated in June of that year, the Rev. J. H. Barb preaching the sermon. This building was demolished in 1916,* and a new brick veneer church was erected. In 1928 there was added to the church a Sunday school auditorium, with class rooms and basement.

The membership of the congregation is 154; that of the Sunday school is 225. The church property is valued at $15,000. The parish owns a good parsonage, located at Churchville, valued at $5000.

The Rev. C. Beard (1879-April, 1881), the Rev. A. C. Gearhart (April to Nov., 1881), and the Rev. J. I. Miller (supply-Nov., 1881-June, 1882), served Pleasant View until in 1882 when it came into the Churchville parish, since which time it has been served by the regular pastors, except occasional supplies during vacancies. See list under St. Peter's.

SALEM PARISH

Salem—The earliest record of Salem congregation, at Seawright Springs is of October 7, 1802, when Samuel and Mary King conveyed to Matthias Link, Sr., and Balser Bumgardner, trustees of the Lutheran and Presbyterian congregations, two acres of land on the south side of Naked Creek, for and in consideration of four pounds. The first infant baptism recorded is that of Samuel, son of Josiah and Dora Shultz, on May 4, 1803, while fifty-one like baptisms were administered from 1805 to 1807. There are twenty-seven names on a communion record of 1805. The name of the minister is not given in any of these records. The first church, a log building, was erected about the time of the King deed. (This building was moved to Mt. Sidney, and is now the colored Methodist church). The Presbyterian (Reformed) withdrew forming St. Michael's, near Bridgewater, and later sold their interest to the Lutheran congregation. In 1859, a new frame church was erected, near the old church, which served as the place of worship, until the brick church was built (1929) on the hill by the cemetery. The auditorium seats 500, while the balcony, Sunday school auditorium and class rooms, facing, will seat 500 additional. Its cost was $35,000. This is the largest rural church and congregation in the Synod.

Salem has three offsprings—Melanchthon Chapel, Pleasant View, and St. James. The membership of the congregation is 451; that of the Sunday school is 432, not including the 57 on the cradle-roll and

---

*On May 9, 1916, while men from the congregation were engaged in this work, the unexpected collapse of one of the walls caused the instant death of W. L. Houff, permanent injury to J. T. Berry, and lesser injuries to C. M. McClune, T. C. McClune and Marshall Sheetz.

CHURCHES OF SALEM CONGREGATION

1st Church built in 1802   2nd Church built in 1859
      Present Church built in 1929

Three Daughters of Mother Salem Church

                                                    St. James' Church
Melanchthon Chapel   Mt. Sidney, Va.
Weyers Cave, Va.

                              Pleasant View Church
                               Near Staunton, Va.

in the home department. The congregation owns a parsonage near Mt. Sidney, valued at $5000.

The following ministers are those known to have served Salem congregation:

G. H. Reimensnyder, 1811-1820	A. C. Gearhart, 1881-1883
M. Meyerhoeffer, 1820-1832	G. A. Long, 1884-1885
J. Hoover, 1832-1839	D. P. T. Crickenberger, 1887-1890
J. G. Reimensnyder, 1839-1842	W. B. Oney, 1890-1897
S. Wagner, 1842-1844	J. C. McGaughey, 1897-1899
P. Shickle, 1845-1847	G. A. Riser, 1899-1902
J. J. Suman, 1847-1849	J. M. Shreckhise, (Supplied)
J. F. Campbell, 1849-1852	D. W. Files, 1903-1913
H. M. Bickle } 1852-1854	A. Richard, 1913-1915
X. J. Richardson } 1852-1854	C. H. Day, 1916-1918
W. S. Bowman, 1854-1856	C. W. Cassell, 1918-1922
V. F. Bolton, 1856-1858	W. W. J. Ritchie, (Supplied)
C. Beard, 1858-1881	L. R. Haus, 1923-1924

D. W. Files, 1925-

St. James, at Mt. Sidney, was organized, out of Salem congregation, November 11, 1882, during the ministry of Pastor A. C. Gearhart. The church, a neat frame structure, stands, in the heart of the village, on the west side of the Lee Highway. It was dedicated, November 2, 1884, the Rev. Dr. T. W. Dosh preaching the sermon. The first trustees were, Peter Dingledine, Samuel Cook, and James Bowman. For many years the parsonage of the Salem parish stood on the adjoining lot.

For two decades or more prior to the organization, the pastor of Salem held occasional services in the old brick schoolhouse at Mt. Sidney. St. James has always been served in connection with Salem, though since 1922 it has not been a part of that parish. Student Russell D. Snyder supplied in the summer of 1923.

The congregation has a membership of sixty-nine and a Sunday school of forty-eight. The church property is valued at $4000. The names of the pastors are given under the record of Salem church.

ZION-ST. JAMES PARISH

Zion-St. James—Here we have one congregation with two churches. Zion, four miles north of Waynesboro, appears to have had its beginning in 1824, when the Rev. M. Meyerhoeffer organized a congregation from the members of Trinity. The Lutheran and Reformed people united and built a church in 1825. The earliest record is of a Communion Service in 1829—sixty persons communing. In 1838 there were forty white, and six colored members, slaves. The first church council consisted of Daniel Keiser, Geo. Shirey, Henry Harner, and Geo. Baylor. That the Lutheran church was stronger than the Reformed is shown by the contributions to repairing the church in 1847, when they contributed $122, while the Reformed contributed $32.56½.

The first parsonage was built in 1855. Pastor W. S. Bowman held a national Thanksgiving service here, November 15, 1855. Between the years 1861 and 1863 the church was improved, the wall was placed around the graveyard and the parsonage remodeled. The cost of these improvements was nearly $1800—a large sum for a small congregation during the Civil War. In 1894 a new church building was erected at the cost of $2632.87.

In 1881, the congregation built St. James on Barren Ridge, several miles northwest, for the accommodation of the members living in that community. In 1913, this building was replaced by a substantial, brick structure, costing $6000. Services are held in the two church buildings on alternative Sundays. The congregation numbers 122 members, with a Sunday school of 141. A total value of church property is $18,000, and that of the parsonage is $7000.

For many years in its earlier history, this congregation was connected in a parish with Salem Church.

The Pastors

M. Meyerhoeffer, 1825-1833	C. Beard, 1857-1881
Wm. Scull, 1834-1835	J. H. Barb, 1881-1887
J. G. Reimensnyder, 1836-1838	V. R. Stickley, 1888-1891
S. Wagner, 1839-1847	D. P. T. Crickenberger, 1892-1896
J. J. Suman, 1847-1849	E. C. Cronk, 1897-1900
J. F. Campbell, 1849-1852	S. L. Keller, 1900-1909
H. M. Bickle, 1853-1854	C. A. Marks, 1910-1920
W. S. Bowman, 1854-1856	K. Y. Umberger, 1920-1923
V. F. Bolton, 1856-1857	J. W. Shuey, 1924-1927

S. L. Nease, 1928-

MIDDLEBROOK PARISH

This group of churches was once known as the Newport Parish (1852) but since 1881 it appears on the record by the name it now bears. The churches are: Mt. Herman, at Newport, near the Rockbridge County line; St. Mark's, at McKinley postoffice; and Holy Trinity at Middlebrook. Mt. Tabor appears to have been the mother church, and the Rev. C. Beard the first regular pastor, with Newport, Pastures, Ludwicks, Mt. Zion and Bunyon's as congregations or preaching points.

The following pastors have served the parish:

C. Beard	W. W. J. Ritchie, 1903-1905
J. M. Shreckhise	E. L. Folk, 1906-1911
W. S. McClanahan	B. S. Dasher, 1911-1913
B. C. Wayman, 1870-1872	J. W. Strickler, 1914-1916
J. M. Shreckhise, 1872-1877	G. C. H. Hasskarl, Ph. D., 1917-1918
J. M. Hedrick, 1881-1884	W. B. Oney, 1918-1921
V. R. Stickley, 1884-1888	J. A. L. Miller, 1922-1925
C. B. Miller, (Supply)	P. L. Snapp, 1926-1927
J. W. S. Shepherd, 1891-1893	J. W. Groth, 1927-1928
C. A. Freed, 1893-1903	A. R. Shumate, 1929-

MT. HERMAN LUTHERAN CHURCH
Newport, Va.

Mt. Herman is believed to have been organized in 1853—the date when it first appears on the register, with the Rev. C. Beard as pastor. The first church, a frame building, was erected in 1857, and the second, also a frame building, in 1912.

The congregation numbers forty-nine members; the Sunday school twenty-five. The estimated value of the church property is $3000.

St. Mark's was dedicated on May 19, 1872, during the ministry of Pastor B. C. Wayman. The land was deeded by John R. Buchanan and wife, to D. C. Arehart, Jacob Runkle, J. R. Buchanan, and Geo. Spitler, trustees. It is a brick structure, surrounded by a beautiful lawn and grove, and seats about 250 people. We have no record of the date of organization, but it is known to have been about the time of the church building. The membership of the congregation is seventy-five; that of the Sunday school eighty-four. The church property is valued at $6000.

Holy Trinity was organized September 29, 1883, by the Rev. Geo. A. Lee. The cornerstone was laid June 14, of that year, and the church, a brick structure, was dedicated on August 2, the Rev. Dr. L. A. Fox, preaching the sermon.

The congregation numbers fifty-four members, with forty-four in the Sunday school. The church property is valued at $5000. The parsonage located in Middlebrook, the property of Holy Trinity, is valued at $3000.

AUGUSTA COUNTY PARISH

Bethlehem, at Ladd, three miles south of Waynesboro, was organized by the Rev. Philip Killian, in 1854, from the members of Trinity living in the community. The church, a brick structure, with gallery for the slaves,* was built that same year. The congregation belonged

*Pastor Killian's interest in the slaves is shown by the records of the slave's births in his Bible.

to the Tennessee Synod until it came into the Virginia Synod at the Convention of 1890, the Hon. Absalom Koiner, prominent in political life of the state, being the lay delegate. The congregation formed an independent parish until 1926, when it united with the Melanchthon Chapel, and is now known as Augusta County parish.

The membership is sixty-five; that of the Sunday school is eighty-five. The church property is valued at $5000, and the parsonage, on the adjoining lot, is valued at $2000.

The following pastors have served this congregation:

P. Killian, 1854-1871	J. A. Huffard, 1900-1903
L. A. Fox, 1871-1882	E. A. Repass, Ph. D., 1903-1907
A. L. Crouse, 1882-1888	P. H. E. Derrick, 1908-1909
J. E. Shenk, 1888-1894	J. W. Strickler, 1909-1914
E. A. Shenk, 1894-1898	W. B. Oney, 1914-1918
W. R. Brown, 1899-1900	D. S. Fox, 1918-1924

M. J. Kluttz, 1927-

Melanchthon Chapel is on the east side of the Keezletown pike, one-half mile south of the North River. It was organized 1851 out of Salem congregation. The church, a frame structure, was dedicated, December 28, 1851. It stands in a beautiful grove, adjoining a large cemetery which has an endowment. Melanchthon was served for three years after its organization by J. J. Suman, of Harrisonburg. From this time until 1922, it was connected with the Salem parish. Following an endeavor to divide the Salem parish, Melanchthon was served partly by Salem pastors and supplied by the Rev. W. W. J. Ritchie, R. D. Snyder, and neighboring pastors until 1926, when it became regularly connected with Bethlehem in the Augusta County parish. The church membership is fifty-three; that of the Sunday school forty-three. The church property is valued at $1500. The Rev. M. J. Kluttz is the pastor.

For pastors other than those named, see Salem.

STAUNTON PARISH

Christ's Church—A decade prior to the organization of the congregation in 1853, a lot was purchased on the corner of Main Street and Central Avenue, and held by trustees appointed by Synod. The Rev. J. B. Davis was the first pastor, and is referred to as the "Missionary at Staunton." In his report to Synod, in 1853, he says, "The Lutheran Observer is taken by each family in the congregation." Sunday school and Church services were held in the Old Bell Tavern, until the basement of the church was ready for use. The corner stone was laid, June 24, 1853—the church completed in 1856, and dedicated as "Central Church" on November 1, the Rev. J. A. Seiss, D. D., preaching the sermon. The building was repaired and stuccoed in 1874. This property was sold in 1888, and the present church, located on Lewis street between Main and Frederick, was completed in 1889, having been dedicated May 26, the Rev. Dr. F. W. Conrad, Editor of the Lutheran

CHRIST'S CHURCH
Staunton, Va.

Observer, preaching the sermon. An enlarged Sunday school room was built in 1911. The auditorium was renovated and beautified in 1919. In 1927, fourteen class rooms were built in the Sunday school portion of the building, and within the past year a lot adjoining has been purchased. The congregation owns a good parsonage on Fayette street. The last report to Synod shows the total value of the church and parsonage property as $39,900. The membership of the congregation is 390; and that of the Sunday school 300.

The following pastors have served Christ's Church:

J. B. Davis, 1853-1859	S. A. Repass, D. D., 1884-1885
D. M. Gilbert, 1859-1862	H. B. Wile, 1885-1886
J. I. Miller, 1862-1869	W. H. Settlemeyer, 1886-1887
D. M. Gilbert, 1870-1871	S. F. Riser, 1887-1888
M. R. Minnich, 1872-1876	H. F. Scheele, 1888-1898
J. B. Haskell, 1876-1881	J. B. Fox, Ph. D., 1899-1900
J. P. Croll, 1881-1883	A. D. R. Hancher, 1901-1917
J. Willis, (Supply)	T. O. Keister, D. D., 1918-1927

C. M. Teufel, D. D., 1928-

WAYNESBORO PARISH

Grace was organized on November 24, 1893, by Pastor J. E. Shenk, of Bethlehem congregation at Ladd. The charter members were Lutherans who had moved to town from the nearby country congregations. Until

GRACE LUTHERAN CHURCH
Waynesboro, Va.

1901 it was served by the pastor of Bethlehem. Since that time it has had full time services of the pastor, except from 1907-1915, when the pastor went one Sunday out of each month to Buena Vista.

The church, a substantial brick building, is located in the heart of the town on Wayne Avenue. The corner stone was laid September 24, 1894. It was completed in 1901, being dedicated on Easter Sunday. The basement was used for church purposes a number of years before the church proper was completed.

The membership is 136, that of the Sunday school is 115. The church property is valued at $28,000, the parsonage on the adjoining lot is valued at $6200.

The Pastors

J. E. Shenk, 1893-1894   Y. Von A. Riser, 1903-1906
E. A. Shenk, 1894-1898   J. G. Graichen, 1907-1911
W. R. Brown, 1899-1900   J. F. Bruch, 1911-1915
E. C. Cronk, 1901-1902   E. L. Ritchie, 1916-1922
          Charles F. Steck, D. D., 1922-

Sons of Augusta County Congregations
Who Have Entered The Ministry

Christian Beard _____ Mt. Tabor
Wm. Rusmiselle _____ Mt. Tabor

J. J. Suman _____ Mt. Tabor
J. A. Snyder, D. D. _____ Mt. Tabor
Geo. W. Holland, D. D. _____ Mt. Tabor
R. C. Holland, D. D. _____ Mt. Tabor
Luther Hogshead, D. D. _____ Mt. Tabor
G. E. Shuey _____ Mt. Tabor
R. A. Helms _____ Mt. Tabor
J. W. Shuey _____ Mt. Tabor
Alex. Cupp _____ St. Peter's
J. H. Cupp _____ St. Peter's
Paul Sieg _____ St. Peter's
A. J. Shumate _____ St. Peter's
A. R. Shumate _____ St. Peter's
J. I. Coiner _____ Zion-St. James'
J. D. Shirey, D. D. _____ Zion-St. James'
C. A. Freed, D. D. _____ Zion-St. James'
J. M. Shreckhise _____ Salem
A. W. Craun _____ Salem
J. J. Brubeck _____ Melanchthon Chapel
H. A. Jackson _____ St. James'
B. F. Landis _____ St. James'
W. H. Berry _____ Pleasant View
C. Armand Miller, D. D. _____ Christ's Church
W. E. Eisenberg _____ Christ's Church
S. W. Berry (Seminarian) _____ Holy Trinity

St. Paul's

St. Paul's at Mt. Solon is in Augusta County, but being associated with
the Rockingham parish the sketch appears there.   Likewise, old Emmanuel
Church.

BEDFORD COUNTY

The pastors of the Botetourt parish appear to have held services at
certain points in Bedford prior to the Civil War.   In 1860 a parish was
formed known as the Bedford Mission, including Union church in
Bedford, Back Creek in Botetourt, Back Creek and Corney's schoolhouse
in Roanoke County.   Union, in Bedford was an organized congregation
worshiping in a union church.   The Rev. A. A. J. Bushong was pastor
from 1860 to 1865.   Owing to the scarcity of ministers following the
Civil War there was a lack of pastoral attention, which caused the congregation to disintegrate.   Another congregation in the county worshiped
in Jeter's Chapel, and was served by the Botetourt pastor in 1898.   It
also has ceased to exist as a congregation.

BLAND COUNTY
BLAND PARISH

Sharon—The first settlers of the County were largely German,
coming either up Walker's Creek, from the New River, or across Walker's
Mountain, from Wythe.   This was as early as, or before, the Revolution.

From these grew the Lutheran congregations of the county. Sharon, the oldest, is one-half mile west of Ceres, on the headwaters of the North Fork of the Holston River. It was a charter member of the Synod of Southwestern Virginia. The Sluss family, several of whom were murdered by the Indians, about 1785, are said to have walked to St. Paul's in Wythe County, a distance of fully fifteen miles, to attend church. The victims of the massacre are buried in the old section of Sharon graveyard. October 14, 1817, Jacob Groseclose deeded to Jacob Spangler and Jacob Kimberlin, elders of the German congregation, forty acres of land. This is believed to have been for the first church, which was built of logs about this time. In 1856, a brick church was built, which was replaced by a frame church building in 1883, and, in 1921, it was torn down and a new frame church built on the location. Most likely Paul Henkel and other pioneer Lutheran ministers visited here. George D. Flohr, Nehemiah Bonham, and Jacob Scherer rendered pastoral services during regular periods. Later, J. A. Brown, J. J. Greever, Stephen Rhudy, H. E. Baily, J. A. Mahood and E. Studebaker served as pastors, but neither congregational nor synodical records give definite dates. Since 1888 pastors served as follows:

D. B. Groseclose, 1888-1890	R. R. Sowers, 1900-1903
J. W. Strickler, 1890-1894	P. H. E. Derrick, 1905-1907
J. A. Mahood, 1894-1895	M. D. Huddle, 1911-1913
C. W. Cassell, 1896-1898	J. L. Deal, 1915-1917

The following have supplied during vacation seasons: J. A. B. Scherer, 1888; J. C. Perry, 1903; J. L. Smith, 1909; O. F. Blackwelder, 1918-1919; P. C. Sigmon, 1920; E. K. Seckinger, 1921; and C. S. Klug, 1926. The present membership is fifty.

St. Matthew's at Bland County Courthouse was organized, in 1873, by the Rev. Stephen Rhudy. The church was built under the pastoral care of Rev. J. A. Brown, D. D., of Wytheville. It is a frame building with a belfry, and stands in the heart of the village. It has always been served by the same pastors as Sharon except in 1888-1889, the Rev. E. Studebaker served as pastor of St. Matthew's, while the Rev. D. B. Grosclose served the remaining part of the parish. The congregation having suffered by removals, now numbers only fourteen, with a Sunday school of forty-six. The property is valued at $2500. The parsonage, at Ceres, is valued at $2000.

Former Congregations

Bethel, stood seven miles west of Bland on the north side of the main road. It was a union church built in 1842, deeded by Daniel Perkey and James Lambert to Lutherans, Presbyterians, and Methodists, Alex. Umberger being the Lutheran trustee. Bethel was a charter member of the Southwestern Virginia Synod, being served at that time by Jacob Scherer. It was always connected with Sharon and Bland. The building was burned in the summer of 1889, but not rebuilt. The Lutheran congregation worshiped in the Gravel Hill schoolhouse after the burning of the church. It was last reported in the minutes of the Southwestern Virginia Synod in 1907.

Red Oak, an old frame building, erected more than a half century ago, used by Lutherans and Methodists, stands about one mile south of Sharon Springs. The congregation belonged to the Bland parish and appeared for the last time on the register of churches of the Synod in 1919.

The Rev. D. B. Grosclose held regular services in the Poor Valley, north of Ceres, while he was pastor at Sharon, and other pastors have held occasional services here, but there is no record of a regular congregation.

The Rev. D. B. Grosclose, the Rev. A. L. Groseclose and Dr. Nellie Cassell, Medical Missionary to India, were confirmed in Sharon congregation.

BOTETOURT COUNTY

Botetourt, formed from Augusta in 1770, had been the home of German settlers for two decades. They were of the Lutheran and Reformed faiths. The first Lutheran minister to visit them is believed to have been Paul Henkel. Their first house of worship was Zion, near Glen Wilton, also called Locust Bottom, built upon land deeded April 11, 1786, by Jacob and Sarah Mayers to the "Dutch Calvanist and Lutherans." It is a brick building, with the old time gallery and pulpit. For more than half century it has not been used by either Calvanist or Lutheran, but the cemetery is well kept. The North Carolina Synod met here in May 1826, and the Virginia Synod, in October 1831.

The Rev. John George Butler, member of the Ministerium of Pennsylvania, who moved to Howrytown about 1796, appears to have been the first resident Lutheran minister. He served churches in the territory of Roanoke, Floyd, and Montgomery Counties, for a period of nine years. Following his removal to Cumberland, Md., in 1805, there was no resident pastor until 1818, however, R. J. Miller and Jacob Scherer, ministers of the North Carolina Synod included Botetourt in their missionary tours to Virginia during this period.

The churches of the County constitute the Botetourt parish. It has been, and is, a large work, from both the number of churches included and the territory covered. Frequently the division of the parish has been considered and at one time was actually carried into effect. In 1872 the Synod formed two parishes, calling one the New Amsterdam, and the other, the James River parish. After two years, however, they were reunited, since neither appeared to be able to support a pastor.

BOTETOURT PARISH

Brick Union was organized by Pastor Butler in 1796, at his own residence. Eighteen articles, based on the Catechism, some of them very strict, are given as the basis of organization. The church, built of brick made on the ground, was erected after 1830, but before 1837. The land was deeded by Christian and Eve Housman, to Henry Star,

George W. Rader, and Christian Housman trustees, for a "Union Meeting House." Brick Union now numbers twenty-eight members, and owns property valued at $1200.

St. Mark's, known as "Copp's," "Old Hickory," and "Jackson's" was organized in 1815, by Missionaries, R. J. Miller and Jacob Scherer. The first church was built during the ministry of Pastor Martin Walther. The present church was begun during the ministry of Pastor C. A. Marks, and completed under his successor, in 1885, at which time it was named "St. Mark's." The land upon which it stands was deeded on March 9, 1885, by Samuel and Lucy Obenshain, to G. W. Styne, C. L. Styne, A. T. Booze, John Dill, and Jacob Bierly, trustees. The membership of the congregation is sixty-four, that of the Sunday school ninety-three. The property is valued at $2000.

Wheatland was organized by Pastor Peter Shickel in 1864. The first worship was held on Timber Ridge. Luther Chapel was built, in 1877, but after the erection of Wheatland church in 1898, it was sold to the County School Board. The congregation numbers 136 and the Sunday school 87. The property is valued at $2000.

Trinity was organized in 1880 under the ministry of Pastor C. A. Marks. Those forming the organization had been worshiping in Shaver's schoolhouse. The church, built in 1878, was burned in 1890, and rebuilt in 1894, on land deeded by Joseph and Lydia Layman, to P. M. Firebaugh, Austin P. Dunbar, and John L. Spiggle, trustees. The congregation numbers thirty-six members, and the property is valued at $2000.

St. Jacob's, six miles northeast of Fincastle, was organized, April 13, 1898, under the ministry of Pastor W. Y. Cline. The church, a frame structure, was built in 1902, on land deeded by Jacob M. and Amanda E. Craft to Jacob M. Craft, Jacob Bierly, George E. Haymaker, M. C. Cahoon and David G. Craft, trustees. The congregation numbers thirty-two members, and the property is valued at $2000.

The parsonage, a seven room frame building worth $4000, is located on the Fincastle and Buchanan turnpike, in the neighborhood of Wheatland. The land was deeded, April 7, 1906, by Jacob L. Cronise and wife, to J. L. Cummings, W. R. Cronise, G. E. Rader and C. M. Firebaugh, trustees, "as a parsonage for the pastor in charge of the Botetourt pastorate."

The following pastors have served the churches of the Botetourt Parish:

Paul Henkel	Samuel Sayford, 1835-1841
R. J. Miller	Gideon Scherer, 1842-1846
Jacob Scherer	Samuel Sayford, 1846-1848
J. G. Butler, 1796-1805	H. G. Bowers, 1848-1852
Daniel Scherer, 1818-1821	V. F. Bolton, 1852-1855
Martin Walther, 1821-1828	Peter Shickel, 1856-1868
D. J. Hauer, 1828-1832	E. J. Jones, 1869-1871
Thomas Miller, 1833-1835	J. B. Greiner, 1871-1873

John F. Keyser, 1873-1874   W. Y. Cline, 1888-1904
F. V. N. Painter, 1876-1878   E. W. Leslie, 1905-1911
C. A. Marks, 1880-1884   J. D. Utt, 1912-1923
E. L. Folk, 1884-1885   H. E. H. Sloop, 1923-1924
                 E. B. Smith, 1925-

The following ministers: E. A. Shenk, C. M. Fox, S. D. Steffey, J. M. Graybill, H. F. Richard, and E. W. Leslie assisted Pastor W. Y. Cline at different times during his ministry in the county. Those connected with Roanoke College have often been called upon to supply the parish. Following the death of Pastor Cline (1904) the Rev. B. W. Cronk, Superintendent of the Orphan Home, and student J. A. C. Hurt of Roanoke College, did supply work in the parish.

The Botetourt Parish has, throughout its entire history, extended beyond the limits of the county, and at times embraced more congregations than those named above. Churches have been established which are not, at present, carried on our register. Mt. Moriah is one of these. It grew out of a preaching station at Zion's Hill, and was organized on April 7, 1894, with twelve members. The church was built in 1893 on land deeded August 16, 1891, by D. L. T. Sizer and wife, and Samuel A. Beamer, to A. H. Hontz, N. S. Cahoon, Walter Luger, Jacob Bierly and Jacob Craft, trustees. Being some distance from the other churches of the parish, the congregation did not receive the services necessary for its growth and dvelopment, and has disappeared from the register of the churches of Synod since 1920.

Glade Creek congregation, near Blue Ridge Springs, organized by the Rev. D. J. Hauer on September 1, 1828, has, through the greater part of its history, been connected with the Botetourt parish, but since 1898 has been connected with Roanoke County churches. Five family names, Kessler, Spickard, Murry, Flook and Henderlight appear in the record of the organization, Benjamin Kessler being an elder, and Henry Spickard a deacon. The church, which belongs to the Missionary Baptist and Lutherans, was built in 1856. The pastors named below are those who have served since it was separated from the Botetourt parish. Those previous to this have been listed under the Botetourt parish.

T. C. Parker, 1899-1902   J. W. McCauley, 1917-1918
E. W. Leslie, (supply) 1903-1904   J. B. Haigler, 1918-1919
J. M. Tise, 1910-1914   H. P. Wyrick, (supply) 1920
L. A. Fox, D. D., (supply)   J. A. Boord, 1921-1923
                 J. D. Utt, 1923-

. Lutheran ministers who were sons of Botetourt County congregation:

E. W. Leslie _____ Brick Union
D. P. T. Crickenberger _____ Brick Union
L. B. Williamson, Seminarian _____ Wheatland
R. L. Booze, Seminarian _____ Wheatland

HOLY TRINITY LUTHERAN CHURCH
Lynchburg, Va.

CAMPBELL COUNTY
Lynchburg

Holy Trinity—Lutheran people have resided in Lynchburg since its early history, as it is evidenced by the founders of some of the oldest business firms of the city, who were Lutherans. The first effort of the Synod of Southwestern Virginia to establish a church here, 1856-1862, was brought to naught by the Civil War. Another in 1870, was abandoned for financial reasons. In 1884, the Synod, sent a commission here to study the question of beginning a mission, but the report was adverse. Again in 1901 the Executive Committee authorized the Rev. C. K. Bell of Salem to visit the Lutheran families known to be living in the city. His work was encouraging, and upon the advice of the Executive Committee he organized Holy Trinity, April 16, 1903, with twenty-five members. Student J. D. Mauney supplied for the summer and the Rev. Dr. L. A. Fox the following winter. Prior to the building of the church on Victoria Avenue, which was dedicated June 16, 1907, services were held in the Y. M. C. A. Hall and in the chapel of St. Paul's Episcopal Church. The church location being found unsatisfactory, the property was sold in 1920. A discouraging vacancy of two years in the pastoral office followed, during which the Sunday school and occasional services were held in the Y. M. C. A. Hall. In March, 1922, they purchased the Rivermont Avenue Methodist Church, which event proved the beginning of a new era for the congregation. From the beginning of the work, the Women's Missionary Society of the Synod rendered a valuable financial and moral support. Through the cooperation of the Board of Home Missions and Church Extension of the United Lutheran Church the purchase of the present splendid church property was made possible. It is valued at $35,000. The parsonage, on the adjoining lot, is valued at $5000. The congregation has a membership of 121, with a Sunday school of 103. The pastors of Holy Trinity have been:

J. C. Peery, 1904-1911   W. H. Riser, 1920-1921
E. C. Cooper, 1912-1914   R. H. Anderson, 1922-1928
C. L. Schreiber, Ph. D., 1915-1918 R. L. Markley, 1928-

GLADESBORO LUTHERAN CHURCH
Gladesboro, Va.

CARROLL AND FLOYD COUNTIES

The churches of the two counties are grouped together in a parish known as the Floyd parish.

Gladesboro, Carroll County, was organized, December 25, 1855, by the Rev. J. C. Repass, pastor in Floyd. There were twelve charter members, seven of the twelve being of the name "Cassell." Barr, Kinzer, Denton, and Weddle, were the other family names. All, or almost all, came from St. John's in Wythe County. They worshiped in a small log schoolhouse until the first church was built in 1856. This was replaced by a larger and better building, frame, in 1890, which was dedicated June 28, 1891.

It is said a Sunday school was established in 1847, with James Hutsell as superintendent, which school has continued without interruption except for a short time during the Civil War—a period of eighty-one years. Capt. James Cassell, W. L. Utt, L. G. Bailey, and W. R. Kinzer have been outstanding laymen in the congregational and Sunday school work.

The membership of the church is 126; that of the Sunday school is 92. The building, valued at $2000, was totally destroyed by a tornado on May 2, 1929. It is now being rebuilt.

Since at times there have been two parishes, at other times there has been but one parish in the two counties, and the Synodical records do not always specify the extent of the pastor's field, it is difficult to give an absolutely correct list of the pastors and the dates of their service. It is likely a number of the pastors of Zion, in Floyd, not named in the list given below have rendered pastoral services at Gladesboro.

J. C. Repass, 1854-1860	P. J. Wade
C. A. Marks	C. J. Sox, 1904-1905
C. A. Rose	J. D. Utt, 1908-1912
J. W. Strickler	A. F. Tobler, 1913-1918
J. M. Hedrick	S. L. Nease, 1924-1925
G. T. Gray, 1889-1898	J. A. L. Miller, 1927-

It appears that E. H. McDonald, I. P. Hawkins, R. R. Sowers, K. Y. Umberger, Isaac Cannaday, L. B. Spracher, W. A. Wade, and R. A. Goodman have supplied Gladesboro at various times.

FLOYD COUNTY

Zion—The earliest records of this, "mother of congregations and ministers," is of infant baptisms in 1793. The date of the organization is given as May 10, 1813, by ministers from North Carolina.* There were twenty-four charter members, Johannes Mayer having been elected elder, and George R. Pflieger deacon. The German language was used until about 1830.

The first house of worship was a small log schoolhouse, built prior to 1813, on ground that is now within the cemetery. This building was replaced by a larger one, built of logs in 1838, at the same location, dedicated on July 29. The brick church was built in 1861, and the present church in 1898.

Zion church was the place of organization of the Southwestern Virginia Synod in May 1842, and has figured largely in the History of the Synod.

The membership of the congregation is sixty-nine; that of the Sunday school is fifty-eight. The church property is valued at $3000, and the parsonage at $4000.

Burke's Fork, in the southwestern part of the county, was organized out of Zion, May 1, 1853, in an old schoolhouse. The names of the families were Wade, Willis, and Gurtherie. From two of these families have come ministers of the Gospel. It was first known as Olive, or Olive Hill. The congregation has always been small, but has maintained a Sunday school during the greater part of its history. The present church is the second one to be used by the congregation. It has been served by the pastors of the Floyd parish.

Willis, in the western part of the county, was organized out of Zion in 1879. The church, a frame building, erected about this time, is yet in use. The present membership is 134; that of the Sunday school, 97.

---

*In certain sketches of Zion these names have been as B. G. Miller and J. S. Jurer, but such names do not appear on the N. C. Synod Roll of Ministers. R. J. Miller and J. Scherer, of the N. C. Synod were missionaries to Va. in 1813.

The church property is valued at $4000, the parsonage at $3000. It has been in the Floyd parish and served by her pastors.

The Pastors of Zion, Burke's Fork and Willis have been:

Martin Walther, 1826-1828	A. J. Bowers, 1887-1888
D. J. Hauer, 1828-1832	W. B. Oney, 1888-1890
Thomas Miller, 1833-1834	C. A. Brown, 1890-1892
J. T. Tabler, 1835-1841	Peter Miller, 1894-1895
Samuel Sayford, 1841-1845	P. J. Wade, 1895-1898
D. M. K. Rader, 1852-1854	R. L. Bame, 1899-1900
J. C. Repass, 1855-1860	T. C. Parker, 1901-1903
Solomon Schaffer (supply)	J. M. Tise, 1904-1906
W. C. Wire, 1862-1867	R. A. Goodman ⎱ (supply)
J. D. Shirey, 1867-1870	W. C. Buck ⎰
J. P. Obenshain, 1871-1874	J. D. Utt, 1908-1912
S. P. Hughs (supply)	A. F. Tobler, 1913-1918
C. A. Marks, 1876-1879	H. P. Wyrick (supply)
N. A. Whitman, 1880-1881	J. M. Tise, 1920-1921
C. A. Rose, 1882-1884	S. L. Nease, 1924-1925
C. A. Marks, 1884-1887	J. A. L. Miller, 1927-

LUTHERAN MINISTERS FROM CARROLL AND FLOYD CONGREGATIONS:

J. W. Smith, D. D.	Zion
J. W. Butler	Zion
B. W. Cronk	Zion
E. C. Cronk, D. D.	Zion
R. R. Sowers	Zion
Isaac Cannaday, D. D.	Zion
James Willis	Burkes Fork
P. J. Wade	Burkes Fork
W. A. Wade, D. D.	Willis
H. E. Poff	Willis
J. D. Utt	Gladesboro
A. F. Tobler	Gladesboro

Rear Admiral Robley D. Evans (Fighting Bob) of the United States Navy, Captain of the "Iowa" in the battle of Santiago, when a young man, attended Sunday school at Zion.

CULPEPER AND PRINCE WILLIAM COUNTIES
MANASSAS PARISH

Bethel, at Manassas; Mt. Zion at Nokesville, in Prince William County; St. Luke's at Elkwood; and Trinity, three miles north of Culpeper, in Culpeper County, form the Manassas parish. The work was begun, and was fostered by the Virginia Conference of the Tennessee Synod. January 1, 1920, it was taken under the care of the Board of Missions of the United Lutheran Church. Lutheran families from the Shenandoah Valley, especially from Page County, having located along

CHURCHES OF MANASSAS PARISH

Trinity Lutheran Church
Elkwood, Va.

Mt. Zion Lutheran Church
Nokesville, Va.

Bethel Lutheran Church and Parsonage
Manassas, Va.
St. Luke's Lutheran Church
Catalpa, Va.

the line of the Southern railroad between Culpeper and Manassas, attracted the Conference to this field.

Bethel—As early as 1885, monthly services were held at Manassas by the Rev. Henry Wetzel. On July 28, 1889, the congregation was organized by the Rev. J. P. Stirewalt, with nineteen members. The Rev. P. C. Wike of Shenandoah County was given pastoral oversight until a regular pastor was called. Services were held in the town hall, other halls, and in the Methodist and Presbyterian churches. A lot for the church building was purchased in December 1895, and a church building program was launched. The church used for the first time in July, 1897, was remodeled and greatly improved in 1919. It is a frame building with belfry, and has art glass windows. The parsonage lot was purchased in 1900, and the parsonage erected in 1904. A one and one-half acre lot, for the cemetery was given by Suffary Whitmer in 1901. The first church council consisted of Henry J. Shaffer, Suffary Whitmer, elders; and J. C. Whitmer and William R. May, deacons. The Sunday school superintendents have been D. F. Bowman, J. L. Kibler, Mrs. J. C. Gregory, Edward Weakhouse, W. J. Young, and J. H. Rexrode. The congregation has sixty-nine members, with a Sunday school of fifty scholars. The church is valued at $5000, and the parsonage at $4000. Pastors having served Bethel congregation and the other congregations of the Manassas parish are as follows:

P. C. Wike, 1889-1890	Moses Grossman, 1899-1904
J. S. Koiner, 1890-1892	J. K. Efird, 1905-1912
A. R. Beck, 1892-1893	O. W. Aderholt, 1913-1915
J. C. Wessinger, 1893 (3 months)	E. Z. Pence, 1916-1924
J. K. Efird, 1895-1899	Luther F. Miller, 1925-

Mt. Zion—Services were held in the schoolhouse at Nokesville, and at times in the union church at Bristow, from the beginning of the work of the parish. In February, 1911, Pastor J. K. Efird organized the congregation with twenty-one members. A lot was purchased in December, 1912. The church, a frame building, with recess for pulpit, and a belfry, was dedicated July 13, 1913, by the Rev. W. L. Darr. The Sunday school was organized with seventy-three scholars this same year. Messrs. F. P. Shaffer, R. A. Wilkins, P. C. Olinger, C. C. Bittle, and Edgar Shaffer have served as superintendents of the Sunday school. The congregation now numbers twenty-eight and the Sunday school has twenty-seven. The church property is valued at $2000.

St. Luke's is three miles north of Culpeper at Catalpa, (Chestnut Fork). Services were held here a number of years prior to building a church, in a schoolhouse, a vacant storeroom, and at times, in the homes of the members. Pastor J. K. Efird formed an organization with twenty-one members in 1906, but because of failure to agree on location and building, little progress was made until the work was re-organized by Pastor O. W. Aderholdt, June, 1913. The church, a frame building, was erected on land purchased from Samuel Rixey, and was dedicated October 24, 1915.

GRACE LUTHERAN CHURCH
Winchester, Va.

First Church built in 1764   Church from 1841 to 1874
Church from 1874 until Sunday school building was added in 1924

The remaining wall of first church building   Present Church and
which was destroyed by fire, Sept. 27, 1858.   Sunday school building
This wall is preserved as a monument and
may be seen at any time in the old church cemetery adjacent Mt. Hebron Cemetery.

The Sunday school superintendents have been Messrs. M. R. Wyant, J. D. Miller, and J. A. Kibler. The congregation numbers twenty-nine members and the Sunday school forty-two. The church property is valued at $1500.

Trinity was organized by Pastor J. K. Efird, October 16, 1891. The church was built in 1894. It is a frame building, with belfry. The first thought was to build at Brandy station on a lot donated by Daniel Wine, but later it was agreed to build at Elkwood on a lot given by H. J. Kite, the lot at Brandy having been deeded back to the donor. The congregation prospered for a number of years. Since the building of St. Luke's and transferring of a number of members, and other serious losses it has been reduced to eight members at present. No Sunday school has been held for several years. The services continue to be held regularly except during the most severe weather. The value of the church property is $1000.

The Rev. J. H. Young is a son of Bethel congregation.

FRANKLIN COUNTY

At present there are no organizations in the county. We find, however, in the Minutes of the Southwestern Virginia Synod, 1879, page 21, "that a congregation recently organized in Franklin County, known as Ninevah, was received into the Synod." It was served at times from Floyd and at other times from Botetourt, or Roanoke County. The Minutes has record of it for about twenty years.

FREDERICK COUNTY

WINCHESTER

Grace—Lutheran people were among the first settlers at Winchester, and very early took steps to provide a place of worship. The deed made by Lord Fairfax to the trustees of the Lutheran church bears the date of May 15, 1753. The congregation was admitted into the Pennsylvania Synod in 1762, and on May 12, 1764, the corner stone of the church was laid. It was no small or temporary structure they planned, but one of large proportions with massive walls of native limestone. They built "with a mind to work," the women carrying water for the mortar; the men working with their guns within reach, because the Indians had torn away some of the work at night and threatened to attack them by day, if they continued. The building so far complete as to serve as a barracks during the Revolutionary War, was used for worship in 1789, and dedicated in 1793. The first pastor was John Casper Kirchner, who died in 1773. Schoolmaster, Anthony Ludi, made himself responsible for the conduct of worship until the coming of Christian Streit in 1785. During this period, J. C. Hartwick, Henry Moller, and C. F. Wilbahn, made occasional visits. In this church the "Special Virginia Conference" was organized in 1793 and the "Synod of Maryland and Virginia, and so forth," was organized here on October 11, 1820. The church was out of town, because, at the time of building there were certain restrictions concerning the non-established churches. In 1842 the present building was erected on Water street between Loudoun and Braddock. It was built of brick, with large pillars and a portico in front. In 1850 a cupola was added, and twenty-five years later the building was enlarged by adding to its length, the walls were raised and the high tower built. The chimes placed in the tower in 1917 to the memory of David Brevitt Glaize by his parents, and the erecting of the Sunday school building in 1924, largely the gift of Mr. G. Casper Fries, are outstanding improvements of recent years.

On the night of September 24, 1854, fire destroyed the old church built almost a century previous. The massive east wall remains standing and is a landmark of much historic interest.

Grace Lutheran church has been, from the beginning, a leader in the religious life of the community and in the work of the church at large. It was the first Lutheran congregation in the South to assume the support of a foreign missionary, having sent the Rev. R. B. Peery to Japan in 1892. She has had many prominent laymen, the late J. E. Cooper deserving special mention. The membership of the congregation is 572, and that of the Sunday school is 521. The church property is valued at $175,000 and the parsonage at $18,000.

Besides those mentioned in the body of the sketch, the pastors have been as follows:

Christian Streit, 1785-1812	Abraham Essick, 1856-1857
Abram Reck, 1813-1827	W. M. Baum, 1858-1861
L. Eichelberger, 1828-1833	T. W. Dosh, 1862-1871
N. W. Goertner, 1834-1835	D. M. Gilbert, D. D., 1873-1887
Theophilus Stork, 1837-1841	L. G. M. Miller, D. D., 1888-1895
J. R. Keiser, 1841-1843	W. L. Seabrook, 1895-1901
J. Few Smith, 1843-1848	G. S. Bowers, D. D., 1902-1918
C. Porterfield Krauth, 1848-1855	A. A. Kelly, 1919-1924

Charles A. Freed, D. D., 1925-1929

Stephens City Parish

Trinity, at Stephens City, first known as Newtown-Stephensburg, is another of the very old congregations. The Joist Hite settlement (largely German), two miles north in 1732, the village having been established in 1750, and trustees having held a lot for the German-Lutheran congregation in 1770,* it is not a mere guess that services were held here before Christian Streit came in 1785. Most likely the first Lutheran ministers to visit Winchester, also visited these people. A log building, on a lot adjoining the old cemetery, on the first street east of the pike, was their first place of worship. In 1812 a brick church was built on the same street, several hundred yards to the north, opposite the present location, which was enlarged in 1851. It was used as a Federal hospital after the battle of Cedar Creek, and greatly damaged. In 1906 this building was demolished, all usable material being worked into the new building

*Cartmell's History of Frederick County, p. 191.

TRINITY LUTHERAN CHURCH
Stephens City, Va.

on the opposite side of the street. The new church, brick, Gothic in style, with Sunday school room, and churchly appointments, was dedicated, August 25, 1907. The bell, cast in Philadelphia, May 16, 1818, is yet in use.

Professor S. C. Wells, Ph. D., teacher in Roanoke College and prominent layman in the church, was born and reared in this community, and in his early life was connected with the congregation.

The parsonage was purchased in 1890. The membership of the congregation is 185; that of the Sunday school is 178. The church property is valued at $25,000, and the parsonage at $6000.

Pastors of Trinity

Christian Streit, 1785-1811   R. A. Fink, 1850-1852
Abraham Reck, 1815   W. F. Greaver, 1852-1855
L. Eichelberger, 1820   J. F. Fahs, 1855-1857
John Tabler, 1830   W. Rusmiselle, 1857-1867
John B. Davis, 1834-1850   Geo. A. Long, 1867-1871

J. F. Campbell, 1872-1876
A. Buhrman, 1876-1876
James Willis, 1877-1882
L. L. Smith, 1882-1894
P. L. Miller, 1894-1896

J. W. Strickler, 1896-1905
C. W. Cassell, 1905-1915
R. H. Cline, 1915-1922
E. O. Graham, 1922-1928
Snyder Alleman, 1928-

ST. PAUL'S LUTHERAN CHURCH
Fawcett's Gap, Va.

St. Paul's, at Fawcett's Gap, nine miles west of Winchester, was organized in 1856, with eight charter members, by the Rev. J. F. Fahs of Newtown (Stephens City). The church, a frame building, was built and dedicated that year, the Rev. Levi Keller preaching the sermon. The first trustees were Ben. Frye, Elijah Rudolph, and Martin Snapp. It has been associated in parishes with Strasburg, Lebanon, and Stephens City. The old church was used by Federal soldiers, and damaged. It was replaced by the present church, also a frame building, in 1903, and was dedicated, September 6, of that year.

The present membership is 77; that of the Sunday school 132. The property is valued at $3000.

The Pastors of St. Paul's

J. F. Fahs
W. Rusmiselle, 1857-1867
Geo. A. Long (supply) 1868

W. Rusmiselle, 1869-1884
L. M. Sibold, 1884-1886
Asa Richard, 1887-1899

J. E. Bushell, D. D., 1899-1901

From this date, see list under Trinity church.

GRAVEL SPRINGS PARISH

This parish consists of five churches—Bethel, at Albin, four miles north of Winchester; Freemont, at Rosenberger; St. John's, thirteen miles southwest of Winchester; Gravel Springs, ten miles southwest of St. John's; and St. James', ten miles further southwest, near the head of

Cedar Creek. Because of the distance between the two extreme churches (about forty miles), it has been called a "Shoe String" parish. St. James' is in Shenandoah County, but is considered here, because it has so long been grouped in a parish with Frederick County churches. Of the five churches, the oldest is

St. John's—The earliest record of St. John's Church is of 1793, however, Christian Streit held services in the community in 1788. Among the early records of baptisms and confirmations, the name of the minister is not given. It was long called "The Furnace Church" or "The Taylor Furnace Church," because of an iron furnace nearby. There seems to have been two log churches on the same location in the old graveyard, the dates not being known. The second was weather boarded, with the high ceiling, the gallery on both ends and one side, and the high pulpit of those early days. The pews were high, straight, and uncomfortable. In the center was a stove, bearing on one side the date of 1763. On the south end, exterior, was a shed in which to store saddles on rainy days. The present church was built in 1873. The first Sunday school was of 1858, with Henry P. Richard, superintendent.

The present membership is 92; that of the Sunday school is 102. The church property is valued at $2000.

The following ministers have served St. John's:

Christian Streit	Jacob Summers, 1882-1884
Abraham Reck	W. J. Smith, 1885-1911
Lewis Eichelberger	Frank Gilbert, 1912-1914
J. B. Davis	H. E. H. Sloop, 1916-1923
Jacob Summers, 1851-1871	J. B. Cassell (supply) 1924
E. H. Jones, 1871-1880	A. F. Tobler, 1925-1927
Webster Eichelberger	J. E. Lowe, 1928

St. James' is believed to have been organized by the Rev. W. G. Keil in 1822. Services were first held in a log house on the same location as the log church built 1840, in what is now a part of the cemetery. In 1884 a frame building was erected on the opposite side of the creek, which building was remodeled in 1913. The congregation has suffered greatly by removals in recent years. The present membership is seventy-three; that of the Sunday school eighty-one. The church property is valued at $1800. The congregation has been connected with this parish almost throughout its history. The pastors have been:

W. G. Keil, 1827-	W. Shepperson
J. T. Tabler, 1830-1834	J. J. Richard, 1840-1850

After this date, see St. John's.

Gravel Springs, known first as "Dry Run," was organized in a log schoolhouse in 1849, by the Rev. J. J. Richard. Since the building of this church shortly after its organization, the congregation has been called "Gravel Springs," because of the character of two nearby springs, and since 1860 the name has been applied to the parish. A Sunday school was conducted before the organization of the congregation, by a Mr.

Tracey and later by Isaac Orndorff. The congregation has suffered greatly by removals. There are thirty-seven members, with forty-two in the Sunday school. The church property is valued at $1000. The congregation seems always to have been associated with St. James' and served by the same pastors.

Bethel appears to have been in existence as a congregation when the Virginia Synod was organized. In 1848, a church, was built of hewed logs, and about forty years later it was replaced with a frame building, which was dedicated, June 5, 1887. In 1921 the congregation moved its place of worship to Albin two miles and a half east, where they erected a neat frame church. The congregation appears to have been served from Winchester, or a nearby church, or a resident pastor in that section of the county, until the coming of Jacob Summers to Gravel Springs parish. Before this it was served by Pastors L. Eichelberger, J. Few Smith, E. G. Procter, and H. G. Bowers. For other pastors, see St. John's.

The congregation numbers 58 and the Sunday school 164. The church property is valued at $4000.

Fremont—Fremont church was built 1853 on land deeded by Wm. F. Marker and wife to P. Raymey, P. H. Richards, J. H. Larrick, A. Larrick, D. W. Larrick, J. Raymey, J. Clowser, trustees. It was named for the great explorer of the West. The occasion was the need of a building for school and church purposes in the communities. It is a small frame building, and since 1876 has been used only for church purposes, while built for a union church, it has for many years been used only by Lutherans. Regular services were held by the Gravel Springs pastors from the time of the building. In 1875 an organization was formed with nineteen members, coming from St. John's. The present membership is thirty-nine; that of the Sunday school is twenty-four. The church property is valued at $1000.

The congregation has always been in the Gravel Springs parish.

The parsonage, located for many years near St. John's, is now at Hayfield. It is valued at $2000.

St. Joseph, or Old Pine Church, a "free church," though built largely by Lutherans and said to have been leased to them by one Mr. Gantz, stood four miles southeast of Stephens City as early as 1800. Few now living remember the old building. It was built of large pine logs, smoothly hewn, and chinked with stone. The interior was ceiled and whitewashed. It had the high goblet pulpit, pews with a narrow board for a back, and was heated with a ten-plate stove. Neither deed to the property nor records of ministerial acts can be found, and the members, if there was ever an organization, appear to have transferred to Trinity in Stephens City.

Sons of Frederick County Congregations
Who Have Entered The Ministry

Isaac Baker _____ Grace
Robert Baker _____ Grace

J. E. Bushnell, D. D. _____ Grace
L. G. M. Miller, D. D. _____ Grace
G. E. Krauth _____ Grace
J. G. Graichen _____ Grace
Luther Yeakley _____ Grace
T. B. Yeakley, D. D. _____ Grace
L. S. G. Miller, D. D. _____ Grace
N. E. Cooper _____ Grace
A. P. Ludden* _____ Trinity
John Guard _____ Trinity
Geo. A. Long _____ Trinity
C. A. Marks _____ Trinity
J. B. Cassell _____ Trinity
James Cadwallader (Seminarian) _____ Trinity
J. W. Richard, D. D., LL. D. _____ St. John's
E. R. Cooper _____ St. John's
P. H. Williams _____ St. John's
Frisby Smith _____ St. John's
E. B. Smith _____ St. John's
Asa Richard _____ Fremont
M. G. Richard _____ Fremont
J. H. Richard _____ Fremont
R. R. Richard _____ Fremont

GILES AND CRAIG COUNTIES

The churches of the two counties constitute the Giles and Craig parish. They are: Bethel, Eggleston, Mt. Carmel, Olivet, Pembroke, and St. Paul's. Throughout their history the churches of the two counties have been closely associated with each other. The pastors from Montgomery County have given much pastoral services to Giles and Craig. The Rev. Solomon Shaeffer, it appears, organized a number of these congregations, and under his supervision a number of the churches were built. Certain of the congregations and churches appear to be as old or older than the Southwestern Virginia Synod. Bethel is said to have been organized in 1830, and in 1845 Stony Creek was received into the Synod. In 1848, we find the Rev. Simeon Scherer serving Stony Creek and Clover Hollow; and Sinking Creek is accredited with a contribution to Synod. Following his withdrawal, the Rev. H. G. Bowers of Botetourt was requested by the Synod to serve Hedings Chapel, and in 1851 the Missionary Society of the Synod assisted in the support of the pastor in Giles. In 1853 the Rev. Samuel Cook, living at Newport was serving the Giles church, and Festus Hickerson was serving at Craig's Creek in 1856 and 1857.

Frequent efforts have been made to maintain two parishes, but in each case it has proved impracticable. From about 1880-1887, we find them

---

*Alonzo P. Ludden came to Virginia from the North when a young man, and taught school for four years at Stephens City. Hence he came out of Trinity into the ministry. He married Miss Caroline Grove of Stephens City.

under the names of Giles pastorate, and Craig mission. The latter was
served by Rev. G. W. Spiggle in 1882-1883 and by Rev. B. W. Cronk in
1884-1887. Again in 1915 two parishes were formed, Pembroke and
Newport (Giles-Craig). They were re-united in 1924. Several of
these churches have been strong and active. As many as six meetings of
the Synod have been held within the parish. Certain congregations, once
upon the register of Synod, have disappeared, being so weakened by
removal of members from the community that those remaining united
with the nearest Lutheran church, and in some cases sold their church
property. This period of transition appears to be yet in progress. To
secure and maintain pastors has been a difficult matter.

Bethel, in Craig County, was organized in 1830. The present
church, the second to stand on this location, was built in 1869.

Stony Creek was organized in 1843 by Pastor Solomon Schaeffer.

Pembroke, also organized by Pastor Schaeffer, first worshiped in a log
schoolhouse. The church built in 1855 was remodeled in 1900.

Eggleston, formerly known as Green Valley, was organized in 1883,
by Pastor G. W. Spiggle. The first officers were: M. L. Sibold, elder;
J. F. Walker, deacon. This congregation, while small, has actively and
loyally co-operated in all church work.

St. Paul's at Newport, is the continuation of a Lutheran congregation
known as Solomon's Temple, which was located four miles north
of the village, and was organized in 1860, by Pastor J. C. Repass.
Later an organization was formed in Newport and worshiped in the
Methodist church. In 1880 they purchased a church building from the
Baptists, which is yet in use. The organization of Solomon's Temple was
disbanded and the church sold.

The pastors given below are those who have served since 1860; the
others having been given above.

J. C. Repass, 1860-1869	B. W. Cronk, 1896-1897
J. B. Greiner, 1870-1872	J. W. Butler, 1898-1902
V. R. Stickley, 1873-1876	L. B. Spracher, 1904-1908
Wm. Stoudenmire (supply)	C. M. Fox, 1909-1913
N. Aldrich, 1880-1882	W. P. Gerberding (sup.) Newport, 1916
G. W. Spiggle, 1882-1884	J. A. Brosius (sup.) Newport, 1919-1920
D. P. T. Crickenberger,	T. C. Parker, Pembroke, 1915-1920
1885-1887	G. Cooper (sup.) Newport, 1923-1924
M. O. J. Krepps, 1888-1893	H. A. Jackson, 1925-1927
J. W. Butler, 1893-1894	L. B. Williamson, (sup.) summer of 1927
	W. H. Kibler, 1929-

GRAYSON COUNTY

There is no Lutheran church in Grayson County, yet it has a place in
these sketches. In the minutes of the 1809 meeting of the Special
Virginia Conference, there is a list of churches known to exist in the
State, and the names of the officers, arranged by Dr. S. Henkel. In this
list appears Elk Creek; John Riede, officer, whose postoffice is Wytheville.

The minutes of the Southwestern Virginia Synod, 1847, page 16, makes mention of a certain lot on Elk Creek in Grayson County in which Lutherans are said to have an interest. The following year, by resolution of Synod, Messrs. Boyers, John Rosenbaum, and Jonas Huddle were named, and the Grayson County court asked to name them trustees of the land belonging to "St. John's Lutheran and Reformed church." Several years later the lot was sold, but litigations arose which continued until the outbreak of the Civil War. In 1860, the Rev. Festus Hickerson was sent to "explore Grayson," and for two years the "Grayson Mission" is entered in the minutes of Synod, but disappears after 1862. In 1872 this Grayson lot was reported sold for $75.90, and the next year $73.00 of this was given to the new church at Wytheville.

The Mountain mission work under the care of the Rev. Kenneth Killinger of Marion, extends into Grayson, where he maintains six preaching points which are listed under the sketch of his work in Smith County.

FIRST EVANGELICAL LUTHERAN CHURCH
Richmond, Va.

HENRICO COUNTY
RICHMOND

First Evangelical Lutheran Church—The story of the efforts of the two Synods of Virginia to establish an English Lutheran Church in the Capital city is fully told in Part I. Therefore, this sketch begins with the organization of the church named above, which took place on March 11, 1869, by the Rev. J. G. Neiffer. There were thirty-six charter members. The two Synods cooperated in the support of the mission in

HEBRON CHURCH (See frontispiece)
Madison, Va.

its early years, and in financing the building of the first church. Prior to having a church home, they worshiped in the homes of the members, in a committee room of the Odd Fellows Hall, Police Court room, and in the Universalist church on Mayo street. The church building, on Seventh and Grace streets was completed in 1877. It was a brick structure with auditorium on first floor and Sunday school rooms above, costing, together with the lot $20,000. The congregation became self-supporting in 1897. In 1908 the property was sold and lot purchased on Monument Avenue, at the Stuart Circle. Upon this was erected, of James River Granite, a most beautiful church, Gothic in style, with churchly appointments, Sunday school rooms and parsonage. No church in the city has a more commanding, nor more churchly appearance. The new church was dedicated on May 21, 1911, the Rev. Dr. Geo. S. Bowers preaching the sermon. The present membership is 806; and the Sunday school membership 447. The church property is valued at $208,000. The Rev. C. L. Brown, D. D., missionary to Japan, was confirmed in the First church. The pastors have been:

J. G. Neiffer, until 1870	J. S. Moser, 1888-1891
D. M. Henkel, 1871-1872	R. E. Livingstone (supply)
R. C. Holland (supply)	J. C. Seegers, 1891-1894
W. Y. Cline (supply)	J. A. Morehead, 1894-1897
W. C. Schaffer, 1875-1888	C. A. Marks, 1899-1906
A. J. Bowers (supply)	J. J. Scherer, Jr., D. D., 1906-

Trinity Mission—A second church was established in the eastern part of the city some twenty years after the organization of the First Church. In 1888 Trinity Lutheran Church, of Richmond, the Rev. George E. Shuey, pastor, applied for admission into the Southwestern Virginia Synod. This being Virginia Synod territory no action was taken until after consulting the Virginia Synod. The Church Extension Society of the Southwestern Virginia Synod and the Synod gave support to the mission, and it afterwards came under the Board of Missions of the United Synod. The Rev. Mr. Shuey withdrew in May, 1891, and the Rev. H. M. Petrea served until in 1893, after which the mission was merged with the First Church.

MADISON COUNTY
MADISON PARISH

Hebron, near Madison, the oldest congregation in the Synod, worshiping in the oldest Lutheran church in regular use in America, had its beginning with the landing of twenty destitute German families on the Virginia coast in 1717. They became indentured servants of Gov. Alex. Spottswood, upon his paying their transportation, and spent eight years of hard service on his land and in his iron works at Germanna, twenty miles above Fredericksburg, on the Rapidan. Having satisfied their obligation to him, they took up land on the Robinson River and the White Oak Run, where they built their homes, and the following year a log church, known as the German Chapel.

Though without a pastor until 1733, they were not unmindful of their spiritual interest. While living at Germanna they worshiped in the blockhouse with other Germans (Reformed), whose pastor was the Rev. John Haeger, and united with them in sending an agent to Europe with a petition to the "Society for the Propagation of the Gospel in Foreign Parts," in London, for the support of a minister. He was promised twenty-five German copies of the Book of Common Prayer, and in Germany he collected some money and books, but was unable to secure a pastor. In 1734 their first pastor, John Casper Stoever, in company with Michael Smith and Michael Holt, having credentials from Gov. Gooch, visited Holland and Germany, to solicit funds with which to build a church and provide for the support of a minister. The subscription book they carried, containing names of places visited, and record of each subscription, is a much prized and well preserved relic. Their mission resulted in collecting well nigh $10,000, after paying all expenses, and also some books. Student Geo. S. Klug, of Elbing, agreed to return with them to become assistant pastor. Pastor Stoever died on the return voyage and young Klug, having been ordained at Danzic, entered upon his duties as pastor immediately after arrival. The money was used to build a church, to purchase a farm and home for the pastor, and to purchase slaves to work the farm.

The church erected in 1740 stands today with little change, except the addition of the annex in 1800. It is a frame building 26 feet wide, 50 feet long and 30 feet high with a small vestry room, 9x13 feet in size, attached to the north side. The interior was ceiled. A gallery extended across the ends and the south side. The annex is an extension 20 feet long and 26 feet wide attached to the south side of the building equally distant from the ends. The church is therefore cruciform in shape. In the gallery, at the south end of the annex facing the pulpit, is the pipe organ, installed in 1800, which is yet in use.

The communion vessels bearing the date of May 17, 1727, were used until a few years ago, and are well preserved. A school promoted by the first pastor, but established by his successor in 1748, continued for well nigh a century. The congregation belonged to the Synod of Pennsylvania, was a charter member of the Maryland and Virginia Synod (1820), and of the Virginia Synod (1829). The early pastors of Hebron visited a number of early Lutheran settlements in the Shenandoah Valley. A colony from Hebron established "Hopeful" church in Boone County, Kentucky, in 1806. The congregation has been active in the general work of the church.

The confirmed membership is 243, with a Sunday school of 125. The total value of the church property is $21,000. The parsonage is located at Madison.

The pastors who have served this parish are as follows:

J. C. Stoever, 1733-1739	Jacob Frank, 1775-1778
G. S. Klug, 1739-1764	Paul Henkel, 1782-1785 (?)
J. Schwarbach, 1765-1774	W. Carpenter, 1787-1813

M. Meyerhoeffer, 1815-1821   W. G. Campbell, 1877-1882
J. Kehler, 1821-1832   G. H. Beckley, 1882-1885
W. Scull, 1832-1834   J. S. Moser, 1885-1888
T. W. Miller, 1835-1847   B. S. Brown, 1888-1891
S. Allenbaugh, 1847-1849   J. A. Flickinger, 1891-1895
A. P. Ludden, 1850-1856   C. B. Miller, 1895-1896
W. S. Bowman, 1856-1859   W. P. Huddle, 1897-1921
Levi Keller, 1860-1867   F. G. Morgan, 1921-1922
R. C. Holland, 1868-1875   V. Y. Boozer, D. D., 1923-1926
              C. K. Rhodes, 1928-

Mt. Nebo at Rochelle, six miles south of Madison, was organized in
1878, by the Rev. L. A. Fox, of Augusta County, from members of
Tennessee Synod churches in Shenandoah and Rockingham Counties, who
had moved here two decades earlier, and the church, a frame structure,
was built the following year. They frequently attended services at
Hebron until 1866, since which time they were served by the following
pastors:

J. E. Seneker, 1866-1877   J. N. Stirewalt, 1882-1887
L. A. Fox, 1877-1881   J. S. Moser (supply)
G. W. Campbell (supply)   J. S. Koiner, 1888-1893

After 1893 the congregation was suppied by the pastors of Hebron
church until it came into the Virginia Synod in 1922,· and has been
regularly a part of the Madison parish.

The confirmed membership is 106, and has a Sunday school of forty-
six. The church property is valued at $5000.

Mt. Pisgah, near Ruth, four miles west of Madison, was organized
April 6, 1894, by the Rev. J. A. Flickinger, and the church was built the
same year. The church lot was deeded by Mr. and Mrs. Uriah S.
Gibbs to J. Utz, Aylette Marshall, and U. S. Gibbs, trustees. The
occasion of the organization and building of Mt. Pisgah was the distance
which the families of Hebron in this section had to travel to church, and
the need of a church for the other people of the community. Pastor
Flickinger held services in a schoolhouse here before the building of the
church. It has always been in connection with the parish with Hebron
congregation. The membership is twenty-eight; that of the Sunday
school is twenty-five. The church property is valued at $1000.

LUTHERAN MINISTERS COMING FROM MADISON COUNTY CONGREGATIONS:

William Carpenter _____ Hebron
Jacob Crigler _____ Hebron
B. C. Wayman _____ Hebron
J. W. Strickler _____ Hebron
J. F. Crigler, D. D. _____ Hebron
T. A. Graves _____ Hebron
W. C. Huddle _____ Hebron
C. Max Huddle (seminarian) _____ Hebron
John H. Fray (seminarian) _____ Hebron

Casper Kipps _____ Mt. Nebo
M. M. Kipps _____ Mt. Nebo

MONTGOMERY COUNTY

There are three parishes in the county—Blacksburg, Price's Fork, and Radford. The history of the churches of the two former parishes have been closely associated with each other, since St. Peter's is the mother church. The earliest pastoral services were renderd by ministers from other states or other counties. The Rev. Solomon Schaeffer who came in 1840, was the first Lutheran pastor to have permanent residence in the county.

BLACKSBURG PARISH

The Blacksburg parish, formerly known as the Montgomery charge, consists at present of New St. Peter's, Mt. Tabor, and Luther Memorial, at Blacksburg.

New St. Peter's, called first, St. Michaels; later St. Peter's and after the building of the present church, New St. Peter's, is one of the oldest Lutheran churches in the state. It originated with the "New River Settlement," the first white people to locate west of the Alleghanies in Virginia, as early as 1745, or possibly 1741.* Leonard Schnell, Moravian Missionary, visited here in 1749, and preached in Adam Harman's house on November 20. That a congregation existed prior to 1755, is evident from the deed made by the executors of the James Patton estate on August 6, 1806, to John Wall and Michael Surface, elders of the "Lutheran Calvanistic church on Thom's Creek—for and in consideration of a promise made unto said church by James Patton in his life time and the sum of one dollar." James Patton died in 1755. The confirmation certificate of Elizabeth Harless (now in possession of her great grandson, Prof. J. E. B. Smith, of Christiansburg) given by the Rev. Peter M. Brugell on June 1, 1788, which also certifies to her baptism twenty years previous, is sufficient evidence of the continuous preaching and administration of the sacrament by Lutheran ministers in this community.

The first church building is believed to have been near Fort McDonald, but the date of its building is not known. Nor is it known when the log church was erected on the land conveyed to the congregation in 1806. The old church was in bad state of repair in 1833, and a brick church was built not many years after this date. New St. Peter's, built in 1895, is about two miles from the old site.

The first rule of organization is the constitution of thirteen articles, prepared by the Rev. W. F. A. Daser, on October 16, 1796. The membership of the congregation at present is fifty-nine; and that of the Sunday school is ninety-six. The church property is valued at $2000.

The following pastors have served St. Peter's:

W. F. A. Daser, — 1800   Daniel Flohr, 1800-1826
John Stanger (assistant)   Martin Walther, 1826-1828

---

*The New River Settlement is separate and distinct from the Adventist or Dunkers Settlement in the neighborhood of Radford about the same time.

Daniel J. Hauer, 1828-1832   M. O. J. Krepps, 1893-1896
Thomas Miller, 1832-1835   D. B. Groseclose, 1897-1903
J. T. Tabler, 1835-1839   J. E. Bushnell, D. D., 1903-1905
Solomon Schaeffer, 1840-1871   J. M. Killian, 1905-1911
J. H. Turner, 1871-1876   R. R. Sowers (supply)
W. E. Hubbert, 1876-1887   B. S. Brown, 1911-1912
J. A. Huffard, 1888-1890   J. A. Brosius, 1913-1921
C. N. A. Yonce, 1890-1892   H. P. Wyrick, 1921-1922
E. R. McCauley (supply)   S. C. Ballentine, 1923-

Mt. Tabor, was organized and the church, a log building, erected in 1843, under the ministry of Pastor Solomon Schaeffer. For several years services had been held in Wall's schoolhouse, in the community. The present church, a frame building, was built in 1878, near the original site. The congregation has been served by the same pastors as St. Peter's. The membership is twenty-nine, and that of the Sunday school eighteen. The church property is valued at $2000.

Luther Memorial, was organized by Pastor W. E. Hubbert, on February 21, 1886. The church, a brick structure, with Sunday school rooms adjoining the auditorium, was dedicated on September 19, of that year. In 1924, the Sunday school building was enlarged. A decade previous to the building of the church, land had been purchased in Blacksburg for a church and a parsonage, and the parsonage erected.

The membership of the congregation is 230, and that of the Sunday school 244. The value of the church property is $30,000. •

PRICE'S FORK PARISH

There are at present but two organized congregations in Price's Fork parish, which was formerly called the New River charge. Following the death of Pastor Solomon Schaeffer, in 1871, the churches of the county were divided into two parishes, known as the Montgomery and New River charges, but were reunited under the ministry of Pastor W. E. Hubbert. In 1890 they were again divided; the New River charge at first being called the Shiloh charge, consisting of St. Mark's, Shiloh and Alleghany. The Rev. S. R. Smith, who had for several years assisted Pastor Schaeffer, was the first pastor of the New River charge. Pastor W. E. Hubbert served these churches from 1876 to 1887 and Pastor J. A. Huffard from 1888 to 1890. The pastors since that date have been:

D. B. Groseclose, 1890-1897   B. F. Landis, (supply) 1908
W. A. Dutton, 1897-1900   B. F. Landis, 1910-1913
James Mahood, 1901-1902   H. J. Pflum (supply), 1918-1920
P. D. Leddin, 1902-1905   T. C. Parker, 1921-1923
George S. Diven, 1905-1906   W. C. Buck, 1927-

Shiloh, was organized and the church built in 1874, under the ministry of Pastor S. R. Smith. A few years later a congregation known as Piney Grove was merged with Shiloh. The church building· was remodeled in 1909, and is valued at $2500. The membership of the congregation is thirty-nine and that of the Sunday school is ninety. Adam Harless, Sr. served fifty years as superintendent of Shiloh Sunday school.

St. Mark's, at Price's Fork, was organized and the church built in 1878, under the ministry of Pastor W. E. Hubbert. The building was remodeled and improved in 1901, and is valued at $3300. The membership of the congregation is 167 and that of the Sunday school 190.

Mt. Zion, organized in 1846, by Pastor Solomon Schaeffer, has been disbanded, but services are held regularly in the church. The first church was built here in 1849; on land given by "Uncle" Sammy Smith. A new church succeeded the old one in 1905. "Uncle" Sammy Smith served as superintendent of the Sunday school here for fifty years in succession.

Vicars—Pastor D. B. Groseclose held services here during the latter part of his ministry in the New River charge. A frame church was dedicated on the thirteenth of May, 1898. The congregation was small and the work not developing as expected, the organization has been abandoned.

CHRIST'S CHURCH
Radford, Va.

RADFORD

Christ's Church has been developed along with the church at Pulaski, the two forming a parish until 1921. In 1887 Synod took definite steps to locate a church here. Services were held in public halls or in one of the other churches by the Rev. W. E. Hubbert of Blacksburg. The Rev. S. S. Rahn of Wytheville took charge March 1, 1891, and on July 19, he organized with twenty-one members. A lot in East Radford was donated by Hon. Hoge Tyler, afterwards Governor of Virginia, and the frame church erected thereon was dedicated August 25, 1895. The location proving undesirable, the property was sold to the colored people five years later. A lot was purchased in Radford and in 1911 a brick building was erected with Sunday school room, and with churchly appointments.

The parsonage on the adjoining lot was built in 1925 and is valued at $6000. The church property is valued at $9000. The membership is eighty-four; that of the Sunday school is fifty-seven.

The pastors have been:

J. A. Huffard, 1891-1901   J. I. Coiner, 1912-1919
P. E. Monroe, 1901-1903   W. P. Cline, Jr., 1919-1921
D. S. Fox, 1903-1906   R. D. Snyder (sup.), summer 1921
Geo. H. Rhodes, 1907-1909   C. E. Kepley, 1922-1923
Paul Sieg, 1910-1912   J. P. Derrick, 1924-1927
H. E. Poff, 1929-

NORFOLK COUNTY

NORFOLK

First Church was organized on April 15, 1894 by the Rev. J. E. Shenk, missionary of the Board of Missions of the United Synod South. Services were held in a rented hall, from before organizing, until the congregation found a home on Charlotte street, purchased in April, 1895, from the Methodist Episcopal Church. It was a stone structure of 200 seating capacity and was, after some interior changes, dedicated free of debt in May 1903. On the following November 1st the church was destroyed by fire. With the insurance money, their own gifts, and some voluntary contributions from congregations of the Synod, the church was restored, and on June 24, 1907, it was dedicated again free of debt. The congregation assumed self-support January 1, 1907. The property was sold in 1920 and a lot was purchased at 15th and Morgan streets upon which a temporary house of worship was erected. This location having proved, not wholly satisfactory, and the congregation having outgrown its home, in 1927 a lot was purchased on Colley Avenue between Maury and Boliver Avenues and the splendid stone Gothic structure "classic in outline, beautiful in proportion" now in process of building was begun on June 1st in 1929. The contract price is $114,000. The church proper, to be used wholly for worship, will seat 500, with

FIRST LUTHERAN CHURCH
Norfolk, Va.

provision for the erection of balconies to seat 300 additional. The Sunday school building, joined to the church, the first unit of which is under construction, will provide for more than 500 pupils. It will be arranged and equipped for the most thorough educational work, and for proper social and recreational purposes, and when all units are constructed will provide for a school of more than 1000. The congregation numbers 386 members and has a Sunday school of 304. The following pastors have served this congregation:

J. E. Shenk, 1894-1901
W. H. Riser, 1902-1911
C. Brown Cox, 1911-1913
E. R. McCauley, D. D., 1913-1922

W. E. Stahler, D. D. (sup.), 1922-1924
F. R. Christ, 1924-1925
W. E. Stahler, D. D. (sup.), 1925-1926
L. W. Strickler, 1926-

PORTSMOUTH

First Lutheran Church—At the 1907 convention of the Virginia Synod a committee was appointed to consider the advisability of establishing a church at Portsmouth, which was given full authority to call a missionary and make provision to finance the movement. Shortly afterwards, the committee visited Portsmouth and being encouraged with their findings, at once extended a call to the Rev. J. W. Shuey of Lexington. The estimated expenses for the remainder of the synodical year were apportioned to the congregations of the Synod. Missionary Shuey entered upon his duties January 1, 1908. Services were held in the Pythian Castle and a Sunday school was conducted. On June 7th, the Missionary assisted by the Rev. W. H. Riser of Norfolk, organized the Luther Memorial (the name given at first and used until 1927), with thirty-eight members. Mr. J. E. Cooper, of Winchester, having visited the mission in the interest of church property, purchased at his own expense and in his own name, a piece of valuable property, upon which were several buildings, and a chapel suitable for church purposes. The congregation was given the use of the chapel, the entire property being held by Mr. Cooper for the benefit of the mission. Owing to the long illness of the owner, and his death (1922), the transfer of the property to the church was delayed. A valuable lot, centrally located has been purchased, and the congregation is looking forward to a permanent church home in the near future.

The mission came under the care of the Board of Missions of the United Synod South in 1912 and later under the Board of the United Lutheran Church.

The 1928 report to Synod shows a membership of 137 and the Sunday school of 118. Since the meeting of Synod there has been a large addition to the membership. The pastors have been as follows:

J. W. Shuey, 1908-1913   P. A. Atkins, 1922-1927
A. W. Craun, 1914-1921   J. I. Coiner, 1927-

PAGE COUNTY

Page County, next to Madison, has the earliest Lutheran history. There were Lutherans among the first settlers at Massanutten, about seven miles west of Luray, near the present highway, in 1726 or 1727. The leader of this colony appears to have been Adam Miller, a Lutheran, who a few years later, located at Bear Lithia Springs, not far from Elkton. The late General J. E. Roller, claimed the "Flatwoods" church near Massanutten, and "Naked Creek" church near Bear Lithia Springs, both to have been Lutheran, and were established within a decade after settlement at Massanutten. It is certain that Pastor Geo. S. Klug of Madison, made regular visits to Massanutten as early as 1748 and likely visited other settlements in these parts. There are at present three parishes and ten congregations in the county. Of the ten, Bethlehem alone was not of the Tennessee Synod. The United States religious census of 1916, the latest published, show the Lutherans to be the second largest group of church people in Page.

STONY MAN PARISH

Mt. Calvary, under the shadow of Stony Man peak, is rightly called the mother church, since there are five congregations in this part of the county organized, directly or indirectly, from her membership: Morning Star, Grace, St. Mark's, St. James', and Beth Eden. The date of the first services held, the first church built, and the first pastor, is not known, the records prior to 1817, having been lost. The earliest record is of August 6, 1765, when Johannes Schwarbach, whom it appears, was rendering pastoral services temporarily, conveyed three acres of land to

LUTHERAN CHURCHES OF PAGE COUNTY

Mt. Calvary Lutheran Church
Stony Man, Va.

Beth Eden Lutheran Church
Near Luray, Va.

St. Mark's Lutheran Church
Luray, Va.

Morning Star Lutheran Church
Five Miles Southeast, Luray, Va.

Bethlehem Lutheran Church
Kimball, Va.

LUTHERAN CHURCHES OF PAGE COUNTY

St. Paul's Lutheran Church
Grove Hill, Va.

St. Luke's Lutheran Church
Alma, Va.

St. Peter's Lutheran Church
Shenandoah, Va.

St. James' Lutheran Church
Rileyville, Va.

Grace Lutheran Church
Ida, Va.

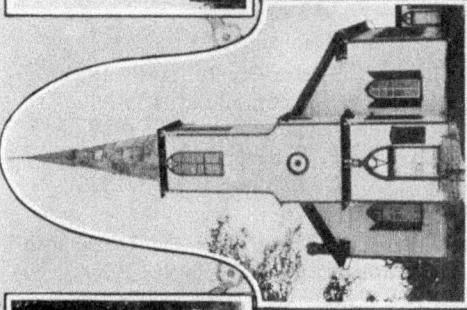

Peter Painter and Jacob Shaffer, trustees. There was both a Lutheran and a Reformed congregation for many years. It was known as the Hoxbiehl, or Gomer's (Comer's) church, and later as Mt. Calvary.

The Lutheran congregation was first a member of the Pennsylvania Synod, Balthaser Sauer having attended a convention as lay delegate. It was one of the five churches in the Valley that united with the North Carolina Synod in 1813, and in 1820, became a member of the Tennessee Synod. The present church, a brick building was built in 1848. The congregation is in possession of a pewter communion set which bears the name of "Thomas Giffin" and dated 1727, but when and how it was brought here is not known. The first pastor is believed to have been Johannes Schwarbach and that other Madison pastors as well as Peter Muhlenberg and Christian Streit, rendered occasional pastoral services. In recent years the congregation has suffered by the removal of many of her members from the community. Regular services are held in the old church, and the property is well kept. The present membership is twenty-nine.

Since 1817 the following have served as pastors:

Peter Schmucker, 1817-1820	Socrates Henkel, 1860-1869
Paul Henkel, 1821	J. N. Stirewalt, 1869-1906
George Leidy, 1822	D. L. Miller, 1907-1909
Ambrose Henkel, 1823-1837	P. L. Snapp, 1910-1921
Jacob Stirewalt, 1837-1860	C. I. Morgan, 1921-1925
A. L. Boliek, 1926-	

Morning Star, five miles southeast of Luray, near the Shenandoah National Park line, was organized November 29, 1873 by the Rev. J. N. Stirewalt, seventy members from Mt. Calvary transferring their membership to the new congregation. The church, a frame structure, erected that year at the cost of $549.99, was dedicated on November 16, the Rev. I. Conder preaching the sermon. The land was conveyed by Henry Shaffer and his wife, Catherine, to Geo. Stombock, Henry Shaffer, and Paul Miller, trustees. A Sunday school has been conducted since the building of the church. The congregation numbers 160, and that of the Sunday school 53. The church property is valued at $2000. A well kept cemetery is in connection with this church. It has been served by pastors of the Stony Man parish.

Grace, seven miles south of Luray, was organized March 10, 1877, by the Rev. J. N. Stirewalt. The charter members came from Mt. Calvary. The first officers were Geo. Sours, Gideon Hoak, John Sours, and D. A. Hoak. The church, brick, built in 1835, by the Reformed people and known as the "Printz" church, was purchased by the Lutherans in 1900, and deeded to Geo. Sours, Simon Sours, and John Hoak, trustees. The membership is eighty-three and that of the Sunday school is seventy-five. The church property is valued at $2000. The congregation has been served by the pastors of Stony Man parish.

Beth Eden, two miles southeast of Luray, was organized by the Rev. J. N. Stirewalt, on December 31, 1896, with twenty-four charter members coming from Mt. Calvary. The land was conveyed by David H. Griffith and wife, Mary B., on May 22, 1895, to David Stombock, Ambrose Fox, and D. F. Griffith, trustees. The church was dedicated on November 14, 1897, the Rev. J. P. Stirewalt, D. D., preaching the sermon. Prior to the building of the church, services were held in Baker's schoolhouse, not far from the present location. The membership is 119, and that of the Sunday school is 53. The church property is valued at $2000. It has been served by pastors from the Stony Man parish.

Stony Man parish owns a parsonage on Blue Ridge Avenue in Luray, which is valued at $6000.

LURAY PARISH

St. Mark's—At a meeting of the Virginia Conference at Mt. Calvary in May 1874, a committee consisting of Pastor J. N. Stirewalt and Messrs. Wm. J. and John A. Shenk, both members of Mt. Calvary church, was appointed to consider building a church at Luray. A lot was purchased off the Wm. Chapman estate, facing the pike east of town (now East Main street), and a frame building erected thereon, which was dedicated April 30, 1876, the Rev. Dr. L. A. Fox preaching the sermon. Shortly thereafter, St. Mark's was organized by pastor J. N. Stirewalt, with twenty-five charter members, all from Mt. Calvary. In the early eighties a vestibule and tower were built, new pews installed, art glass put in the windows, and the floor carpeted.

Shortly after these improvements the chapel, a frame building almost as large as the church, was erected for the Sunday school and like purposes.* In 1926 the church was replastered, the church and chapel connected by extending the church vestibule, and a pipe organ installed.

During the ministry of the Rev. Dr. J. I. Miller, he erected on the church property a large building and conducted a girls school known as "Von Bora College." Part of this building is now used as the parsonage. In 1897 the congregation united with the Virginia Synod.

The membership of St. Mark's is 174; that of the Sunday school is 124. The church and parsonage property is valued at $20,000. The pastors have been:

J. N. Stirewalt, 1876-1881	F. C. Oberly, 1893-1895
J. I. Miller, D. D., 1882-1893	D. P. T. Crickenberger, 1897-1901
D. P. T. Crickenberger, 1890-1892	J. A. Huffard, D. D., 1903-1922
	C. W. Cassell, 1922-

Students T. B. Yeakley and L. P. Pence, the Rev. J. E. Bushnell, D. D., and the Rev. S. W. Kuhns, have each done supply work for the congregation.

---

*The extensive improvements and beautifying of the church was due largely to the beneficence of B. F. Deford, of the Deford Tannery.

Bethlehem—The records of Bethlehem church, four miles east of Luray on the Lee Highway, prior to 1851, cannot be found, and since then are incomplete. The brick church now in use was erected in 1851. A log schoolhouse, one-fourth mile north of the present location, on an elevation just west of the home of J. W. Alther, was the place of worship before the day of the brick church. The early history of the congregation appears to have been intimately associated with Hebron church at Madison. In the minutes of the Virginia Synod it appears as Pass Run church until about 1868.

The congregation has suffered many loses by removal. The membership is sixty-three; that of the Sunday school thirty-four. The church property is valued at $1500.

We have not been able to find the names of all the early pastors of the congregation. In the forties, S. Wolfersberger, S. Allenbaugh, A. R. Rude, each was pastor for a short time. A. P. Ludden of Madison served as pastor from 1850 to 1856, and A. J. Kibler, from 1857 to 1860. Following them were J. M. Shreckhise, J. F. Campbell, X. J. Richardson, L. Keller, R. C. Holland, C. Beard, and J. S. Moser. Since 1882, when Dr. J. I. Miller became pastor at Luray, the congregation has been served by St. Mark's pastors. Pastor J. N. Stirewalt, of the Stony Man parish, supplied at times during vacancies.

Shenandoah Parish

The Shenandoah parish consists of St. Peter's at Shenandoah; St. Paul's at Grove Hill; St. Luke's at Alma; and St. James' at Rileyville.

St. Peter's is the continuation of the Naked Creek church, and old St. Peter's west of the river.*

When the Rev. I. Conder in 1873 began holding services at old St. Peter's, he found the church in bad state of repair, and the congregation much disorganized. Two years later he effected reorganization and had the church extensively repaired. In 1884, under his ministry, twenty-five of the members had their membership transferred to the town of Milnes (now Shenandoah) and continued their organization under the name of St. Peter's. The church was completed two years later and dedicated on the third Sunday in August, 1886.

The early synodical connection of this congregation is not certain, but most likely it was the Tennessee Synod. Before the Civil War we find Naked Creek, St. Paul's and Pass Run constituting a pastorate of the Virginia Synod, and served by Pastors Samuel Allenbaugh, W. S. Bowman, and others. After 1875, it was in the Tennessee Synod until 1925, except from 1898 to 1903, when it was connected with the Virginia Synod.

---

*"The Naked Creek church, a Lutheran church, was founded 1733. In 1747 it was moved west of the river and given the name of St. Peter's. Under the lid of the pulpit was found the name of the builder of the pulpit, Christian Konrad, and the names of the building committee; John Mueller, William Biederfisch, John Ziegler, Frederick Ziegler, and Gerhard Koyte. Among the pastors were: Christian Stoever, Samuel Godfrey Ziegler, Emanuel Rudebush, and Gerhard Mueller."—From Gen. J. E. Roller.

The present membership is 198; that of the Sunday school 270. The church property is valued at $8000. A movement is on foot to build a larger and better church on another location. The pastors since 1873 are:

I. Conder, 1873-1893

R. H. Cline, 1893-1899

D. P. T. Crickenberger, 1899-1901

L. P. Pence } Supply until 1903

J. E. Bushnell, D. D. } Supply until 1903

M. A. Ashby, 1903-1919

A. R. Beck, 1920-1921

A. L. Boliek, 1921-1926

C. L. Hunt, 1926-

St. Paul's, on the Shenandoah-Luray road, four miles north of Shenandoah, long known as Monger's church (from a family in the community), appears to have been established in the latter half of the eighteenth century. The earliest date is 1782. The log church, which stood on the west bank of the river one mile southeast of the present church was built prior to 1792. It has been known as St. Paul's since 1807. The brick church, begun in 1860, was not completed until in 1868. This building was demolished 1927, to make way for the present splendid brick structure, with churchly appointments, Sunday school rooms and basement, which was dedicated in March 1928. It was at first both Lutheran and Reformed. A number of the earlier pastors given below are evidently of the Reformed faith. St. Paul's was one of the five churches of the Valley which united with the North Carolina Synod in 1813 and later with the Tennessee Synod. About the middle of the last century it was served part of the time by Virginia Synod pastors. The membership is 127; and that of the Sunday school is 148. The church property is valued at $23,000. The pastors are given in the church record as follows:

Peter Schmucker, 1818-1821

John Brown, 1821-1825

F. W. Vandesslord, 1825-1827

J. P. Cline, 1827-1833

Sam. Oswald, 1833-1836

G. F. Staehlin, 1836-1842

S. J. Fitzer, 1842-1845

Jacob Stirewalt, 1845-1847

J. P. Cline, 1847-1856

J. A. Kibler, 1857-1860

W. H. Cone, 1860-1868

S. Henkel, 1868-1876

J. W. Hausenfluck, 1877-1892

S. Henkel, 1892-1893

R. H. Cline, 1893-1899

John Stirewalt, 1899-1903

M. A. Ashby, 1903-1920

A. R. Beck, 1920-1921

A. L. Boliek, 1921-1926

C. L. Hunt, 1926-

St. Luke's, at Alma, is, according to an authority already cited, the continuation of the "Flatwood's" church near Massanutten. Some of the names of the old families were: Neuman, Koyte, Stoneberger, Bomberger, Jurie, and Biederfisch. The congregation was worshiping in the Stoneberger church on Stony Run, two miles west of Stanley, in 1795. The deed to this property was made on August 12, 1795, by Frederick Stoneberger and Matthias Friermood to John Nowman and Daniel Snyder, trustees, for the Lutheran and Presbyterian (Calvanistic) congregations. At this time there was a church on the lot known as the "William's"

202   A History of the Lutheran Church

church, which no doubt, accounts for it having been called "St. William's" at one time. The Lutheran congregation withdrew from here in 1873,* and purchased part interest in the Union church at Alma, known as Fairview. The Union church having burned in 1892, the Lutheran congregation purchased the other interest and rebuilt under the name of "St. Luke's." This property is valued at $3000. The membership of the congregation is fifty-four, and that of the Sunday school is seventy.

The names of the pastors of this congregation prior to 1837 are not known, but it is safe to say they were those Lutheran ministers who served other congregations in these parts.

The pastors since 1837 are:

Jacob Stirewalt, 1837-1839	John Stirewalt, 1899-1903
Socrates Henkel, 1860-1871	M. A. Ashby, 1903-1920
J. N. Stirewalt, 1871-1880	A. R. Beck, 1920-1921
J. W. Hausenfluck, 1880-1892	A. L. Boliek, 1921-1926
R. H. Cline, 1893-1899	C. L. Hunt, 1926-

St. James'—In 1877, the Virginia conference appointed J. N. Stirewalt and J. W. Hausenfluck to give pastoral services to a number of Lutheran families living at Cedar Point (now Rileyville). The old Union church was used as a place of worship. In 1882, the congregation was organized; Good, Sours, and Miller were the names most numerous among the members. In a short time they bought one-half interest in Union church and later rebuilt. The membership is seventy-four. Not having full use of the church, the congregation is limited to but little Sunday school work. The value of the property is $2000. The last sermon preached by the Rev. J. N. Stirewalt, was here on November 4, 1906.

The pastors have been:

J. W. Hausenfluck, 1884-1891	M. A. Ashby, 1911-1919
J. N. Stirewalt, 1891-1906	A. R. Beck, 1920-1921
D. L. Miller, 1908-1909	A. L. Boliek, 1921-1926
	C. L. Hunt, 1926-

The Lutheran Ministers From Page County

J. E. Shenk	St. Mark's
E. A. Shenk	St. Mark's
C. E. Hershberger	St. Mark's
Glen G. Boliek (seminarian)	St. Peter's
A. J. Stirewalt, D. D.	Mt. Calvary
L. L. Huffman	St. Luke's
W. H. Swaney	Mt. Calvary
Dennis Swaney	Mt. Calvary

*The great flood on the Shenandoah River in September 1870, swept away the home, the family and the mill of Noah Kyte, the most prominent family in the congregation. This together with the moving of a number of families to the West, about this time greatly weakened the congregation.

PITTSYLVANIA COUNTY

DANVILLE

It was brought to the attention of the 1921 convention of the Synod of Southwest Virginia that a · number of Lutheran families living at Danville were interested in establishing a church in their city. The matter was referred to the Executive Committee, but, did not receive immediate attention because of lack of funds available for that purpose. In the meantime these families arranged with pastors from North Carolina and Virginia to hold occasional services for them. A religious census of the city at this time revealed more than three score Lutherans living there. Being assured of the support of the Home Mission Board of the United Lutheran Church, Mr. H. A. Schroder, student of the Southern Seminary, assumed pastoral care for the summer months of 1922. On June 18th, the Rev. E. H. Copenhaver, President of the Synod, organized the Church of the Ascension, with thirty-two members, and at the evening services administered the Holy Communion. The Every Member Canvass that fall showed a commendable liberality on the part of the members. An unused Jewish Synagogue, centrally located, was offered as a place of worship, and later the congregation was given the use of this building for a period of years, for its upkeep. Certain industrial changes in the city, the removal of many of the charter members and the period of the unrestricted use of the Synagogue having expired, have resulted in discouragement; however, the recent purchase of a well located lot, and the prospect of a church home, makes the outlook much brighter.

The present membership is forty-six and the Sunday school fifty-five.

The Rev. J. W. Link served the parish from 1923 to 1927. Seminarian A. K. Yount supplied during the summer of 1927 and the Rev. Paul Sieg the following winter, after which the Rev. A. K. Yount accepted the work as permanent pastor in 1928.

PULASKI COUNTY

Women's Memorial—The establishing of Women's Memorial congregation is an outstanding accomplishment of the Woman's Missionary Society of the Synod of Southwest Virginia, the work having been fostered, and for many years maintained by that organization. In the eighties when Martin's Tank, a railroad flag-stop, became Pulaski, and began to be a town, which by the vote of the people in 1893, became the county seat, Lutheran people from Wythe, Montgomery and other adjoining counties came here to establish homes. The Rev. W. E. Hubbert of Blacksburg, assisted at times by the Rev. Dr. L. A. Fox, held services as early as 1887, and organized the congregation in 1888. On August 1, 1889, the corner stone of the church was laid, the Rev. Dr. W. B. Yonce, President of the Synod, officiating, the Rev. J. L. Murphy being pastor at the time. The church, a brick building, with Sunday school room, was dedicated July 27, 1890. It came under the support of the

Board of Missions of the United Synod August, 1897. On January 1, 1925, it became self-supporting. A pipe organ was installed in 1915, partly the gift of Andrew Carnegie. The congregation having kept pace with the growth of the town, is looking forward to a larger church, and better Sunday school equipment. The church property is valued at $10,000. The parsonage, on the adjoining lot, is valued at $8000.

The membership of the congregation is 109, and that of the Sunday school 122. Since January 1, 1921, the congregation has had full time service of the pastor. Before this date it was connected with Radford. The pastors of Women's Memorial besides those mentioned above have been:

J. A. B. Scherer, 1890-1891	J. B. Moose (supply)
J. A. Huffard, 1892-1901	J. I. Coiner, 1912-1919
P. E. Monroe, 1901-1903	W. P. Cline, 1919-1920
D. S. Fox, 1903-1906	W. G. Cobb, 1921-1922
Geo. H. Rhodes, 1907-1909	C. J. Rice, 1923-1928
L. A. Fox, D. D. (supply)	C. Brown Cox, D. D., 1928-

ROANOKE COUNTY

The Lutheran congregations of Roanoke County have been closely associated with those of the mother county, Botetourt. The pioneer resident Lutheran pastors were: John George Butler in Botetourt County 1796-1805; Daniel Scherer on Peter's Creek in Roanoke County 1818-1821; Martin Walther in Botetourt County 1821-1835; and Dan J. Hauer living in a parsonage near Zion in Roanoke County 1828-1832. These and several of their successors, part of the time served St. Peter's in Montgomery County, and Zion in Floyd County, as well as visiting and preaching at other points at which churches were established later.

The first congregation in the county was *Zion* which was in existence in 1828, when the twenty-third convention of the North Carolina Synod was held here, at which time the church was dedicated. Pine Grove was organized in 1845, and the church built about the same time. These two were the strong churches of Roanoke County parish for many years; Lowry's Chapel, later called Southview, and Cave Spring having been organized later. Zion, rebuilt in 1905 on a nearby location and called New Zion, was merged with College Church at Salem in 1920. Pine Grove continued on the Register of Churches until 1891 after which the members were gradually transferred to St. Mark's in Roanoke. Southview and Cave Spring have also been erased from the roll, the members having almost all moved into the towns. The Roanoke County parish disappeared from our roll with the organization of Emmanual in Roanoke, in 1922.

Besides these mentioned above, the following ministers have served the churches of the former Roanoke County parish. In some cases the dates are uncertain and during vacancies they were supplied by ministers and students at Salem.

Thomas Miller, 1833-1835   J. W. Butler, 1887-1892
Samuel Sayford, 1835-1842   J. M. Moser, 1896-1897
Gideon Scherer, 1842-1851   B. W. Cronk, 1897-1899
D. F. Bittle, D. D.⎫   T. C. Parker, 1899-1903
P. Shickel   ⎪   J. M. Tise, 1909-1914
A. A. J. Bushong ⎬1852-1882   J. W. McCauley, 1915-1917
J. L. Buck   ⎭   J. B. Haigler, 1918-1919
          J. A. Boord (Bourde), 1921-1922

COLLEGE CHURCH.
Salem, Va.

SALEM PARISH

College Church, the first town church within the Southwestern Virginia Synod, was organized on December 18, 1852, by the Rev. C. C. Baughman, with seven charter members. The church building, erected in 1856, an imposing and commodious brick structure, standing on the corner of College Avenue and Main Street was replaced in 1921 by the beautiful and more commodious Gothic building constructed of Catawba sandstone, and located further south on College Avenue. The life and history of the congregation are interwoven with that of Roanoke College. The first pastor was connected with the College, and the first president of the college was, for fourteen years, pastor of the congregation. It has been the church home of a great majority of the members of the college faculty, and of many of the students during their college days; and, also, the church home of the staff and the children of the Orphan Home. Her pastors and members have done much to nourish and strengthen the work of the churches of the county. The most prominent of her members in public life have been the Hon. John McCauley, the Hon. A. M. Bowman, Sr., and the Hon. William McCauley.

The pastors of College church have been:

C. C. Baughman, 1852-1853   D. F. Bittle, D. D., 1861-1869
D. F. Bittle, D. D., 1853-1859   S. A. Repass, 1869-1872
J. P. Smeltzer, 1860-1861   E. E. Sibole, 1873-1875

L. G. M. Miller, 1875-1888	C. K. Hunton, 1905-1920
C. A. Miller, 1888-1896	L. A. Fox, D. D., (supply)
L. A. Fox, D. D.	J. S. Kleckner, 1923-1926
F. V. N. Painter, D. D.	(supply) F. C. Longaker, Ph. D., (supply)
C. K. Bell, 1897-1905	Roy T. Troutman, 1927-

The membership of the congregation is 243, while that of the Sunday school is 311; and the value of the property is $87,600.

ST. MARK'S LUTHERAN CHURCH
Roanoke, Va.

St. Mark's Parish

St. Mark's, the mother church in Roanoke, first appears on the Synodical records in 1875, when it was received into Synod. However, regular services had been held by the pastor of College church since 1869, and a small frame church was built there in 1873. It is believed that Gideon Scherer, when he was pastor of Zion and Pine Grove congregations from 1846 to 1852, held services at Big Lick, (Roanoke, since 1880), it being his home, and from an early date a community center because of the intersection of roads. The Trouts, the Terrys, and the Howberts were some of the Lutheran families. The Hon. John Trout gave the land for the first church, which stood on the site of the present High Street Colored church, and again donated the land for the new church built in

1883, on Commerce and Church streets. The congregation was a part of the College church parish until 1883. The magic growth of the city making necessary a larger building, that of 1883 gave place to the commodious and costly stone church completed in 1891. In 1903, this property was exchanged for the former Greene Memorial (Methodist), the former St. Mark's becoming Greene Memorial Methodist church. St. Mark's property is valued at $150,000, exclusive of the parsonage on Church avenue. The membership of the congregation is 668, and that of the Sunday school 495.

Since the congregation became a separate parish the pastors have been as follows:

W. J. Smith, 1883-1885	Oliver C. Miller, 1892-1894
J. E. Bushnell, 1885-1890	L. G. M. Miller, D. D., 1894-1905
J. A. Huffard, 1890-1892	T. O. Keister, D. D., 1905-1913

J. Luther Sieber, D. D., 1914-

VIRGINIA HEIGHTS PARISH

Virginia Heights congregation in Roanoke was organized by the Rev. J. W. McCauley, on May 10, 1916, with twenty-nine members. A frame chapel with churchly furnishings was erected in 1917 on Grandin Road, near Virginia avenue. This was enlarged in 1922 and a pipe organ installed. The seating capacity is 275 and the value is $15,000.

The membership is 337, while that of the Sunday school is 220.

Dr. Nellie Cassell, medical missionary in India, has been for several years a member of the congregation.

The pastors have been:

J. W. McCauley, 1916-1918	O. F. Blackwelder, 1920-1925
C. O. Lippard, 1918-1920	J. M. Lotz, 1926-1927

H. Edgar Knies, 1928-

EMMANUEL PARISH

Emmanuel, in Villa Heights, Roanoke, was organized on August 6, 1922, by the Rev. J. A. Boord, with thirty-five members. The following Sunday a Sunday school was organized with an enrollment of 80. The frame chapel, seating 250 people, was erected by the members of the congregation out of lumber donated by St. Mark's. It is located on Lafayette Boulevard and Staunton Avenue, N. W. It is valued at $2500. The congregation numbers 133, while the Sunday school numbers ninety-one.

The Rev. J. A. Boord resigned in 1923, since which time the Rev. J. D. Utt has been pastor. Pastor Utt also serves Glade Creek, in Botetourt County.

KITTINGER'S

Kittinger's, fourteen miles southwest of Roanoke, first known as Back Creek, is said to have been organized by Pastor A. A. J. Bushong in 1868. It is a small congregation and belonged to the Roanoke County parish until a few years ago. Later it was connected with Virginia Heights and St. James at Vinton, but is now detached. Since separating from the old pastorate it has been served by Pastors J. W. McCauley, C. O. Lippard, O. F. Blackwelder, W. C. Huddle, E. W. Leslie, and J. D. Utt. The Rev. J. M. Tise is the pastor at present.

VINTON

St. James', in Vinton, an eastern suburb of Roanoke, organized by Pastor J. E. Bushnell in 1889 chiefly from members of St. Mark's, was merged with the mother church in 1923. A neat frame church building dedicated in November 1891, served as the house of worship. St. James' had the full time service of a pastor, for, but a small part of its history, which no doubt accounts to a large extent for its slow development. The proceeds from the sale of the property is held in trust with a view to using it, in a like work in southeast Roanoke. Those who served as pastors and supplies here, are: J. E. Bushnell, J. A. Morehead, T. S. Brown, J. M. Moser, J. M. Grabill, H. F. Richards, T. C. Parker, E. W. Leslie, T. O. Keister, D. D., L. A. Fox, D. D., J. M. Tise, J. W. McCauley, C. O. Lippard, O. F. Blackwelder, W. C. Huddle, and J. D. Utt.

St. Paul's, on Peter's Creek, two miles east of Salem, was organized in 1913 by pastor J. M. Tise, and the church erected the same year. A Sunday school has been conducted here, continuously. The congregation was first served by the pastors of the Roanoke County parish, but in 1927, it was placed under the care of College church and is served by Dr. H. J. McIntyre, Synodical Lay reader. The congregation has seventeen members with a Sunday school of forty-one members. The church property is valued at $1500.

LUTHERAN MINISTERS FROM ROANOKE COUNTY CONGREGATIONS:

C. N. A. Younce	College Church
Geo. W. McClanahan	College Church
E. R. McCauley, D. D.	College Church
Victor McCauley, D. D.	College Church
J. Luther Frantz	College Church
C. M. Fox	College Church
J. H. Turner, D. D.	College Church
J. W. McCauley	College Church
John Boone	
Miss Mary Markley, Missionary to Porto Rico	St. Mark's
Miss Jessie Cronk, Missionary in Training	College Church

ROCKBRIDGE COUNTY

Rockbridge County, although settled largely by Scotch-Irish and, therefore a Presbyterian stronghold, has had a Lutheran history for almost a century. When S. Filler was licensed as a minister by the Virginia Synod in 1842, he was directed to embrace in his field of labor vacant congregations in Rockbridge County, working under the direction of the Rev. D. F. Bittle. The location of these congregations is not known, but it appears the pastors from Augusta County had been visiting them.

BETHANY LUTHERAN CHURCH
Rockbridge County, Va.

BETHANY PARISH

Bethany, five miles northeast of Lexington, had its beginning with the services held in Rehoboth schoolhouse, in the early fifties, by Pastors C. Beard, X. J. Richardson, and D. F. Bittle, a group of Lutheran families having recently moved from Augusta County to this community. The church was built, and the congregation organized in 1859, under the ministry of the Rev. J. M. Shreckhise. The first church council consisted of H. Teaford, J. P. Cook, Geo. B. Shaner, J. H. Teaford, and the trustees were J. P. Houseman, Philip Engleman, and J. P. Cook. The present church, located a short distance west of the former site, was erected in 1904, and is valued at $10,000. The parsonage stands quite near. The membership of the congregation is 127, while that of the Sunday school is 111.

The following pastors have served this parish:

J. M. Shreckhise, 1859-1860   J. W. Shuey, 1897-1907
W. S. McClanahan, 1860-1866   J. I. Coiner, 1908-1913
J. M. Shreckhise, 1867-1897   J. W. Shuey, 1913-1924
J. P. Obenschain (Assistant)   W. B. Oney, (supply)
R. H. Cline, 1926-

The Rev. A. B. Obenschain is a son of Bethany congregation.

New Mt. Olive, called Mt. Olive until 1900, appears on the register of churches, in the minutes of Synod in 1880, since which time a list of individual congregations of the Synod has been carried continuously. The congregation is believed to be much older than this, and is likely one of the vacant congregations to which the Rev. S. Filler, was sent in 1842. When the new church was erected in 1900, it took the place of a very old church which stood on a nearby location. It has been served in connection with Bethany during the greater part of the time of which we have record. While not formerly a part of the Bethany parish it is being served by the Bethany pastor, the Rev. R. H. Cline. The church, a neat frame chapel, is valued at $4000. The membership is forty-four with a Sunday school of eighty-four.

Buena Vista

Trinity congregation was organized in September, 1891, shortly after the town began to build. The church, brick, the first good church to be erected in the town, was dedicated November 20, 1892. Few missions established by the Virginia Synod have begun with better promise than this one, however, the collapse of the boom and the final closing of certain large industries caused the removal of many members, which migration continued until few were left. Having no parsonage, it was difficult to keep a resident pastor. Much of the time services were held but once each month. The effort to make the congregation self-sustaining continued until 1923, when it was disbanded and the church sold.

Those who served as pastor or temporary supply, are as follows: J. W. S. Shepherd, E. E. Shantz, V. R. Stickley, J. I. Miller, D. D., R. A. Helms, A. D. R. Hancher, W. B. Aull, J. M. Shreckhise, J. G. Graichen, J. F. Bruch, W. A. Craun, Peter Miller, J. A. Morehead, D. D., L. A. Fox, D. D., J. C. Seegers, D. D., Paul Sieg, J. A. Shealy, C. W. Cassell, and P. A. Atkins.

Spring Valley—A congregation by this name, was established three miles east of Fairfield, and a small frame church built in 1890. D. B. Foltz and O. S. Strole were the trustees. Those composing the congregation had recently moved from Page County, and prior to building the church worshiped in Donalds schoolhouse. It belonged to the Tennessee Synod until 1897, after which it came into the Virginia Synod. The people having moved away the congregation was disbanded in 1912, and the property sold. The pastors were:

J. W. Hausenfluck, 1891-1897 W. B. Aull, 1902-1904
J. M. Shreckhise, 1897-1901 J. M. Shreckhise, 1904-

ROCKINGHAM COUNTY
Rockingham Parish

There are two parishes by the same name in the county—that of the old Virginia Synod belonging to the Staunton conference, and that of the old Tennessee Synod which is now in the New Market conference.

The former consists of Frieden's, Trinity at Bridgewater, and St. James' at Mt. Sidney, in Augusta County, (St. James', although in the parish since 1922, is being served in connection with Salem).

Frieden's, nine miles southwest of Harrisonburg, was established as early as 1749, since in that year, a small building was erected to be used as a church and schoolhouse. The Lutherans and Reformed have shared equally in ownership and use of the property, although the Reformed appears to have been the stronger from the beginning. The second church, larger and better than the first, built of hewed logs, was torn away and built into a residence in 1819, when the brick church was erected.

This building originally, was very similar to that at McGaheysville, built fifteen years earlier. It could be entered by either of three doors, one in each end and one on the east side. A gallery extended across each end and the east side. The pulpit, nine feet from the floor, against the west wall, was reached by a stairway of fourteen steps, on each side of which was a railing of hand carved bric-a-brac work painted green. A sounding board was over the pulpit, and under was a small inclosure, one step above the floor, in which the singing-master sat. This was also used by the clerk to record the communicants, and later, at times when there were but few hearers, it was used by the preacher. The interior was modernized in 1874, by closing two of the doors and removing the side and north gallery and the high pulpit.

We know little of the early pastors of either Lutheran or Reformed congregations. The Rev. Daniel Huffman, whose death occurred in 1798, and who is buried in the cemetery, had labored here a number of years, but it is not certain to which denomination he belonged. The Rev. Dr. John Brown of the Reformed church was pastor from 1799 to 1850. In 1801, he drew up a series of "Church Articles and Fundamental Rules" which has served as a constitution. At this time Jacob Zander and John Early were the Lutheran elders. The Lutheran congregation has suffered from a number of long pastoral vacancies, while the Reformed church has been well supplied. Regular Lutheran services are not being held at present, though the congregation retains all its property rights and privileges.

The following pastors have served the Lutheran congregation in the order here given, but dates are too uncertain to give, prior to 1856: Gotlieb Deshler, Daniel Huffman (?), John G. Butler (Botler), Peter Ahl, Adolph Spindle, Geo. Reimensnyder, Jacob Stirewalt, Jesse Hoover, D. F. Bittle, J. J. Reimensnyder, Peter Schickel, J. J. Suman.

The following pastors served after 1856:

V. F. Bolton, 1856-1857	I. P. Hawkins, 1886-1890
J. M. Graybill, 1858-1860	J. L. Buck, 1891-1893
G. W. Holland, 1860-1872	J. W. Strickler, 1893-1896
J. H. Barb, 1873-1881	C. E. Hershberger, 1897-1900
G. W. Campbell, 1882-1883	W. B. Oney, 1900-1906
M. G. G. Scherer, 1885-1886	G. E. Shuey, 1908-1914

N. E. Cooper, (supply) 1917   C. C. Snyder, (supply) 1919
J. A. L. Miller, 1920-1922

Trinity. When Peter Shickel was licensed by the Virginia Synod in 1838, he, having received a call to certain vacancies in Rockingham County, took up his residence at Bridgewater, where he labored until 1855. Samuel Dinkle, being delegate to Synod in 1839, indicates there was already a congregation at Bridgewater. The deed to the church lot was made in 1848, and the first church built in 1868; the second and present church having been built on the same lot in 1881. A female Seminary was conducted here by the Rev. W. H. Dinkle and the Rev. G. W. Holland, in 1866, and several years following. The membership of the congregation has been decreased by removals to such an extent, that regular services are not being held at this time. The parsonage of the parish is located at Bridgewater. The pastors of these congregations have been, almost in every case, those who have served at Frieden's.

St. James'. The sketch of this congregation appears in connection with Salem in Augusta County.

Union Church at Cross Keys. Services were held here by Lutheran ministers at a very early date. The church figured in the meetings, of the Special Virginia Conference from 1793 to 1817—the last meeting of which we have record adjourned to meet in this church. The Lutherans had equal interest with the Presbyterians in the property. The last reference in the minutes of Synod is of 1850, the Rev. S. Filler, being the pastor. It is now Cross Keys Presbyterian church.

Dayton. A Lutheran church built here in 1853, and for a number of years served by the pastors of old Rockingham parish of the Virginia Synod, was later sold to the church of the Brethren, the members transferring their membership to the nearest Lutheran church.

ROCKINGHAM PARISH
New Market Conference

The Rockingham parish of the New Market conference consists of: McGaheysville, Bethany (St. Jacob's), Trinity, St. Paul's, at Mt. Solon in Augusta County, and St. John's.

McGaheysville is called by the name of the village, or the "Peaked Mountain" church, from the peaked appearance of the southern end of the Massanutten mountain overshadowing it. Here, prior to 1750, German people of the Lutheran and Reformed faiths established homes, and as early as 1763 built a church. The first church was built of logs and in it was conducted a school taught by Gottfried Christian Luthmanns Leondardt. In 1768, the second church was dedicated by the Rev. John Schwarbach. The third church, a large frame building, with high ceiling, extended gallery and high pulpit was dedicated on May 27, 1804, by Christian Streit, Lutheran minister, and the Rev. John Brown, Reformed minister. This church, with some alteration is yet standing and is used as a place of worship by the few Lutherans yet remaining in the community. It was used by both congregations, until 1885, when the Reformed congregation withdrew and built the Brown Memorial church on an adjoining lot. The church records, written in German until 1825, are said to be the most complete of any old church in the county. The agreement entered into by the two congregations on October 31, 1769 is one of the most interesting documents of its kind anywhere to be found. As complete as are the records of this old church not all of the names of those who ministered unto the spiritual welfare of the people have been preserved. The following pastors' names have been recorded:

John Schwarbach, 1768-   Henry Wetzel, 1852-1858
Jacob Frank, 1776-   J. E. Seneker, 1864-
——— Schmidt, 1783-   Jacob Killian, 1864-1865
Christian Streit, 1788-   Irenaeus Conder, 1865-1895
William Carpenter, 1789   R. H. Cline, 1896-1898
V. G. C. Stockus, 1795-1797   M. A. Ashby, 1902-1907
Geo. Riemenschnieder, 1812-1817   C. K. Rhodes, 1913-1920
Michael Meyerhoeffer, 1821-1827   H. D. Chapman, 1921-1925
                  H. E. H. Sloop, 1925-

Bethany, six miles south of Harrisonburg, called St. Jacob's, or Spader's church was organized about 1843, by the Rev. Henry Wetzel. The congregation has had two church buildings, both frame, the first was erected about the time of the organization and was used much of the time as a schoolhouse; the second, much larger than the first, was built in 1874. It has been remodeled and improved to such an extent that it appears quite new, and is valued at $4,000. The membership of the congregation is forty-five with a Sunday school of eighty-five.
The pastors who have served Bethany congregation are:

Henry Wetzel, 1842-1858   J. W. Hausenfluck, 1892-1911
J. E. Seneker, 1863-1865   C. K. Rhodes, 1913-1920
Irenaeus Conder, 1867-1892   H. D. Chapman, 1921-1925
                  H. E. H. Sloop, 1925-

Trinity, seven miles east of Harrisonburg, was first known as Armentrouts, then as St. Phillip's in 1825, but as Trinity, since 1864. The list of subscribers toward a church building in 1787 and constitution adopted in 1807, at which time Armentrout's church was standing, are the two outstanding dates in the early records of this congregation. The name Gottlieb Deshler, a scholarly Lutheran minister of that day, appears on this subscription list in 1787, but no other minister's names appear on existing records until 1851, when Pastor Ambrose Henkel administered a baptism. The present church built about 1864, is more than a mile northwest of the old location.
The membership of the congregation is thirty-six and that of the Sunday school is thirty-two. The church property is valued at $800. The following pastors have served this congregation:

Ambrose Henkel, 1850-1852	P. C. Wike, 1895-1899
Henry Wetzel, 1853-1861	E. H. Kohn, 1900-1901
Jacob Stirewalt ⎰ 1863-1864	J. W. Hausenfluck, 1901-1913
J. E. Seneker ⎱	C. K. Rhodes, 1913-1920
Irenaeus Conder, 1867-1894	H. D. Chapman, 1920-1925
H. E. H. Sloop, 1925-	

St. Paul's, at Mt. Solon, belonging to the Rockingham parish of the New Market conference, was formed from a colony from Koiner's church early in the eighteenth century. The first entries in the record book are those made in 1838 by Jacob Killian, who began to serve them shortly after he became pastor at Koiner's. The name at first was the Lutheran Chapel, but later it was called by the name it now bears. The first church was dedicated in 1844, by the Rev. Henry Wetzel, and the Rev. Ambrose Henkel. The present membership of the congregation is fifty, while that of the Sunday school is thirty-two. The property is valued at $3,000. The following pastors have served the congregation:

Jacob Killian, 1838-1841	J. W. Hausenfluck, 1878-1912
Henry Wetzel, 1841-1861	C. K. Rhodes, 1913-1920
J. E. Seneker, 1863-1867	H. D. Chapman, 1921-1925
Irenaeus Conder, 1868-1874	H. E. H. Sloop, 1925-

Emmanuel—According to an old record book, a congregation by this name existed at an early date near Mt. Solon. The records are written in two forms of handwriting, one in a crude, imperfect German, beginning in 1803, the other in a very fine and beautiful script, beginning in 1801. Three ministers are named, but they are known to be Reformed. Two lists are found headed, "Communicants of the Evangelical Lutheran Church" but these are of a later date. The prominent names found are: Rader, Kirchhof, Heise, Pfleiffer, Hoffart, Hoffman, Fleming, Grim, Messerschmidt and Degen.

It is believed that Emmanuel congregation was the forerunner of St. Paul's mentioned above. The church in which Emmanuel congregation worshiped is now used by the church of the Brethren. Burials are still made in the cemetery by some of the old Lutheran families.

St. John's, nine miles northeast of Harrisonburg, originally Lutheran and Reformed, bears a date upon its records of 1808, but dates upon the stones in the old cemetery show burial as early as 1790. The small log church standing here in 1812, was the place of worship until 1870, when it was torn down and rebuilt, the old side logs being used for the ends of the new building and new and longer logs were used for the sides. The recent incomplete reports, owing to pastoral vacancies, prevents us from giving the present numerical strength, and an estimated value of the property.

From the best that we can gather, the congregation was served by those Lutheran ministers who visited and labored in Rockingham County, until after the Civil War. Those recorded are:

Geo. W. Holland, 1867-1871
J. H. Barb, 1872-1881
W. G. Campbell, 1882-1883
M. G. G. Sherer, 1885-1886
I. P. Hawkins, 1886-1890

J. L. Buck, 1891-1892
J. W. Strickler, 1893-1896
C. E. Hershberger, 1897-1900
W. B. Oney, 1900-1906
Geo. E. Shuey, 1908-1914

J. A. L. Miller, 1920-1922

Since 1922 the congregation has been supplied chiefly by the pastor at Harrisonburg, and W. W. J. Ritchie, until this past summer (1929) the congregation was connected with Rockingham parish, the Rev. H. E. H. Sloop, pastor.

RADER'S CHURCH
Timberville, Va.

TIMBERVILLE PARISH

Rader's is located one half mile west of Timberville. On May 20, 1765, Adam Reider and Alexander Painter deeded to Michael Neice a parcel of land, "in behalf of the church called the Lutheran church." This is the first record of Rader's, and is given as the date of its organization. From the words in the deed, "beginning back of said meeting house where it now stands," it is evident a church building already stood upon this land, therefore, we know that Rader's church, which name is taken from one of the parties deeding the land, is older than 1765. The old deed, written in German script, has been preserved. The dates of the building of the first and second churches are not known, but the third church, a log building, was erected in 1806. The fourth and present building, erected in 1878, on land purchased on the opposite side of the road for church and additional cemetery space, is a large building with interior walls frescoed. The first communion record, which carries twenty-four names, is of November 25, 1798.

The first Synodical connection of this congregation was to the North Carolina Synod in 1813. In 1820, it became a charter member of the Tennessee Synod and remained in the Virginia Conference until the merger with the Virginia Synod in 1925. There are no records to show who was the pastor when the church was organized and until 1783. The congregation numbers 157, and has a Sunday school of 60. The property is valued at $10,000.

The following is the list of the pastors since 1783:

Paul Henkel, 1783-	Jacob Stirewalt, 1858-1869
Ambrose Henkel, 1829-1837	John S. Bennick, 1869-1881
Jacob Stirewalt, 1837-1839	J. P. Stirewalt, D. D., 1882-1919
Ambrose Henkel, 1839-1855	V. L. Fulmer, 1920-1923
Socrates Henkel, 1855-1858	L. L. Lohr, D. D., 1923-1925
	A. W. Ballentine, 1927-

St. Paul's located three miles southeast of Timberville, was organized in 1891, by Pastor J. P. Stirewalt, with thirty-eight members, who came largely from Rader's. Two years previous services had been held by the Rev. Dr. S. Henkel, and by Pastor Stirewalt, in the groves and in a room over a paint shop. The church, a frame building, erected on land purchased from J. D. Mills, was first used in June, 1891, and dedicated in September of that year. The Sunday school was begun shortly after the organization and now numbers twenty-four. The membership of the congregation is seventy-four. The church property is valued at $2,000. It has throughout its history been connected with the Timberville parish and served by her pastors.

St. John's, at the foot of the Shenandoah mountain, northwest of Timberville, was organized in the home of Harrison Branner, by the Rev. H. Wetzel on September 25, 1870. The members came out of Rader's church, following their leader, who, not being in harmony with the Tennessee Synod, united in a movement to establish the Concordia Synod of Virginia. After nine years, however, they returned to the Mother Synod, and Pastor Wetzel continued to serve them until 1889, since which time they have been regularly connected with the Timberville parish.

The old church, a log building, was improved by weatherboarding and plastering in 1907. The membership of the congregation is sixty-nine. The property of the church is valued at $700.

HARRISONBURG PARISH

Muhlenberg—when J. A. Seiss was licensed "To perform the duties of a minister of the Gospel," in May 1842, and was directed to visit Union Church in Rockingham County and such other churches as are unsupplied in that region, he took up his residence at Harrisonburg, and shortly thereafter, began holding regular services in the town. At the next convention of Synod the "enterprise at Harrisonburg was commended and Brother Seiss encouraged to go forward." Following the withdrawal of Pastor Seiss in 1843, Pastors J. Suman and P. Shickel appeared to have been in

MUHLENBERG CHURCH
Harrisonburg, Va.

charge of the work for well nigh a decade. The congregation was received into Synod in 1849, a lot purchased in 1850, and the church, a brick building, dedicated May 8, 1851. During the Civil War it was used as a Federal hospital, and not again used for worship until 1868. A new brick building was erected on the same location in 1888. There followed a long, hard struggle and many discouragements, until 1925 when the congregation became self-supporting. There has been a steady and substantial growth in membership and at present the congregation is looking forward to a larger house of worship. The present membership is 315, with a Sunday school of 165. The property is valued at $15,000, exclusive of a $7,000 parsonage.

The following pastors have served this congregation:

J. A. Seiss, 1842-1843   J. J. Suman
S. Filler   V. F. Bolton
Isaac Baker   J. M. Graybill, 1856-1860

Geo. W. Holland, 1860-1862	G. E. Krauth, 1899-1902
W. H. Dinkle	G. E. Shuey, 1903-1908
W. S. McClanahan, 1867-	E. L. Folk, 1911-1915
Geo. W. Holland, -1872	E. A. Repass, Ph. D., 1915-1917
J. H. Moser, 1879-1883	J. L. Smith, 1917-1920
T. O. Keister, 1886-1890	E. W. Leslie, 1921-1922
H. E. Ebling, 1890-1891	H. E. Beatty, 1922-1927
C. N. A. Yonce, 1892-1894	P. A. Atkins, 1927
G. E. Shuey, 1895-1899	C. M. Coffelt, 1927-

Lutheran Ministers From Rockingham County Congregations:

S. Filler _____ Frieden's
W. H. Dinkle _____ Frieden's
J. I. Miller, D. D. _____ Frieden's
Peter Miller _____ Frieden's
J. S. Bennick _____ Rader's
J. P. Stirewalt, D. D. _____ Rader's
M. L. Pence _____ Rader's
A. M. Pence _____ Rader's
M. A. Ashby _____ Rader's
C. H. Pence _____ Rader's
E. H. Jones _____

SHENANDOAH COUNTY

Shenandoah is the strongest Lutheran county in the State. Within its boundaries are twenty-seven congregations of the Synod of Virginia, aggregating 3842 members, and two of the Joint Synod of Ohio, Patmos near Woodstock and Mt. Zion in the Fort Valley. Eight of the twenty-nine are centenarians. As is the case in Rockingham County, the sketches of Shenandoah are arranged according to location rather than the date of organization.

New Market Parish
New Market Conference

Emmanuel had its origin in the Davidsburg church (St. Matthew's). The date of its organization is usually given as 1840, when the first lay-delegate attended the Tennessee Synod from New Market, but the congregation has an earlier history. The controversies disturbing the Lutheran churches in the county, the first half of the century, rent the Davidsburg church in twain, in 1820. The two tendencies—one toward and one away from strict adherence to the historic Lutheran Confessions, each had a following in the congregation. Paul Henkel's convictions were decidedly with the former tendency. When the Rev. S. S. Schmucker, whose convictions were with the latter, came to New Market, the feeling was intensified, and found outward expression in the church doors being closed against the organizer and former pastor of the congregation, the Rev. Paul Henkel. Those in sympathy with Mr. Henkel, ·

attended services at Armentrout's and Rader's (both Tenn. Synod churches) and at times gathered for worship at such places as could be secured in New Market, frequently in Solomon's schoolhouse, resulting in the formation of Emmanuel congregation.

The first church was built in 1848, on ground donated by Samuel Godfrey Henkel. It was a brick structure, with gallery across the rear. In 1892, this building was replaced by a larger and better brick building, with churchly appointments, and Sunday school rooms, separated from the church by sliding doors. A pipe organ was also installed. In 1920 a brick porch was added as an entrance to the vestibule. Surrounding the church is a well kept cemetery, Paul Henkel and his wife, being buried near the entrance.

In 1898 a commodious and comfortable parsonage was built. The membership of the congregation is 230, that of the Sunday school is 154. The church property is valued at $15,000, the parsonage at $6,000.

The following is a list of the ministers who have served the congregation:

Paul Henkel, 1822-1825	Socrates Henkel, 1850-1896
Ambrose Henkel, 1825-1838	Ernest H. Kohn, 1897-1903
Jacob Stirewalt, 1838-1843	E. L. Wessinger, 1903-1908
Ambrose Henkel, 1843-1859	Enoch Hite, 1909-1911

William J. Finck, D. D., 1912-

Mt. Zion—The Rev. Socrates Henkel began preaching at Kipp's schoolhouse in August, 1853, and six months later organized Mt. Zion congregation (Feb., 12). Services continued to be held in the schoolhouse, except in the summers they were held in the grove, until 1872, when the church was built on ground given by George Lohr. It is a medium sized frame building, with gallery across the rear. Extensive improvements were made in 1917, and a bell, the gift of S. Frank Hess, was placed in the tower. The church stands in a grove facing the road. The congregation has since its organization been served by the same pastors as Emmanuel. The membership is 125, with a Sunday school of 79. The property is valued at $2,000.

NEW MARKET PARISH
Winchester Conference

The New Market parish of the Winchester Conference, formerly of the Potomac Conference of the old Virginia Synod, is composed of St. Matthew's, standing on the northern edge of New Market; St. Mark's, at Forestville, and St. Martin's at Maures Mill, two miles northwest of New Market. The parsonage, an attractive residence, is located at New Market, across Main Street from the church.

St. Matthew's congregation is the fruit of the labors of Paul Henkel and the result of his moving to New Market in 1790. Upon his arrival in this community he found but a very few Lutherans, but the Zirkles had settled to the west and southwest of the former "Cross Roads."

CHURCHES OF NEW MARKET PARISH

St. Mark's Church	St. Matthew's Church	St. Martin's Church
Forestville, Va.	New Market, Va.	Maures Mill, Va.

With the aid of Lewis Zirkle he selected a proper site for a church and Mr. Zirkle donated a half-acre lot for the purpose of building a church. In the spring of 1791, he began to preach in the neighborhood; in June of that year the first timbers were cut, and in April, 1792, Paul Henkel held the first services in the new church. It was built of logs and provided with glass windows, hauled by Paul Henkel himself from Philadelphia in 1793. Later a tower with a 220 pound bell was erected in front of the church. It was known as the Davidsburg Church. Paul Henkel was the first pastor and continued to serve the congregation until 1820, though with a number of necessary interruptions, since he moved to Staunton in 1794, to North Carolina in 1800, to Point Pleasant in 1811 and again in 1816, each time returning to New Market after an absence of a few years, and taking up his work again. Even while away he would visit the congregation, administer the sacraments and preach to the people both in German and English. John Foltz frequently supplied the congregation from 1794 to 1806. Beginning with 1811, J. Nicholas Schmucker, and his brother, John Peter, supplied the church. In December, 1820, S. S. Schmucker began his work in New Market, at the direction of his two uncles, J. N. and J. P. Schmucker. A school was established in connection with the church in 1806. The old church was replaced by a larger and better one in 1848. In 1890, the present brick church was built.

During the battle of New Market, May 15, 1864, a Federal battery was planted in the cemetery of St. Matthews. The shell which lodged in the lamp post in front of the church during the battle, may be seen there today.

The membership of the congregation is 194, and that of the Sunday school is 167. The property is valued at $12,000.

The following pastors have served the congregation:

Paul Henkel, 1792-1794	J. P. Cline, 1828-1832
John Foltz, 1794-1797	Samuel Oswald, 1833-1844
Paul Henkel, 1797-1800	J. P. Cline, 1847-1866
John Foltz, 1801-1802	J. A. Snyder, D. D., 1866-1907
Paul Henkel, 1806-1811	E. A. Repass, Ph. D., 1907-1915
Paul Henkel, 1813-1816	J. B. Derrick, 1916-1919
Peter Schmucker, 1817-1819	J. W. Link, 1919-1922
S. S. Schmucker, 1820-1925	T. A. Graves, 1924-1927
S. K. Hoshour, 1825-1827	R. S. Poffenberger, 1927-

St. Mark's was organized by Pastor J. A. Snyder, in 1873, from those members who withdrew from Solomon church because of internal dissensions growing out of doctrinal differences. For a short time they worshiped in the old church and afterwards in the Zirkle schoolhouse, at Forestville, until the present church, a frame building, was completed in 1874. The congregation was, from the beginning, connected with St. Matthews and has, throughout its history, been served by her pastors.

The membership of St. Mark's is seventy-four and it maintains a Sunday school of eighty. The church property is valued at $4,000.

St. Martin's was organized by J. A. Snyder, in 1890, out of members of St. Matthew's church. Services were first held at Oak Shade schoolhouse near Maures Mill, until the church, which was begun in that same year, was completed. It has always been in the New Market parish and served by her pastors.

The membership of the congregation is 125, while that of the Sunday School is 122. The church property is valued at $4,000.

FORESTVILLE PARISH

St. Mary's, three miles west of Mt. Jackson, was known as Pine Church until the present building was erected. Prior to 1783 the Lutheran people of the Forest appear to have worshiped at Rude's Hill on the Valley Pike three miles south of Mt. Jackson. This old church was probably built as early as 1760 and was the meeting house of the entire community. It is believed to have been one of the regular appointments of Peter Muhlenberg, there being a tradition that he repeated here the famous War Sermon, first preached at Woodstock, at which time a large number of the Forest people enlisted in the Colonial army. On July 25, 1787, John Pennywitt deeded five acres of land for (Pine) church and graveyard, the church, Lutheran and Reformed, already standing on the ground having been built in 1783. In 1873 the Lutheran congregation built the church now standing about one-quarter of a mile northeast of the old church. About the same time the Reformed congregation built Grace Church, one and one-half miles north. St. Mary's is built of heavy pine timber, with interior walls beautifully frescoed. The property is valued at $4,000. The congregation belonged to the Tennessee Synod, and came into the Synod of

CHURCHES OF FORESTVILLE PARISH
Solomon's Lutheran Church
Forestville, Va.   St. Mary's Lutheran Church
Mt. Jackson, Va.

Virginia with the other congregations of the Virginia Conference in 1925. The congregation numbers 123 with a Sunday school of 81.

The following are the pastors of St. Mary's:

Paul Henkel, 1783-1825	J. P. Stirewalt, 1882-1904
Ambrose Henkel, 1825-1855	A. R. Beck, 1904-1911
Jacob Stirewalt, 1857-1869	D. L. Miller, 1912-1916
J. S. Bennick, 1869-1881	F. M. Speagle, 1917-1925
D. W. Zipperer, 1925	

It appears that John Foltz and Adam Miller were assistants to the Rev. Paul Henkel, and J. P. Cline and Socrates Henkel to the Rev. Ambrose Henkel.

Solomon's, a daughter of Pine Church, appears to have been organized about 1793 under the leadership of Paul Henkel. The first church built in 1793 on land deeded by Henry Rausch and wife, was dedicated November 15, 1795 by Paul Henkel and Christian Streit, Lutheran, and Jacob and Daniel Hoffman, Reformed, ministers. About fifty years later members of the Reformed congregation withdrew to the County Line Reformed Church. Shortly after this a portion of the Lutheran members withdrew for doctrinal and practical reasons, and later organized St. Mark's at Forestville. Since then Solomon's congregation has had the full use of the church property. The present church was built by the Lutherans of Solomon's congregation in 1876. It is built of heavy pine timbers and presents an imposing appearance, with interior beautifully frescoed. The old building was sold at auction in 1879 and the proceeds divided equally between the Lutheran and Reformed, the two Lutheran congregations sharing equally. Solomon's became a member of the North Carolina Synod in 1813 and of the Tennessee Synod in 1820 and came into the Virginia Synod with the other congregations of the Virginia Conference in 1925.

The membership of the congregation is 278 and of the Sunday school 165. The church property is valued at $4500.

The parsonage of this parish, a frame dwelling valued at $4000, is located near Mt. Jackson. The pastors of Solomon's have been as follows:

Paul Henkel, 1793	Samuel Oswald, 1836
J. N. Schmucker, 1807	Jacob Stirewalt, 1845-1869
John Foltz, 1809	J. S. Bennick, 1869-1881
Paul Henkel, 1812	J. P. Stirewalt, 1882-1904
J. P. Schmucker, 1814-1820	A. R. Beck, 1904-1911
S. S. Schmucker, 1821-1825	D. L. Miller, 1912-1916
S. K. Hoshour, 1826	F. M. Speagle, 1917-1925
J. P. Cline, 1828	D. W. Zipperer, 1925-

MT. JACKSON PARISH

Mt. Jackson parish, composed of Mt. Calvary, in Mt. Jackson; Bethel, near Hamburg; and St. James at Hudson's Cross Roads, was so constituted in 1884, when the Rev. W. E. Stahler became pastor of these three churches. The parsonage of the parish located at Mt. Jackson, was built in 1889, and is a substantial frame structure, valued at $6,000.

The pastors serving the parish have been:

W. E. Stahler, 1884-1887	M. L. Canup, 1907-1910
L. A. Mann, 1888-1890	B. A. Copenhaver, 1911-1918
E. L. Folk, 1891-1900	P. L. Royer, 1919-1923
E. L. Folk, 1902-1906	R. L. Haus, 1924-1927
	C. J. Rice, 1928-

Mt. Calvary, at Mt. Jackson, first appears on the Register of Churches in 1844, being served together with Zion, Solomon's, and Cross Roads, by Pastor A. R. Rude, but it is believed that services were held here much earlier than this date by the pastors at New Market and Woodstock. "The brick church," a community landmark, built by Lutherans and Reformed more than a century ago, was their first place of worship. The first Lutheran church, a frame building located on Main Street opposite the present site, was built in 1860. The building was destroyed by fire October 18, 1882; a second church, a brick building erected in 1884 on the same site, was also burned October 10, 1885. The present structure was begun at once and completed that year. The Rev. J. G. Morris preached the sermon at each dedicatory service.

It is believed that the Rev. J. P. Cline served this congregation until his death in 1866; the Rev. J. A. Snyder, until 1878; and the Rev. J. S. Moser labored here until 1883, serving also the Lutheran congregation in Harrisonburg. Since this date it has been a part of the Mt. Jackson parish, whose pastors are named above.

The membership of the congregation is 118; that of the Sunday school is 120. The value of the property is $12,000.

St. James, at Hudson's Cross Roads, was in existence as early as 1842, an old log church (Lutheran, built in 1844), being used by both the Reformed and Lutherans until 1852, when the former built to themselves. The present Lutheran church, a frame building, valued at $2,500 was built in 1898. The early history of this congregation and that of Mt. Jackson appears to have run parallel. The following pastors are known to have served the congregation prior to the formation of the present Mt. Jackson parish—J. Summer, A. R. Rude, W. H. Cone, Levi Keller, 1867-1871; Peter Miller, 1871-1879. The Rev. G. W. Spiggle, the Rev. J. A. Snyder, and the Rev. M. G. G. Scherer, supplied until 1884.

*Bethel,** near Hamburg, northwest of Mt. Jackson was formed by those who withdrew from old Zion church (Tennessee Synod) in 1858, because of internal dissensions, the Rev. W. H. Cone being the organizing pastor. The new congregation united with the Virginia Synod, but it continued to worship in the old church for a period of about two years, at which time it was closed to them. They at once took steps to build, the cornerstone of the church having been laid on the day of the firing upon Fort Sumter, but owing to the war disturbances the building, a frame structure, was not completed until 1867. In 1909, the church was extensively improved and beautified, which makes it quite attractive and churchly in appearance both as to the exterior and the interior. On January 1, 1861 the congregation was given its share (225 acres) of land granted from Lord Fairfax to Zion church in 1781. The church not including the farm is valued at $5,000. The membership is seventy-four and the Sunday school numbers eighty. The Rev. Levi Keller, was pastor of this congregation from 1867 to 1871; the Rev. Peter Miller, from 1871 to 1879; the Rev. M. G. G. Scherer served from 1882 to 1883. In 1884 Bethel came into the Mt. Jackson parish.

Edinburg Parish

The Edinburg parish as it is now constituted, consists of Zion, five miles west of Edinburg, St. Jacob's near Conicville, Salem northwest of Mt. Jackson and St. David's in the Fort Valley. These churches have not been associated in a parish for a long period, and therefore it is necessary to give a separate list of pastors for each.

Zion—The recorded history of this congregation begins on January 9, 1781, when Lord Fairfax granted 465 acres of land to the Lutheran people living on Stony Creek. The grant was to the Lutherans alone, however, they and the Reformed united in building a church. It was

---

*Dr. Wayland in the History of Shenandoah County, tells of "Old Bethel" on the river below Red Bank, which tradition says was a Lutheran church, and was built as early as the old Rude Hill church. It may have been a forerunner of Zion. The old church was burned. A Methodist church was built on the site, in which building Bishop Asbury preached in 1790.

dedicated on June 22, 1788, Pastors Abraham Gottlieb Deschler for the Lutherans, and Bernhard Willy for the Reformed, conducting the services. This church, a log building was burned, and the second church being found unsatisfactory was replaced by another in 1840. The present building was erected in 1894. In 1892 the Reformed congregation withdrew and built St. John's church. When the division of sentiment arose between the Virginia and Tennessee Synods, the land belonging to the congregation was, by mutual agreement, divided, Bethel receiving 225 acres and Zion retaining 240 acres. A commodious dwelling and a ten acre lot near the church are set aside for the pastor's use. In recent years the congregation has lost many members by removals from the community. The present membership is fifty-six. The church property, exclusive of the farm is valued at $3000.

The body of Pastor John Henkel, a brother of Paul Henkel, was buried under the pulpit of the church.

The pastors serving Zion have been as follows:

A. G. Deschler, 1786-1800	Ambrose Henkel, 1854-
John Henkel, 1800-1804	J. H. Hunton, 1857-1861
John P. Schmucker, Supply	Henry Wetzel, 1861-1869
J. N. Schmucker, Supply	J. S. Bennick, 1870-1876
Geo. F. Steahlin, 1835-1837	J. P. Stirewalt, 1877-1881
J. P. Cline, 1837-	S. Henkel, D. D., 1883-1884
George Schmucker, 1838-	P. C. Wike, 1887-1888
John Hamilton, 1840-1841	A. L. Crouse, 1889-
A. R. Rude, 1842-1844	R. H. Cline, 1890-1894
Jacob Stirewalt, 1845-	A. L. Boliek, 1894-1902
Thomas Miller, 1846-1850	J. L. Deaton, 1902-1906
Levi Keller, 1850-	W. L. Darr, 1907-

St. David's—Powell's Fort, in which is St. David's—a valley of peculiar charm in the Massanutten Mountains east of Woodstock, was not only an early settlement, but also an early Lutheran preaching point. The first church built in the Fort was largely Lutheran in building and in use, and in it the patriot-preacher Muhlenberg is said to have preached.* Paul Henkel confirmed a class here on August 24, 1788, and John Foltz administered Baptism in 1809. While there are few records available, and the names of the early ministers are not known; except as mentioned, it appears certain that St. David's developed parallel with the other early churches in the County and was cared for by the same pastors. Being somewhat isolated, it was never numerically strong but has taken its place in the work along with the other congregations of the Tennessee Synod. A log building served as schoolhouse and church until 1877, when the present church was built. Internal dissension in 1882 led to the withdrawal of certain members, and the organization and building of Mt. Zion as a member of the Joint Synod of Ohio. The present membership of St. David's is forty-five and the property is valued at $900.

---
*Wayland's History of Shenandoah County, page 179.

The pastors since 1834 are:

G. F. Staehlin, 1834-1835	J. E. Seneker, 1882-1884
J. N. Schmucker, 1836-	J. W. Hausenfluck, 1885-1900
Jacob Stirewalt, 1851-1860	A. L. Boliek, 1900-1902
H. Wetzel, 1863-1866	J. L. Deaton, 1902-1903
Jacob Stirewalt, 1867-	M. L. Pence, 1903-1907
W. H. Swaney, 1868-1869	O. W. Aderholt, 1909-1910
H. Wetzel, 1870-1875	J. S. Wessinger, 1911-1914
J. E. Seneker, 1876-1878	L. L. Huffman, 1915-1918
G. W. Lose, 1879-1880	M. A. Ashby, 1919-1921

W. L. Darr, 1922-

St. Jacob's, called also, Jacob's* church was built in 1838. The land was given to the Lutheran and Reformed churches by Lord Fairfax in 1755, and a church is supposed to have stood here prior to 1838, the first definite date of building. In 1884 the two churches divided the property, and the Lutheran church now in use was built in 1887. The membership is 101 and the property is valued at $2000.

The pastors serving the congregation have been:

George Schmucker, 1838-1842	S. Henkel, 1882-1883
Jacob Stirewalt, 1843-1855	P. C. Wike, 1887-1890
A. Henkel, 1855-1857	R. H. Cline, 1890-1892
Jacob Stirewalt, 1858-1869	A. L. Boliek, 1893-1902
J. P. Stirewalt, 1874-1886	J. L. Deaton, 1902-1906

W. L. Darr, 1907-

Salem congregation was organized on August 20, 1898 by the Rev. J. P. Stirewalt. The church was built in 1876 as a Disciples church. In 1898 it was purchased by Geo. W. Minnick and given to the Lutheran congregation. The dedication took place on August 21. The congregation has always been very small. The property is valued at $600.

The pastors have been:

A. L. Boliek, 1898-1902   J. L. Deaton, 1902-1906

W. L. Darr, 1907-

Orkney Springs Parish

St. Paul's, at Jerome, thirteen miles west of Mt. Jackson; Powder Springs, near Orkney Springs; Morning Star, at Hepners; and Bethel, near Bergton in Rockingham County, have constituted the parish since 1913, all of the churches being, at that time, in the Tennessee Synod.

The parsonage is located at Orkney Springs. The pastors since the formation of the present parish have been:

J. W. Hausenfluck, 1913-1916   J. A. Bourde, 1925-1927
M. L. Pence, 1918-1924   Russel D. Knoebel, 1927-

---

*The name is believed to have been given because of three prominent laymen in the Rinker family named "Jacob," grandfather, father and son, members of the Reformed congregation worshiping here.

CHURCHES OF ORKNEY SPRINGS PARISH

Bethel Lutheran Church
Bergton, Va.

Powder Springs Lutheran Church
Orkney Springs, Va.

St. Paul's Lutheran Church
Jerome, Va.

Morning Star Lutheran Church
Hepners, Va.

St. Paul's came into being in 1827, under the ministry of the Rev. Ambrose Henkel. A log schoolhouse served as a place of worship until the building of the church in 1854. It stood on the land of Godfrey Miller—Lafayette and Jacob Miller being the trustees. The present church, a frame building, larger and better than the former, was built in 1891, and extensively repaired in 1927. It is valued at $5,000. The present membership of the congregation is 223, and the Sunday school is 238. Prior to the formation of the parish the pastors were:

Ambrose Henkel, 1827-1836	J. P. Stirewalt, 1882-1886
Jacob Stirewalt, 1837-1867	P. C. Wike, 1887-1898
W. H. Swaney, 1868-1870	M. L. Pence, 1899-1908
J. S. Bennick, 1870-1879	A. R. Beck, 1908-1911

Powder Springs was organized by the Rev. J. S. Bennick, about 1871 (so called because these are sulphur springs). The Rev. J. N. Schmucker, while pastor at Woodstock, 1806-1846, frequently held services here, and it was also an outpost of "Hudson Cross Roads" church during the term of Pastor Peter Miller (1871-1879). The old schoolhouse was the place of worship. In 1872, a church was built of logs and weatherboarded, and is valued at $1,000. The congregational membership is 137, and that of the Sunday school is 75. The pastors before the present parish was formed were:

J. S. Bennick, 1870-1881	A. L. Boliek, 1893-1902
J. P. Stirewalt, 1882-1888	J. L. Deaton, 1903-1906
A. L. Crouse, 1888-1889	J. P. Stirewalt, 1906-1907
R. H. Cline, 1890-1893	W. L. Darr, 1907-1912

Morning Star was formed in 1887, by those members of Powder Springs living in the Hepners community, the Rev. J. P. Stirewalt being the organizing pastor. The church, a frame building, was erected near the time of the organization and is valued at $1,000.

The membership of this congregation is eighty-four, while that of the Sunday school is sixty-four.

The pastors earlier than 1913 have been:

J. P. Stirewalt, 1887-1893	J. L. Deaton, 1903-1906
A. L. Boliek, 1893-1902	J. P. Stirewalt, 1906-1907
	W. L. Darr, 1907-1912

Bethel, in Rockingham County, was formed by those members of Phanuel church who declined to go with the old congregation into the Ohio Synqd in 1880, the Rev. A. L. Crouse, being the organizing pastor. The church, a frame building, was erected in 1884. Its value is $2,000. The congregation numbers twenty-seven members. The pastors until 1913 were:

A. L. Crouse, 1884	A. L. Boliek, 1893-1902
R. H. Cline, 1890-1893	Vacant, 1902-1913

THE SHENANDOAH COUNTY PARISH

The Shenandoah County Parish includes: Lebanon, west of Strasburg; Mt. Zion, west of Woodstock; and St. Luke's, southwest of Woodstock. The pastor lives in the parsonage near Mt. Zion, which is the property of the Mt. Zion congregation. It is a neat frame residence, electrically lighted. The parish, as it is at present, was so constituted in 1904, and since has been served by the following pastors:

V. R. Stickley, 1904-1905	D. S. Fox, 1915-1918
J. M. Tise, 1905-1909	L. W. Gross, 1918-1923
W. B. Oney, 1909-1914	P. E. Shealy, 1925-

Lebanon church was organized December 2, 1848, in Cross Road schoolhouse by the Rev. John F. Campbell, pastor at Strasburg, with five members, namely: Rev. John Richard, Jacob Windle, Catherine Windle, Mary A. Funkhouser and Catherine Keller. At the end of the second year the membership had increased to forty. Within the year 1858, the church, a frame building, was begun, completed, paid for and dedicated. This building, with some improvements has been used continuously as the house of worship. It is valued at $3,500. The membership now numbers 171, and the Sunday school 153. The pastors previous to the formation of the present parish are:

John F. Campbell, 1848-1849	William Rusmiselle, 1857-1884
Levi Keller, 1849-1856	L. M. Sibole, 1884-1886

Asa Richard, 1887-1899   John E. Bushnell, D. D., 1899-1900
A. M. Smith, 1900-1903

St. Luke's was organized in 1878 by Pastor Peter Miller, and the church was built about that time. It is a frame building valued at $2,500. The membership of the congregation is 95 and of the Sunday school is 112. Prior to the formation of the present parish the following were the pastors:

Peter Miller,   -1879   R. A. Longanecker, 1898-1899
A. A. J. Bushong, 1880-1895   W. H. Riser, 1899-1901
R. A. Longanecker, Supply 1896   J. A. Boord, 1902-1903

Mt. Zion first appears on the roll of congregations in 1891, as a part of the Woodstock parish, under the care of Pastor A. A. J. Bushong. The church, a frame building was dedicated on November 4, 1884. In 1925 a Sunday school room was added and the chancel was remodeled. The estimated value of the property is $4,000. The membership of the congregation is 184, and that of the Sunday school is 115. The congregation has from the beginning been united with St. Luke's, and served by the same pastors.

WOODSTOCK PARISH

Emanuel—The date usually given as that of the organization of Emanuel congregation is 1767, which date is found on the old communion set, and on the old embroidered altar cloth. There is, however, record of an infant baptism four years prior to this date. The first regular pastor was the Rev. J. P. G. Muhlenberg, whose ministry began in 1772 and closed in 1776 when he enlisted in the Colonial army. There seems to have been no other regular pastor until 1804. Those Lutheran ministers who visited Winchester and other points in the lower Valley before and after the Revolution appear to have been at Woodstock also, but they were visitors rather than regular pastors. Paul Henkel was here also, but not as pastor. Mr. Muhlenberg, a regularly authorized Lutheran minister came in response to an urgent call of the German Lutheran people, but that he might not be hindered by the Virginia laws pertaining to religious ordinances, he, upon the advice of certain influential parties in the Colony, accepted ordination by the established church and therefore became the accredited rector of the parish in which Woodstock was located—the Beckford parish. Having met the requirements of the established church, no complaint could be registered against his zeal in behalf of the Lutheran people here, and at the many other points he is known to have visited and preached. The church in which he preached the famous war sermon at Woodstock stood in Main Street at the intersection of Court Street. It was built about 1761, as a kind of a community church, and is known to have stood until 1848.* After the war, when Mr. Muhlenberg returned to Woodstock, he gave his clerical robe to Paul Henkel who appears to have been the only Lutheran minister

*See Wayland's History of Shenandoah County, page 403.

EMANUEL LUTHERAN CHURCH
Woodstock, Va.

EMANUEL LUTHERAN CHURCH
Woodstock, Va.
Built in 1803, Removed 1884

in the community at the time. Not until two decades after the Revolution did the Lutherans take definite steps to build a church of their own, the delay due, no doubt, to the disorganized conditions following the War and the fact that they continued to use the old church. The building begun in 1803 was not completed until two decades afterwards. It was dedicated in 1829, at the organization of the Virginia Synod. The location was 200 feet east of the present church, now a part of the cemetery. A larger and better brick building was erected in 1884, to which a Sunday school room was added in 1904. The first parsonage was purchased during Pastor Levi Keller's second term. The property owned by the congregation, church, parsonage and sexton house is valued at $35,000. The present membership of the congregation is 165, and that of the Sunday school is 154. She has had a number of laymen prominent in the work of the Synod. M. Coffman, who for a long period was Treasurer of the old Virginia Synod, served also as Superintendent of the Sunday school of the congregation for fifty-five years.

The pastors who have served the congregation are:

J. P. G. Muhlenberg, 1772-1776	J. P. Cline, 1848-1853
J. Nicholas Schmucker, 1804-1833	Levi Keller, 1856-1860
J. Ulrich, 1834-1835	J. A. Snyder, 1860-1865
J. Nicholas Schmucker, 1835-1846	Levi Keller, 1867-1870
J. F. Campbell, 1844-1848	Peter Miller, 1871-1879

A. A. J. Bushong, 1880-1901   W. J. D. Scherer, 1907-1909
J. E. Shenk, 1901-1904   S. W. Kuhns, 1911-1922
J. W. F. Kitzmeyer, 1905-1907 R. H. Cline, 1923-1927
                J. P. Derrick, 1927-

MT. CALVARY LUTHERAN CHURCH
Near Woodstock, Va.

Mt. Calvary—In 1850, certain members of the Lutheran and Reformed churches, living in the neighborhood of Sheetz' Mill, three miles northeast of Woodstock, united to build Mt. Calvary. The church was built in 1854. The Lutheran congregation belonged to the Tennessee Synod. About thirty years later a portion of the members under the leadership of the Rev. Henry Wetzel, withdrew and established Patmos, several miles north, which connected itself with the Joint Synod of Ohio. Mt. Calvary, not large from the beginning, is quite near other Lutheran churches and has not had a large numerical growth. Since 1921, it has been served in connection with Emanuel at Woodstock, though not officially in the parish.

Pastors J. E. Seneker, H. Wetzel, D. E. Snapp, and Detrick served this congregation until 1887. From that time until 1921 the following ministers are given as having served.

J. N. Stirewalt, 1887-1889   O. W. Aderholt, 1909-1912
S. Henkel, 1889-1891   J. S. Wessinger, 1912-1915
P. C. Wike, 1891-1899   L. L. Huffman, 1915-1918
M. L. Pence, 1899-1909   M. A. Ashby, 1920-1921

Toms Brook Parish

St. Peter's—The Lutheran people in the Toms Brook community appear first to have worshiped at Borden's schoolhouse near Saumsville, a preaching point of J. N. Schmucher in 1806, and later at Hottle's schoolhouse, one mile south of Mt. Olive, where was built in 1824, Frieden's, a Lutheran and Reformed church. In 1842, they built Brook Union one mile west of the village of Toms Brook, which was dedicated on the fifth Sunday in May of that year, in connection with a meeting of the Northern Conference of Virginia Synod. The first St. Peter's Lutheran church, a frame building, was erected in the village in 1869. The large and attractive brick church with Sunday school room, and churchly appointments, was dedicated in April, 1905. The congregation was served in connection with Strasburg from 1894 to 1922, at which time an independent parish was formed, St. Matthew's of the Tennessee Synod uniting with St. Peter's. The church property is valued at $15,000. It has a membership of 226 and a Sunday school of 195.

The pastors since 1842, which seems to be the date of organization are:

J. N. Schmucker,   -1844   A. A. J. Bushong, 1880-1895
J. F. Campbell, 1844-1849   L. L. Smith, D. D., 1895-1911
Levi Keller, 1850-1860   J. W. Link, 1911-1918
J. A. Synder, 1860-1865   R. Homer Anderson, 1919-1922
Levi Keller, 1867-1871   Geo. S. Bearden, 1922-1925
Peter Miller, 1871-1879   W. C. Huddle, 1925-

St. Matthew's is a continuation of the Lutheran congregation worshiping at Frieden's. The church, a frame building, valued at $4,000, stands one-half mile south of the old church. The parsonage in which the pastor lives at Toms Brook is owned by St. Matthew's and St. Stephen's. The pastors who served this congregation prior to 1922, when it was united with St. Peter's, are given below. After this date they are given under the preceding sketch.

J. N. Schmucker, 1806-184— (?)   J. Paul Stirewalt, 1876-1882
Socrates Henkel, 1849-1854   P. C. Wike, 1886-1899
Joel Swartz, 1854-   M. L. Pence, 1899-1907
John H. Hunton,   -1861   O. W. Aderholt, 1909-1910
Henry Wetzel, 1861-1874   J. S. Wessinger, 1911-1914
J. N. Stirewalt, 1875-1876   Lester L. Huffman, 1915-1918
                    M. A. Ashby, 1919-1921

St. Stephen's was built as a Lutheran and Reformed church in 1842 by members of Frieden's church living in the community. The organizing minister was J. N. Schmucker, pastor of Lutheran congregation worshiping at Frieden's. The meeting at which steps were taken to build, was held at the home of Isaac Baker, on February 12, 1842, when a building committee, consisting of Paul Rosenberger, Joseph Baker and Lawrence Hammon, was appointed. The need for a church being greatly felt by these people, and contributions of money, timber and labor from the members, resulted in the erection of a frame building upon the land set apart by Paul Rosenberger. It was completed in October of that year.

The congregation having increased, and the building being in a bad state of repair, a new church was begun in 1860, but owing to the interruptions caused by the Civil War, was not completed until 1867.

In 1872, the Lutherans bought the interest of the Reformed and the church was re-dedicated as "St. Stephen's Evangelical Lutheran Church" on November 3, 1872.

The membership of the congregation numbers forty and the Sunday school seventy-one, and the church property is valued $2,000.

The pastors who have served St. Stephen's congregation are:

J. N. Shmucker, 1842-1850	O. W. Aderholt, 1909-1910
S. Henkel, 1851-1853	J. S. Wessinger, 1911-1914
Joel Swartz, 1853-	L. L. Huffman, 1915-1918
H. Wetzel, -1885	M. A. Ashby, 1919-1921
P. C. Wike, 1886-1899	F. M. Speagle, 1922-1924
M. L. Pence, 1899-1907	W. C. Huddle, 1927-

ST. PAUL'S LUTHERAN CHURCH
Strasburg, Va.

STRASBURG PARISH

St. Paul's—The first records of this congregation are of 1760. It is known, however, that a church building, most likely built by Lutherans and Reformed, was standing in the village in 1747. The Rev. Michael Schlatter of the Reformed church visited the Reformed congregation here in 1748. The name of the first Lutheran minister rendering pastoral services is not known, but it is almost certain that one of the earliest was the "patriot-preacher," Muhlenberg. A Lutheran church building appears to have been erected of logs, in 1769, in which was installed a pipe organ. Lord Fairfax deeded 200 acres of land on the "North River of Shenandoah," December 23, 1771, to Hieronomus Baker, Martin Roller, Laurence Snapp and Henry Felkner, "elders of the Lutheran church and congregation." The first brick church was erected in 1844, which was used as a hospital, arsenal, and stable by the Federal Army during the Civil War; the pews being used to make coffins. The church was rebuilt in 1893, and a Sunday school room added in 1902. The membership of the congregation is 192 and that of the Sunday school 322. The total value of the church property is $37,500, exclusive of the $14,000 parsonage in Strasburg.

The following pastors have served the congregation:

John P. G. Muhlenberg, 1772-1776	William Rusmiselle, 1866-1869
Christian Streit, 1785-1812	Andrew Long, 1869-1871
Abram Reck, 1813-1824	J. F. Campbell, 1871-1876
J. Nicholas Schmucker, 1827-1832	James Willis, 1877-1882
William Godfrey Keil, 1832-1834	L. L. Smith, D. D., 1882-1911
John Barton Davis, 1834-1844	John W. Link, 1913-1919
J. F. Campbell, 1844-1849	R. Homer Anderson, 1919-1922
Levi Keller, 1849-1860	Geo. S. Bowden, 1922-1929
J. A. Snyder, 1860-1865	C. F. Steck, Jr., 1929-

MINISTERS FROM SHENANDOAH COUNTY CONGREGATIONS

T. O. Keister, D. D.	St. Paul's, Strasburg
C. J. Smith, D. D.	St. Paul's, Strasburg
G. Morris Smith, D. D.	St. Paul's, Strasburg
G. W. Campbell	St. Paul's, Strasburg
E. E. Sibole, D. D.	St. Paul's, Strasburg
J. L. Sibole	St. Paul's, Strasburg
L. M. Sibole	St. Paul's, Strasburg
Harry Kibler	Lebanon
C. M. Coffelt	Mt. Zion
H. F. Coffelt	Mt. Zion
C. W. Hepner	Mt. Zion
S. L. Keller	Emanuel, Woodstock
R. L. Miller	Emanuel, Woodstock
W. S. Bowman, D. D.	St. David's
Martin Walther	St. David's

R. E. Golladay, D. D. _____ St. David's
L. P. Pence _____ St. Mary's
D. I. Offman _____ Emmanuel, New Market
W. H. Kibler _____

SMYTH COUNTY

Two of the churches of the county, St. James' and Pleasant Hill, are considered along with the Washington and Wythe County churches because of their long connection with those parishes. The only parish wholly within the county is that which follows:

MARION-EBENEZER PARISH

The parish consists of Ebenezer, northwest of Marion; the congregation in Marion, and Attoway, four miles southeast of Marion. Of these Ebenezer is the oldest, and also the oldest in the county. The congregations have been associated together throughout their history and served almost all the time by the same pastor. The development of the work of the parish since the early seventies, has been intimately connected with the life of Marion College, the president of the college and other ministers connected with it having served either as pastor or as supply of one or all of the churches very much of the time. In the late eighties and early nineties, Marion was a separate parish. There has been overlapping which neither Synodical nor congregational records fully show, making it very difficult to give a list of pastors in their order and with proper dates.

The following is a full list of the pastors, but dates are uncertain.

George Flohr, 1799-1820	J. B. Greiner, 1879-1881
Andrew Secrist, 1820-	J. J. Scherer, D. D., 1881-
Jacob Scherer, -1830	J. P. Brodfuhrer, 1882-
Elijah Hawkins, 1830-	I. P. Hawkins, 1884-1886
J. K. Rader	W. P. Huddle (Marion) '90-'92
John Boone, 1855-1856	H. N. Miller, Supply, 1893
W. C. Sloop, 1857-1861	E. C. Cronk, Supply, 1894
L. A. Mann, 1861-1868	J. B. Grenier, D. D., 1907-1911
W. E. Hubbert, 1868-1869	R. E. Kern, 1912-1914
E. H. McDonald, 1870-1871	E. H. Copenhaver, 1915-1929
J. J. Scherer, 1871-1879	Hugh J. Rhyne, 1929-

Ebenezer, the mother church of the parish, was organized and worshiped first at Mt. Zion, a log church two miles northwest of the present Ebenezer church. It is believed that the congregation was in existence in 1799 and that the Rev. George Flohr, was their first pastor. The present church was built in 1848, since which time it has borne the name Ebenezer. Being in the Chilhowie (Chilhowee). neighborhood, the congregation is often referred to in the early records as the Chilhowie church. The two most numerous family names have been Copenhaver and Rosenbaum. The membership of the congregation is now seventy-one and that of the Sunday school is sixty-eight. The property is valued at $2,000.

Marion—In 1874, twenty-four members from either Ebenezer or Cedar Grove church united, under the leadership of Pastor J. J. Scherer, in forming a congregation at Marion. Messrs. G. D. H. Killinger, T. M. Rosenbaum were elected elders; Thomas Copenhaver and M. M. Musser deacons. The congregation worshiped in the Methodist church until 1887, in the Episcopal church until 1896, and in the College Chapel until 1910 when the church was built. The membership of the congregation is 194, and the Sunday school 269. The property is valued at $7,500.

Attoway, four miles southeast of Marion, on Staley's Creek, for a number of years a preaching point, became an organized congregation in 1910, under the ministry of Pastor J. J. Scherer. A schoolhouse was used as a place of worship until the building of the church, the same year of the organization. The membership is fifty-one, and the Sunday school seventy-seven. The church property is valued at $2,000.

St. Matthew's, at Atkins, six miles east of Marion, has ceased to exist as a congregation. It was the continuation of the "Cullops church," (Collups, Colleps) of the early part of the last century, which stood on the creek a mile southwest of Atkins, known also as Cedar Grove. The church preceding the present one was built in 1857, and was dedicated by E. Hawkins, and W. D. Roedel. With the building of the church in 1888, at Atkins, the name, St. Matthew's was given. The property is held by the trustees. It was long a part of the Marion-Ebenezer parish.

MOUNTAIN MISSION WORK

The mountain mission work, under the care of the Rev. Kenneth Killinger, began with his holding Sunday schools, and lay-services in certain mountain communities, south of Marion, less than a decade ago. The success attending his efforts led to his appointment to the work, under the direction of the pastor at Marion, and to the support of the Synod and the Woman's Missionary Society, and later, to the Synod granting him license to preach and administer the Sacrament in this particular field. The work now extends to a large part of Smyth County, and also into Grayson and Washington Counties. Curran Valley, Furnace Hill, Slemp's Creek, Bear Creek, and Mitchell Creek, in Smyth; Mill Creek, Cabin Creek, Helton, White Top, and Fairview, in Grayson and Washington are the chief preaching points. Preaching, prayer services and Sunday schools are held at these places, and in a great many isolated homes, the Sunday school lessons are being studied. On Bear Creek, north of Atkins, a congregation has been organized known as the Church of the Atonement, where those who have been baptised and confirmed hold their membership. The membership is seventy-four, but in all there are more than one thousand, in the various Sunday schools, and the home department. Several small church buildings have been

erected and where there is no building in which to gather, services are
held in the open air.

Ministers From Smyth County Congregations

Levi Groseclose	Pleasant Hill
W. C. Buck	Pleasant Hill
R. G. Rosenbaum	Ebenezer
E. H. Copenhaver	Ebenezer
J. J. Scherer, Jr., D. D.	Marion
B. A. Copenhaver	Marion
Kenneth Killinger	Attoway

TAZEWELL COUNTY

There are three congregations in the county, Central church in
Burke's Garden, the congregation at Tazewell, and Wartburg, at Bluefield, Virginia. The mother church is that in Burke's Garden.
Wartburg has been developed along with Bluefield, West Virginia, and
Tazewell has been associated part of the time with Wartburg, and Bluefield, West Virginia. "Poor Valley," southwest of Burke's Garden, and
"Concord," an old union church between Burke's Garden and Tazewell,
frequently mentioned in the minutes of Synod, have been preaching
points, rather than organized congregations.

Burke's Garden Parish

Burke's Garden, named for its first settler, and the fertility of the
soil, is a great basin, the bottom of which is scores of square miles of level
land, the rim being mountains towering more than a thousand feet above.

Central Church, had its beginning in the early decades of the past
century. A church building was erected as early as in 1826, and the
Rev. Christian Bergman, who was the first person to be buried in the
churchyard, is believed to be the first preacher. It is more than likely,
that George Daniel Flohr, and other pioneer Lutheran ministers rendered
occasional pastoral services here prior to the date given above. The first
church, built of hewed logs, with the old time gallery, and the elevated
goblet pulpit, reached by steps, was used by all denominations. In 1875,
a new frame church was erected, owned by the Lutherans, but used by all.

There is a Lutheran and also a Methodist chapel in the Garden, but
all services are held at the Central church. The membership of the
congregation is ninety-four, and the Sunday school forty-eight. The
church property is valued at $5,000. The parsonage in Burke's Garden,
owned by the congregation is valued at $3,500.

The following ministers have served the congregation:

Jacob Scherer	E. H. Kohn, 1895-1896
——— Tolbert (?)	J. H. Wyse, 1898-1904
J. J. Greever, 1841-1877	J. P. Miller, 1905-1907
H. E. Baily, 1878-1890	E. L. Ritchie, 1907-1913
J. A. Mahood (supply)	Student L. L. Huffman (supply)
J. A. Morehead, 1892-1894	R. H. Anderson, 1915-1918

S. W. Hahn, 1919-1922   Student Geo. A. Metz (supply)
E. L. Baker, 1922-1925   J. A. Shealy, 1928-

Tazewell (Jeffersonville)—In 1890, under the leadership of the Rev. J. B. Greever, a brick church was built in North Tazewell, near the railroad station. This property was sold in 1899, and in 1902, a neat frame building, costing $4,000, was erected in Tazewell. The congregation was received into Synod in 1895. The membership numbers nineteen, with a Sunday school of fifteen.

The pastors have been the same as those serving Burke's Garden since 1892, except that W. H. Greever and E. C. Cronk served either as pastor or supply at various times prior to 1897, and from 1900 to 1903, it was connected with the church at Bluefield, West Virginia.

Wartburg, at Bluefield, Va. (Graham). The congregation grew out of the labors of the Rev. J. B. Greever, who came here in 1886, and established Wartburg Seminary. In a short time he began holding services in the Methodist Church for the many Lutheran families who were coming to the new town. After the erection of the school building (1888), they began worshiping in the chapel, which they continued to use until the completion of the church, a frame building, with adjoining Sunday school rooms, in 1904. The organization was formed about 1888. The congregation grew rapidly at first, but with the collapse of the Graham boom, the discontinuance of Wartburg Seminary, and the sale of the school property, its growth and development were greatly retarded. It has been, at times, an independent parish under the care of the United Synod Mission Board, whose pastor also did pastoral work in the coal fields, but at other times has been connected with Bluefield, West Virginia or Tazewell. The present membership is forty-one and that of the Sunday school seventy-two. The church property is valued at $5,000. The following pastors have served the congregation:

J. B. Greever,   -1894   K. Y. Umberger, 1912-1915
W. H. Greever (supply)   J. B. Moose, 1915-1917
E. C. Cronk, 1895-1897   A. W. Ballentine, 1917-1918
C. L. Brown, summers of '97-'98   K. Y. Umberger (supply)
C. W. Cassell, 1898-1905   Stu. G. F. Weissling (supply)
J. B. Greever (supply)   Supplied from Bluefield, W. Va.
C. W. R. Kegley, 1907-1911   J. A. Shealy, 1928-

MINISTERS FROM TAZEWELL COUNTY CONGREGATIONS

J. J. Greever _____ Burke's Garden
Stephen Rhudy _____ Burke's Garden
J. B. Greever _____ Burke's Garden
R. B. Peery, D. D. _____ Burke's Garden
W. H. Greever, D. D., LL. D. _____ Burke's Garden
J. C. Peery, D. D. _____ Wartburg, Bluefield, Va.
L. B. Spracher _____ Wartburg, Bluefield, Va.
R. Homer Anderson _____ Wartburg, Bluefield, Va.

WARREN COUNTY

A goodly number of Lutherans have lived in Warren since its early history, although Ebenezer at Browntown, nine miles south of Front Royal, is the sole congregation. The Rev. J. I. Miller, of Luray, effected the organization in 1885, the congregation using the union church, built in 1882, and in which they have one-fourth interest. In 1897, under the leadership of Mr. F. P. Cover, proprietor of the Browntown tannery, a Lutheran Church was built, at which time the congregation was quite prosperous. Following the closing of the tannery and the removal of many families from the village, the membership of Ebenezer has been greatly decreased. Pending probable development in the community, it is thought wise to continue services and the organization. This, however, has been attended with special difficulties because of the distance from other Lutheran Churches. The congregation has been served by the pastors at Luray, except for a brief period during the nineties, when it was connected with Stephens City. Although, not at present, a part of Luray parish, pastoral attention is given by the Luray pastor.

WARWICK COUNTY

Newport News

Holy Trinity—by direction of the Board of Missions of the United Synod South, the Rev. J. E. Shenk of Norfolk made a canvass of the city of Newport News in 1897 finding a number of Lutheran families desirous of, and ready to cooperate in, the establishment of a church. Action on the part of the Board was delayed by the outbreak of the Spanish American War. In response to a call from the Mission Board the Rev. E. A. Shenk of Waynesboro entered upon the work in November, 1898, and on the day of his installation, December 4th, he and the Rev. Dr. L. L. Smith, President of the Virginia Synod, organized Holy Trinity congregation. In the following September, the Presbyterian church at 111-113, 27th St., a frame building seating 300 people, with an adjoined two roomed Sunday school department, was purchased at the cost of $7000. With the assistance of the Board the indebtness was paid off in May, 1907, at which time the congregation declared itself self-supporting. The Synod found it necessary, however, to give some financial support at times for the next decade. During the World War, Trinity Church was the leading one in the city and perhaps in the entire section in serving and befriending the men in uniform; the Lutheran Brotherhood service house, furnished by the National Lutheran Council being their sole retreat in their hours of leisure, and the congregation also gave bi-weekly socials. The Sunday school room and the church were always crowded for Sunday services. In this work the Rev. Dr. G. M. Diffenderfer and Miss Mary Markley rendered valuable service. Sixteen of the sons saw active war service. One, Carl H. Wiegel, gave his life.

HOLY TRINITY LUTHERAN CHURCH
Newport News, Va.

In 1920 the congregation purchased the parsonage on 24th Street. The entire church property is valued at $30,000. The membership of the congregation is 271, that of the Sunday school is 133.

W. T. Stauffer, Esq., member of the congregation, has been outstanding in the work of the Virginia Synod and of the United Lutheran Church. The pastors have been as follows:

E. A. Shenk, Nov. 1898-June, 1908
A. C. Karkau, July, 1909-Sept., 1911
I. D. Worman, Apr., 1912-July, 1914
W. W. Frey, Oct., 1914-May, 1915
J. A. Shealy, 1916-1920
P. H. Pearson, Dec., 1920-July, 1924
C. M. Teufel, Dec., 1924-Jan., 1927
P. J. Bane, Jan., 1928-

The following ministers have done supply work here. Rev. M. C. Horine, D. D., 1908-'09; George H. Cox, D. D., winter of 1911 and

1912; J. A. Ainsworth, summer 1915; W. E. Stahler, D. D., autumn 1927.

WASHINGTON COUNTY

The three churches of the parish are, Lutheran Chapel, on South Fork of the Holston River; St. James', four miles south of Chilhowie, in Smyth County; and Mock's Chapel, at Damascus, nine miles south of Abingdon. For a number of years there were four churches in the parish but Geisler's Chapel, near Meadow View, has disbanded. No doubt services were held, by pioneer Lutheran missionaries, at various places in the county where Lutheran people are known to have lived, prior to the organization of the Synod of Southwestern Virginia, in 1842. The year following the organization of the Synod, an effort was made to have a pastor "visit the congregations in Washington County" and the records, for years, show this to have been esteemed missionary territory. The list of the pastors are given at the close of the sketches.

Luther Chapel was organized in 1845, by the Rev. J. A. Brown, of Wytheville, who from the beginning of his ministry appears to have given special attention to the field. There have been three churches: the one built of logs about the time of the organization, the second and present church, both of frame construction. The church property is valued at $2,000. The membership of the congregation is twenty-six, but does not maintain a Sunday school. The tenth convention of the Synod was held in Luther Chapel.

St. James'—The organization and building of the first church occurred in the year of 1859, under the ministry of the Rev. F. Hickerson. There were seven charter members. The deed to the land was made on March 11, and the church dedicated in October, the Rev. D. F. Bittle, of Roanoke College preaching the sermon. The church was repaired in 1882 and again in 1892. The present church, which is valued at $3,000, was built in 1908. The membership of the congregation is fifty-three. St. James' is the home church of the Hon. H. L. Bonham, who has represented his county in the State Legislature, and is prominent in the political, industrial and religious life of the state.

Mock's Chapel, came into being as an organization on February 10, 1893, under the ministry of the Rev. W. B. Oney. The church was built about the time of the organization. It is a frame building, to which Sunday school rooms were added during the ministry of Pastor S. C. Ballentine. Damascus is an important center in the lumber industry and the congregation has had a large place in the life of the community. The membership is sixty-seven and the church property is valued at $3,000. The parsonage of the parish, a good residence, is located at Damascus.

The following ministers have served the parish, but it is not certain that each of them has served all the churches.

J. A. Brown, 1844-1851

John K. Rader, 1851-1852

J. A. Brown, 1853-1854

John Boon, Supply

William G. Sloop, 1856-1857

F. Hickerson, 1857-1861

L. A. Mann, 1861-1866

J. A. Bell, 1866-1875

S. R. Smith, 1876-1878

J. A. Bell, 1879-1880

W. B. Oney, 1881-1887

D. S. Fox, 1887-1888

J. W. Strickler, 1889-1890

S. D. Steffey, 1891-1893

J. C. Repass, 1894-1901

P. D. Leddin, 1902-1903

M. Q. Boland, 1903-1904

E. H. Copenhaver, 1904-1907

W. C. Buck, 1909-1910

B. W. Cronk, 1911-1913

J. B. Greiner, D. D., 1914-1917

S. C. Ballentine, 1917-1923

P. E. Seidler, 1924-1925

S. L. Nease, 1925-1928

A. L. Hahn, 1929-

WYTHE COUNTY

Many Lutherans were among the early settlers of Wythe County, but who the first ministers were is not known. Paul Henkel visited here in the nineties of the eighteenth century, however, there were others before him. Four congregations, St. Paul's, Zion, Kimberlin, and St. John's, each a mother church, St. Paul's the mother of them all, were centenarians before the close of the last century. The twelve congregations of the county are grouped into five parishes. Within the past twenty-five years, six congregations of the county have discontinued as organizations because of mergers, in each case the discontinuance proving an advantage to the work. The county has given a large number of her sons to the Lutheran ministry. One congregation, Pleasant Hill, located in Smyth County, is included with the sketches of Wythe, because of its connection with Kimberlin parish.

RURAL RETREAT PARISH

St. Paul's, three miles northeast of Rural Retreat and Grace, in Rural Retreat constitute the parish. Grace, while the offspring largely of St. Paul's, has been associated in a parish with the mother church but for a few years.

St. Paul's—The written history of this congregation, the oldest Lutheran church in Virginia west of the New River, begins with 1776— the date of several baptisms, by one whose name is not given. A record book was purchased in 1779, and the communion cloth made of home grown flax upon which is embroidered the initials: C. A. D.; R. I. N.; and N. A. K. and the name of Mrs. Kregger, bears the date of 1784. The old communion set, solid silver, is evidently of as early date. The first minister's name in the records of the congregation is that of Paul Henkel, who administered communion in August, 1793, and it is likely, that W. F. A. Daser, also ministered to the Lutheran people here, about this time. The first church, which stood between the present church site and cemetery, was built of chestnut logs, and is believed to have been standing at the time of the first baptisms. A second church was dedicated

ST. PAUL'S LUTHERAN CHURCH
Wythe County, Va.

in 1829, by Jacob and Daniel Scherer, Henry Graber preaching the sermon. The brick church, built in 1854, was damaged by a storm in 1876, and rebuilt in 1877. This was replaced in 1916, by a brick building with Sunday school rooms, and churchly appointments, it being, at present, one of the best rural churches in this section of the state. In the thirties and forties of the past century there were serious internal dissensions in the congregation, which greatly hindered its life and development, due largely to the doctrinal controversy disturbing the Lutheran churches in Virginia about that time. St. Paul's was associated with Kimberlin and Pleasant Hill in the Mt. Airy parish for fully a half century, until 1905, after which, it, with Pleasant Hill, formed the Mt. Airy parish until 1920, when the present parish lines were formed. The membership is 110, with a Sunday school of 94. The property is valued at $10,000.

The following pastors have served the congregation:

Leonard Willy, 1799
Geo. D. Flohr, 1799-1824
Jacob Scherer, 1827-1844
James A. Brown, 1846-1854
E. Hawkins, 1855-1868
L. A. Mann, 1868-1869

J. C. Repass, 1870-1882
F. Studebaker, 1882-1885
W. P. Huddle, 1886-1889
D. S. Fox, 1889-1893
W. R. Brown, 1894-1898
D. S. Fox, 1899-1902

GRACE LUTHERAN CHURCH
Rural' Retreat, Va.

J. A. Arndt, 1903-1905   G. H. Rhodes, 1909-1920
J. B. Greiner, D. D., 1906-1907 J. H. Richard, 1921-1926
B. A. Barringer, 1927-

Grace—Hawkin's Chapel, the Lutheran church at Rural Retreat, and since 1924, Grace, are the names given this church in the minutes of Synod. The congregation grew out of the services held for a number of years by Lutheran pastors of the county, at various schoolhouses, and especially at Oak Grove on the site of the present church. Regular preaching and Sunday school services were held by Pastor Elijah Hawkins, and L. A. Mann, and steps taken to build a church prior to 1868. Under the leadership of the Rev. E. H. McDonald, the church was completed in 1872. The congregation was organized that year by Pastor J. C. Repass, of the Mt. Airy parish, and listed on the Parochial Report of Synod, as of the parish. The Rev. J. B. Greever, having established an academy at Rural Retreat, using the basement of the church until the school building was completed, a desire arose on the part of some that the congregation, be separate from the Mt. Airy parish. The outcome was two congregations of the same name, using the same church, each with a pastor, one belonging to the old parish, and the other independent of it. This continued for more than a decade, when in 1886, an agreement was reached by which the congregations were united with Pastors W. P. Huddle, of Mt. Airy parish, and J. W. S. Shepherd, successor to Pastor J. B. Greever, serving as co-pastors. By the end of the second year (1888), both had accepted calls to other fields, and the reunited congregation extended a call to another—its connection with the Mt. Airy parish ceasing at this time. The present church was built in 1910, to which the Sunday school house was added in 1913, and a pipe organ put in the church by Mr. and Mrs. J. S. Etter, a few years later. The congregation numbers 312 members, and the Sunday school 226. The value of the church property is estimated at $30,000. The parsonage, belonging to the congregation, and valued at $6,000, is located at Rural Retreat.

The following pastors have served this congregation:

J. C. Repass, 1872-1881	J. B. Greiner, D. D., 1888-1904
J. B. Greever, 1872-1886	S. C. Ballentine, 1905-1908
E. Studebaker, 1882-1885	G. H. Rhodes, 1909-1920
W. P. Huddle, 1885-1887	J. H. Richard, 1921-1926
J. W. S. Shepherd, 1885-1888	B. A. Barringer, 1927-

Fairview—In 1889 one-fourth interest was purchased in Fairview church, which is located on the main road south of Rural Retreat. The congregation was received into Synod in 1894. It was served by the pastor of the mother church at Rural Retreat almost throughout its history. After about twenty years the organization disbanded, the members returning to Rural Retreat.

Berea—In 1898 Berea was built to accommodate the members of the congregation living in the "Glade," southwest of Rural Retreat. The congregation was received into Synod in 1903. Like Fairview, the congregation was small, and later found it of no advantage to continue the organization. It merged with the mother church in 1925. It was served almost all the time by the pastor at Rural Retreat.

Cripple Creek Parish

Zion, five miles southwest of Crockett, known in its early history as the German Church on Cripple Creek, is probably the second oldest congregation in the county. The earliest record is of the baptisms of Catharine Lits, January 1791, and Eve Huddle, April, 1791. The first church, a log building, was dedicated on Whitsunday 1794, the Rev. John Stanger, Lutheran, and the Rev. Daniel Repass, Reformed, officiating. The Rev. Anthony Frank, of Reed Creek, a Lutheran minister who had recently come from Germany, but of whom we know little, was present. At that time there were twenty-eight male members; sixteen Lutheran, and twelve Reformed. Christopher Spraker and Henry Vaught were the Lutheran officers, and Peter Spangler was the Reformed officer. Rev. John Stanger, who lived a few miles north of the church, appears to have been the first regular pastor.

The North Carolina Synod met here in May, 1838. The congregation became a charter member of the Southwest Virginia Synod at its organization in 1842. The present church building, a substantial and neat frame structure was erected in 1856. The congregation was for many years in the Central parish of Wythe county, now known as the Cripple Creek parish.

It numbers 102 members and has a Sunday school of 91. The church property is valued at $1200.

The following pastors have served Zion congregation:

John Stanger, 1791-1824	C. M. Fox, 1899-1902
Jacob Scherer, 1828-1845	K. Y. Umberger, 1902-1906
J. A. Brown, 1846-1882	D. S. Fox, 1906-1915
N. A. Whitman, 1883-	K. Y. Umberger, 1915-1917
J. C. Repass, 1884-1894	A. F. Tobler, 1918-1925
D. S. Fox, 1895-1898	F. M. Harr, 1925-1929

St. Peter's, nine miles southeast of Crockett, which has been associated in the parish with Zion, was organized in 1830 by the Rev. Jacob Scherer. The first church, a small frame structure with gallery and an elevated pulpit, was erected in 1839 and dedicated by a committee appointed by the Synod. It was the place of the last meeting of the North Carolina Synod held in Virginia (1841), at which meeting it was agreed that the churches in Virginia should organize themselves into a separate Synod. The church building now standing was erected in 1885, and is a frame structure, seating about 300 people. The present membership is fifty-eight and that of the Sunday school is seventy-five. The church property is valued at $1500. The pastors of St. Peter's have been, since its organization, the same as those who served Zion, except that Gideon Scherer appears to have been pastor from 1841 to 1842, Elijah Hawkins 1842-44, E. McDonald, 1866-68 and N. A. Whitman appears not to have served St. Peter's.

Rosenbaum's Chapel is located on an elevation south of the railroad at Crockett. It was organized in 1875 by the Rev. J. A. Brown. The church, a substantial frame building with belfry, was erected in 1875 on land donated by Stephen Rosenbaum, who contributed very largely to its building. It has been throughout its history associated with Zion and St. Peter's. The congregation has always been numerically small. The church property is valued at $2000. The pastors are the same as those which have served Zion and St. Peter's.

Bethany, six miles southeast of Crockett, was organized by the Rev. K. Y. Umberger in 1904. The church, a frame building, was dedicated in May, 1905, and was enlarged and remodeled in 1926. The membership of the congregation is seventy-one; that of the Sunday school is seventy-seven. The church property is valued at $2000. The pastors are those who have served Zion and St. Peter's.

The parsonage of the Cripple Creek parish is located near Rosenbaum's Chapel at Crockett. It is a frame dwelling with six rooms, and is valued at $3000.

St. Andrew's, at Speedwell, disbanded as an organization in 1927. The members transferred to other churches of the Cripple Creek parish, but the property was retained. This was a preaching point for a number of years prior 1904, when the old Quaker church was purchased and St. Andrew's organized. The congregation was small and owing to the changed economic conditions in the community, had little numerical growth. It was in the Cripple Creek parish from its organization.

KIMBERLIN PARISH

The Kimberlin Parish lies west and north of Rural Retreat; Kimberlin, four miles northwest, Pleasant Hill six miles west, on the Lee Highway, and Corinth four miles north. The mother and two daughters constitute the parish—the name being taken from the mother church. The parsonage, a comfortable frame residence, valued at $4,500, is located at Rural Retreat.

In 1869 the Mt. Airy parish, consisting of St. Paul's, Kimberlin, and Pleasant Hill, purchased a farm of 108 acres near Kimberlin church and erected a dwelling thereon for the use of the pastor. When the parish was divided in 1905 the parsonage farm was sold and the money apportioned to the congregations for parsonage purposes. The parsonage of the Kimberlin parish was located near Corinth until 1917, when it was sold and the present parsonage of Rural Retreat purchased. The Kimberlin cemetery is one of the oldest and largest church cemeteries in the county.

Kimberlin—The first written record of the congregation is of the dedication of the church in August, 1797. The land (6¾ acres) was deeded by Martin Kimberlin, to George Weaver and Adam Dutton, trustees. (Martin Kimberlin, most likely the same person, was an officer at St. Paul's about this time.) The name of the organizing pastor is not ·known, but Leonard Willy drew up a constitution for Kimberlin, St. Paul's, St. John's and St. Mark's (Collep's in Smyth County), in 1798. The first church, which stood south of the present location, in the cemetery, was repaired in 1834, and rededicated by Henry Graber and William Artz, of North Carolina, the Rev. Graber preaching the sermon. The second church, a frame building, was built in 1854, and the third, also frame, and valued at $4,500, was built in 1913.

The membership of the congregation is ninety-seven, and that of the Sunday school is ninety-three.

Jonas Huddle, a member of Kimberlin, whose death occurred in 1881, was an outstanding layman of the Synod. He attended the 1836 and 1838 conventions of the North Carolina Synod as delegate, was a delegate to the convention preliminary to the organization of the Synod of Southwestern Virginia in 1841 and, except the meeting of 1842, was a

CHURCHES OF KIMBERLIN PARISH
Near Rural Retreat, Va.
Kimberlin Church
The Mother

Pleasant Hill Church   Corinth Church
Daughter   Daughter

member of every convention, either as delegate or as an officer, until his death. Also, he served as superintendent of the Sunday school for fifty years.

The following pastors have served the Kimberlin church and parish, except as noted under Pleasant Hill.

Leonard Willy,   -1799   W. R. Brown, 1894-1898
Geo. D. Flohr, 1799-1826   D. S. Fox, 1899-1902
J. A. C. Schoenberg (supply)   J. A. Arndt, 1902-1905
—— Kyle (supply)   H. P. Counts, 1909-1911
Jacob Scherer, 1827-1837   J. L. Smith, 1912-1913
Elijah Hawkins, 1838-1868   W. W. J. Ritchie, 1914-1916
L. A. Mann, 1868-1869   S. W. Hahn (student supply)
J. C. Repass, 1870-1882   W. G. Cobb, 1919-1920
E. Studebaker, 1882-1885   P. E. Shealy, 1921-1925
W. P. Huddle, 1886-1889   Frank H. Miller, 1925-1927
D. S. Fox, 1890-1893   P. L. Snapp, 1927-

Pleasant Hill was received into Synod in 1843, the congregation "having lately built a comfortable church in connection with several other denominations, and having organized under the pastoral care of the Rev. Elijah Hawkins." The members came very largely, from Kimberlin. It was a preaching point for a great many years. The present church, frame, valued at $3,000, was built in 1907. The pastors of Pleasant Hill are the same as those serving Kimberlin since 1843, except that the Rev. Dr. J. B. Greiner served it in connection with St. Paul's from 1905 to 1907, and in 1916, the Rev. Geo. H. Rhodes supplied. Since 1917 it has been regularly in the Kimberlin parish. The membership of the congregation is 79, and that of the Sunday school is 110.

Corinth was organized in 1892, largely from members of Kimberlin, living in the Black Lick community, by Pastor D. S. Fox, of the Mt. Airy parish. For a half century, or more, Lutheran ministers had held occasional service in the "old Brick church," and later in the schoolhouse, and at times a community Sunday school was conducted. In 1893, the congregation built a frame church with several small rooms adjoining the church auditorium—it being at that time one of the best rural churches in the county. The lot upon which it is built was purchased from the Presbyterians by Michael Cassell, and donated to the congregation. The present membership is sixty, with a Sunday school of eighty-five. The church property is valued at $3,000. The pastors of Corinth have been those who served Kimberlin church since 1892.

HOLY TRINITY CHURCH
Wytheville, Va.

WYTHEVILLE PARISH

Trinity, in Wytheville, was organized in 1876, out of St. John's under the leadership of the Rev. A. Phillippi. Shortly thereafter, the church, a beautiful, Gothic brick structure with churchly appointments, was built on Main Street. The private school, Trinity Hall, for boys and girls, conducted by Pastor Phillippi, in the eighties and nineties, contributed much to the growth and development of the congregation. With the merger of St. John's and Trinity, in 1924, Trinity becomes the successor of the historic mother congregation.

The membership is 207, with a Sunday school of 115. The value of the property is $18,000. The parsonage, an attractive modern residence, is valued at $10,000.

The pastors serving this congregation have been:

A. Phillippi, D. D., 1876-1915   Geo. W. Spiggle, 1918-1923
H. N. Miller, Ph. D., 1916-1917   Fred J. Lottich, 1924-1927
J. P. Miller, D. D., 1928-

OLD ST. JOHN'S LUTHERAN CHURCH
Near Wytheville, Va.

St. John's—one of the historic spots of Wythe County is old St. John's church and cemetery, one mile northwest of Wytheville, where have worshiped, and where lie buried, many of the early leaders of the county. The life and labors of the Rev. Geo. D. Flohr, the Rev. J. A. Brown, D. D., and the Rev. A. Phillippi, D. D., covering a period of more than a century, are inseparably connected with St. John's church.

When the congregation merged with Trinity (1924), an endowment was created for the unkeep of the cemetery and church property, provision made for the holding of an occasional service, and a special "Home Coming" on the last Sunday in August of each year. St. John's appears to have been organized when Father Flohr came in 1799, the Rev. Leonard Willy having prepared a constitution for this and the other churches he was serving in 1798. The first house of worship was built about 1800, by the Lutherans and Reformed, although the Reformed congregation seems not to have continued very long. A pipe organ was placed in this church in 1814, and in 1855, the old church was replaced by the present frame building. This building has been repaired several times and is well preserved. St. John's, while not the oldest, has been perhaps the most influential congregation in the county. She has given an unusually large number of her sons to the ministry.

The following ministers have served this congregation:

George Daniel Flohr, 1800-1826	Alexander Phillippi, 1866-1889
John Jacob Scherer, 1828-1836	S. S. Rahn, 1889-1892
J. A. Tabler, 1837-1839	Paul Sieg, 1893-1903
J. J. Greever, 1841-1847	W. A. Julian, 1904-1905
James A. Brown (ass't), 1842-1845	Paul Sieg, 1905-1909
James A. Brown, 1858-1862	K. Y. Umberger, 1910-1912
W. D. Roedel, ⎱ 1862-1866	B. E. Petrea, 1913-1920
E. H. McDonald ⎰	C. J. Rice, 1920-1923

L. J. Lottich, 1924

St. Mark's—In 1891, under the leadership of Pastor A. Phillippi, a congregation was organized, and a small frame church built, three miles east of Wytheville, by members belonging to Trinity, living in the community. With the coming of better roads and transportation facilities, the need of the church and organization being no longer apparent, after an existence of about twenty years it was disbanded and property sold, the members returning to Trinity. The congregation had but the one pastor, Dr. A. Phillippi, who served in connection with Trinity.

WYTHE COUNTY PARISH

The Wythe County parish, lies west and north of Wytheville, consisting of Lebanon, four miles west, on the Lee Highway; St. Luke's, five miles north, in the Cove; and Holy Advent, four miles northwest, on the Lakes-to-Florida Highway. Formerly, St. Luke's and Holy Advent were in the Wytheville parish, and Lebanon in the Central parish.

Lebanon was organized by Pastor Jacob Scherer in 1851. The first church, built about that time, was located north of the Lee Highway, not far from the present location. The present church, a frame building, was erected in 1882, and is valued at $2,000. The membership is fifty-four, and the Sunday school forty-nine.

Following are the pastors who have served the congregation:

J. A. Brown, 1854-1882	K. Y. Umberger, 1902-1906
N. A. Whitman, 1883-	Paul Sieg, 1906-1909
J. C. Repass, 1884-1894	K. Y. Umberger, 1910-1912
D. S. Fox, 1894-1898	B. E. Petrea, 1912-1919
C. M. Fox, 1899-1902	C. J. Rice, 1920-1923

K. Y. Umberger, 1924-1927

St. Luke's—In 1894, Pastor A. Phillippi, in order to provide for the members of St. John's and Trinity, living in the Cove community, built a church and organized a congregation, which is known as St. Luke's. The congregation has been small from the beginning, but has met a real need in the community.

He was the pastor until his death, in 1915, after which it was served by the pastor of Trinity until 1920 when it became a part of the Wythe County parish. The membership numbers fifty, and the property is valued at $2000.

Holy Advent—A group of the members of St. John's and Lebanon living in the Bald Hill community united in building Holy Advent church in 1912. The organization was completed and received into Synod in 1916. The congregation was connected with Trinity until 1920 when it came into the Wythe County parish. There is a membership of forty-six and the property is valued at $2000.

Poplar Grove, on Stony Fork, several miles northwest of Holy Advent, was organized in 1897 by Pastor D. S. Fox. It was connected with the Central parish. With the organization of Holy Advent the need of the Poplar Grove organization no longer existed, hence its discontinuance.

MEN ENTERING THE LUTHERAN MINISTRY FROM WYTHE COUNTY

Simeon Scherer	St. Paul's
Gideon Scherer	St. Paul's
A. Copenhaver	St. Paul's
J. J. Scherer, D. D.	St. Paul's
H. Wetzel	St. Paul's
A. Phillippi, D. D.	St. Paul's
J. L. Buck	St. Paul's
W. R. Brown	St. Paul's
M. D. Huddle	St. Paul's
W. A. Dutton	Kimberlin
C. W. Cassell	Kimberlin
E. A. Repass, Ph. D.	Kimberlin
J. A. Brown, D. D.	St. John's
J. C. Repass	St. John's
W. B. Yonce, Ph. D.	St. John's
S. A. Repass, D. D.	St. John's
C. B. King, D. D.	St. John's
T. S. Brown	St. John's
J. A. Huffard, D. D.	St. John's
J. B. Umberger	St. John's
J. A. Morehead, D. D., LL. D.	St. John's
C. R. W. Kegley	St. John's
K. Y. Umberger	St. John's
W. P. Huddle	St. Peter's
J. N. C. Park	Grace, Rural Retreat
S. D. Steffey	Grace, Rural Retreat

H. P. Wyrick _____ Grace, Rural Retreat
J. T. Huddle, D. D.* _____ Trinity
J. A. C. Hurt _____ Trinity
P. A. Atkins _____ Trinity

J. T. Crabtree, who for eighteen years was Superintendent of the Orphan Home at Salem, was a son of Kimberlin.

WEST VIRGINIA

BERKELEY AND JEFFERSON COUNTIES

Lutheran people are believed to have lived and held worship in this section earlier than 1750. Much of the history of the churches at Martinsburg (Berkeley County), and Shepherdstown (Jefferson County), runs parallel. Both appear to have been organized about 1750, and were served by the same pastors, almost all the time, until, during the ministry of Pastor B. M. Schmucker, 1848 to 1852. The first connection of these congregations with the Virginia Synod, was in 1820, when the Synod of Maryland and Virginia was organized. Pastor C. P. Krauth, Sr., was serving the two congregations at the time. In 1829, Pastor Jacob Medtart, whose address was given at Martinsburg, but who was also serving at Shepherdstown, took his place as a member of the Synod of Virginia. At the next convention of the Synod (1830) he, together with three other pastors, withdrew, when the resolution was adopted by the Synod to withdraw from the General Synod, and united with the Maryland Synod.** The Potomac River was the recognized line between the two Synods, however, certain congregations along the border appear to have affiliated with which ever of the two Synods to which the pastor belonged when he became pastor. Martinsburg was generally recognized as belonging to the Virginia Synod until the outbreak of the Civil War, St. Paul's which is carried on the roll of the Synod along with Martinsburg, was near Greensburg, and was organized during the ministry of Pastor Reuben Weiser, 1835 to 1837. Shepherdstown, since 1866, has been continuously in the Virginia Synod.

St. Peter's—It is believed the Lutheran people had a house of worship at Shepherdstown, as early as 1750. The old brick church which stood near the railroad was built in 1795. It stood for more than one hundred years, and in 1924, sixteen years after it ceased to be used, it was destroyed by fire. The present church, a beautiful and churchly stone building, was completed in 1908. The value of the property is $25,000. The parsonage, belonging to the parish, a commodious residence located at Shepherdstown, is valued at $4,000. The membership of the congregation is 267, and that of the Sunday school is 150.

In the following list of pastors the abreviations of "Va." and "Md." after certain names between 1829 and 1866, indicate the Synod to which the pastor belonged.

---

*Confirmed while at school. The family belonged to Kimberlin.
**The Maryland Synod, in 1830, again took up the name "The Synod of Maryland and Virginia," which is carried until 1833.

ST. PETER'S LUTHERAN CHURCH
Stepherdstown, W. Va.

Pastors—Bauer, C. F. Wilbahn, Nicodemus, J. Geo. Young, and Weyman, served the congregation prior to 1790.

Christian Streit, 1785-1790
J. D. Young, 1790-1800
F. William Jasinski, 1800-1802
J. C. Rebenach, 1808-1814
John Kaehler, 1817-1819
C. P. Krauth, Sr., 1819-1827
Jacob Medtart, 1827-1835
Reuben Weiser, 1835-1837 (Md.)
Charles Martin, 1837-1842 (Md.)
Samuel Sprecher, 1842-1843 (Md.)
J. A. Seiss, 1843-1846 (Va.)
C. P. Krauth, Jr., 1847-1848 (Md.)
B. M. Schmucker, 1848-1852 (Va.)

J. P. Smeltzer, 1852-1860 (Md.)
J. I. Miller, 1860-1865 (Va.)
J. F. Campbell, 1866-1868
D. H. Bittle, D. D., 1868-1872
J. Hawkins, 1872-1875
R. C. Holland, 1875-1878
D. M. Moser, 1878-1893
C. H. Rockey, 1893-1900
H. Max Lentz, 1900-1903
H. C. Haithcox, D. D., 1903-1914
I. D. Worman, 1914-1924
R. D. Synder, 1924-1927
Walter V. Simon, 1928-

ST. JAMES' LUTHERAN CHURCH
Uvilla, W. Va.

St. James', at Uvilla, east of Shepherdstown, is first on the roll of congregations of Synod in 1900. Services were held here as early as 1847, and in 1856, under the leadership of Pastor J. P. Smeltzer, the first church was built. The congregation was formed from members of the church at Shepherdstown, living in the community. It has always been associated with the mother church, and served by the same pastor. The present church, a beautiful brick building, standing in a beautiful grove of oaks, was erected in 1897. The church property is valued at $3,500. A community hall stands on the church ground. The membership of the congregation is 155, and that of the Sunday school 110.

Smithfield—The Smithfield parish, consisting of Smithfield, fifteen miles southwest of Shepherdstown, Gerrardstown, seven miles southwest of Martinsburg, and Stone Chapel had its place on the roll of the old Virginia Synod until in the early years of the present century. Smithfield, which seems to have been the main church of the parish, was an early preaching point, Paul Henkel having preached here in January, 1783 and repeatedly thereafter. The farewell letter of Pastor J. D. Young dated November 8, 1800 and recorded in the church record, is a high tribute to the Smithfield people.*

The church, yet standing but not in regular use, was built in 1798. The pastors as given in the record are:

Christian Streit	J. R. Keiser
J. D. Young, 1792-1800	J. J. Suman, 1843-1846
W. F. Jasinski	E. G. Proctor
—— Melsheimer	H. G. Bowers, 1852-
J. C. Rebenach	A. Copenhaver, 1856-
—— Kohler	J. Frazier, 1859-
C. P. Krauth	D. A. Kuhn, 1866-
J. Winter	W. S. McClanahan, 1869-
D. Eyster	G. A. Long, 1871-1884
Jacob Medtart	W. Eichelberger, 1885-1888
R. Weiser	L. M. Sibole, 1890-1896
Theo. Stork	E. H. Jones, Jr., 1896-1898

J. W. Strickler, 1898-1900

MINISTERS WHO ARE SONS OF JEFFERSON COUNTY CHURCHES

L. L. Smith, D. D. _____ Shepherdstown
W. J. Smith _____ Shepherdstown
E. L. Folk _____ Shepherdstown
J. W. Link _____ Uvilla

HARDY AND HAMPSHIRE COUNTIES
THE CAPON-NORTH RIVER PARISH

The churches in Hardy and Hampshire Counties, West Virginia, and Fairview on Timber Ridge near the state line in Frederick County, Va.,

*The letter is written in beautiful German script. The English translation by Dr. W. J. Finck is filed with the old record book in the Archives of our Synod.

constitute the Capon-North River parish. It is a large, mountainous territory, thinly populated. A number of the congregations are small. It has been necessary for the pastor to travel long distances to reach certain of the churches and therefore his visits to these communities have not been frequent.

Hebron, near Capon Bridge in Hampshire County, is the mother church. It is not unlikely that Johannes Schwarbach and Peter Muhlenberg visited the Capon Valley. The earliest record at Hebron is of the confirmation of twelve young people in 1786. The ministry of Christian Streit and Abram Reck in and around Winchester extended to the "Capon Church." The church site was deeded to the German congregations, meaning Lutheran and Reformed. The ministry of the latter ceased about 1813. A log church built about 1786 served as the house of worship until 1849 when the brick church was built. The Rev. John Hamilton, M. D. was the first resident pastor. The present membership is sixty-eight; that of the Sunday School is thirty-one. The property is valued at $4,000.

Fairview, in Frederick County, Virginia, was organized about 1846 by the Rev. John Richard, in the home of Jacob White. The church owned by Lutherans and Methodists was built 1854 and was remodeled 1899. The membership is twenty-eight. The church property is valued at $2,000.

St. Peter's—The organization, St. Peter's, formed at Wardensville in Hardy County by X. J. Richardson about 1850, had ceased to function before Peter Miller located here in July, 1858. He reorganized the next year with twenty-three members. The old Union church was used as the place of worship until the completion of the new church, brick, dedicated September 4, 1870, the Rev. Dr. T. W. Dosh preaching the sermon. The membership is 104; that of the Sunday school 126. The church property is valued at $7,000.

Mt. Vernon—Rev. Peter Miller began to hold occasional services in the Trout Run Valley in 1861 and three years later organized a congregation with eleven members. A small log building used also as a schoolhouse served as their place of worship until 1899 when a union church was built. The church has filled a real need in this community which, because of its isolation due to the ruggedness of the mountains and the character of some of the citizens, was called the "Devil's Hole." The membership is at present less by one than when organized.

Ebenezer, at Rio, in Hampshire County, first known as North River Mills, was first organized by X. J. Richardson about 1850. He also effected an organization at Mt. Zion near this point. Both had ceased to function when Peter Miller began his ministry in these parts. He reorganized at North River Mills, as Ebenezer, in 1866, with twenty-five members. Throughout his ministry he had held occasional services at a number of points in this territory. Since there were few churches and little preaching, Rev. Abram Reck and W. G. Keil are said to have visited the Dutch Hollow during the first quarter of the last century. The North River meeting house, a very old log building, was the place of worship until the church was built in 1905. The membership is 68; that of the Sunday school is 113. The property is valued at $3,000.

St. James'—The Laurel chapel was built in 1865 and the congregation, with twenty-six members, was organized the following year by Peter Miller. The church burned in 1881 and was rebuilt the next year as St. James'. Few people are now living in this community and the membership has decreased to nine.

Mt. Moriah—The community known as the "Baughman" settlement in Hardy County had received occasional visits from the earlier Lutheran ministers. In 1861 Peter Miller began to visit it more frequently. He organized Mt. Moriah 1885 with fifteen members and completed the church building later. The present membership is sixty-two. The property is valued at $600.

Trinity, which was organized by Peter Miller in 1898 with fifteen members and the church built 1901, was, because of the removal of members from the community, disbanded in 1916, the church sold, and the church records placed in the archives of Synod.

* * * * * *

The outstanding figure of this territory has been the Rev. Peter Miller, who for sixty years almost continuously was recognized as everybody's pastor and under whose ministry nearly all of the churches were established. These churches have been throughout their history closely associated. In 1898 the parish was divided, placing in the Capon parish Hebron, St. Peter's, Trinity, Trout Run, and Fairview, and in the North River parish, Ebenezer, St. James', and Mt. Moriah. These were united in 1923. There was a parsonage at Wardensville, and one at Rio. Although there were two parishes, there was an overlapping in pastoral services.

The pastors of these churches have been:

W. G. Keil, 1822-1827	Wm. Rusmiselle, 1853-1858
Lewis Eichelberger, 1828-1840	P. Miller, 1858-1871
John Hamilton, M. D., 1840-	Webster Eichelberger, 1871-1877
Issac Baker	L. M. Sibole, 1878-1883
Wm. Shepherdson	P. Miller, 1884-1890
John Richard	J. P. Wade, 1890-1896
John Tabler	D. W. Michael, 1896-1898
X. J. Richardson -1853	W. H. Riser, 1898-1900

Capon Parish

J. K. Efird, 1900-1902	A. M. Smith, 1908-1909
C. M. Fox, 1902-1905	H. E. H. Sloop, 1911-1914
J. P. Wade, 1905-1908	Peter Miller, 1915-1918

D. W. Files, 1919-1925

North River Parish

Peter Miller, 1898-1914   H. D. Chapman, 1914-1917

N. E. Cooper, 1918-1921

Capon-North River Parish

G. A. Stoudameyer, 1927-

IMMANUEL LUTHERAN CHURCH
Bluefield, W. Va.

MERCER COUNTY

Immanuel grew out of the services which the Rev. J. B. Greever began to hold in Bluefield, shortly after he located at Graham, in 1886. A small frame church was built on Raleigh and Monroe streets, in 1890, which was the place of worship until the property was sold in 1906. The congregation worshiped in the Y. M. C. A. building, and in the basement of the First Presbyterian church, until the property on Mercer and

Duhring streets, consisting of two dwellings was purchased (1908), one of which was converted into a chapel. The church, a brick structure, with churchly appointments, and basement for Sunday school purposes was completed in 1915. The chancel was re-arranged and a pipe organ installed in 1922, and three years later the parsonage on the adjoining lot was turned into a parish house. Bluefield was a mission of the United Synod South, from 1897 to 1917, when it became self-supporting. During the greater part of the time, the congregation has enjoyed the full time service of a pastor. The present membership is 194 and the Sunday school 167. The value of the church is $45,000, and the parish house $10,000. The pastors have been as follows:

J. B. Greever, 1887-1890	S. P. Koon, 1902-1903
J. L. Buck, 1890-1891	C. W. Cassell, 1904-1905
H. E. Bailey, 1891-1892	C. W. R. Kegley, 1908-1911
J. B. Greever (supply)	K. Y. Umberger, 1912-1915
W. H. Greever, 1894-1900	J. B. Moose, 1915-1917
C. W. Cassell (supply)	K. Y. Umberger, 1917-1920
W. C. Seidel (supply)	C. F. Steck, Jr., 1921-1923

P. L. Royer, 1923

The Coalfields—Shortly after the Rev. J. B. Greever located at Graham (1886), he began holding services at various points, ·where Lutheran people were living, in the Flat Top coalfields. The Bluefield and Graham pastors continued the work, and in 1898 the field was made a part of the Graham parish under the care of the United Synod Mission Board. Had there been ample support to make possible one or more full time workers in the field, permanent churches could have been established. Pocahontas, Bramwell, Maybeury, Elkhorn, North Fork, Arlington, Keystone, Eckman, Vivian and Welch were at times preaching points. A church built at Maybeury in 1891 was afterwards sold, and congregations organized at Keystone in 1904, and North Fork in 1922, were discontinued because of the removals of members and the lack of pastoral attention. For several years there has not been regular preaching appointments in the field.

TENNESSEE

BLOUNTVILLE PARISH

Immanuel Church is located on Reedy Creek in Sullivan County, Tennessee, about five miles north of Blountville. Tradition puts the date of the organization about the year 1796. Probably by the Rev. Paul Henkel or the Rev. John G. Butler. It was first known as Union Church and was owned jointly by the Lutherans and Presbyterians.

It has had three houses of worship, the first was a frame structure built of hewn timbers with a stone chimney at one end and a fireplace large enough to receive a good size log. The pulpit was about six feet high with steps leading up to it from each side. When it was replaced by a better building it was used for many years as a schoolhouse. It was in this old church that the writer of this brief sketch was baptized.

IMMANUEL LUTHERAN CHURCH
Blountville, Tenn.

In 1865 a new brick building was erected about three hundred yards from where the first church stood. It was a large church 60x40. It frequently happened on special occasions that it would not hold more than half of the people who had gathered for worship. It was erected under the pastoral supervision of the Rev. A. J. Brown, D. D., and was dedicated by him soon after its completion. The cost was negligible. The present building was erected in 1903. It is constructed of brick with a seating capacity of about 500. It is one of the most commodious rural churches in all the surrounding country. It is valued at $5,000. It was dedicated the 3d Sunday in November, 1903, the Rev. J. A. Morehead, D. D. preaching the dedicatory sermon.

Near the church is located the parsonage, an eight roomed frame building neatly finished both inside and outside. The cost of erection was $4,000. The present membership is 162.

The following ministers were members of this congregation: William Hancher, Joseph Harr, J. K. Hancher, Geo. H. Cox, W. G. Wolford, Geo. B. Hancher, A. D. R. Hancher and F. M. Harr.

Pastors:

Adam Miller, Sr., 1818-1844	W. H. Roof, 1906-1913
William Hancher, 1844-1857	W. G. Cobb, 1914-1918
A. J. Brown, D. D., 1858-1894	B. S. Brown, Sr., 1918-1921
H. E. Bailey, 1899-1901	W. H. Roof, 1922-1926
S. D. Steffey, 1902-1905	K. Y. Umberger, 1927-

New Haven Church is located about eight miles west of Blountville in Sullivan County, Tennessee. It was organized sometime prior to 1811, for in that year it was received into the North Carolina Synod under the name of Roler's Church. Its first elders were Martin Roler and George Lideke. It is very probable that it was organized by the Rev. Charles Z. H. Schmidt, who was the pastor at the time of its reception into the North Carolina Synod.

It has had two houses of worship. The first was a log building with a high pulpit and chancel. It was located about half a mile from where the present church stands. The present church is a frame building about 40x30 feet in size and was erected under the pastoral supervision of the Rev. W. G. Wolford in 1874, and dedicated by him on June 27th of the same year. The cost was negligible, most of the material and work being donated. It is valued at $600.

During its connection with the Tennessee and Holston Synods up until the building of the present church, it was known as New Hope Church.

The present membership is fifty-six.

It has been served by the following pastors:

Charles Z. H. Schmidt	S. D. Steffey
William Hancher	H. A. Kistler
J. K. Hancher	H. D. Chapman
W. G. Wolford	J. A. Bourde
H. E. Bailey	K. Y. Umberger

Zion Church is located about eight miles west of Bristol, in Sullivan County, Tennessee. The exact date of its organization is not known. It is evident, however, that it was sometime prior to 1811, for it was received into the North Carolina Synod at its 9th convention held at Lincolnton, North Carolina of that year. It is very probable that it was organized by the Rev. Paul Henkel or the Rev. John G. Butler.

This congregation has the honor of being the birthplace of the Holston Synod which occurred on January 1, 1861.

It has had three houses of worship. The first was a log building, the second a frame structure with a seating capacity of about 300, the third and present building is also a frame structure about 60x40 feet in size and of modern church architecture. It is valued at $2,000. It was erected under the pastoral supervision of the Rev. W. H. Roof.

In 1902, because of a very unpleasant disruption, this congregation withdrew from the Holston Synod and united with the Southwestern Virginia Synod. It remained in this connection until 1917 when it was again received into the Holston Synod.

The present membership is forty-two.

The following ministers—Jacob Shaffer, J. A. Seneker, John P. Deck and Joseph Seneker were children of this church.

It has been served by the following pastors:

C. Z. H. Schmidt   W. G. Wolford
Jacob Zink   J. B. Greever
William Hancher   J. W. Link
J. K. Hancher   W. H. Roof
                K. Y. Umberger

BLUFF CITY PARISH

Silver Grove Church is located about nine miles south of Bristol in Sullivan County, Tennessee, near the banks of the Holston River. It was first known as Cedar Grove Church, and was organized by the Rev. A. J. Brown, D. D. It was received into the Holston Synod in September, 1877. Twenty years later in 1897 a lot was purchased on the pike leading out from Bristol into the Holston Valley, and a new church built with a seating capacity of about 300. This is one of the neatest rural churches of the community. We have no record of its dedication. The cost of erection was $1000. The present membership is fifty.

One the same plot of land near this church is located the parsonage of the Bluff City parish. It is a very neat building of the bungalow type, and was erected at a cost of $1250.

Pastors:

A. J. Brown, D. D.   H. A. Kistler
J. K. Hancher   H. D. Chapman
W. G. Wolford   J. A. Bourde
J. B. Greever   B. W. Cronk

Buehler Church is located about six miles south of Bristol in Sullivan County, Tennessee. It is very probable that it was organized by Rev. Adam Miller, Sr., early in the 18th century. It belonged to the North Carolina Synod prior to the organization of the Tennessee Synod.

It has had three houses of worship. The first was a log building and the second was a brick structure with a seating capacity of about 300. It was erected in 1863, and dedicated soon after its completion by the Rev. A. J. Brown, D. D. The present edifice is a frame building about 40x50 feet in size. It was erected about the year 1900. The date of its dedication is not known. Valued at $1500.

The Rev. J. L. Murphy is a child of this church.

The membership is fifty.

Pastors:

Adam Miller, Sr.   J. W. Link
William Hancher   H. A. Kistler
A. J. Brown, D. D.   H. D. Chapman
K. Y. Umberger   J. A. Bourde
                B. W. Cronk

Holston Grove Church is located in Sullivan County, Tennessee, about eight miles south of Blountville on the banks of the Holston River. It was organized in 1903 by the Rev. S. D. Steffey. It has a history previous to its organization. There is an old church just across the Holston River from where this church stands that was organized by the Rev. William Hancher. It is still standing, but has long since been abandoned. In the course of time most of its members resided on the opposite side of the river somewhat isolated from the old church, which was first known as the Dutch Meeting House then as South Fork and finally as Luther Chapel.

On June 15, 1890, these isolated members were organized into a congregation, known as Fair View Church by the Rev. J. K. Hancher, with thirty-three members. It was located some three or four miles west of where the present church is located. Hence it has had three church buildings. Th membership consisting of members in part of each of the former churches. It is a frame building with a seating capacity of about 200. It is valued at $2000.

The present membership is forty-three.

Pastors:

J. K. Hancher	H. D. Chapman
S. D. Steffey	J. A. Bourde
W. H. Roof	B. W. Cronk

Oak Grove Church is located about six miles north of Bristol in Washington County, Virginia.

It was organized by the Rev. William Hancher about the year 1840, and was first known as Liberty Church and later as Mumpower Church. It has had two church edifices, both of them practically on the same site. The present church is a frame structure, 40x30 feet in size. It is valued at $1000.

The present membership is twenty-four.

Pastors:

William Hancher	H. A. Kistler
J. K. Hancher	H. D. Chapman
W. G. Wolford	J. A. Bourde

B. W. Cronk

Sugar Grove Church is located about one mile east of Benham's on Abram's Creek in Washington County, Virginia. It was first known as Rich Valley Church, and was probably organized by the Rev. Jacob Zink, who was the first pastor of which we have any record. Its first house of worship was about five miles east of the present site, and has been abandoned for many years. In 1882, a reorganization was effected by the Rev. J. K. Hancher in Sugar Grove schoolhouse near where the present church is located. Services were held here until 1906 when the present church was erected under the pastoral supervision of the missionary Superintendent of the Holston Synod, the Rev. W. C. Davis and' the supply pastor, the Rev. W. G. Wolford. It was dedicated in August, 1906, by Rev. W. C. Davis.

It is valued at $500.   Present membership fifteen.

Pastors:

Jacob Zink	William Hancher
Adam Miller, Sr.	J. K. Hancher

W. G. Wolford   H. D. Chapman
H. A. Kistler   J. A. Bourde
                 B. W. Cronk

Bristol Parish

The Church of the Redeemer had its beginning in 1891* with the work of the Rev. J. L. Murphy, missionary of the Holston Synod. He established a Sunday school and preached regularly, but did not give full time services to the mission. Following his withdrawal two years later the mission did not receive the pastoral attention necessary to rapid development, only occasional services being held by visiting pastors. Within the decade the Rev. J. B. Greever of the Holston Synod and the Rev. A. Phillippi of the Southwestern Virginia Synod were frequent visitors. The growing importance of the field and the urgent need of immediate financial aid, led the mission to apply to the Southwestern Virginia Synod for admission in 1903.

The church was built in 1904. It is a brick structure seating 300 people, and has adjoining Sunday school room. The value of the Church property is $65,000, and that of the parsonage is $2300. The membership of the congregation is 160.

The pastors other than those named have been:

Paul Sieg, 1903-1906   J. L. Yost, 1917-1920
K. Y. Umberger, 1907-1910   J. L. Smith, 1921-1923
J. W. Link, 1910-1912   E. B. Smith, 1923-1925
E. L. Ritchie, 1913-1916   H. E. Henning, 1926-1929

Chattanooga Parish

The Lutheran Church of The Ascension—The initial beginning of this congregation was made by the Lutheran church in Atlanta, under the leadership of Rev. W. Carl Schaeffer, Jr. Their kindly offices interested Father W. C. Schaeffer, D. D., then of Knox County, Tennessee, to enter the Chattanooga field and do the pioneer work in gathering and organizing the congregation, which was done October 12, 1913, with thirty-nine charter members. Rev. R. S. Patterson, D. D., Secretary of the Home Mission Board of the United Synod of the South, and Rev. W. C. Schaeffer, Jr., Atlanta, assisted Father Schaeffer in the organization proper.

The Rev. L. B. Spracher, of Salisbury, North Carolina, took charge of the work as first resident pastor, October 1, 1914. Three months later, January 15, 1915, Pastor Spracher, while in the faithful discharge of his duties, contracted smallpox—an epidemic then raging in the city—and died a day or two later, in his own home, his wife being a lone attendant upon his death. He was buried without ceremony by a squad from the health office, detailed for that duty, in Forest Hill cemetery. He slept in an unmarked grave until a few years ago, when the local

---
*Bristol was a preaching point, and visited by Dr. A. J. Brown of Blountville, two decades prior to this date.

CHURCH OF THE ASCENSION
Chattanooga, Tenn.

congregation solicited funds and placed a modest marker at his grave. The altar in the church is also dedicated to his memory by his admiring friends. The pulpit is a memorial gift to the memory of Father Schaeffer, by his own loving sons.

It was fittingly appropriate that the next pastor should be the younger son of Father Schaeffer, the Rev. H. Brent Schaeffer, now President of Lenoir Rhyne College. He took up the work immediately after his graduation from the seminary, May 17, 1915.

With his introduction into the work, definite steps were taken for obtaining a church home. The Holston Synod and the Home Mission Board of the United Synod of the South were interested in the cause, and a substantial piece of property was purchased for $8500 at the corner of MaCallie and Central Avenues. Here the congregation worshiped in an improvised chapel for some time, expecting, ultimately, to build a church on this lot. But God had other plans. The World War was in full swing. In August, 1918, young Pastor Schaeffer resigned to enter war service.

In January, the following year, Pastor Charles A. Phillips took up the duties of the pastoral office, and served the congregation efficiently for eighteen months.

On Trinity Sunday, July 11, 1922, Pastor C. L. Miller took up the duties of shepherding the flock, after a vacancy of two years. With his coming it was the plan to start the erection of the church building at once. Three months later, however, the congregation came into possession of the present church property, buying it from Centenary congregation of the Southern Methodist church, at a very satisfactory price. The church building was renovated and remodeled to conform to Lutheran usage, and the whole plant, from first to last, has cost the congregation $35,000. The property is well worth today more than twice that price. The congregation owes $6000 still on the property. Until the congregation purchased this property, it had worshiped in eight different buildings in the ten years of its existence from its organization. The membership consists of about one hundred members today, although more than twice that number have held membership here and have passed on to other localities. Some day this congregation will be one of the strong congregations of Lutheranism on this outpost of our Synod, and will likely be the mother congregation for a number of missions in this growing commercial territory.

Cocke County Parish

Luther Memorial Church is located on Oven Creek about three miles north of Parrottsville in Cocke County, Tennessee. It was organized in 1811 by the Rev. H. Grady Davis.

It has had two houses of worship. The first was a frame building about 30x40 feet in size, and was erected under the pastoral supervision of the Rev. H. Grady Davis. The congregation not being satisfied with the style of this building tore it down and erected a more commodious edifice after the modern style of Lutheran church architecture which was cleared of debt and dedicated on June 26, 1927. The dedicatory services were conducted by the pastor, the Rev. B. D. Castor, assisted by the Rev. C. M. Teufel. It is one of the most beautiful churches in that section of the country. The present membership is 107.

The parsonage, located at Salem Church, is owned jointly by this and Salem congregations, and valued at $3000.

Pastors:

H. Grady Davis, 1911-1913   B. S. Brown, Jr., 1916-1924
W. H. Roof, 1913-1915   B. D. Castor, 1926-

Salem Church is located in Cocke County, Tennessee, five miles east of Parrottsville.

It was organized in 1845 by The Rev. A. J. Fox. Prior to the organization services were held at the home of Mr. Michael Ottinger near where the present large church stands. These services were held by the Rev. A. J. Fox.

It has had two church buildings. The first was a small frame building with no heat. The members would build log fires in front of the building and warm until time for services and then go in. In 1873 it was enlarged and improved. It had an old fashioned pulpit on the side of the building. It was rededicated in 1874 probably by the pastor, the Rev. J. C. Barb, D. D.

The present church is a frame structure with a seating capacity of about 400. It is modeled after the modern style of Lutheran church architecture, with a pulpit and chancel arranged accordingly. It was erected in 1906. On the 7th day of October of the same year it was dedicated, the Rev. R. C. Holland, D. D., preaching the sermon, and the pastor, the Rev. H. E. H. Sloop, reading the dedicatory service. Cost $3000.

The parsonage of the Cocke County parish is located a few hundred yards from this church on a plot of land containing some thirty or forty acres. It was purchased on the 5th day of August, 1920. The Holston Synod was then in session at the church and there being a need for parking space for vehicles and automobiles, some four or five of the leading members got busy during the noon recess and in less than one hour the purchase price of $1200 was secured. It is a neat, commodious building of the bungalow type, and is owned jointly by the Salem and Luther Memorial congregations. It is valued at $3000.

This congregation is one of the most progressive and loyal churches within the territory of the old Holston Synod. Its present membership is 234.

Pastors:

A. J. Fox, 1844-1846	J. B. Rogers, 1891-1893
J. K. Hancher, 1846-1851	J. H. Summit, 1893-1895
A. Rader, 1852-1870	J. C. Barb, D. D., 1896-1900
J. C. Barb, D. D., 1871-1876	F. M. Harr, 1900-1903
J. C. Miller, 1876-1879	J. A. Linn, 1903-1905
J. C. Barb, D. D., 1880-1882	H. E. H. Sloop, 1905-1907
J. B. Fox, 1884-1886	W. C. Davis, D. D., 1911-1913
J. C. Miller, 1887-1888	W. H. Roof, 1913-1915
J. M. Moser, 1889-1890	B. S. Brown, Jr., 1916-1924
B. D. Castor, 1926-	

GREENE COUNTY PARISH

St. James' Church is located in Greene County, Tennessee, thirteen miles south of Greeneville near the foothills of the Unaca Mountains. It was organized sometime prior to 1811. It was received into the

ST. JAMES' LUTHERAN CHURCH
Greene County, Tenn.

North Carolina Synod, September 24, 1811, the Rev. Charles Z. H. Schmidt being the pastor. It is very probable that it was organized by him. It was first known as St. Jacob's Church.

It has had three church edifices. The first was a log building, the second a frame structure 60x40 feet in size, with low overhead ceiling and a high pulpit. For many years it withstood the ravages of wind and rain until it became very much dilapidated. In 1901 an effort was made to erect a new church which met with considerable opposition. The majority of the people were, however, willing and the enterprise was launched, and in a few weeks the material for the erection of the new building was on the ground.

On the third Sunday in May, 1901, the pastor preached from Nehemiah 2:20, "The God of heaven he will prosper us, therefore, we his servants will arise and build." So powerful was the truth of the text brought to bear upon the minds and hearts of the people that they were willing, with a shout, to adopt the proposal of Nehemiah as their own. On Monday following ninety-three of the members assembled to tear down the old building. Three days later 104 people gathered to raise the frame of the new building. The enthusiasm was so great that it silenced the sneers of objectors and they fell in line with the others and the work went forward with leaps and bounds.

Two months later, on the third Sunday in July, the new church was dedicated complete and free of debt. The dedicatory sermon was preached by the Rev. C. B. Cox, and the service read by the Rev. F. M. Harr. It has a seating capacity of about 400, and is valued at $3500. The present membership is 388.

·This church has had an interest in two parsonages. The first was erected about three miles west of the church on an eminence overlooking the village of Cany Branch. It was a one story building with five rooms. It was owned jointly by St. James', Solomon, and Salem churches.

While the Rev. F. M. Harr was pastor of these churches he bought a four-acre lot adjacent to the church lot at St. James' and erected on it an eight room two-story building at his own expense. In 1903 he sold it to the parish for a parsonage at a loss of $250. It is now owned jointly by St. James' and Solomon churches; the latter two congregations having bought the interest of Salem Church in 1908. It is valued at $3500.

Two ministers have gone out from this congregation, namely, the Rev. George Easterly and the Rev. A. Rader.

It has been served by the following pastors:

C. Z. H. Schmidt	J. H. Summitt, 1893-1895
Philip Henkel	J. C. Barb, D. D., 1896-1900
George Easterly	F. M. Harr, 1900-1903
A. Rader, 1852-1870	J. A. Linn, 1903-1905
J. C. Barb, D. D., 1871-1876	H. E. H. Sloop, 1905-1907
J. C. Miller, 1876-1879	W. C. Davis, D. D., 1907-1911
J. C. Barb, D. D., 1880-1882	H. Grady Davis, 1911-1913
J. B. Fox, 1884-1886	W. H. Roof, 1913-1917
J. C. Miller, 1887-1888	E. B. Smith, 1918-1921
J. M. Moser, 1889-1890	J. A. Shealy, 1924-1928
J. B. Rogers, 1891-1893	B. S. Dasher, 1928-

SOLOMON'S LUTHERAN CHURCH
Greene County, Tenn.

Solomon's Church is located in Greene County, Tennessee, about ten miles south of Greeneville on the banks of Cave Creek. The probable date of its organization is 1797. It was received into the North Carolina Synod at its ninth convention, held at Lincolnton, North Carolina, in 1811. Its first elders were Frederick Godshall and Peter Richter. It was served at that time by the Rev. Charles Z. H. Schmidt.

It has had three houses of worship. The first was a log house located near where the present church stands, the second was a brick building about 36x50 feet in size, and was erected about the year 1843. The present building is a frame structure 50x50 feet in size, with a class room cut off from the main auditorium by folding doors. It was erected in 1912 under the pastoral supervision of the Rev. H. Grady Davis. It was dedicated the 4th Sunday in June, 1913, the Rev. W. C. Davis, D. D. preaching the dedicatory sermon from these words, "What mean ye by these stones," and the Rev. H. Grady Davis reading the dedicatory service.

This church has the honor of being the birthplace of the Tennessee Synod. It was here on the 17th day of July, 1820, that the following ministers and lay-delegates met and organized the Evangelical German Lutheran Tennessee Synod.

The ministers were the Rev. Paul Henkel, the Rev. Jacob Zink, the Rev. Adam Miller, Sr., the Rev. Philip Henkel and the Rev. George Easterly.

Lay delegates—John Keicher, Conrad Keicher, Michael Kapp, John Nehs, John Ottinger, Philip Easterly, John Kock, Philip Ebert, Frederick Godshall, John Froschauer, John Renner, John Bauer, Frederick Shaeffer, Peter Gabel, Jacob Hermann, Henry Herchelroth, Jacob Deck, Nicholas Eley and George Boessinger. They were all noble veterans of the cross and deserve having their names perpetuated on the pages of history.

This congregation holds a half interest in the parsonage of the Green County parish, valued at $3000. The church is valued at $4000.

The present membership is 140.

Pastors:

C. Z. H. Schmidt	J. C. Miller
Philip Henkel	J. M. Moser
David Henkel	J. B. Rogers
J. E. Bell	J. C. Barb, D. D.
George Easterly	F. M. Harr
A. J. Fox	J. A. Lynn
J. K. Hancher	H. E. H. Sloop
Adam Flenor	W. C. Davis, D. D.
J. A. Seneker	W. H. Roof
Andrew Rader	H. Grady Davis
J. M. Wagner	E. B. Smith
J. C. Miller	J. A. Shealy
J. B. Fox	B. S. Dasher

Greeneville Parish

Church of the Reformation is located in Greeneville, Tennessee. It was organized in 1893 by the Rev. J. L. Murphy. In 1895 a lot was purchased on Depot Street, and a house of worship was begun under the supervision of the Rev. J. C. Barb, D. D. He resigned before it was completed. The Rev. F. M. Harr as supply pastor was instrumental in

completing the building. It was a small church with a seating capacity of about 200. It has recently been sold, and a new site is now under consideration if not already purchased on which a·new church will be erected in the near future. The present membership is fifty-two.
It has been served by the following pastors:

J. L. Murphy   C. B. Cox
J. C. Barb, D. D.   W. C. Schaeffer, D. D.
F. M. Harr   J. G. Graichen
                    B. S. Dasher

KINGSPORT PARISH

Holy Trinity Church is located at the corner of Broad and Sevier Streets, Kingsport, Tennessee. It was organized by the Rev. H. Grady Davis in 1918.

Previous to the organization services were held in the public school building by the Rev. N. D. Yount, student from Southern Seminary at Columbia, S. C.

In the spring of 1918, Rev. H. Grady Davis was officially called by the Mission Board of the United Lutheran Church as pastor. The Board assumed control of the work as a mission under the care and supervision of said Board.

During the pastoral care of the Rev. Davis, a lot on which to erect a church was purchased from Mr. R. S. Walker at the very moderate price of $6000. On this lot there was a large, commodious dwelling and a three-room servants' cottage. The cottage was converted into a temporary chapel in which services were held until 1928, at which time the first unit of a permanent house of worship was begun, and is now completed.

It is constructed of brick, after the Gothic style of architecture as approved by the Board of Architecture of the United Lutheran Church. The building is 26 feet wide by 66 feet long, including vestibule. The estimated cost about $13,000.

There is a bright future for this mission as it is located in a town which has grown in a little more than a decade, from a mere village to a modern city of several thousand inhabitants. It has also developed into one of the leading manufacturing centers of East Tennessee, and affords ample material for rapid growth, not only in material wealth, but in the extension of God's Kingdom and the saving of immortal souls.

Pastor J. A. Huffard, D. D., whose death occurred while he was in the service of the mission in 1927, is worthy of special mention.

The mission has been served by the following ministers:

W. G. Cobb, 1916-1917   J. A. Huffard, D. D., 1922-1927
H. Grady Davis, 1918-1921   J. W. Shuey, 1927-

KNOX-MONROE PARISH

Miller's Church is located about seven miles northeast of Knoxville, Knox County, Tennessee. The date of its organization is not known. It was first known as Lonas Church, and was received into the North

HOLY TRINITY LUTHERAN CHURCH
Kingsport, Tenn.

Carolina Synod in 1811, the Rev. C. Z. H. Schmidt being its pastor. Its first elders were Henry Lonas, Henry Mauck, Nicholas Gibbs and Henry Lauer. (See history of North Carolina Synod, page 167.) There is, however, a large marble monument standing in the church yard on which is carved the following memorial, "Founded by Rev. Adam Miller on land donated by Jacob Miller." No date is given. If this record is correct then the organization did not take place until sometime after 1815, because the Rev. Miller was not ordained deacon until that year. He was ordained pastor by the Tennessee Synod at the time of its organization at Solomon's Church, Greene County, Tennessee, July 17, 1820. It is very probable that the record of the North Carolina Synod is correct, and that the Rev. Adam Miller was the first regular pastor. All previous services had been held by traveling missionaries.

It has had three church edifices. The first was very likely a log building and the second a frame structure about 40x30 feet in size. The present building is a neat frame building modeled according to the plan of Lutheran church architecture with a seating capacity of about 250. It was erected under the pastoral supervision of the Rev. J. M. Moser, and was dedicated soon after its completion by the Rev. A. J. Brown, D. D. It is valued at $2500.

The present membership is eighty-three.

This congregation has now in process of erection a parsonage to cost $4000. It is being erected from bequests made to the church by Mrs. L. R. Gibbs and Mr. R. F. Young for that purpose. It is located on the Washington Pike, about one mile west of the church. When it is completed it will be one of the most commodious and convenient parsonages of any of our rural churches.

This church has been served by the following pastors:

C. Z. H. Schmidt	J. C. Miller
Adam Miller	J. C. Wessinger
Jacob Shaffer	H. L. Seagle
J. M. Wagner	J. C. Miller
George H. Cox, D. D.	W. C. Schaeffer, D. D.
J. M. Moser	F. M. Harr
J. B. Rogers	J. A. Booher

M. L. Minnick

St. Mary's Church is located six miles west of Madisonville, the county seat of Monroe County, Tennessee. The date of the organization is not known. It is evident, however, that it was early in the 18th century.

It has had two church buildings, which were erected on the same plot of land. The writer of this brief sketch knows nothing of the first building. The present church is about 36x48 feet in size, a frame structure, and was erected in 1879 and dedicated October 26th of the same year, the Rev. A. J. Brown, D. D. preaching the dedicatory sermon from Jude 3:5, "Earnestly contend for the faith once delivered to the saints," and I Peter 3:15, "And be ready always to give to every man that asketh you a reason of the hope that is in you with meekness and fear,"

The property is valued at $1000, and the congregation has a membership of fifteen. This congregation together with St. Paul's Church own jointly a five room parsonage, located in Madisonville, the county seat of Monroe County, Tennessee. Valued at $1000.

Pastors:

Jacob Cloninger	W. G. Wolford
J. C. Miller	W. C. Davis, D. D.
J. M. Moser	W. C. Schaeffer, D. D.
J. B. Rogers	F. M. Harr
P. L. Miller	J. A. Booher
	M. L. Minnick

St. Paul's Church is located in Monroe County, Tennessee, three miles west of Vonore on the L. & N. R. R. It was probably organized about the year 1817 by the Rev. David Henkel, who was sent out by the North Carolina Synod in that year to Tennessee as traveling missionary. The earliest date of which we have any record is 1820. It is certain, however, that the organization was prior to that date.

It has had two houses of worship. The first was located about half a mile south of where the present church stands in one of the most uncouth sites that could have been selected. It was a frame structure, 30x40 feet. The building had become old and dilapidated. At the suggestion of the pastor, Rev. F. M. Harr, a new church was erected on a beautiful site on the pike leading from Vonore to Sweetwater. It is a neat church, and an ornament to any community. It is valued at $3000. It was dedicated on October 31, 1920, the Rev. W. C. Davis, D. D. preaching the sermon and Pastor Harr conducting the dedicatory service.

Present membership is forty.

The following ministers were members of this church, Rev. J. H. Summitt, Rev. J. Morgan Moser, Rev. W. C. Davis, D. D., and the Rev. H. Grady Davis.

It has been served by the following pastors:

Jacob Shaffer	W. G. Wolford
Jacob Cloninger	C. E. Hershberger
J. C: Miller	W. C. Schaeffer, D. D.
J. M. Moser	F. M. Harr
J. B. Rogers	J. A. Booher
P. L. Miller	M. L. Minnick

Zion Church is located in Knox County, Tennessee, about six miles south of Knoxville near Nubert's Springs. It is not known when and by whom it was organized.

It has had three church buildings. The first was a log building, the second a frame building with a seating capacity of about 200. The present church is a frame structure about 36x48 feet in size. It was erected under the pastoral supervision of the Rev. W. C. Davis, D. D.,

in 1907, and dedicated the second Sunday in August of the same year
by the Rev. R. C. Holland, D. D. It is valued at $3000. Present
membership is seventy-seven.

The Rev. Joseph Howser was a child of this church.

Pastors:

Adam Miller, Sr.	J. C. Wessinger
Jacob Shaffer	H. L. Seagle
Geo. H. Cox, D. D.	W. C. Davis, D. D.
J. M. Wagner	W. C. Schaeffer, D. D.
J. C. Miller	F. M. Harr
J. M. Moser	J. A. Booher
J. B. Rogers	M. L. Minnick

ST. JOHN'S CHURCH
Knoxville, Tenn.

KNOXVILLE PARISH

St. John's Church is located on the corner of Fourth Avenue and
Broadway in Knoxville, Tennessee. It was organized in 1889 by the
Rev. L. K. Probst, under the direction of the Mission Board of the United
Synod in the South.

It has had two church edifices. The first was a frame structure on
the corner of 5th Avenue and Broadway. It was purchased from the
M. E. Church. The present building is constructed of Tennessee
Marble. It was erected by Mrs. Martha J. Henson as a memorial to
her sainted husband, Mr. J. A. Henson, at a cost of $63,000. It has a
seating capacity of about 500 including the gallery; a large Sunday
school room in the basement with a study, robe room, and other modern
conveniences. In beauty and architecture it ranks high among the city's
churches.

From its organization it has enjoyed a reasonable degree of prosperity,
and has a bright future before it.

It has a large commodious parsonage, located on Gratz Street, one block from Broadway. It too was donated to the church by the Hensons. The church property is valued at $150,000 and the parsonage at $6500.

It has been served by the following pastors:

L. K. Probst, 1889-1893	J. Luther Frantz, 1913-1915
A. D. R. Hancher, 1894-1900	W. C. Davis, 1916-1920
E. C. Witt, 1901-1903	George H. Rhodes, 1920-1923
M. M. Kinard, D. D., 1903-1906	C. F. Steck, Jr., 1923-1928
V. C. Ridenhour, 1908-1912	Arthur M. Huffman, 1929-

Mosheim Parish

Blue Spring Church is located in the town of Mosheim, Greene County, Tennessee. It was first known as Patterson's Church, later as Golden Springs, and finally as Blue Spring. The date of its organization is not known; it was, however, previous to 1811, for in the year it was received into the North Carolina Synod, the Rev. C. Z. H. Schmidt being its pastor. It is very probable that it was organized by him. In the early history of the Lutheran Church in east Tennessee, there was a church just a few miles north of this church on Lick Creek, first known as Lick Creek Church, then as Bethesda, and finally as Immanuel Church. The eleventh convention of the Tennessee Synod was held in this church on September 13, 1830. Like many of the old churches its membership gradually diminished until only a handful remained, and they were merged with the Blue Spring Church and the old church abandoned.

This congregation has had three church buildings. The first was a log building, the second was of brick about 50x40 feet in size. The date of its erection not known. The present building was erected under the pastoral supervision of the Rev. F. M. Harr in 1893 and dedicated on the second Sunday in May, 1894, the Rev. A. D. R. Hancher preaching the dedicatory sermon and the pastor loci reading the dedicatory service. The church is valued at $1500. The present membership is thirty-eight.

The parsonage of the Mosheim parish is located just a few hundred yards from the church, and is owned jointly by Blue Spring and Sinking Springs congregations.

It has been served by the following pastors:

C. Z. H. Schmidt	J. B. Rogers
A. J. Fox	F. M. Harr
A. Rader	C. B. Cox
J. K. Hancher	Noah Bible
Geo. H. Cox, D. D.	O. C. Peterson
J. M. Wagner	H. J. Matthias
J. C. Barb, D. D.	R. R. Sowers
J. B. Fox	J. C. Miller
A. C. Gearhart	C. L. Hunt

L. A. Wertz

Luther Zion Church is located about five miles east of Limeston in Washington County, Tennessee. It was organized by the Rev. William Hancher about the year 1849, and was received into the Tennessee Synod on September 14, 1850. It was organized under the name of Union Church, and retained that name until the erection of its second house of worship.

The first building was a log house, the second is a frame structure 42x32 feet in size, modeled after the churches of its day. It was erected in 1875 and is valued at $2000.

As early as 1811, there was a Lutheran church, located a few miles south of where the present church stands. It, too, was known as Union Church. Its first elders were Abraham Shnep and Elias Bowman. To the personal knowledge of the writer of this brief sketch fragments of the old church were to be seen in 1897—a relic of a generation who have long since passed away. It is very probable that the membership of the present church at the time of its organization was made up, in part, at least, of the fragmentary membership of this old church.

The Rev. L. M. Wagner of the Missouri Synod is a child of this congregation. The present membership is thirty-three.

It has been served by the following pastors:

William Hancher	C. M. Fox
A. J. Brown, D. D.	Noah Bible
W. G. Wolford	O. C. Peterson
J. B. Rogers	H. J. Matthias
F. M. Harr	C. L. Hunt
C. B. Cox	L. A. Wertz

Sinking Springs Church is located three miles south of Midway, Tennessee, near the head waters of Mink Creek. Its first house of worship was erected about seven miles south of the present location at Timber Ridge. The present location at that time was owned by the Presbyterians. In the course of time, however, it came around that the majority of the Lutherans resided in the vicinity of Sinking Springs and the majority of the Presbyterians at Timber Ridge, so they exchanged properties, and in doing so they must have exchanged names for their churches; for each retains the name of the latter location. The date of the transfer is not known. It is evident, however, that it was previous to the reception of this congregation into the North Carolina Synod which occurred September 24, 1811, for it was entered upon the minutes of Synod as Sinking Springs Church. The date of its reception into the North Carolina Synod is the earliest date of which we have any record.

Its first pastor on record was the Rev. C. Z. H. Schmidt.

The second house was a brick building, 60x40 feet in size, with a comparatively low overhead ceiling and an elevated pulpit. The date of its erection was sometime previous to the year 1870. The eighth annual convention of the Holston Synod convened in this church on August 27, 1870. In lieu of the regular synodical sermon, the President, the Rev.

A. J. Brown, D. D., preached a dedicatory sermon of highly interesting and instructive character from Eph. 2:20, after which the Rev. J. C. Barb, D. D. read the dedicatory service.

The present building is a wooden structure erected practically on the same site as the second building, and is valued at $8000. It was dedicated on October 28, 1923. The Rev. Geo. H. Rhodes preached the dedicatory sermon from Psalms 26:8 and the Rev. C. L. Hunt, the pastor loci, read the dedicatory service. It is one of the most beautiful churches in all that section of the country.

Two ministers have gone out from the membership of this congregation, the Rev. M. L. Thornburg and the Rev. Noah Bible. The present membership is 110.

The parsonage located at Mosheim, Tennessee, is owned jointly by this and the Blue Spring congregations.

The following ministers have served this church:

Charles Z. H. Schmidt	J. B. Rogers
Phillip Henkel	F. M. Harr
George Easterly	C. M. Fox
A. J. Fox	Noah Bible
A. Rader	F. M. Harr
A. Fleenor	H. J. Matthias
Jacob Cloninger	R. R. Sowers
J. B. Fox	J. C. Miller
A. C. Gearhart	C. L. Hunt

L. A. Wertz

Bethel, is located four miles south of Knoxville, on the property of the Williams-Henson Home for boys. The congregation was organized by the Rev. Geo. H. Cox, in 1874, and the church was dedicated on June 6, 1875, the Rev. J. C. Barb preaching the sermon. It was erected at a cost of $2000, and will seat 250 people. The site was donated by L. E. Williams and much of the means for building was furnished by him. For a number of years the congregation enjoyed a reasonable degree of prosperity, but owing to the lack of a regular pastor the membership has declined until few remain. The church which stands about 200 yards from the Williams-Henson Home can be used as a chapel for the institution.

OHIO SYNOD CHURCHES

Phanuel, at Bergton, (in Brock's Gap), Rockingham County. The minutes of the Pennsylvania Ministerium show that John Foltz of Rockingham County was licensed in 1796 to serve four preaching points, one of which was in Brock's Gap. There is frequent mention of Brock's Gap in the minutes of early conferences and Synods. At the Special Virginia Conference of 1817, J. N. Schmucker was requested to visit Brock's Gap and preach. Peter Schmucker and his nephew, George, are known to have visited and preached for people in the mountains west of the valley. Ambrose Henkel and Jacob Stirewalt are believed to have made special visits to Brock's Gap community. The written records begin with the work of Socrates Henkel, on July 9, 1849. A log church was built and on July 13, 1851, was dedicated by the pastor. The congregation was admitted into the Tennessee Synod in 1855, Martin Sondhaus, being the pastor. During the ministry of Pastor Henry Wetzel (1859-1872) and under his influence the congregation united with the Ohio Synod. In 1888, the log church was removed and a larger and better church building erected on the same site, two small rooms being added to rear in 1908—and in 1928 it was remodeled and improved. A parsonage was built in 1896 on a two-acre plot of ground purchased for that purpose.

Following are the names of the pastors who have served the church:

John Foltz, 1796-1810	J. H. Lutz, 1894-1904
Ambrose Henkel, supply	P. L. Snapp, 1904-1905
Socrates Henkel, 1849-1853	S. H. Puffenberger, 1907-1914
Martin Sondhaus, 1853-1859	W. L. Ridenour, 1914-1916
Henry Wetzel, 1859-1872	H. F. Richard, supply
W. M. Sibert, 1872-1891	Frederick Kittel, 1918-1921
L. J. S. Carpenter, 1891-1894	R. A. Dapper, 1922-1926
Arthur Blank, 1927-	

Patmos congregation, near Woodstock, which withdrew from Mt. Calvary in 1882, and *Mt. Zion*, in the Fort Valley which withdrew from St. David's about the same time, are also members of the Joint Synod of Ohio.

MISSOURI SYNOD CHURCHES

Bethlehem Evangelical Lutheran Congregation of Richmond was organized October 3, 1852 "by the Rev. W. Schmogrow, a member of the Virginia Synod." There were 39 charter members. Names prominent in the early history of the church were E. O. Nolting; Ernest Franck; Carl Spott; Albert Spott; Carl Feitig. On June 1, 1855 the Rev. Schmogrow resigned. On February 7, 1856 the congregation severed its connection with the Virginia Synod and united with the Missouri Synod. Carl Gross became pastor of the church in June, 1856.

In 1868 the church at Sixth and Clay Streets was built. During August of this year the Eastern District of the Synod of Missouri, Ohio, and other States met in this church. Dr. C. F. W. Walther, for many years the outstanding man in the Missouri Synod, preached the convention sermon.

The following pastors have served the congregation—since affiliated with the Missouri Synod.

Carl Gross, 1856-1867	C. Oehlschlaeger, 1883-1902
L. Lochner, 1867-1877	F. H. Meuschke, 1903-1920
F. Dreyer, 1877-1883	O. A. Sauer, 1921-

Since the organization of the church 1011 have been baptized, 711 have been confirmed, 417 couples have been married, and 549 persons have been buried. At the present time the congregation numbers 400 active communicant members.

Other churches of the Synodical Conference in Virginia—

Bethany and Trinity, Waynesboro; This is an old and substantial congregation, having a very beautiful new church.

Immanuel, Charlottesville, Pastor J. H. Miller, established 1869.

Immanuel, Alexandria, Pastor C. J. Goette, small but self-sustaining.

Trinity, Norfolk, Pastor L. J. Roehm, mission congregation organized in 1920. Pastor Roehm also serves a mission organized in Hopewell a year ago.

Farmville, Cumberland, Amelia, Meherrin are mission stations served by pastor residing at Farmville.

A congregation was organized at Scottsville, in Albemarle County in July, 1929, and is served from Charlottesville.

Colored mission at Meherrin, L. G. Dorpat, pastor. Old mission station.

Slovak Lutheran Church at Emporia, M. Havlir, pastor.

Bethlehem, Richmond has maintained a parish school without interruption since 1867. Mr. C. F. Reuss is the present principal. Tuition $2.00 per month to such as are not members of the church.

Trinity Church, formerly known as the Koiner Church, earliest records bear the dates 1771 and 1772, and it is supposed there was a congregation here at that time, or that it was at least a preaching point.

John Schwarbach was then pastor at the Hebron church, and no doubt he visited this community. A log house of worship was built in 1789. The first pastor's name found is that of Adolph Spindler, who was pastor in Augusta County from 1796 far into the next century. After him the following records of pastors are found:

Paul Henkel, 1793-1797	Ambrose Henkel, 1836
E. G. Naiman, 1796-1800	Jacob Killian, 1836-1866
John Foltz, 1800-1810	J. E. Seneker, 1866-
G. H. Riemenschneider, 1810-1823	T. S. Swinehart, 1877-1879
Ambrose Henkel, 1823-	F. Kuegele, 1879-1916
John N. Stirewalt, 1831-1836	E. J. Frederick, 1916-1923

H. E. Plehn, 1924-1926

A brick church succeeded the old log church in 1838. In 1881, another brick structure was erected more modern in style, and located about 200 feet north of the first.

PART III

History of the Educational Activities
of Synod

EDUCATIONAL ACTIVITIES

How beautiful is youth! how bright it gleams
With its illusions, aspirations, dreams!
Book of beginning, story without end,
Each maid a heroine, and each man a friend!
—*Longfellow.*

THERE never was a time in the history of the Lutheran Church in Virginia, when its members did not feel a deep concern for the education of their children. The first pastor in the State as early as 1734 projected a system of education for the Hebron congregation in Spottsylvania County (now Madison County), which his successor put into operation, and it is said that in so doing he opened the first popular school for both sexes in the Dominion. Almost all of the early congregations had schools connected with them, in some cases the pastor himself was the teacher, while in others it was his assistant.

It cannot be claimed that wonderful things were accomplished, or that immense sums were invested, but it is only just to say that considering the limitations and privations of our people in many parts of the Commonwealth of Virginia and State of Tennessee, a fair and reasonable effort was made to provide the rudiments of learning in private and parochial schools, or synodical institutions.

Especially is this true of the years preceding the Civil War and the years during its course and immediately following its end. Instruction was imparted in both secular and religious branches, in the German and English languages. Pastors often served as teachers of children, as well as of young men preparing for the ministry. Often ministers took the lead in organizing schools in towns and at the side of churches in the country, and superintended their operation, or served as members of boards appointed to control an institute or academy. Often Lutheran ministers united with other local teachers or forces in organizing schools, like Christian Streit in Winchester, Socrates Henkel in New Market, and many others as will appear in reading the history of education in Virginia. On the territory of the Virginia Synod stood the cradle of Roanoke College. A number of schools for girls were conducted on the same territory for brief periods that demonstrated the individual willingness on the part of promoters and teachers to labor and to suffer for the good of the daughters of our land.

In southwest Virginia the spirit of education inspired the hearts of our Lutheran leaders with a vision that led after many hardships to permanent results in the educational activities for both men and women. It was undoubtedly the indomitable will and the irrepressible persistency that enabled the Southwestern Virginia Synod to bequeath with justifiable pride two valuable institutions to the Lutheran Synod of Virginia, Roanoke College and Marion Junior College for young women, even though its territory has become the graveyard for two institutions that in their time gave promise of living and thriving in perpetuity, Wytheville Female Seminary and Elizabeth College. The sacrifice, the labor, the gifts of love, the hopes, built into these two institutions were enough to give them an undying existence of usefulness, but as they did not survive, History must mention them as well as those that remain. Thousands of dollars were cheerfully given and lost; services were rendered with insufficient compensation. It is necessary to record not only the heartfelt thanksgiving for our two thriving schools of learning, but also a deep appreciation of the good done by the two that are no more.

The congregations connected with the Tennessee Synod but located in Virginia, through their pastors and members, cooperated in providing for the needs of ministerial education by giving private instruction in homes and schools, and in later years by making generous contributions in students and support to Lenoir College, Hickory, N. C. Many of these students educated at home or in Lenoir College labored in the bounds of the Virginia Conference of the Tennessee Synod, and thus these educational activities resulted in making a substantial contribution to the advancement of the Lutheran Church in Virginia. After the union with the Lutheran Synod of Virginia and the expiration of the time limit, the interests and support of the New Market Conference were transferred heartily to Roanoke and Marion Colleges.

In eastern Tennessee efforts were made in the education of young men that were contemporaneous with the early operations of Hartwick Seminary in New York, and that consequently antedated the work inaugurated at Gettysburg in 1826, but unfortunately personal vacillation and synodical troubles brought this noble enterprise to a premature and regrettable end. In later years on the same territory an institution for young men and women was conducted with synodical approval and support that furnished for a number of years opportunities of securing an education for many, and made it possible for a number of young men to study for the ministry, but its existence met with no permanent success, and eventually brought great loss and distress to the promoters, and the Holston Synod that had encouraged it for many years. But in spite of these failures the fruits of personal labors in this field were significant, and Tennessee produced its great teachers, like Dr. Cox, as well as its great preachers, like Dr. Brown and Dr. Hancher.

In addition to the synodically and semi-synodically established and maintained schools, there have been a large number privately owned which have existed for the Church, have done its educational work, and may well be classed as having been Lutheran contributions to the great cause of education. They were founded and maintained at great personal sacrifice of time and money by those who were worthy of being leaders in greater movements. Each of these endeavors served a useful purpose in meeting local and general educational needs.

In this chapter are enumerated the schools that have been maintained on the territory embraced by the compass of this History, together with those now in existence. The story of both classes will be read with interest. With all the patrons of education the motive has been the same, remembering, as Carl Hilty wrote, that "true education rests on two foundations, love of truth and courage for the right." Sustained by these lofty sentiments, the Christian educators of the Lutheran Church in Virginia and Tennessee have labored hard, often as pioneers, without due reward, each one helping directly or indirectly to prepare the way for the future success of all Lutheran educational activities.

The Virginia Institute
The Forerunner of Roanoke College

When David F. Bittle of Maryland was licensed and ordained for the pastorate of Mt. Tabor Church, Augusta County, in 1837 and 1839, he soon realized that there was

ROANOKE COLLEGE
Salem, Va.

a great need for education among the young men of the community in which he labored. Fortunately a young minister from the same State had come to the more genial climate of Virginia for his health, and while he could not preach he could teach. The two united their interests, and in the fall of the year 1842, they began to teach in a classical school that they had organized. The Rev. Christopher C. Baughman taught the classics three days in the week and Pastor Bittle mathematics for two days. Prof. Baughman was made principal. Friends came to their help and provided school buildings. B. F. Hailman, Esq., donated an acre of ground near his home, and made large contributions in lumber, which he hauled to the selected site for the school. Captain George Shuey led the neighbors in the raising of the buildings and in many other ways aided in the initial work of the Institute. The school was located eight miles southwest of Staunton, Virginia.

Two buildings were erected, the first a one-story structure, divided into two rooms; the second two stories high, consisting of four rooms and called "The Brotherhood," because it furnished the place for eating and sleeping.

There were twelve to fifteen pupils the first winter, but the number rose rapidly. When the report was made to the Synod in May, 1843, all was encouraging and the Synod made the school a synodical school and invited the Southwest Virginia Synod to cooperate. Soon there were seventeen pupils. In 1845, Prof. Bittle returned to Maryland, and he was succeeded by Mr. John E. Herbst as instructor of mathematics. A forward step was taken just before the leaving of Prof. Bittle, by incorporating the Institute. The charter bears the date January 30, 1845. The name was changed to The Virginia Collegiate Institute.

The school continued in its good work, but gradually the feeling was strengthened that the location was not favorable, and in the early days of 1847, it was decided to move to Salem. In the May-June vacation of that year the change was made, and for a year or more the school was held first in a dismantled Baptist church, and then in the Presbyterian Academy in Salem, but in the meantime the trustees had bought a four-acre lot and in the center of it erected a three story brick building, that forms the center of the present administration building of Roanoke College. Prof. Baughman bought an adjoining lot of the same size for himself and erected a home upon it. In the fall of 1848 the school began its work in the new building. The attendance rose at once to forty, and much enthusiasm was aroused on all sides and in 1851 a wing (the west wing) was added to the edifice to accommodate the increased interest in students and class work.

Again the sentiment made itself manifest that more should be done than the Institute could do with its Junior College curriculum, and the motion prevailed, in the midst of considerable opposition, that the Institute be raised to a full college. A new charter was secured bearing the date March 14, 1853, and the name of the Institute was changed to Roanoke College.

The charter was secured through the activity of the Hon. John McCauley, member of the Virginia Legislature from Roanoke County. The trustees named in the charter were: Dr. John H. Griffin, John P. Kizer, the Rev. John B. Davis, the Rev. James A. Brown, the Rev. A. R. Rude, the Rev. Elijah Hawkins, the Rev. A. P. Ludden, George Shuey, Benjamin F. Hailman, Jacob Baylor, John Grosclose, Michael Miller, George W. Rader, Abraham Hupp, John B. I. Logan, Nathaniel Burwell, and George P. Tayloe.

The Rev. C. C. Baughman having been called to the presidency of Hagerstown Female Seminary, the Rev. D. F. Bittle was elected president of the College. At the first meeting of the Board of Trustees, N. Burwell was elected its president, Prof. S. C. Wells (elected on the Board at this meeting) was made secretary, and J. P. Kizer was elected treasurer. The first faculty was constituted as follows: President Bittle, in charge of the Department of Intellectual and Moral Science; Prof. S. C. Wells, of the Department of Mathematics and Natural Philosophy, and Prof. Henri G. Von Hoxar of the Department of Ancient and Modern Languages and Literature. The first session enrolled thirty-eight pupils, four of the number being Juniors—the highest class in the college. Through the efforts of the president sufficient money was raised to purchase additional books for the library, and geological and mineralogical collections, and to build the east wing of the main building. Before the outbreak of the Civil War the West Hall was erected and the faculty increased to five members. With much difficulty and amid many interruptions the college was kept open throughout the Civil War; the fact of its being in operation is believed to have saved it from destruction. The year following the close of the War the East Hall was erected, and the Library Building was completed in 1879. Dr. Bittle served as president until his death in 1876; the Rev. Dr. T. W. Dosh, 1877 to 1878; Prof. J. D. Dreher, Ph. D., 1878 to 1903; the Rev. Dr. J. A. Morehead, 1903 to 1920; and the Rev. C. J. Smith since the year of 1920.

Near the close of Dr. Dreher's administration the Main building was enlarged by adding another story. During Dr. Morehead's administration the Dormitory, Gymnasium and College Commons were erected. The building plans for the future include a new and larger Gymnasium (now in process of erection), converting the old Gymnasium into a Library Building and the present Library Building into a Chapel. The faculty at present numbers twenty-eight members, and the student body 254, which is the full capacity of the institution. The College is fully accredited by the State Board of Education and also belongs to the Southern Association of Colleges.

Thus about the self-sacrificing labors of its early teachers and patrons, the four acre campus and the three story hall of learning, has been built a noble institution for the training of young men for service in the church and in the nation.

SCHOOLS FOR YOUNG WOMEN

The Southwestern Virginia Synod was the first of the group forming the present Synod of Virginia to begin the work of female education. In 1854, following a resolution to extend the educational operations of the Synod by establishing classical schools for boys in each conference district, Synod took this significant action: "Inasmuch as the time is not far distant when we should have a female Seminary of superior order in connection with the Synod, be it resolved that a committee be appointed to adopt plans, inspect locations, and if expedient make proposals to different localities for the establishment of such institution." The committee, consisting of the Rev. D. F. Bittle, the Rev. J.

A. Brown and L. D. Hancock, Esq., reported at the next convention that Wytheville had been selected as the location, buildings leased for the coming session (the Gibbony residence on Main Street), the Rev. W. D. Roedel had been elected principal, and the time set for the opening of the school. Although privately owned, and controlled by a self-perpetuating board of trustees, the aim and hope was that the school should be owned and controlled by the church. With this end in view the Rev. John Boon was elected financial agent to visit the congregations and solicit funds. The first session opened on October 1, 1855, with an enrollment of forty-five. A later session had an enrollment of one hundred and thirty-one. Provision was made for forty boarders. Property was purchased for the permanent location. The school continued its career of usefulness until 1866, when because of the untimely death of the principal, the Rev. W. D. Roedel, and financial embarrassment growing out of the distress of the Civil War, its doors were closed. Under the leadership of the Rev. E. H. McDonald an effort was made to continue the school, but without success.

The loss of the Wytheville Female Seminary to the church, was also a personal loss to certain individuals, especially to the Rev. J. A. Brown who had contributed large sums to it, but even these losses did not prevent them from making further efforts in behalf of the daughters of the church. Those who were active in promoting Wytheville Female Seminary were also active in promoting Marion Female College.

Marion Female College—In 1871 the Synodical committee having the question of female education under consideration, brought the interesting information that the Rev. J. J. Scherer, a member of the Synod living and conducting a school at Columbus, Texas, had returned to Virginia and would have charge of the "Marion Male and Female High School." The committee expressed it as their judgment that Prof. Scherer would endeavor to build such a school as the Synod desired, if proper encouragement is given, and that the town and community of Marion will heartily

MARION JUNIOR COLLEGE
Marion, Va.

cooperate. Two years later we find offers from Marion
and Rural Retreat being submitted to Synod—the former
being accepted by a majority vote. The following year
Marion Female College was chartered by the state as a
Liberal Arts College. The home of the institution was the
Smith residence, in the heart of the town. Sufficient money
was contributed to purchase additional land and add to the
building as need arose, the largest addition being the
McMullen Hall in 1883. Since 1912 the college has been
conducted in the splendid and splendidly equipped new brick
building, modern in every particular. The capacity is 125,
to which number the enrollment is limited. The standard
is that of a "Junior College," accredited by the State Board
of Education. It is a member of the American Association
of Junior Colleges. The school offers the four year

standardized High School course and two years of standardized College work. The graduates receive the Junior College diploma, which entitles them to admission to the Junior class of the leading colleges, and to teach in the High Schools of the state.

The first Board of Trustees consisted of twenty-five men, nominated by the Synod, the majority being members of the Lutheran Church. They represented every portion of the Synod and were of the best citizenship of Southwestern Virginia. They were J. W. Sheffey, Dr. H. C. Stevens, M. Jackson, Jas. H. Gilmore, Jas. Copenhaver, N. L. Look, G. H. D. Killinger, Stephen Groseclose, John Copenhaver, C. K. Coley, Wm. McCauley, Valentine Vanhuss, Peter Schaeffer, the Rev. J. J. Scherer, John S. Copenhaver, Benjamin Phlegar, the Rev. J. A. Brown, the Rev. J. B. Greiner, Jos. Groseclose, Jacob Cassell, John Groseclose, Jas. H. Francis, Nelson Fudge, the Hon. Fayette McMullen, Judge J. A. Kelly. Judge J. W. Sheffey was the first president of the Board of Trustees. The Rev. J. J. Scherer, D. D. was the first president of the College, and served until his retirement in 1909, when he became president emeritus. His successors have been the Rev. J. C. Peery, the Rev. J. P. Miller, the Rev. H. N. Miller, Ph. D., the Rev. C. Brown Cox, D. D., and the Rev. E. H. Copenhaver. Since 1925 the board members have been elected by the Synod. Selections are made from a list submitted by the Board. Two-thirds of the Trustees are members of the Lutheran church.

The tenor of the College has been distinctively Christian and is characterized by an earnest endeavor to induce each student to crown her intellectual attainments with the Christian graces. The finest tribute to her worth is the place her graduates fill in the life of the communities in which they live.

The *Virginia Synod* was not without her champions of female education. The story of their activities and self-sacrificing labors is one of great interest.

In his report to Synod in 1845, President J. B. Davis said—"The subject of female education so long and so shamefully neglected among us, we are pleased to see is exciting some interest in the church." He called attention to the female seminary under the care of the Rev. Mr. Eichelberger at Winchester, and suggested that it might be made to serve the church of the entire Valley. The following year, he, as President of the Synod, again called attention to the subject, but no definite steps were taken. We have no information as to the Winchester Female Seminary.

In 1858 President X. J. Richardson in his report to Synod called attention to the importance of the education of the daughters of the church and urged that steps be taken toward establishing a female seminary. His suggestion was indorsed by the Synod and referred to the President. The following year he again urged the matter, at which time a committee consisting of himself, the Rev. A. R. Rude, Messrs. George Pifer, George Baylor and W. H. Cline was appointed to give it earnest consideration. At the next convention (1860) the committee reported that New Market, Strasburg and Winchester were interested in securing the proposed seminary. Nothing more was done during the Civil War period, but the Minutes of 1867 show that the Rev. W. H. Dinkle had conducted successfully for one session a female seminary at Bridgewater, and would open the second session the following September with the Rev. George W. Holland assisting him. The Bridgewater Female Seminary received the hearty endorsement of the Synod and was commended to the people. It appears to have continued for several sessions having an attendance of from thirty to fifty pupils. Little is known of this educational endeavor beyond the brief record in the Minutes of Synod.

Staunton Female Seminary opened its first session in September, 1870 with the Rev. J. I. Miller as principal. The school was owned by a joint stock company and controlled by a Board of Trustees. It was incorporated under the State laws, and was recognized as the female school of the Virginia Synod, but the Synod was in no way financially responsible for it. Annual reports by the principal were rendered to the Synod, and a committee from the Synod annually visited the school. The catalog of 1871 names a Faculty of nine members. The departments were Juvenile, Preparatory, Academic and Collegiate, there being two years of College work. The plan of instruction and course of study was that followed by the best colleges of the land. Being under the auspices of the Lutheran Church the religious instruction and services were in harmony with her teaching and usage. President Miller withdrew in 1882, and the Rev. James Willis succeeded him. The school was housed in a good building at a desirable location in Staunton, and the attendance was always good. The Board finding the income did not meet the expenses, and the appeals to the church for financial aid not being heeded, it became necessary to close the school in 1896. A committee from Synod, appointed to consider the whole question of female education, reported it inadvisable to attempt to reopen the institution. The Rev. Christian Beard was a large contributor to the Staunton Female Seminary.

Von Bora College, at Luray, was established by the Rev. Dr. J. I. Miller in 1883 and continued for a period of ten years. A large frame building was erected for this purpose on the lot of St. Mark's Lutheran church, and part of the time a nearby residence was rented for additional room. There were four departments in the school—Juvenile, Preparatory, Academic and Collegiate. The Collegiate course extended over four years. There were ten in the Faculty, and at times as many as ninety pupils. At one session there were forty boarders. The school rendered a very great service to the Lutheran church in Page and adjoining counties, as well as to the community at large.

After leaving Luray, Dr. Miller conducted a similar school at Buena Vista, in a large hotel building. This continued but for a few sessions. Later he purposed to open a school at Basic, now a portion of Waynesboro, but he was too advanced in years for further school work.

Elizabeth College at Salem, Virginia, was established in 1910, as Roanoke Women's College, by the joint action of the two Synods of Virginia. The objective, a "high grade college for young women owned and controlled by the church," was a most worthy one. The charter required the Board of Trustees to be elected by the Synods. The first session opened in the fall of 1912. The college building, the first of a contemplated group, was a handsome and commodious white stone structure, at a superb location on the eastern suburbs of Salem. Conditional rating as an "A College," was "secured from the State Board of Education, and each year saw progress toward meeting these conditions." In 1915, Dr. C. B. King, President of Elizabeth College in Charlotte, North Carolina, offered the goodwill, the name, and a portion of the equipment to Roanoke Women's College. The offer having been accepted it was henceforth known as "Elizabeth College."

The financial demands of so large an educational program proved heavy. Some advantage came with the cooperation of the Synod of Maryland and the Synod of West Virginia. Efforts were being made to enlist the interest and cooperation of a larger number of Synods when a disastrous fire cut short the life of the institution. During the Christmas vacation of 1921, December 22, the College with all of its equipment was destroyed by fire of an undertermined origin. The following March at a joint meeting of the Synods it was agreed to "discontinue the operation of the College and liquidate its affairs as soon as possible." This having been done by the Board of Trustees, the College grounds were purchased by the Orphan Home, and the net assets were distributed to various institutions of the church.

The Rev. J. C. Peery was president of the College until 1918, after which the Rev. Paul Sieg was the acting president. More than 500 students were enrolled during the decade of its existence. Fifty-three were graduated with the A. B. degree and sixty-six others were awarded certificates for having completed certain courses.

CO-EDUCATIONAL SCHOOLS

Mention is here made of several activities of Lutheran educators primarily for Lutheran young people. In each of these the methods and courses of instruction were sound, and approved by the best educators. Positive religious instruction based on Luther's Catechism, was given as part of the course. Each of these schools was well patronized and each is recognized as having made a distinct contribution to the cause of Christian education.

The Rural Male and Female Academy was established at Rural Retreat by the Rev. J. B. Greever in 1872. The basement of the Lutheran Church was used until school buildings were erected. The school did chiefly Preparatory and Academic work. A boarding department was maintained in the residence of the principal, where also was the girls' dormitory. The boys' dormitory and school rooms were in the "Academy" building on the opposite side of the railroad, nearly one half mile below the railroad station. The school continued until 1886 when the principal moved to Graham, now Bluefield, Va., and established the

Wartburg Seminary—This school was the private property of Prof. J. B. Greever until he conveyed it as a gift to the Lutheran Church, to be used for the purpose of conducting a "high grade college." It was controlled by a Board of Trustees, the majority of whom were Lutherans. The property consisted of twenty acres of land, upon which was a large three story brick building containing chapel, class rooms and girls dormitory; and a large frame building used as a boys boarding house, besides several other buildings. The catalog of 1895 shows an attendance of 112, and a faculty of ten. The departments maintained were Elementary, Preparatory and Collegiate. The location was strategic, at the gateway of the Flat Top coal fields. A debt, contracted by having certain improvements made on the College building, coming due during the financial stringency of the nineties, led to the closing of the school and finally to the sale of the property.

Trinity Hall, at Wytheville, was established and conducted by the pastor of the Lutheran church, the Rev. Dr. Alexander Phillippi. It opened in the fall of 1878 and continued for about twenty-five years. The course included chiefly Academic and Collegiate studies. The principal

used his own property and the basement of the Lutheran
church. For a period there were both day and boarding
pupils, but later the enrollment was limited to boarding
pupils.

The mind of the *Holston Synod* toward the education
of young men and women under church influences, may be
read in the resolutions adopted at its first meeting—"We
will labor to create and foster a spirit of education in our
churches and the community in general. * * * * We will,
as we may acquire the means, and as the wants of our church
and community may demand, deem it our imperative duty to
establish schools under our own control." He who reads
the Minutes of the Synod is persuaded that they earnestly
endeavored to do as they had resolved. In the report of the
President, the Rev. Dr. A. J. Brown in 1868, attention is
called to the need of a female school in their midst, and to
the opportunity at that time presenting itself at Blountville.
His suggestion resulted in favorable action. An option was
secured on property and some subscriptions made, but it
appears nothing further was accomplished.

About this time steps were taken to purchase a controlling
interest in Mosheim Institute, a privately owned school
being operated by the Rev. J. M. Wagner, a member of the
Synod. The purchase was made, and the school under the
control of Synod continued with varying success under the
management of the following principals: The Rev. J. M.
Wagner, the Rev. J. C. Barb, the Rev. A. C. Gearhart and
Prof. W. T. Guthrie, until in 1897 the Rev. J. B. Greever
was elected president and a determined effort was made by
the Synod to establish a standard college to be known as
"Mosheim Synodical College." The cost of building and
maintaining the institution proved very great for so small a
constituency. The difficult of meeting the pledges together
with misunderstandings and misinterpretations led to
disunion and finally to the sale of the property and the loss
of the school to the Synod.

Shenandoah Lutheran Institute—For eight years the
Virginia Conference of the Tennessee Synod conducted a
graded and high school in New Market, Va., under the title,

The Shenandoah Lutheran Institute. The school began its first session September 9, 1913, in the large brick mansion just north of New Market, known as the Gideon Koiner home. The teachers for the first two years were Prof. W. J. Stirewalt and Mr. Henry L. Seay, assisted by the pastors, J. P. Stirewalt, E. A. Repass and W. J. Finck. After the end of two years, Mr. Seay resigned and Mrs. William J. Finck assisted and, in 1918, Mrs. Finck was elected principal. Dr. C. O. Miller taught science in the high school department, and Mrs. C. W. Bennick was elected teacher of the grades, assisted by Miss Linda P. Baker.

The management of the school rested in a Board of Directors, elected annually by the Conference. The following are the members that served during the eight years: The pastors, P. L. Snapp (first president), D. L. Miller, J. S. Wessinger, W. J. Finck (second president), L. L. Huffman, C. K. Rhodes, W. L. Darr, and F. M. Speagle; laymen, Dr. C. O. Miller, Dr. W. P. Crickenberger, Mr. E. M. Minnick, and Mr. C. A. Pence.

The course of studies covered the regular schedule arranged for the grades and a four year high school by the State, to which were added for each class lessons in Christian knowledge, based on the General Council Graded Series. The number of pupils reached an enrollment of sixty-five in the best year, but the average ran from forty-five to fifty-five. War, epidemics, lack of patronage in the outlying districts of the Conference, and the constant improvement of the public school system, prevented the Institute from having a sufficient number of pupils to justify the continuance of the school.

The sessions of the last six years were held in the Polytechnic Institute building. After the Institute ceased to exist as a Conference school, a parochial school was continued for a few years by Emmanuel congregation of New Market.

The above is the only distinctively Lutheran school maintained at New Market, however, Lutherans have been leaders in both private and community schools. The New Market Academy, the New Market Female Seminary, The

New Market Polytechnic Institute, and Stanley Hall, have had the following Lutheran leaders connected with them: Joseph Salyards, W. H. Swaney, J. L. Stirewalt, Socrates Henkel, Solomon Henkel, J. D. Zirkle, Noah I. Henkel, Samuel G. Henkel, David S. Henkel, Robert H. Cline, W. H. Smith, Casper G. Henkel, Francis E. Rice, and Thomas L. Williamson.

THEOLOGICAL SEMINARIES

In the year 1816, Philip Henkel in his labors in Greene County, Tennessee, discovered a young Englishman well versed in the classics, Joseph E. Bell by name. He recommended him to the Synod for authority to preach and to catechise, in order that he might assist in the great missionary work in the district in which he lived. In 1817, Pastor Henkel reported to his Synod that he had begun a small seminary in Greene County, Tennessee, with the aid of Mr. Bell, in which theology, Greek, Latin, German and English were taught. For several years these two men labored together, but in 1821, Mr. Bell returned to the Presbyterian Church, from which he had come, and Mr. Henkel was unable to carry on the seminary alone, though his Synod had encouraged him with the promise of contributions for the work from the various congregations.

The Southern Theological Seminary—In 1872, the South Carolina Synod transferred its theological seminary, conducted in connection with Newberry College, to the General Synod South. The seminary was opened in Salem, with Dr. Stephen A. Repass as the president and main professor, assisted by the Rev. Dr. T. W. Dosh. Members of the Roanoke College faculty also assisted. Here the school continued for twelve years, the only time that a Lutheran Theological Seminary existed on the soil of Virginia. It gave a great inpetus to the work in Virginia, especially to the Southwestern Virginia Synod, on whose territory it was established. In 1884, the General Synod South discontinued the Seminary, and its students went to Philadelphia and Gettysburg to complete their studies.

LUTHERAN ORPHAN HOME
Salem, Va.

THE KONNAROCK TRAINING SCHOOL

The Konnarock Training School, while not an institution of the Synod of Virginia, is within the territory of the Synod, being located in Washington County, Virginia, at the foot of the White Top Mountain. It is an institution for the boys and girls of the Southern mountains—established and maintained by the Women's Missionary Society of the United Lutheran Church in America. The initial steps were taken at the Biennial Convention of the Society held in Pittsburgh in 1922.

The land was donated by Mr. and Mrs. L. C. Hassinger. Miss Mary P. Smith was the first principal. The first session opened in a farm house in December, 1924. The building, erected by the gifts of the women of the church, was dedicated on May 19, 1926. Mrs. Catherine Cox Umberger is the present principal. Accommodation are provided for as many as thirty boarding pupils, and an equal number of day pupils.

* * *

THE LUTHERAN ORPHAN HOME OF THE SOUTH

> I count this thing to be grandly true:
> That a noble deed is a step toward God,
> Lifting the soul from the common sod
> To a purer air and a broader view.
>
> *—Holland.*

In the benevolent work of caring for the orphan, the Lutheran Church is a leader among the Protestant denominations in America. The early date of 1738 marks the beginning of the loving care for the fatherless and the widows among the Salzburgers in the Ebenezer Colony on the Savannah, Ga. This is undoubtedly the first orphanage established among Protestants in America. It did not continue its existence as the prosperity in the colony removed the need, and the building constructed for an orphanage was converted into a schoolhouse. One hundred and forty years passed before another effort was made in the South to care for needy and friendless children, but this effort resulted in giving the United Synod in the South a home for the orphans that it can well be proud of.

To Virginia belongs the credit of originating and fostering this child of mercy in the days of its precarious infancy. When its usefulness began to reach beyond the bounds of Virginia and its capacity increased it was offered to the United Synod in the South and it became the child of the southern synods, who elected the members for its Board of Trustees and united in its support.   This was in 1894.

The Home had its beginning in the reception of. two homeless children into the home of the Rev. W. S. McClanahan, September 11, 1888. Pastor McClanahan was appointed the first superintendent, and with the aid of five colaborers the work was carried on for five years, when Mr. McClanahan resigned and the home was moved to the property of Mr. Trout. There were now ten children to be cared for. Mrs. Davidson was appointed matron and Dr. F. V. N. Painter was made non-resident superintendent. Both these homes were located east of Salem, between Roanoke and Salem.

In 1897 the S. F. Simmons property in Salem was bought for the home and the name of the home was changed from "The South View Orphan Home" to "The Lutheran Orphan Home of the South." The Rev. B. W. Cronk was now superintendent. He had served one year in the Simmons building with twenty-six children and continued for six more years in a new location. At the end of his term there were fifty-six children in the home.

On March 9, 1899, the Board met in special session and decided to buy the "Hotel Salem" property on the east side of College Avenue for $14,500. Roanoke College advanced the money so that the property could be secured and used at once. With a number of changes the hotel adapted itself remarkably well for the purposes of the Home. The Rev. J. H. Wilson was appointed financial agent and he succeeded in securing the amount of the cost in cash and subscriptions.

Upon the resignation of Mr. Cronk, Prof. J. T. Crabtree was elected. He was well adapted for the position and was ably assisted by his wife. He served from September 15, 1904, to the time of his death, November 4, 1922. At the time of his death there were one hundred children in his care. He increased the material value of the property in many ways, by improvements, by the purchase of tracts of adjoining farm land, and by establishing endowment and building funds. The Rev. E. W. Leslie and Mr. George F. Santmiers were his two successors in office. Upon the resignation of Mr. Santmiers, the Rev. Paul Sieg served as acting superintendent, until the Rev. Turner Ashby Graves took up the position in 1927.

In December, 1921, during the Christmas holidays, the chaste and substantial stone building of Elizabeth College was completely destroyed by fire. The loss so thoroughly discouraged the patrons and participating synods that it was decided to discontinue the college. The Board of the Orphan Home resolved to secure the property consisting of seventy-seven acres of farm land, and use it for the site of the new home under contemplation. The purchase was made and the work of establishing the orphanage on the cottage plan was outlined by the architect, George C. Baum of Philadelphia. The corner stone was laid for five buildings October 25, 1925, and on November 9, 1926, these buildings were dedicated by the President of the Board, the Rev. Dr. J. Luther Sieber, assisted by many coworkers and the Secretary-Treasurer, the Hon. R. W. Kime. The orphans were moved from the old hotel property under the supervision of the Rev. Paul Sieg. The furniture in the new home was all new. The transmigration marked a new day in the life of "The Lutheran Orphan Home of the South." The five substantial brick buildings presented a most beautiful cluster of magnificent homes, ideally located. The total cost was about $200,000. The Home furnishes room for one hundred and forty children with their teachers and caretakers.

THE WILLIAMS-HENSON HOME

The youngest institution within the bounds of the Synod is the Williams-Henson Home for boys, located on the Knoxville-Maryville highway six miles south of Knoxville.

It is the fruit of the beneficence of Lewis E. Williams, whose death occurred in 1925. The will provided that all funds accruing from the estate, "shall be used perpetually for the establishment and maintenance of a home for delinquent boys, known as the Williams-Henson Home, and that the ownership and control shall be vested in the Evangelical Lutheran Holston Synod, or its legal successor." The estate consisted of 165 acres of land, the usual farm buildings, and some money.

At the 1926 Annual Convention of the Synod the gift was accepted, and trustees of the proposed home were elected. Progress in its development has not been rapid because of legal complications of a minor nature, the lack of buildings for an institution of this character and the necessity of equipping and improving the farm. Contact has been formed with the Inner Mission Board of the United Lutheran Church. Mr. I. Sears Runyon of New York served as superintendent for a short period, since which time the Rev. C. F. Steck, Jr., has been at the head of the institution.

EDUCATION THROUGH PUBLICATION

The history of Virginia Lutheranism would be incomplete without an account of the work done by the Henkel Publication House in New Market. Though of private ownership the character of its output was always educational and religious to such an extent that it played a prominent part in the conservation and the advancement of the Lutheran Church in Virginia and throughout America.

The date of the establishment of the printery in New Market is given as 1806, but its mental creation is a few years older. Not many years after the return of Solomon Henkel from Philadelphia in the fall of 1793, he opened a drug store in New Market, and became a practical pharmacist. It was a simple matter to add to his medical supplies, writing materials and books. He became the agent for John Gruber of Hagerstown, Maryland, secured subscribers for his publications, and sold many copies of "J. Gruber's Hagerstown Town and Country Almanack," which was first published in 1797. From the buying and the selling of books it was a short step to the wish to produce them. He first revealed his plans of starting a printery in New Market to his father, Paul Henkel, in a letter in 1805, while the father was in North Carolina. Solomon had been informed that there was a printing outfit offered for sale not far from the place where Paul Henkel was located, but it was soon learned to the regret of both father and son that the outfit had been sold.

Paul Henkel returned to New Market in the summer of 1805 with his family, excepting his second son Philip, who remained in North Carolina to serve his charge as an ordained minister. He brought with him an order for printing from the Synod of North Carolina. A Special Conference was held at Woodstock in October, and it was decided at the meeting that the minutes should be published, including the doctrinal articles of the Augsburg Confession. It was necessary to send these two orders to John Gruber to have the printing done. However, father and son felt that it should be the last work in printing done away from New Market. Through the help of Mr. Gruber himself, who sold them a quantity of old type and the necessary equipment, and took young Ambrose Henkel into training that he might learn to set up type, they succeeded in establishing the long desired printery in New Market in 1806. Paul Henkel gave the use of a room for the enterprise. The business was carried on under the name of Ambrose Henkel. The first extended publication that came from the press was the copy of the minutes of the Special Conference held in the new Röder's Church, October 5-6, 1806. For the services of dedication, hymns had been printed on separate slips, and these hymns were incorporated in the minutes when they appeared in print a few weeks later. All this work of printing referred to in these lines, done in Hagerstown and in New Market, was in German. The copy of the minutes now in possession of the writer consists of twenty-four pages. Due apologies are made on the last page for the author, who was Paul Henkel, and for the compositor, who was his son Ambrose, in the following words: "The author was compelled to prepare these pages under the stress of many other duties. The young printer, whose first work now appears in these pages, lacked much needful equipment as well as experience. They hope to do better in the future."

This in brief is the history of the beginning of the Henkel printery in New Market. It developed favorably. The young printer served a long apprenticeship, working at various places away from home, like Hagerstown and Frederick, Hanover and Reading, that he might learn all the branches of the business, including even the making of cuts and binding of books. In the fall of 1807, he was called home by his older brother Solomon, for the time had come to enter upon another project. Ambrose urged his brother to postpone the beginning of the new enterprise until January 1, 1808, but Solomon was urgent, and thus it happened that on Wednesday, October 7, 1807, the first German weekly in Virginia and the South was issued from the Henkel press with Ambrose Henkel as editor and pub-

lisher. It appeared under the title, *"Der Virginische
Volksberichter und Neumarketer Wochenschrift."* (The
Virginia Popular Reporter and New Market Weekly
Record.) The first number issued served as the prospectus
and sample copy, and it was followed by seventy-seven other
issues, continuing to June, 1809, when it was discontinued
for lack of a sufficient number of subscribers and advertisers.
It consisted of four large pages, was well edited, gave
domestic and foreign news, and contained but few adver-
tisements, chiefly notices and announcements. Dr. Solomon
Henkel advertised the religious books he had for sale in his
book store, and as postmaster published quarterly a list of
the uncalled-for letters in his office. These official lists
were the only part in the paper printed in English.

Upon the suspension of the weekly, Ambrose Henkel
was again free to leave home and perfect himself in his
chosen calling. First he entered once more the employ of
Mr. Gruber, and towards the close of the year, 1809, he
went to Baltimore and spent almost the whole of the year
1810 in that city. In the meantime his younger brother
Andrew was following the trade at home, and another
brother David, was also helping in the printery. When
necessary, journeymen were employed to assist. One of
these John Wartmann by name, became a partner in the
business and the firm's name from 1810 to 1814 was
Ambrose Henkel and Company.

Before returning home late in 1810, Ambrose Henkel
went to Philadelphia and bought a new press for $135.
The object of this investment was to enable the firm in New
Market to enter upon the publication of a German Hymnbook, of which Paul Henkel had prepared the copy. The
published up to this time, and was made possible by the
ductions of the Henkel printery. It was the largest work
published up to this time, and was made possible by the
purchase of the new press and the achievements of Ambrose
Henkel. Before this time primers and readers, minutes
and catechisms, practically all in German, marked the height
reached by the output, but from this time on larger under-
takings became the order of the day. The printery devel-

oped into the champion of the Lutherans of the Valley, and began to issue all books needed that could not be secured by purchase; first German books, and then, giving more attention to the needs of the English-speaking people, books and pamphlets in English. Readers and catechisms were also printed in German-English editions. In 1816 the first English hymnbook was sent forth as edited by Paul Henkel. After the organization of the Tennessee Synod all the synodical printing required by the Synod was done by the Henkels. Between 1820 and 1831, the works of David Henkel, who was a prolific writer, were published in New Market. This was a great boon to the pastors of the Tennessee Synod laboring in the Valley of Virginia, as well as all other Lutheran ministers, struggling to solve the language question in their congregations.

As Dr. Solomon Henkel, who had taken over the printing business about the year 1814 in his own name, advanced in years, he entrusted to his four sons the desire of his heart to publish the Book of Concord in the English language. After the father's death in 1847, the sons kept their father's estate undivided in order that their combined means and efforts, together with the self-sacrificing contributions of their wives, might enable them to carry out the father's wish. The unanimous approval of the Tennessee Synod had been secured in 1845, but Dr. Henkel passed away without seeing the fulfillment of his plan. The four sons, Dr. Samuel G. Henkel, Mr. Siram P. Henkel, Mr. Solomon D. Henkel, and Dr. Solon P. C. Henkel, united under the firm name of Solomon D. Henkel and Company, and continued the work with untiring energy. After seven years of arduous labors the long-looked-for volume left the press in 1851, followed by a second edition with all translations revised in 1854. In 1848, the same Synod was asked to approve the plan of issuing Luther on the Sacraments. In 1851, the Synod was asked to give its approval to the publication of Luther's Small and Large Catechism in one convenient volume in the English language. In 1855, once more Synod was asked, through the spokesman of the firm, Dr. Samuel G. Henkel, for its approval, and this time it was for the publication of a translation of Luther's Church Postil, a series of sermons on the Epistles of the Church Year. It is needless to state that in every case the Synod gave its hearty and unanimous approval to all these proposals, and promised its united cooperation in the distribution of these important volumes.

These books were all doctrinal in their character and served to inform and fortify the growing membership of the Lutheran Church in the principles of their religion. They were issued at a time when the people were using the English language, and the Confessions of the Church were available only in the languages of the Lutheran countries of Europe. The translation and publication of these standard writings came therefore at an opportune time and helped to conserve the membership of the Church and to bring many from the unchurched in the various communities into a living knowledge of the true faith and into union with the Lutheran Church.

The greatest of the volumes issued by the Henkel printery was "The Book of Concord, or Symbolical Books of the Evangelical Lutheran Church." It was an undertaking of prodigious magnitude, involving not only the ordinary work of the printer and bookbinder, but also the duty of selecting the original works in German and Latin, and of finding the men who were able to make a correct translation, expressed in pure and idiomatic English. When completed it proved to be a monumental achievement. A volume well bound, clearly printed, consisting of 775 octavo pages, was put into the hands of the Lutheran public. It found a ready acceptance in all parts of the country. The South eagerly welcomed it, and Pennsylvania and Ohio absorbed many copies. It attracted the attention of the professors in Gettysburg Seminary, and the Lutheran educators of the North and East. In the preparation of the second edition Lutheran scholars like Charles Philip Krauth, of Gettysburg, W. F. Lehman, of Columbus, Ohio, J. G. Morris, of Baltimore, and C. F. Schaeffer, of Easton, Pa., gave their valued assistance.

For the first time in its history, in any part of the world, the Book of Concord appeared in an English dress, and the Henkel printery in New Market, Virginia, had the honor of publishing this standard work of the Lutheran Church to the world.

This work of doctrinal confirmation and information, performed by the Book of Concord and the other publications mentioned above, was followed by a continuous practical influence flowing from a religious weekly. About 1870, or a little later, the desire was expressed by Lutherans of North Carolina to secure the publication of a conservative periodical. A delegation was sent to New Market and the negotiations with the Henkels resulted in the starting of "Our Church Paper," beginning January 3, 1873, and continuing until 1904, when it merged with the *Lutheran Visitor* to form the *"Lutheran Church Visitor,"* official organ of the United Synod in the South.

Dr. Socrates Henkel was the editor-in-chief from the beginning, assisted by W. E. Hubbert, L. A. Fox, Elon O. Henkel and Ambrose L. Henkel. It was widely read and exerted a powerful influence for constructive Lutheranism in the South. It was largely instrumental in paving the way for the formation of the United Synod in the South on a conservative basis of union.

* * *

The Virginia Lutheran

The official paper of the Synod—the Virginia Lutheran —as an agency of information and inspiration, has rendered a valuable service in unifying the Synod in thought and action, and in strengthening the faith and aspirations of the people. The paper, as an inheritance from the former Virginia Synod, the oldest of the merging bodies, has been of the Synod from the beginning. The idea of a synodical paper of this character is older than the date of the first issue of the Virginia Lutheran. In 1900 the Southwestern Virginia Synod was publishing each quarter the "Monitor," as a medium of communication between the officials of the Synod and the people. The plan was for the congregations to subscribe for each family and pay it from the current expenses, sending the paper through the mail to each, direct from the office of publication. The idea was conceived and promoted by the Rev. W. H. Greever, at that time Secretary of the Synod. Though the publication was not made permanent its value was fully demonstrated, and when the Virginia Synod at the convention of 1921 instructed the Executive Committee to begin publishing a synodical paper, the secretary of the committee, having assisted in launching the Monitor twenty years previous, had part in embodying the Monitor idea in the Virginia Lutheran. The union of the Virginia Conference with the Synod in 1925 added a field in which the fruits of a synodical paper were already growing. The Lutheran Messenger, the official organ of the Conference which had been published since 1921, was discontinued, her subscription list and good-will being transferred to the Virginia Lutheran.

The editor of the Virginia Lutheran is the Superintendent of Synod. It is published monthly by Shenandoah Publishing House, Inc., Strasburg, Va., the company publishing this volume, the business manager being a member of the office staff of the company. Two of the four pages are given to the work of the Synod itself and one page is given to each the Women's Missionary Society and the Luther League. It is growing in patronage and in favor with the people. A goodly number of congregations subscribe through the church budget for each family of the congregation. With an increased number of readers will come an increased number of those who heartily support the entire program of the church.

PART IV

Auxiliary Organizations of the Synod

THE WOMEN'S MISSIONARY SOCIETY

THE story of the development of the Women's Missionary Society on the territory now occupied by the Lutheran Synod of Virginia is a story of small beginnings leading to ever larger accomplishments; a story of the development of the women of the Church from a timid distrust of their own ability and the fear of the sound of their own voices in public, to a position of assured leadership; a story of a continual uniting of smaller bodies into larger ones; a story that parallels that of the Lutheran Church in the South. It begins in the southwestern corner of Virginia; extends to North and South Carolina when three societies merged into the Women's Missionary Conference of the United Synod South; then reaches across into eastern Tennessee and to the rest of Virginia; embraces the merging of the three English speaking bodies of Lutherans into the United Lutheran Church of America, and ends in the formation of the present Lutheran Synod of Virginia.

The missionary interests of the Lutherans on this terrain did not originate with the women of the church nor in the beginning did the women have to clamor for permission to form missionary societies. In the constitutions adopted by two of the synods when organized we find the following section which after quoting the Lord's last command, Matt. 28:19 reads:

> "The synod shall regard it as a sacred duty to adopt from time to time such measures as they may deem best calculated to execute this solemn injunction."

In 1834 the Virginia Synod organized Educational and Missionary Societies. The Educational Society was for the purpose of gathering funds to aid young men in their studies for the ministry, that of the Missionary Society to provide funds for home mission work within the Synod. This

Missionary Society met in connection with the Synod with
more or less regularity for a half century or more until the
more modern method of gathering funds for such benevo-
lences through apportionment became fixed.

The Southwestern Virginia Society

The first convention of the Synod of Southwestern
Virginia, held in Floyd in 1842, passed a resolution soliciting
the Educational and Missionary Societies of Wythe and
adjacent counties to hold their next annual meeting in
connection with the Synod.   This indicates that prior to the
organization of the Synod such societies were already in
existence possibly under the auspices of the North Carolina
Synod.   These organizations in the beginning were auxiliary
to a general organization of the same name in the General
Synod.   At the next annual meeting of the Synod, the
Society united with it.   Six years later provision was made
for the dissolution of the joint society and the formation of
two societies, one educational and the other missionary.
The object of the Missionary Society was given "to supply
the destitute portions of our Church in the bounds of the
Synod with the preached Gospel and the Holy Scriptures."
It was called the Home Missionary Society.   A few years
later the two societies were again united and continued to
function until 1878 when it was resolved to disband and
"that all the interests, responsibilities and assets be handed
over to Synod which shall carry on the work contemplated
in the work of the Society."

Efforts were evidently made to further the work in the
Sunday Schools and at the Conference meetings, but appar-
ently the desired results were not encouraging, for an item
relative to the work of the Society in President Greiner's
report in 1879 was referred to a committee consisting of
Rev. J. J. Scherer and Rev. L. G. M. Miller to report at the
next meeting of Synod.   Accordingly we find that in Pine
Grove Church, Roanoke County, 1880, the committee
reported as follows:

Ladies' Cooperative Association

In view of the pressing necessities of Synod in the prosecution of our Missionary and Educational Operations, and knowing the characteristic devotion of woman in every good work:

Resolved, 1. That we earnestly appeal to the female portion of our congregations to form cooperative associations in each congregation or pastorate in our connection, to aid us in raising the funds so much needed.

Resolved, 2. That a committee of three be appointed to carry out the object of this proposition.

Resolved, 3. That the amounts so raised shall be credited in the Minutes to the ladies of the congregations severally so raising them.

Resolved, 4. That our pastors be required to read this paper at their earliest opportunity to all the congregations of their respective charges and give counsel and direction in the accomplishment of the object proposed.

The committee appointed to.carry out these resolutions was Revs. W. E. Hubbert, L. G. M. Miller and J. J. Scherer.

At the next meeting of Synod the committee presented a form of constitution to be adopted by the Synod. In this the name, Ladies' Cooperative Association, was changed to Woman's Synodical Missionary Society. The constitution provided name, membership fee, officers and appropriations. Article VI read: "All moneys raised shall be appropriated to the support of Home Missions in our Synod." A resolution was adopted by Synod "requiring the pastors to call attention to this action and urge the organization of auxiliary societies."

The Synod elected Miss Kate G. Haller, President; Miss Fannie A. Yonce, Secretary; Mrs. J. A. Brown, Treasurer; with Miss Hattie E. Martin and Mrs. C. A. Marks additional members of the Executive Committee. At this same meeting the estimate made for money needed for Home Missions was $170 and for Foreign Missions $50. This was what was expected from the whole Synod! At the next meeting of Synod five societies had been organized, St.

John's, Wythe County; Marion; Rural Retreat; Blacksburg, and Newport. A revised form of the constitution was adopted providing that the funds could be used for either Home or Foreign Missions. The treasurer reported $9.50 which was devoted to the Carroll mission.

Perhaps because three of the women had the courage to appear in person at the next meeting of Synod as delegates, the organization of the Women's Missionary Society is dated from the meeting in 1883 at Marion. The three representatives were Miss Ella Yonce, Mrs. Ella Copenhaver, Mrs. Virginia Slusser. They appear to have had no voice in the preceedings, however. The report of the Secretary of the Executive Committee was read and mention is made in it of the organization of a society in College Church, Salem. At this meeting Dr. David A. Day of the Muhlenberg Mission, Africa was present and additional interest and impetus was given by the fact that a young man from the South, Rev. W. P. Swartz, had offered himself for work in India.

The following year, Missionary-elect Schwartz himself was present and afterwards visited a number of congregations and organized women's societies. At this meeting Mrs. L. A. Fox was elected president, an office which she filled most acceptably for twenty-two years. Associated with her during the pioneer years were Mrs. J. J. Scherer, Misses Fannie and Ella Yonce, Mrs. W. E. Hubbert, Mrs. J. A. Brown, Mrs. Jno. A. Kizer, Mrs. W. J. McCauley and others.

The new Executive Committee felt that the constitution prepared for the women by the synod was inadequate and gave notice through the Church papers that a constitution prepared by the Board of Missions of the United Synod, South would be proposed for consideration at the next session. Up until this time, the annual meetings had been but an incidental part of the program of Synod. The reports of the Executive Committee and of the Treasurer were read by one of the pastors and an address on missions constituted the program. At the meeting held in College Church, Salem in 1885, the President was asked to read her own report before Synod and at the close of it she asked that the constitution be adopted. This constitution provided for the election of officers by the women delegates and that the funds for missionary purposes be remitted to the treasurer of the Board of Missions. The annual meetings were to be held near the time and place of the meeting of Synod.

After a lively discussion this constitution was approved by Synod and the President, Dr. J. J. Scherer, always a warm supporter of the work of the women, addressed them as follows:

"When we organized the Women's Missionary Society, several years ago, I clearly foresaw the action which was taken today, but I did not then think the time would come so soon.

"The President of the Executive Committee has carefully consulted me during the year, and from time to time asked my advice upon matters pertaining to the Society.

"I sincerely hope that no one will misunderstand the action taken today, and impede the progress and usefulness of the Woman's Work by withdrawing his influence and support.

"I most heartily bid the Women's Missionary Society 'God speed!' "

At 2:30 that afternoon, August 14, 1885, the women met apart from Synod in the basement of College Church and proceeded to organize under the new constitution.

The members of Synod builded more wisely than they knew in furthering the missionary interest among the women of the churches and then generously giving over into their hands the direction of the work. The most cordial relations have always existed between the officers of the two bodies and the women have always carried an item of synodical home missions on their budget.

Indeed, in the beginning the work was almost exclusively for home missions either on the territory of the Synod or that of the United Synod of the South.

Home Missions

The first special object was at Knoxville, Tenn. and then the women united with great enthusiasm on building the Women's Memorial Church at Pulaski, Va. for which $3,000.00 was raised and next $1,200 on a church at Radford. They united with the other southern women in helping at Augusta, Ga. and Winston-Salem, N. C. The pastors' salaries at Bluefield, Bristol, Lynchburg, Radford, and Virginia Heights were supplemented from time to time. A pledge of $5,000 was paid in yearly installments of $1,000 each on the property at Lynchburg. Chattanooga and Kingsport have been helped in the same way. In the minutes of 1896 we find an appropriation of $50.00 for work among the Swedes at Saltville.

Foreign Missions

During the early years the Foreign Mission contributions were divided between Africa and India and the money sent through the General Synod but after the Board of Missions of the United Synod South was formed, a regular sum of $100.00 a year was appropriated for Foreign Missions and the same for Home Missions. With the beginning of the mission in Japan by the southern church and the sending out of Revs. J. A. B. Scherer and R. B. Peery interest in foreign missions was greatly increased and when Rev. C. L. Brown was called as a missionary to Japan resolutions were offered to pay one third of his salary provided the Board agreed and the women of the North and South Carolina Societies would assume the remainder. These arrangements were satisfactorily perfected and the item of Dr. Brown's salary was a fixed one on the budget until after the death of Dr. Holland, he resigned as a missionary to become secretary of the Board of Foreign Missions. After the U. L. C. A. merger all contributions for Foreign Missions have been paid through the General Society and the foreign mission interests were widened to include India, Africa, South America and China.

Training the Younger Generation

In addition to the organization of the women's societies, much attention has been paid to the development of the children's societies and later to the organization of groups of young women. The children were usually given some definite object for which to raise funds and in time their contributions added materially to the total income. Some of the leaders in developing this branch were Miss Alice V. Fox (Mrs. C. K. Bell), Miss Mae Scherer, Miss May Greiner, Miss Rose Hankler (Mrs. W. W. Walker) and Mrs. E. H. Copenhaver.

In 1911, a Young Women's Hour was introduced in the Convention program and since that time has become one of the most attractive features of the conventions. The hour had expanded into an entire session. The number of separate organizations for the young women has never been large but the younger women have always helped in all departments of the work.

Literature

The need for special literature for the use of the societies was early recognized. A number of excellent papers were prepared to be read at Conventions and public meetings but lack of funds prevented their use in leaflet form. A little book of Bible readings and prayers was published under the title of "A Common Service Book for the use of Missionary Societies." This little volume served a real need at the time it was issued since few of the women were accustomed to lead in prayer in public. It went through several editions and was adopted by the other southern societies. The studies were prepared by several of the women and Mrs. M. S. Evans and Mrs. Fox acted as editors. Mrs. Evans was Chairman of the Literature Committee for a number of years and was much interested in her department.

Much of the success of the Society during the years was due to the untiring pen of Miss Fannie Yonce, who as corresponding secretary wrote hundreds of letters in answer to requests for advice and information and various papers for use in programs and for publication. The question of an official organ as a means for communication was for a long time a vexed one. The Board of Missions distributed free a publication known as *Home Mission News*. The *Lutheran Home* published originally in Salem by J. T. Crabtree and afterwards sold and combined with other papers had a department set apart for the Women's Missionary Work. Many of the women subscribed for the organ of the General Synod women known first as the *Missionary Journal* and afterwards as *Lutheran Woman's Work*.

When the *Lutheran Visitor* became the official organ of the United Synod South, it carried a page devoted to the women's work. Mrs. B. E. Copenhaver, Mrs. L. A. Fox and Mrs. W. F. Morehead were appointed as editors or assistants from time to time until the management secured the services of Mrs. M. O. J. Kreps as permanent editor.

Week of Prayer and Self Denial

In the President's report for 1887 we find the following: "In order to increase our contributions and for our own spiritual growth and development it might be well for us to set apart one week during the year for special prayer and self-denial." The convention took action on this item setting apart the last week in October for this purpose. A paper, "Love Gifts to the Lord," by Miss Fannie Yonce read at this meeting seemed to have deepened the impression that the President's suggestion made on the minds of the delegates. The observance of this week became more and more the custom among the local societies. It was adopted by the women of North and South Carolina, joint envelopes and topics were prepared for use at the daily meetings during the week. When the Women's Missionary Conference was organized, the time for holding the Week of Prayer was changed to the first full week in Lent. At the time of the merger it was carried over into the program of the General Society. The observance of it has played a large part in developing the prayer life of the women and the offerings made are usually most generous.

An undue space has perhaps been allotted to the Society of the Synod of Southwestern Virginia. It was, however, the pioneer organization in the south and as such, influenced largely the subsequent development of the work. The following have served as presidents: Miss Kate Haller, Mrs. L. A. Fox, Mrs. W. F. Morehead, Mrs. John G. Bringman, Mrs. W. R. Brown. Mrs. Bringman in one capacity or another has perhaps served continuously longer as a member of the official family than any other for forty years.

Contribution of the Women of Southwest Virginia to the Church at Large

Mrs. B. E. Copenhaver is at present a member of the Literature Committee of the General Society; Miss Mae Scherer is on the Executive Committee of the National Luther League; Mrs. Bringman was a member of the first Executive Board of the W. M. S. of the U. L. C. A. Mrs. W. F. Morehead was the first President of the Women's Missionary Conference and has been on the Executive Board of the General Society from the beginning as Recording Secretary, Vice-President and President. Mrs. E. C. Cronk was chairman of Literature of the Women's Missionary Conference, Editor of *Tidings,* a children's missionary paper, member of the Literature Committee and head of the Light Brigade of the General Society and the author of many pageants and leaflets. Mrs. M. O. J. Kreps, who was born on the territory and served as pastor's wife there for several years, has had an active career as President of the South Carolina Society and as author of many leaflets and articles for publication. Sister Alice Fisher is serving as deaconess in the Philadelphia Motherhouse and Miss Chloe Sibold is in training at Baltimore. Dr. Nellie Cassell is a missionary in India.

The territory formerly comprised in the Synod of Southwestern Virginia is now in the Marion and Roanoke Conferences.

The Women's Missionary Conference of the
United Synod South

In connection with a meeting of the United Synod of the South held in Dallas, N. C., July, 1906, representatives from the Southwest Virginia, the North Carolina, and the South Carolina Societies met and organized the Women's Missionary Conference of the United Synod South.

The idea of uniting the three synodical societies into a general organization was nothing new. Twenty years before, a resolution had been passed by the Southwest Virginia Convention looking towards such a step and a committee was appointed to carry out the resolution. At the next Convention the committee reported "no progress" and the resolution was made a standing one. Reference is made to the project from time to time but finally the report is brought in that "it is not possible to do anything."

The meeting at Dallas was doubtless brought about by the common interest in the Japan mission and especially in the $20,000.00 movement. Such a sum was reported as necessary to establish a boy's school in Japan. The Board of Missions hesitated to appeal to the southern church for such an amount! One interested woman said, "There are approximately 20,000 women in the United Synod South; surely we can get a dollar from each of them!" Permission was asked of the Board of Missions and at a meeting of the United Synod in 1904 a hearty approval was voiced and the women started out to raise the money. As everyone who has ever worked out a per capita scheme knows, we did not reach everyone of the 20,000 women nor did we raise the $20,000 over and above our regular pledges in one year or three, but we did give sufficient impetus to the movement for the Board to take heart and prosecute the campaign with vigor and more than twice the original amount was finally raised by the Church, and the Kyushu Gakuin became a reality. In addition the women discovered the value of cooperation and the difficulty of reaching the women who were not organized into missionary societies.

No attempt was made to effect a close organization at Dallas. The biennial meetings were to be for inspiration largely. The work of publishing joint programs and leaflets and week of prayer topics, of getting out our own thank-offering boxes, of having a common life membership pin of promoting mission study and of organizing the women in the other Synods was undertaken. Our organization soon brought us into much closer contact with the women of the other general bodies. We had long used the material prepared by the General Synod women. Mrs. E. C. Cronk was Chairman of Literature and one of her leaflets fell into the hands of Mrs. Charles L. Fry, of the Ministerium of Pennsylvania, who was at that time much interested in forming a Federation of the Women's Missionary Societies of the General Council. Correspondence soon resulted in a friendship which eventually meant much for the development of literature for all the women of the United Lutheran Church. Mrs. Fry was invited to one of our Conventions and after the organization of their Federation there was a regular exchange of "fraternal" delegates. The General Council Federation adopted our programs and soon a Joint Literature Committee composed of Miss Sallie Protzman of the General Synod, Mrs. Fry of the General Council, and Mrs. Cronk, of the United Synod, South anticipated by several years the closer union which was formed in 1918.

The southern women had often begged to be allowed to send young women missionaries to Japan but were always told that "the time was not yet ripe." When the Board of Missions finally decided to send out Miss Mary Lou Bowers (Mrs. Louis Grey) and Miss Martha Akard the women eagerly pledged their support, and when Misses Anne and Maude Powlas were sent some years later their salaries, too, were added to the women's budgets. After the organization of the Conference the funds were still handled through the synodical treasurers and each society made off its own budget.

At the time of the U. L. C. A. merger a Silver Jubilee Fund had been raised for the erection of a home for our women missionaries in Japan and a beginning had been made on a fund for a girls' school there. By the time of the merger, too, organizations of women's societies had been effected in all of the other eight southern Synods.

During its fourteen years of existence, the Women's Missionary Conference had only two presidents, Mrs. W. F. Morehead and Mrs. M. O. J. Kreps.

The Women's Conference of the Holston Synod

It is often difficult to trace the beginnings of the missionary impulse in any locality because it usually begins with the work of one individual which may be lost sight of entirely in the final results. One of such beginnings may be noted in the Holston Synod territory. In the Minutes of the Southwest Virginia Convention of 1895 Mrs. A. D. R. Hancher, whose husband was then pastor at Knoxville, reported the organization of a woman's and a children's Society at Knoxville, and greetings were sent by the Convention to the women of the Holston Synod.

It was not until 1907, however, that any concerted attempt was made to organize. Miss Dora Kinzer, of Madisonville, Tenn. attended the meeting of the Women's Missionary Conference at Dallas, and went home full of enthusiasm for a society among the women of the Holston Synod. Accordingly, at a meeting of the Synod of Madisonville, August 2, 1917 the women were called together in the church grove while Synod was in session. Dr. R. C. Holland, Secretary of the Board of Missions, and Rev. W. C. Davis, Field Missionary of the Holston Synod, presented the possibilities of Women's work for the Church. A number of women present pledged themselves to do all in their power to effect organizations in their home churches. A constitution was adopted, officers were elected and the society launched.

In 1908 contributions amounting to $29.10 are listed from six societies. The interest in the cause of missions increased rapidly, but owing to the lack of experience and timidity of the women it was difficult to find leaders who were willing to go ahead. For several years Mrs. E. C. Cronk representing the Literature Committee of the W. M.

C. and Mrs. W. F. Morehead, the President, attended the Conventions and helped the young society through the difficult first years. Finally, Mrs. W. J. Lintz, an energetic leader, was found who combined an accurate knowledge of conditions on the field with practical ability and great consecration and devotion. The work of organization and the development of the women was done largely through her administration. Mission study classes were formed. Department Secretaries were appointed and the objects supported by the Conference kept steadily before the women. The name of the organization was changed to the Women's Missionary Society of the Holston Synod and the funds which had at first been paid to the treasurer of Synod were sent to the treasurer of the Society. They were much interested in the Japan Mission and in home mission work on their own territory.

Their contributions increased rapidly and in 1914 we find them pledging $500.00 a year for four years to Morristown and assuming $500 a year on Martha Akard's salary. They have the honor of furnishing the church with the first woman missionary sent out from the territory of the present Virginia Synod—Martha Akard, who has done such signal service for our women's work in Japan and who is now head of the Janice James School in Kumomota.

The following have served as presidents: Mrs. W. L. Brakebill, Mrs. W. C. Schaeffer, Mrs. John R. Cloyd, Mrs. W. J. Lintz, Mrs. W. J. Caldwell, Miss Mary Brown. In 1922 after fifteen years of active service the Holston Society merged with the other two on our territory to form the Virginia Society. The Societies on this territory now form the Knoxville Conference of the Virginia Society. Mrs. W. J. Caldwell was elected on the first Executive Board of the General Society but afterwards resigned.

The W. M. S. of the Virginia Synod

The organization of the women in the Virginia Synod as in the Synod of Southwestern Virginia was first authorized by the Synod itself, but it is an interesting comment on the difference in the temper of the times to note that while the committee appointed in 1881 was composed of pastors, that appointed thirty years later was made up of women. Dr. George S. Bowers, President of the Virginia Synod in 1911 appointed as a committee to organize the women's societies already existing into a Synodical Society, Mrs. A. D. R. Hancher, Mrs. E. L. Folk, and Mrs. E. A. Repass.

That the women themselves were quite ready for such a step is evidenced by the promptness with which they went to work. The Synod met in August; the committee was called together in Christ Church Staunton in December but there were more present than just the committee. We quote from the report of the first President: "Invitations were sent to all Missionary Societies in the Synod, asking for cooperation, also to congregations expecting to organize such societies.

"Two meetings were held on December 7th, one at 5 p. m. for prayer and guidance in our new undertaking. Seventy-five women were present, representing societies from Zion; St. James'; Mt. Sidney; Mt. Tabor, Middlebrook; Grace Church, Waynesboro; New Market; Harrisonburg; Bethany (Lexington); Norfolk; St. Peter's, Shepherdstown; Richmond; Madison; Woodstock; Christ Church, Staunton.

"At the afternoon session the Bible Study was in charge of Miss Mattern, teacher in charge of Bible instruction at Mary Baldwin Seminary. Greetings from the editor of our Missionary Department of *The Visitor* were read by Mrs. W. C. Eisenberg of the Staunton Society. Mrs. A. M. Howison, treasurer of the Presbyterian Synodical Organization of Virginia, gave a most encouraging and stimulating talk, congratulating us on the remarkably full attendance of our women upon such an occasion.

"At 8 p. m. the business session was called to order by the committee in charge. The Constitution of the Synodical Society of the Southwestern Virginia Synod was read and adopted. The nominating Committee brought in a recommendation that the appointed committee act as officers until the first meeting of the Synodical Convention."

With such an enthusiastic start we are not surprised to find that the first Convention held in Christ Church, Staunton, August, 1912 should have been a most successful one. A fine inspirational program had been arranged by the committee. Some of the speakers being Rev. A. J. Stirewalt, Missionary to Japan; Dr. R. C. Holland, President of the Board of Foreign Missions; Rev. G. S. Bowers, President of the Virginia Synod; Dr. J. A. Morehead, President of the United Synod South; Mrs. C. F. Kuder, former missionary to India; Mrs. E. C. Cronk and Mrs. W. F. Morehead, of the Women's Missionary Conference; Mrs. W. C. Schaeffer, of the Holston Synod.

Eleven societies sent delegates and $496.18 was reported as having been sent to the Treasurer of Synod. The money contributed by the women's societies up to this time had been counted by the local congregations as part of their apportionment.

The high standard in program building set by the first Convention was maintained and at each subsequent Convention some outstanding speaker from among the missionary women of the church as well as pastors, missionaries on furlough and Board Secretaries were always invited to be present.

A number of the societies thus brought together had been active for years. At the 1914 Convention, that of St. Matthews, New Market, organized by the Rev. W. P. Schwartz in 1884 celebrated its 30th anniversary.

The new Society soon began to report new organizations and to assume their share of the work done by the Women's Missionary Conference. A number of individual societies assumed special objects such as contributions for buildings in Africa, leper colony, building in India, support of native workers, kindergartens in Japan, etc. In 1914, $200 was pledged to Martha Akard's salary and $50 for the children on the Rev. Stirewalt's salary. In 1915, Mrs. M. O. J. Kreps was the principal speaker and Dr. J. A. Morehead made an appeal for help in educating a Japanese student then in Roanoke College. The Convention pledged $50 for this purpose and established a scholarship fund in memory of the little daughter of Mrs. Kreps who had died in early childhood known as the Irma Kreps Scholarship Fund. The amount pledged for this fund was increased from year to year until the merger meeting of the Virginia societies when it had reached the sum of $400 and it was requested that this fund be taken over by the merged society. At this time the latest recipient, Mr. Kishi, had graduated from Roanoke College and since activities of the women's societies had been directed chiefly in the channels of work for women and children, the scholarship was given by the merged society first to Nellie Cassell to help in her medical education and for the past two years has been voted to Jessie Cronk who also has the mission field in view. A scholarship in Elizabeth College in honor of Mrs. Hancher was devoted to a young Korean student until that institution was discontinued. A memorial scholarship in Kyushu Gakuin was established in honor of Dr. R. C. Holland.

Regular appropriations were made to the Boards of Foreign and of Home Missions and at one Convention it was decided to appropriate a minimum sum of $300 for Synodical Home Missions. In the eleven years of its organization the women had progressed from giving a few hundred dollars each year to apply on the apportionment to a budget of over $4,000.00 a year. The various departments of work were well looked after by the Department Secretaries and special attention was paid to mission study classes.

The Presidents were Mrs. A. D. R. Hancher, Mrs. I. D. Worman, Mrs. J. L. Smith, Mrs. E. L. Ritchie (acting for one year) and Mrs. E. C. Cronk.

The societies formerly included in this organization now form the Staunton and Winchester Conference Societies of the Lutheran Synod of Virginia.

The Mergers—1918 and 1922

The strength that lies in united forces has been demonstrated again since the Missionary Societies of the former General Synod, General Council and United Synod South followed the lead of the Church and merged. To the

southern women especially it has meant an enlarged mission-
ary horizon and increased opportunities for service. On the
committee to arrange for the merger meeting the Women's
Missionary Conference was represented by Mrs. J. G.
Bringman and Mrs. I. D. Worman. At the Merger
Convention Mrs. Bringman was elected to the Executive
Board, Mrs. E. C. Cronk to the General Literature Com-
mittee and Mrs. W. F. Morehead as Recording Secretary.

Although small in numbers as compared to the other
two groups the southern women have been most loyal to the
merged society and feel that they have given as well as
received benefits from the union.

Four years later the merging of the Southwest Virginia,
the Holston and the Virginia Societies into the Women's
Missionary Society of the Lutheran Synod of Virginia
touched us more nearly since it meant a breaking up of
former groups and the forming of new combinations. As
usual the women were ready before the Synods were, but at
length we were told that we might go ahead and a Joint
Merger Committee consisting of the Presidents of the three
Societies and three additional members was appointed. The
following members met in Richmond, April 19, 1922, and
made the necessary arrangements for the merger Convention,
Mrs. W. F. Morehead, Chairman; Mrs. Louis Krause,
Secretary; Mrs. E. C. Cronk, Mrs. J. G. Bringman, Mrs.
W. R. Brown, Mrs. E. H. Copenhaver.

The Merger Convention was held in Virginia Heights
Church, Roanoke, Virginia, September 11-13, 1922. At
that time the three merging bodies reported a combined
membership of 2163 women, young women, and children.
The contributions from the three societies for that year
totalled $9,457.34. The total receipts for the year 1927-28
were $12,919.37.

Since the merger, the work in Virginia has gone steadily
forward with no phenomenal growth in membership but with
all pledges met each year. In addition to the dues and
offerings turned into the treasury of the General Society,
synodical specials amounting to nearly $2,000 each year have
been assumed. The specials authorized by the General

Society such as the Japan School, the Fund for Mountain Missions, and the Tenth Anniversary Fund have had liberal support.

The merged Society finished out the pledge assumed by the Southwest Virginia Society of $5,000.00 for Lynchburg and then assumed at different times $2,500 for Chattanooga and $2,500 for Kingsport which will be completed except for $500 by the 1929 Convention. The list of synodical specials for 1929 reads as follows: Chattanooga Mission, $500.00; Kingsport Mission, $500.00; Irma Kreps Scholarship, $400.00; Pastor at Furnace Hill, $300.00.

On the homebase side the first big task before the new organization was the establishment of the Conference Groups. This has been most successfully accomplished and an additional Conference, New Market added. This is composed of societies in churches formerly belonging to the Tennessee Synod on Virginia territory. This conference with the others is actively at work.

The following have served as Presidents of the merged society: Mrs. W. F. Morehead, Mrs. E. H. Copenhaver and Mrs. J. G. Bringman.

It has not been possible in this brief sketch to make mention of many other women who as officers and department chairman in the synodical and local societies have contributed as much to the success of the organization as those chosen to head it from time to time, but their names are listed in a much more permanent record in God's book of remembrance.

The Women and the Mission Boards

From the time when the Board of Missions of the United Synod of which Rev. Edward Horn, D. D. was President and Rev. L. K. Probst, Secretary prepared the first Constitution for the Women's Missionary Societies, the relation of the women to the Board of Missions has been closer than to the Synods as such. The President of Synod was usually consulted about any new work and he frequently honored the Conventions with his presence but this relationship was more or less casual. The Secretary of the Board of

Missions, however, never failed to make the rounds of the women's meetings. Dr. L. K. Probst and later Dr. R. C. Holland were always welcomed and both were the trusted friends and advisors of the women. When a separate Home Mission Board was organized, Dr. R. H. Patterson and Dr. A. D. R. Hancher were welcomed just as cordially and given a place on the programs. The representatives of synodical home mission interests did not wait usually to be invited; they came anyway. For years the women's societies made regular contributions to the two Boards of Missions in addition to special work which was undertaken under their direction.

When the Board of Foreign Missions decided to send out the first young women missionaries, Dr. Holland did an unheard of thing. He invited representatives from each of the three synodical societies then organized to meet with the Board of Foreign Missions to consider names of possible young women. Only one accepted the invitation, Mrs. W. F. Morehead. It was her privilege at that time to suggest the name of Martha Akard.

At the time of the U. L. C. A. merger the women of the other synodical societies were of the opinion that this had been an established custom and they pushed the matter of having women as advisory members on the Church Boards. Accordingly the W. M. S. was granted the privilege of naming two advisory members on each of the Church Boards to which the Society contributed. This custom has proved of great advantage to the women in their better understanding of the work of the Church as a whole and I believe that the Church has never regretted this step, since it has resulted in better understanding and in increased support of the women of all of the Church's activities. Some of the best informed Lutherans in the whole Church are to be found on the Women's Executive Board since they hear reports at their meetings from each Board. The keen interest with which the women present followed the proceedings of the last Convention of the U. L. C. A. bore evidence to their intelligent interest in all that concerns the church at large.

The President of the Women's Missionary Society is given a place on the program of the Church Convention, Synodical Presidents are invited to speak on the floor of Synods and our traveling secretaries are invited to address Brotherhoods, Luther Leagues and frequently to speak at a morning service. It is a far cry from the day when the pastors read the reports of the Women's Missionary Societies before the Synods. The Women's Missionary Society has done a great service in training the women to help in other ways than in washing dishes at church suppers and they have not in the meantime lost the art of washing dishes, or of training their own children in the home.

* * *

OTHER AUXILIARY ORGANIZATIONS

The other auxiliary organizations of the Synod, the Synodical Luther League and the Synodical Luther Brotherhood, each having come into existence since the Synod was organized, but brief sketches are given of them. It appears these should be placed along with the other auxiliary organization. The following sketches were written by a member of the Committee.

THE SYNODICAL LUTHER LEAGUE

Luther Leagues and other young peoples societies have existed in a number of the congregations of the Synod for several decades, and at times there were steps taken looking toward district and synodical organizations. A short time prior to the merger forming the present Synod, there was formed a "Federation of Young Peoples Societies" in Southwest Virginia, which immediately after the Merger called a convention of all the young peoples societies within the Synod. This convention, held in St. Mark's, Roanoke, Virginia, November 3-5, 1922, was the First Convention of the Luther League of the Lutheran Synod of Virginia.

The first task was to bring into the organization all the societies within the Synod, and to establish a relationship with the Synod whereby the League would cooperate in carrying out the full program of the church. The objective of the Virginia Synodical Luther League is "educational, inspirational and consecrational, rather than financial." The League having representation on eight important committees of the Synod, and the two organizations cooperating understandingly, there is every promise of continued usefulness.

The first president was Mr. F. A. Bostian, of Roanoke. He was succeeded by Mr. F. C. Hamer, of Staunton, and he in turn by Mr. G. C. Henrickson, of Richmond. The present president is Miss Vivian Cronk, of Salem. The Convention of 1928 reported seventy leagues and 1945 members.

Each of the six conferences of the Synod has a conference organization of the Luther League. Conference conventions are held once or twice a year, and are inspirational, educational and consecrational in character.

THE LUTHER BROTHERHOOD

The youngest auxiliary organization of the Synod is the Luther Brotherhood, organized at Roanoke in 1928, just prior to the opening of the annual convention of Synod. Mr. Frank Walters of Salem was elected president. Thirteen organizations were enrolled as members. The First Annual Convention was held at the opening of the Synod in 1929. Mr. F. C. Hamer of Staunton is the president. The organization is laboring to effect organizations in a greater number of the congregations of Synod, and will undoubtedly serve as the agency for the enlisting of the men of the church to greater activity.

The Brotherhood sponsored the Laymen's Banquet held in Patrick Henry Hotel on the evening of January 30, 1929, in connection with the convention of Synod, at which addresses were made by Dr. E. Clarence Miller, of Philadelphia, and Judge John F. Kramer, of Mansfield, Ohio.

PART V

TABLES

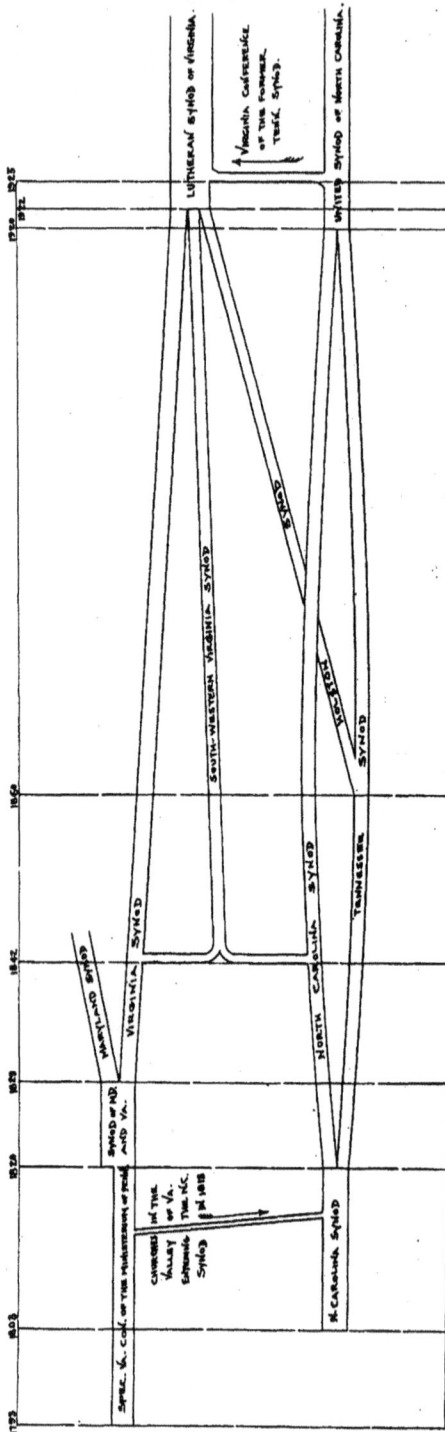

SOURCES OF THE LUTHERAN SYNOD OF VIRGINIA

1793—Organization of the Special Virginia Conference of the Ministerium of Pennsylvania.

1803—Organization of the North Carolina Synod.

1813—Five congregations in the Shenandoah Valley enter the North Carolina Synod. These formed the nucleus of the Virginia Conference of the Tennessee Synod.

1820—Organization of the Synod of Maryland and Virginia.

1820—Organization of the Tennessee Synod, occasioned by a rupture in the North Carolina Synod. The Tennessee Synod had churches in Virginia, North Carolina, South Carolina and Tennessee.

1829—By Mutual agreement the churches in Virginia belonging to the Synod of Maryland and Virginia, formed the Synod of Virginia; the remaining part of the old Synod assuming the name of the Maryland Synod, which name she has carried continuously since 1833.

1842—Organization of the Synod of Southwestern Virginia out of the North Carolina Synod churches in Virginia, and the Virginia Synod churches in and west of the county of Botetourt.

1860—Organization of the Holston Synod out of the churches in the state of Tennessee, belonging to the Tennessee Synod.

1920—Merger of the North Carolina and Tennessee Synods, forming the United Synod of North Carolina.

1922—Merger of the Virginia, Southwestern Virginia and Holston Synods, forming the *Lutheran Synod of Virginia*.

1925—The Virginia Conference of the United Synod of North Carolina, formerly the Virginia Conference of the Tennessee Synod, united with the Lutheran Synod of Virginia.

NAMES OF MINISTERS

ON THE ROLLS OF THE BODIES FORMING THE PRESENT
LUTHERAN SYNOD OF VIRGINIA

Abbreviations. The current abbreviations for the individual synods are used. Tr.—transferred; D'cd.—deceased; D.—dismissed; Dm.—demitted the Ministry; W.—withdrew; Dp.—deposed.

In many cases the synodical records are not full as to admissions, dismissals, etc.

THE EVANGELICAL LUTHERAN SYNOD OF VIRGINIA

NAME	Received Into Synod				Removed		REMARKS
	Date	Licensed	Ordained	Tr. from	Date	How	
J. N. Schmucker	1829				1847	W.	Health failed. Left the territory. Died 1855.
Martin Walther	1829				1834	Tr.	N. C. Synod.
M. Meyerhoeffer	1829				1833	D'cd.	In Rockingham Co.
John Kehler	1829				1830	W.	To Md. later Episcopal Church.
Jacob Medtart	1829				1830	W.	
John P. Cline	1829				1834	Tr. Md.	Returned 1847. D'cd 1866.
Daniel J. Hauer	1829				1834	Tr. Md.	
Lewis Eichelberger	1829				1830	W.	Returned in 1838. Tr. S. C. Syd. 1852.
G. H. Reimensnyder	1830	L			1831	D.	
David Eyster	1830			Md.	1830	W.	Moved to Dansville, N. Y.
John Dagey	1830	L			1835	Tr.	
Thomas Miller	1832	L			1860	D.	Returned 1879. D'cd 1880.
William Scull	1832	L	1833	E. Pa.	1836		Left Lutheran Ch.
J. T. Tabler	1833		1833		1888	Tr. N. C.	
A. Babb	1833	L	1834		1838	Tr. E. Pa.	
Samuel Oswald	1833	L	1834		1844	W.	Health failed.
J. Hoover	1833	L	1834		1838	Tr. Syd. of West	
J. Ulrich	1833	L	1834		1835	Tr.	
J. B. Davis, D. D.	1834	L	1837		1875	Tr. N. C.	Ordained at special service Strasburg, Nov. 5, 1837.
G. F. Staehlin	1835	L		E. Pa.	1840	D.	
Samuel Sayford	1835	L	1839		1842	Tr. Sw. Va.	
Solomon Oswald	1835	L			1888	Tr. Md.	
Geo. Schmucker	1835	L			1838	W.	
David F. Bittle	1838		1839		1846	Tr. Md.	
John Hamilton, M. D.	1838				1842	Tr. O.	
Isaac Baker	1838	L	1843		1876	D'cd.	Name removed 1847. Restored 1851. Part time written J. Baker
Theo. Stork	1838		1839		1841	Tr. Pa.	
J. G. Reimensnyder	1838	L	1839	Ohio	1842	Tr. Md.	
Peter Shickle	1839	L	1841		1856	Tr. Sw. Va.	
Geo. Diehl	1840	L			1841	Tr. Md.	
Samuel Wagner	1840	L	1841		1848	D.	
Peter Glenn	1840	L			1841		License conditional. Not renewed.
Sol. Shaeffer	1841	L			1845	Tr. Sw. Va.	
Wm. Shepperson	1841	L	1843		1859	Tr. to E. O.	
J. R. Keiser	1842	L	1842		1844	Tr. N. Y.	
S. Filler	1842	L	1846		1862	D'cd.	
J. A. Siess	1842	L	1844		1847	Tr. Md.	

THE EVANGELICAL LUTHERAN SYNOD OF VIRGINIA
(Continued)

NAME	Received Into Synod				Removed		REMARKS
	Date	Licensed	Ordained	Tr. from	Date	How	
S. Allenbaugh	1842				1849	Tr. Ill.	Came from United Brethren.
A. R. Rude	1842	L	1843		1863	Tr. Ga.	Name erased 1847. Reentered 1848. Tr. S. C. 1863.
C. C. Baughman	1843	L	1843	Md.	1853	Tr. to Md.	
J. Wolfersberger	1843	L			1843		License discontinued.
J. Few Smith	1844	L	1845	N. Y.	1848	D.	
J. J. Suman	1844	L	1845	Md.	1854	Tr. Md.	
J. F. Campbell, D. D.	1844	L	1845		1852	Tr. Md.	Returned 1866. D'cd 1892.
A. P. Ludden	1845	L	1846		1856	Tr. N. Y.	
J. Summers	1845	L	1847		1871	Tr. Md.	Returned 1879. D'cd 1884.
J. Richard	1846	L			1851	Tr. Md.	Came from United Brethren
C. M. Shepperson	1846	L			1847	Tr. Pg.	Returned in 1851. Went to Ga. that year.
E. G. Proctor	1848	L	1850		1851	D'cd	
X. J. Richardson	1848	L	1850		1866	Tr. Mel.	
C. P. Krauth	1849			Md.	1856	Tr. Pg.	
B. M. Schmucker	1849	L	1849	E. Pa.	1852	Tr. Pa.	
J. W. Miller	1850	L	1851	W. Pa.	1891	D'cd	
L. Keller	1850	L	1851	W. Pa.	1871	Tr. Md.	
R. A. Fink	1850	L	1851		1856	Tr. Ill.	
C. Beard	1850	L	1852	Md.	1890	D'cd	
M. M. Bachtell	1850	L			1851	Tr. Al.	
G. A. Nixdorff	1851			Md.	1854	Tr. Pa.	
H. M. Bickel	1852	L	1852	E. Pa.	1854	Tr. O.	
H. G. Bowers	1852	L		Sw. Va.	1856	Tr. Md.	
Geo. W. Anderson	1852	L			1854	Tr. Md.	
Wm. Rusmiselle	1852	L	1854		1892	D'cd.	
W. M. Schmogrow	1852	L	1852	Md.	1856	Tr. O.	
W. F. Greaver	1853		1853	Sw. Va.	1856	Tr.	
G. Haines	1853	L	1854	W. Pa.	1855	Tr. Pa.	
J. H. Cupp	1853	L	1855	Pa.	1864	Tr. S. C.	Returned 1866. D'cd 1884.
W. S. Bowman	1854	L	1856		1859	Tr. S. C.	
D. H. Bittle, D. D.	1855			E. Pa.	1859	Tr. Sw. Va.	Returned 1868. Tr. Ga. 1871
E. Lubkert	1855		1855	Pa.	1856	Tr.	
S. P. Fink	1855	L			1856		License not renewed
W. Kopp	1856			Al.	1857	Tr. W. Pa.	
J. F. Fahs	1856				1857	Tr. Pa.	
A. Essick	1856				1858	Tr. Md.	
V. F. Bolton	1856		1856	Sw. Va.	1858	Tr. Hartwick	
A. Copenhaver	1856	L	1857		1859	Tr. Mel.	
J. M. Shreckhise	1856	L	1858		1861	Tr. S. C.	Returned 1866. D'cd 1916
J. S. Rosenberg	1856	L			1856		
A. J. Kibler	1856	L			1860	D.	
J. P. Smeltzer	1857			Md.	1860	Tr. Sw. Va.	
John Fortham	1857			Md.	1860	Tr. Al.	
H. Keller	1857	L			1858	Tr. N. Y.	
E. Dorsey	1858			Md.	1860	Tr. E. Pa.	
W. H. Baum	1858		1858	E. Pa.	1862	Tr. W. Pa.	
J. M. Grabill	1858	L	1859	Md.	1860	Tr. Mel.	
Geo. A. Long	1858	L	1860		1887	D.	Entered the Presbyterian church.
Peter Miller	1858	L	1860		1880	Tr. S. C.	Returned 1884. Tr. N. C. 1890. Returned 1896. D'cd 1918.
T. W. Dosh, D. D.	1858	L	1859		1872	Tr. S. C.	Tr. from N. C. 1877. Tr. Md. 1886.

THE EVANGELICAL LUTHERAN SYNOD OF VIRGINIA
(Continued)

NAME	Date	Licensed	Ordained	Tr. from	Date	How	REMARKS
J. A. Snyder, D. D.	1858	L	1859		1917	D'cd.	
W. H. Cone	1859			Sw. Va.	1864	Tr. N. C.	
J. Winecoff	1859			W. Pa.	1865		
Jacob Frazier	1859	L	1861		1863	D.	
C. Martin	1860	L			1861		
G. A. Compton	1860				1866	Tr. M.E. Church	Came from Methodist church and returned to the same.
L. G. Bell	1860			W. Pa.	1861		
J. I. Miller, D. D.	1860			Mel.	1884	Tr. Tenn.	Returned 1908, Tr. Sw. Va. 1909. D'cd 1912.
D. M. Gilbert, D. D.	1860		1860	W. Pa.	1863	Tr. Ga.	Returned 1871. Tr. 1887 to E. Pa.
J. D. Shirey	1860	L	1861		1868	Tr. Sw. Va.	
G. W. Holland	1860	L			1873	Tr. S. C.	
W. Eichelberger	1860	L			1863	Tr. S. C.	Returned 1869. Tr. Ind. 1879. D'cd 1886.
W. S. McClanahan	1861			Sw. Va.	1877	Tr. Sw. Va.	
W. H. Dinkle	1865	L	1866		1875	D'cd.	
R. C. Holland	1868	L	1869		1881	Tr. Md.	
B. C. Wayman	1868	L	1870		1874	D'cd.	
A. A. J. Bushong	1868			Sw. Va.	1908	D'cd.	
J. G. Neiffer	1869			Min. Pa.	1870	Tr. N. C.	
J. W. Tressler	1870	L	1871		1873	Tr. N. I'll.	
D. M. Henkel	1871			Min. Pa.	1873	Tr. N. C.	
J. H. Barb	1872	L	1874		1887	Tr. Md.	
J. Hawkins	1872			S. C.	1875	Tr. Md.	
E. H. Jones	1872			Sw. Va.	1883	Tr. Md.	
M. R. Minnich	1873		1873		1903	Tr. Min. Pa.	
R. E. McDaniel	1874			Tr. Pa.	1875	Tr. to Ill.	
J. P. Obenshain	1874			Sw. Va.	1877		Later in Sw. Va.
P. H. Miller	1874	L	1875		1875	Tr. Md.	
J. E. Cooper	1874	L			1875		License not renewed because of ill health. Returned 1899, died 1915.
A. M. Smith	1875	L	1876		1882	Tr. Md.	
A. Burham	1876			Md.	1877	D'cd.	
W. Y. Cline	1876		1876		1888	Tr. Sw. Va.	
W. C. Schaeffer	1876			Md.	1887	Tr. S. C.	
W. G. Campbell	1877		1877	Sw. Va.	1885	Tr. Al.	
James Willis	1877		1877		1900	Tr. Md.	
L. M. Sibole	1877	L	1880		1896	D'cd.	
J. B. Haskell	1878			S. C.	1881	Tr. S. C.	
J. M. Hedrick	1878			Sq.	1884	Tr. N. C.	
Asa Richard	1878	L	1889		1899	Tr. Md.	Returned 1913.
D. M. Moser	1879			Hartwick	1893	Tr. E. Pa.	
J. S. Moser	1879			Sw. Va.	1884	Tr. S. C.	Returned 1885. Tr. Cal. 1892.
A. C. Gearhart	1879	L	1880		1883	Tr. Neb.	
L. L. Smith, D. D.	1880	L	1880	Sw. Va.	1911	D'cd.	
Geo. A. Lee	1881			Miami	1887	Tr. Witt.	
John Croll	1881			E. Pa.	1884	Tr. E. Pa.	
G. H. Beckley	1882			Md.	1885	Tr. Md.	
J. E. Bushnell, D. D.	1882	L			1883	Tr. S. C.	Returned 1900. Tr. Sw. Va. 1903.
W. P. Beerbower	1882	L	1883		1884	D'cd	
M. G. G. Scherer	1882	L	1883		1884	Tr. Ga.	Returned 1885. Tr. Md. 1886.
V. R. Stickley	1884			N. C.	1892	Tr. N. C.	Returned to Va. 1904. Tr. N. C. 1906.
J. W. S. Shepherd	1884			S. C.	1899	D'p.	Tr. Sw. Va. 1886. Returned 1889.
R. G. Rosenbaum	1884			Sw. Va.	1885	Tr. Pg.	
W. E. Stahler	1884			E. Pa.	1887	Tr. W. Pa.	

THE EVANGELICAL LUTHERAN SYNOD OF VIRGINIA
(Continued)

NAME	Received Into Synod				Removed		REMARKS
	Date	Licensed	Ordained	Tr. from	Date	How	
S. A. Repass, D. D.	1884			Sw. Va.	1885	Tr. Min. Pa.	
W. J. Smith	1885			Sw. Va.	1911	D'cd	
G. W. Spiggle	1885			Neb.	1894	Tr. Pg.	
G. E. Shuey	1885	L	1886		1887	Tr. E. O.	Returned 1894, died 1917.
W. H. Setlemeyer	1886			Md.	1888	Tr. Al.	
T. O. Keister, D. D.	1886			Min. Pa.	1890	Tr. S. C.	Returned 1918.
J. W. Smith	1886			Min. Pa.	1891	Tr. Md.	
I. P. Hawkins	1887			Sw. Va.	1891	Tr. Al.	
D. P. T. Crickenberger	1887			Sw. Va.	1901	Tr. Pg.	
S. T. Riser	1887			S. C.	1888	D'cd	
L. G. M. Miller, D. D.	1888			Sw. Va.	1895	Tr. Sw. Va.	Returned 1910. D'cd 1918.
C. B. Miller	1888			N. C.	1890	Tr. N. C.	
L. A. Mann	1889			Md.	1891	Tr. W. Pa.	
H. F. Shealy	1889			S. C.	1890	Tr. Kan.	Returned 1900. Dm. 1907. Spelled Sheele after 1896.
J. E. Shenk	1889	L	1890		1904	Tr. N. C.	
B. S. Brown	1889			N. C.	1892	Tr. N. C.	
A. F. Richardson	1889			Md.	1893	Tr. Md.	
H. E. Ebeling	1890			Md.	1894		Name erased from roll.
W. B. Oney	1890			Sw. Va.	1896	Tr. N. C.	Returned 1900. Tr. E. O. 1906. Returned 1909.
J. L. Buck	1891			Sw. Va.	1893	Tr. Al.	
J. A. Flickinger	1891	L			1895	Tr. Md.	
E. L. Folk	1891			Al.	1901	Tr. N. C.	Returned 1902. Tr. N. C. 1916.
P. J. Wade	1891	L	1891	Sw. Va.	1895	Tr. Sw. Va.	Returned 1906. Tr. Md. 1908.
P. L. Miller	1891	L	1895		1897	Tr. N.C.	
C. N. A. Yonce	1892			Sw. Va.	1896	D'p	
J. C. Seegers	1892			Hol.	1895	Tr. Min. N. Y.	
W. H. Berry	1892			Md.	1893	Tr. Neb.	Returned 1895. Tr. E. O. 1899.
R. B. Peery, Ph. D.	1892		1892		1904	Tr. E. Pa.	
Paul Sieg	1892		1892		1893	Tr. Sw. Va.	
H. E. Bailey	1893			Sw. Va.	1895	Tr. Hol.	
C. H. Rocky	1893			N. Ind.	1900	Tr. Md.	
S. L. Keller	1893			S. C.	1895	Tr. Can.	Returned 1900. Tr. 1910 Neb.
C. A. Freed	1893			Min. Pa.	1903	Tr. S. C.	
D. W. Files	1893	L	1896				
J. W. Strickler	1894			Sw. Va.	1905	Tr. N. C.	Returned 1909. D'cd 1916.
J. A. Morehead, D. D.	1895			Sw. Va.			
E. A. Shenk	1895		1895		1908	Tr. N. C.	
W. L. Seabrook	1895			Kan.	1902	Tr. S. C.	
D. W. Michael	1896			N. C.	1898	Tr. Pg.	
C. A. Marks	1896			N. C.			
R. A. Helms	1896		1896		1899	Tr. N. C.	
J. C. McGauchey	1897			Neb.	1900	Tr. Pg.	
E. C. Cronk, D. D.	1897			Sw. Va.	1903	Tr. Ga.	Returned 1921
C. E. Hershberger	1897			Hol.	1907	Dm.	
J. W. Shuey	1897		1897				
W. P. Huddle	1897			N. C.			
W. H. Riser	1898		1898		1911	Tr. N. C.	
W. R. Brown	1899			Sw. Va.	1902	Tr. Sw. Va.	
J. B. Fox, Ph. D.	1899			S. C.	1900	D'cd	
E. A. Repass, Ph. D.	1900			Min. Pa.	1917	Tr. N. C.	
G. E. Krauth	1900			Pg.	1902	Tr.	
G. A. Riser	1900			N. C.	1902	D'cd	
J. K. Efird	1900			Tenn.	1901	Tr. Tenn.	

THE EVANGELICAL LUTHERAN SYNOD OF VIRGINIA
(Continued)

NAME	Received Into Synod				Removed		REMARKS
	Date	Licensed	Or'ained	Tr. from	Date	How	
H. Max Lentz	1901			Miami	1902	D'cd	Drowned
J. A. Huffard, D. D.	1901			Sw. Va.	1927		
A. D. R. Hancher,D.D.	1901			Hol.			
W. B. Aull	1901		1901		1904	Tr. S. C.	
C. M. Fox	1902			Sw. Va.	1904	Tr. N. C.	
J. A. Boord	1902			S. C.	1904	Tr. Pg.	(Bourde)
Y. von A. Riser	1903			S. C.	1906	Tr. Ga.	
W. W. J. Ritchie	1903			N. C.	1914	Tr. Sw. Va.	Returned 1919.
Geo. S. Bowers, D. D.	1903			Md.	1919	Tr. Md.	
H. C. Haithcox, D. D.	1904			Ind.	1914	Tr. Md.	
J. H. Wyse	1905			Sw.Va.	1908	D'cd	
C. W. Cassell	1905			Sw.Va.	1915	Tr. Sw. Va.	Returned in 1917.
J. M. Tise	1906			Sw. Va.	1910	Tr. Sw. Va.	Returned in 1915. Tr. Sw. Va. 1920.
J. F. W. Kitzmeyer	1906			N. Y.	1908	Tr. N. Y.	
J. G. Graichen	1907			S. C.	1912	Tr. Hol.	
W. W. Frey	1907			Pg.	1908	Tr. Pg.	
J. J. Scherer, Jr., D. D	1907			Md.			
W. J. D. Scherer	1907			E. Pa.	1910	Tr. Md.	
M. L. Canup	1907		1907		1910	Tr. N. C.	
L. S. G. Miller, D. D.	1907		1907				Missionary to Japan.
P. H. E. Derrick	1908			Sw. Va.	1909	Tr. S. C.	
J. I. Coiner	1908		1908		1913	Tr. Sw. Va.	
J. F. Bruch	1909			Min. Pa.	1915	Tr. Min. Pa.	
A. C. Karkau	1909			Min. Pa.	1911	Tr. N. Y.	
S. W. Kuhns	1911			N. C.			
H. E. H. Sloop	1911			N. C.	1915	Tr. Sw. Va.	Returned 1916.
C. Brown Cox	1911			N. C.	1918	Tr. Sw. Va.	
B. A. Copenhaver	1911		1911		1918	D'cd	
B. S. Dasher	1911		1911		1914	Tr. N. C.	
I. D. Worman	1912			Md.			
J. W. Link	1912			Sw. Va.			
Chas. W. Hepner	1912		1912				Missionary to Japan.
Frank Gilbert	1912			Sq.	1915	Tr. Md.	
E. R. McCauley, D. D.	1914			Pa.		Tr. N. C.	
W. A. Craun	1914		1914				
H. D. Chapman	1915		1915		1917	Tr. Hol.	
D. S. Fox	1915			Sw. Va.	1917		
R. H. Cline	1916			Tenn.			
C. H. Day	1916			S. Ill.	1918	Tr. N. C.	
E. L. Ritchie	1916			Sw. Va.			
J. B. Derrick	1916			S. C.			
J. A. Shealy	1916		1916		1921	Tr. S. C.	
G.C.H.Hasskarl,Ph.D.	1917			Min. Pa.	1920		
T. Aoyama	1917						Japanese Minister
N. Yamanouchi	1917						Japanese Minister
R. Yamanouchi	1918				1918	D'cd	Japanese Minister
D. Honda	1918						Japanese Minister
J. L. Smith	1918			N. C.	1921	Tr. Sw. Va.	
N. E. Cooper	1918		1918				
A. A. Kelly	1919			E. Pa.			
L. W. Gross	1919			Olive B.			
R. H. Anderson	1919			Sw. Va.			
Paul L. Royer	1919		1919				
J. A. L. Miller	1920			N. C.			
James Oosterling	1920			N. Ill.			
E. W. Leslie	1921			S. C.			
Grover Morgan	1921			N. C.			
P. H. Pearson	1921			E. Pa.			
P. L. Snapp	1921			N. C.			
K. Y. Umberger	1921			Sw. Va.			
Jacob Scherer	1842				1854	Tr. Texas	Reentered 1855; Died 1860
Samuel Sayford	1842				1848	Tr. Ind.	

THE EVANGELICAL LUTHERAN SYNOD OF
SOUTHWESTERN VIRGINIA

NAME	Date	Licensed	Ordained	Tr. From	Date	How	REMARKS
		Received Into Synod			Removed		
Elijah Hawkins	1842				1868	D'cd	
John J. Greever	1842		1842		1877	D'cd	
Gideon Scherer	1842		1842		1854	Tr. Tex.	Reentered 1 8 5 5 ; Died 1861
Stephen Rhudy	1842	L	1846		1894	D'cd	
James A. Brown, D. D.	1843	L	1844	W. Pa.	1900	D'cd	March 4.
Solomon Schaeffer	1845	L	1846	Va.	1871	D'cd	
Simeon Scherer	1848	L	1850		1852	Tr. N. C.	
H. G. Bowers	1848	L	1850		1852	Tr. Va.	
L. C. Groseclose	1849	L	1850		1851	Tr. N. C.	
Wm. F. Greaver	1851	L			1853	Tr. Va.	
John K. Rader	1851	L	1854		1860	D'cd	
Samuel Cook	1851	L	1854		1856	Tr. Ind.	
J. C. Repass	1854	L	1856		1903	D'cd	
V. F. Bolton	1854	L		Va.	1856	Tr. Va.	
D. F. Bittle, D. D.	1854			Va.	1876	D'cd	
W. D. Roedel	1855			E. Pa.	1866	D'cd	
John Boon	1855	L	1857		1861	Tr. Mich.	
Festus Hickerson	1885	L	1858		1870	D'cd	In S. C. 1864.
Amos Copenhaver	1855	L					No report
Wm. G. Sloop	1855	L	1857	·	1859		Honorably dismissed
John J. Scherer, D. D.	1855	L	1856		1919	D'cd	
Wm. S. McClanahan	1856	L	1859		1861	Tr. Va.	Returned 1878. D'cd 1910
Wm. B. Yonce, Ph. D.	1857	L	1859		1895	D'cd	
Peter Shickel	1858			Va.	1884	D'cd	
William H. Cone	1858		1858		1859	Tr. Va.	
J. G. Frey	1860	L	1861		1873	D'cd	
J. P. Smeltzer	1860			Va.	1861	Tr. S. C.	
John A. Bell	1861	L	1864	M. E. Ch.	1888	D'cd	
L. A. Mann	1861	L	1862		1869	Tr. Md.	
S. R. Smith	1861	L	1865		1880	D'cd	
A. A. J. Bushong	1861	L	1862		1868	Tr. Va.	
A. Phillippi, D. D.	1861	L	1861		1916	D'cd	
E. H. McDonald	1861	L	1862		1878	D'p.	
W. C. Wire	1862	L	1864		1868	Tr. Mel.	
D. P. Cammann	1863	L		Germany	1867	Tr. S. C.	
J. L. Weaver	1865	L			1865		License revoked.
D. H. Bittle, D. D.	1866			N. C.	1868	Tr. Va.	
James Mahood	1867	L	1870		1914	D'cd	
J. D. Shirey	1868			Va.	1871	Tr. S. C.	
W. E. Hubbert	1868	L	1870		1876	Tr. N. C.	Returned 1877. D'cd 1916.
L. A. Fox, D.D.,LL.D.	1869			Tenn.	1870	Tr. Pa. .	Returned 1887.
S. A. Repass, D. D.	1869			Min. Pa.	1884	Tr. Va.	
E. H. Jones	1869			M. E. Ch.	1871	Tr. Va.	
J. B. Greiner, D. D.	1870		1870		1917	D'cd	
J. P. Obenshain	1871	L	1874		1874	Tr. Va.	Returned 1877. Died 1917.
C. C. Mayer	1872			Tex.	1876	D'cd	
J. B. Greever	1872	L	1874		1897	Tr. Hol.	
J. H. Turner	1873			Hol.	1876	Tr. Md.	
E. E. Sibole	1873		1873		1875	Tr. Min. Pa.	
J. F. Kiser	1873			Min. Pa.	1879	Tr. S. C.	
V. Stickley	1873	L	1876		1876	Tr. N. C.	
L. G. M. Miller, D. D.	1875			Min. Pa.	1888	Tr. Va.	Returned 1895.
C. A. Marks	1876	L	1877		1886	Tr. S. C.	
F. V. N. Painter, D. D.	1877	L	1878		1920	Dm.	
L. E. Busby	1877	L					
H. E. Bailey	1877	L	1878		1893	Tr. Va.	Returned 1901.
J. S. Moser	1877	L	1878		1878	Tr. Va.	
W. G. Campbell	1877	L			1877	Tr. Va.	

THE EVANGELICAL LUTHERAN SYNOD OF SOUTHWESTERN VIRGINIA
(Continued)

NAME	Received Into Synod				Removed		REMARKS
	Date	Licensed	Ordained	Tr. from	Date	How	
J. L. Buck	1877		1878		1882	Tr. N. C.	Returned 1890; Tr. Va. 1891; Returned 1896; Tr. Ga. 1899.
William Stoudemire	1878	L			1880	W.	To S. C.
N. Aldrich	1880			Ind.	1885	Tr. Md.	
N. A. Whitman	1881			Sq.	1882	Tr. N. Ind.	Returned 1883, Tr. Ind. 1884.
Geo. W. Spiggle	1881		1881		1885	Tr. Neb.	Returned from Pg. Syd. 1918.
W. B. Oney	1881	L	1882		1890	Tr. N. C.	
J. C. Brodfuhrer	1882			Neb.	1885	Tr. S. C.	
E. Studebaker	1882			M'd.Tenn	1907	D'cd	
Geo. T. Gray	1882			M. E. Ch. South	1898	D'cd	
Charles A. Rose	1882	L			1884	Tr. N. C.	
T. Shannon Brown	1882	L			1883	Tr. N. C.	
J. W. Strickler	1882	L			1886	Tr. N. C.	Returned 1890; Tr. Va. 1894.
W. J. Smith	1883			N. C.	1885	Tr. Va.	
D. P. T. Crickenberger	1883	L	1884		1888	Tr. Va.	
R. G. Rosenbaum	1884		1884		1884	Tr. Va.	
B. W. Cronk	1884	L	1885		1887	Tr. N. C.	Returned 1896; Tr. N. C. 1908; Returned 1911; Tr. S. C. 1914, R. 1918.
I. P. Hawkins	1885			S. C.	1886	Tr. Va.	
E. L. Folk	1885		1885		1886	Tr. Al.	
W. P. Huddle	1885	L	1888		1893	Tr. N. C.	
C. B. King	1885	L					Tr. to E. Pa. or Md.
D. S. Fox	1886	L	1890		1915	Tr. Va.	
J. W. S. Shepherd	1886			Va.	1888	Tr. Va.	
J. E. Bushnell, D. D.	1886			S. C.	1892	Tr. Md.	Returned 1903, S. C. 1916.
A. J. Bowers	1887			S. C.	1888	Tr. S. C.	
J. M. Hedrick	1887			N. C.	1889	Tr. N. C.	
James W. Butler	1888	L	1890		1892	Tr. S. C.	Returned 1894, Tr. Wis. 1903.
C. Armand Miller	1888	L	1889		1896	Min. Pa.	
J. Brown Umberger	1888	L	1889		1890	Tr. Kan.	
D. Bittle Groseclose	1888	L	1892		1903	Tr. S. C.	
M. O. J. Kreps	1889			S. C.	1896	Tr. S. C.	
W. Y. Cline	1889			Va.	1905	D'cd	
James A. Huffard	1889			Min. Pa.	1901	Tr. Va.	
S. S. Rahn	1889			S. C.	1893	Tr. Tenn.	
P. J. Wade	1889	L			1891	Tr. Va.	Returned 1896, Tr. N. C. 1899.
G. E. Shuey	1889			E. O.	1891	Tr. Aug. Syd.	
L. P. Scherer	1890			Md.	1908		Dropped from Roll.
J. A. B. Scherer	1890	L			1898	Tr. S. C.	
S. D. Steffey	1891		1892		1896	Tr. N. C.	
C. N. A. Yonce	1891				1892	Tr. Va.	
C. A. Brown	1891			N. C.	1892	Tr. N. C.	
R. B. Perry	1891						Ordained by Va. Synod, 1892.
J. A. Morehead, D. D., LL. D.	1892		1892		1895	Tr. Va.	
C. M. Fox	1892	L	1893		1895	Tr. S. C.	Returned Hol. Syd. 1899, Tr. N. C. 1909; Returned N. C. 1914.
O. C. Miller	1893			Cal.	1905	Tr. Kan.	
Paul Sieg	1893			Va.			
W. A. Dutton	1893	L	1897		1894	Tr. Kan.	Returned Neb. 1896, Tr. N. C. 1899.
Peter Miller	1894			N. C.	1896	Tr. Va.	
W. R. Brown	1894			N. C.	1899	Tr. Va.	Returned 1902.

THE EVANGELICAL LUTHERAN SYNOD OF
SOUTHWESTERN VIRGINIA
(Continued)

NAME	Received Into Synod				Removed		REMARKS
	Date	Licensed	Ordained	Tr. from	Date	How	
W. H. Greever	1894	L	1896		1901	Tr. S. C.	
E. R. McCauley	1894	L			1895	Tr. to Sq.	
J. Luther Frantz	1894	L					
E. H. Kohn	1895			Min. Pa.	1897	Tr. Tenn.	
E. C. Cronk	1895		1895		1897	Tr. Va.	
J. M. Moser	1896			Hol.	1897	D'p.	
C. W. Cassell	1896		1896		1905	Tr. Va.	Returned Va. 1915,
					1916	Tr. Va.	
J. M. Killian	1896	L			1898	Tr. Md.	Returned 1905.
E. W. Leslie	1896	L	1898		1899	Tr. N. C.	Returned 1903, Tr. S. C. 1910.
J. M. Grabill	1898			Md.	1899	Tr. Md.	
John H. Wyse	1898			S. C.	1905	Tr. Va.	
C. L. Brown, D. D.	1898		1898				Missionary to Japan
R. R. Sowers	1898	L	1901		1903	Tr. N. C.	
C. K. Bell	1899			Md.	1905	Tr. Tenn.	
T. C. Parker	1899		1899		1903	Tr. N. C.	Returned 1915.
R. L. Bame	1899			N. C.	1901	Tr. N. C.	
P. E. Monroe	1901		1901		1902	Tr.	
C. R. W. Kegley	1901		1901		1902	Tr. N. C.	Returned 1908, Tr. Chicago.
P. D. Leddin	1902			N. Y.	1905	Tr. N. Y.	
K. Y. Umberger	1902		1902		1921	Tr. Va.	
S. P. Koon	1902		1902		1904	Tr. S. C.	
O. C. Peterson	1902		1902		1903	Tr. Hol.	
J. A. Arndt	1903			Tenn.	1906	Tr. Tenn.	
M. Q. Boland	1903			Tenn.	1907	Tr. Miss.	
E. H. Copenhaver	1904	L	1906		1908	Tr. Chicago	Returned from Ga. 1915.
J. M. Tise	1904			Eng. Syd. of N. W.	1906	Tr. Va.	Returned 1910, Tr. Va. 1915. Re't 1920.
S. C. Ballentine	1905			S. C.	1909	Tr. S. C.	Returned 1918.
Geo. S. Diven	1905			N. Y.	1908	Tr. C. Pa.	
T. O. Keister, D. D.	1905			Pa.	1914	Tr. Pg.	
L. B. Spracher	1905		1905		1908	Tr. N. C.	
J. C. Peery	1905		1905		1918	Tr. N. C.	
C. J. Sox	1905		1905		1906	Tr. S. C.	
P. H. E. Derrick	1906			S. C.	1908	Tr. Va.	
C. K. Hunton	1906			E. O.			
J. P. Miller	1906			S. C.	1908	Tr. N. C.	Returned 1911, Tr. N. C. 1914.
H. P. Counts	1907			Ga.	1915		
E. L. Ritchie	1907			N. C.	1916	Tr. Va.	
G. H. Rhodes	1907		1907		1921	Tr. Hol.	
J. D. Utt	1908		1908				
W. C. Buck	1909		1909		1910	Tr. N. C.	
B. F. Landis	1910		1910		1916	D'p.	
J. A. C. Hurt	1910		1910				
M. D. Huddle	1910		1910		1914	Tr. S. C.	
J. W. Link	1910		1910		1911	Tr. Va.	
J. I. Miller, D. D.	1910			Va.	1911	Tr. Va.	
B. S. Brown	1911			N. C.	1913	Tr. N. C.	
J. L. Smith	1912			N. C.	1914	Tr. S. C.	Returned 1921.
R. A. Kern	1912			Min. Pa.	1914	Tr. Min. Pa.	
E. C. Cooper	1912		1912		1915	Tr. Min. Pa.	
H. N. Miller, Ph. D.	1913			Ohio	1918	Tr. Ga.	
J. I. Coiner	1913			Va.	1919	Tr. Miss.	
B. E. Petrea	1913			N. C.	1919	Tr. Md.	
W. A. Sadtler, Ph. D.	1913			Neb.	1915	Tr. N. Y.	
W. W. J. Ritchie	1914			Va.	1920	Tr. Va.	
J. Luther Seiber	1914			N. Y.			
J. A. Brosius	1914			Sq.	1921	Tr. Al.	
J. F. Deal	1915			Tenn.	1921	Tr. N. C.	

THE EVANGELICAL LUTHERAN SYNOD OF SOUTHWESTERN VIRGINIA
(Continued)

NAME	Date	Licensed	Ordained	Tr. From	Date	How	REMARKS
	Received Into Synod				Removed		
O. L. Schreiber, Ph. D.	1915			N. Y.	1919	Tr. N. Y.	
John B. Moose	1915			N. C.	1917	Tr. N. C.	
R. H. Anderson	1915			S. C.	1919	Tr. Va.	
A. F. Tobler	1915		1915				
J. W. McCauley	1916			Md.			
A. W. Ballentine	1917			Miss.	1918	Tr. Ga.	
J. L. Yost	1917			N. C.	1921	Tr. N. C.	
J. B. Haigler	1917			Ga.	1919	Tr. N. C.	
W. G. Cobb	1918			Hol.			
C. O. Lippard	1918		1918		1920	Tr. Tenn.	
Paul A. Atkins	1918	L					Ordained after merger 1922.
Jacob Pflum	1918	L		.			Student, returned to his home Synod.
Herman Wyrick	1918	L	1921				
C. Brown Cox	1918			Va.			
S. W. Hahn	1919		1919				
W. P. Cline, Jr.	1919			Ga.	1921	Tr. Ga.	
W. H. Riser	1920			S. C.	1922	Tr. N. C.	
O. F. Blackwelder	1920			N. C.			
C. J. Rice	1920		1920				
J. A. Boord	1921			Pg.			(Bourde)
J. H. Richard	1921			E. Pa.			
C. F. Steck, Jr.	1921			Ohio			
E. R. Byers	1921			Neb.			

THE EVANGELICAL LUTHERAN HOLSTON SYNOD

NAME	Date	Licensed	Ordained	Tr. From	Date	How	REMARKS
	Received Into Synod				Removed		
Wm. Hancher	1861				1870	D'cd	
A. J. Brown, D. D.	1861				1894	D'cd	
J. M. Shaffer	1861				1885	D'cd	
J. K. Hancher	1861				1898	D'cd	
J. B. Emmert	1861				1874	D'cd	
James Fleenor	1861				1888	D'cd	
J. A. Seneker	1861				1870	D'p	
J. Cloninger	1861				1890	D'cd	
J. C. Barb, D. D.	1861				1882	Tr. Ind.	Returned 1895; Died 1900.
H. D. Giesler	1861		1861		1865	D'cd	
A. Fleenor	1861				1870	D'cd	
J. M. Wagner	1867			Tenn.	1890	D'cd	
A. Rader	1867			Tenn.	1873		Hon. Dismissed.
Joseph E. Bell	1867				1871	D'cd	
Wm. G. Wolford	1868	L	1869		1919	D'cd	
J. H. Turner	1870		1870		1872	Tr. Sw. Va.	
G. H. Cox	1871	L	1872		1888	Tr. N. C.	
Joseph Houser	1871	L	1874				Withdrew to Mo. Syd.
J. C. Miller	1871	L	1874		1891	D'm	Reordained 1901.
M. L. Thornburg	1872	L	1875		1878	Tr. Mo. Syd.	
G. J. Greer	1873	L			1879		Dropped from roll.
L. M. Wagner	1874	L	1875		1877	Tr. Mo. Syd.	
Samuel Booher	1874	L			1879		Dropped from roll.

THE EVANGELICAL LUTHERAN HOLSTON SYNOD
(Continued)

NAME	Date	Licensed	Ordained	Tr. from	Date	How	REMARKS
J. G. Schaidt	1875			Min. Pa.	1888	Tr. N. C.	
C. A. Bruegmann	1878				1881	D'p	No record of how admitted.
F. M. Ottinger	1878	L			1880		Dropped from roll.
J. H. Summitt	1880		1880		1897	Tr. M. E. Ch.	
J. P. Deck	1881		1881		1882		Hon. Dismissed
G. B. Hancher	1883		1883		1891	Tr. Min. Pa.	
J. B. Fox	1884		1884		1887	Tr. S.C.	
J. B. Rodgers	1884	L	1886		1900		
J. M. Hayes	1885	L			1886	Tr. Bapt. Ch.	
A. C. Gearheart	1886			Neb.	1888	Tr. Sw. Va.	
J. M. Moser	1886		1887		1896	Tr. Sw. Va.	
J. M. Boyd	1888	L	1894		1894		Went to the Baptist Church.
F. M. Harr	1888	L	1891		1904	Tr. N. C.	Returned 1911.
J. L. Murphy	1891		1891		1894	Tr. Aug.	
J. C. Seegers	1891		1891		1892	Tr. Va.	
A. D. R. Hancher	1892		1892		1901	Tr. Va.	
C. E. Hershberger	1895	L	1896		1897	Tr. Va.	
H. E. Bailey	1895			Va.	1901	Tr. Sw. Va.	
J. B. Greever	1897			Sw. Va.	1902	D'p	Reinstated later.
C. M. Fox	1898				1899	Tr. Sw. Va.	
Noah Bible	1900			M. E. Ch. South	1917	D'cd	
C. Brown Cox	1901			N. C.	1903	Tr. N. C.	
E. C. Witt	1901		1901		1903	Tr. Ga.	
S. D. Steffey	1902			N. C.	1905	Tr. Sw. Va.	
M. M. Kinard, Ph. D.	1903			S. C.	1907	Tr. N. C.	
O. C. Peterson	1903			Sw. Va.	1908	Tr. S. C.	
J. C. Wessinger	1904			Tenn.	1905	Tr. Tenn.	
J. A. Linn	1904			N. C.	1907	Tr. N. C.	
H. L. Seagle	1905		1905		1906	Tr. Tenn.	
W. C. Davis	1905		1905		1911	Tr. Chicago	Returned 1916, Tr. 1920 Olive Branch.
H. E. H. Sloop	1905			Miss.	1908	Tr. N. C.	
W. H. Roof	1906			S. C.			
V. C. Ridenhour	1907			S. C.	1913	Tr. N. C.	
W. C. Schaeffer, D. D.	1908			Ga.	1921	D'cd	
H. J. Mathias	1909			Chic.	1910	Tr. Ga.	
M. C. Riser	1909		1909		1914	Tr. S. C.	
H. G. Davis	1910		1910		1916	Tr. Min. Pa.	Returned 1918 to Kingsport Mis.
P. L. Miller	1911				1912	Tr. Miami	
H. A. Kissler	1911			Tenn.	1920	Tr. S. C.	
J. G. Graichen	1912			Va.			
J. Luther Frantz	1913			Md.	1916	Tr. Al.	
W. G. Cobb	1914			N. C.	1917	Tr. Va.	
L. B. Spracher	1914			N. C.	1915	D'cd	
H. B. Schaeffer	1915		1915		1919	Tr. Tenn.	
B. S. Brown, Jr.	1916		1916				
R. R. Sowers	1918			S. C.	1919	Tr. S. C.	
E. B. Smith	1918			N. S.			
C. A. Phillips	1918			Ga.			

VIRGINIA SPECIAL CONFERENCE OF THE EVANGELICAL LUTHERAN TENNESSEE SYNOD

The dates given are as of the name appearing on, or disappearing from, the roll.

NAME	ADMITTED	REMOVED	REMARKS
Ambrose Henkel	1856	1870	Deceased.
Henry Wetzel	1856	1868	United with Joint Synod of Ohio.
	1885	1890	Deceased.
Jacob Killian	1856	1871	Deceased.
Socrates Henkel, D. D.	1856	1901	Deceased.
Joel Swartz	1856	1857	Ordained by Conference. Moved to Ohio.
J. L. Stirewalt	1856	1857	Ordained by Conference. Lived in Ohio.
Martin Sondhaus	1857	1865	Moved to Ohio.
Jacob Stirewalt	1858	1872	Deceased.
J. H. Hunton	1858	1866	Ordained by Conference. Moved to Canada.
G. Schmucker	1858	1867	United with Joint Synod of Ohio.
J. E. Seneker	1865	1868	United with Joint Synod of Ohio.
T. Miller	1865	1878	Transferred to Virginia Synod.
W. H. Swaney	1865	1869	Ordained by Conference. Moved west.
J. S. Bennick	1865	1882	Ordained by Conference. Deceased.
I. Conder	1868		
J. N. Stirewalt	1870	1906	Ordained by Conference. Deceased.
L. A. Fox, D. D.	1872	1887	Transferred to Southwest Virginia.
J. P. Stirewalt, D. D.	1873		Ordained by Conference.
J. W. Hausenfluck	1877	1922	Ordained by Conference. Deceased.
A. L. Crouse	1882	1890	Moved to North Carolina.
J. I. Miller, D. D.	1885	1894	Transferred to Virginia Synod.
P. C. Wike	1886	1899	Moved to South Carolina.
J. S. Koiner	1890	1899	Withdrew to Maryland Synod.
R. H. Cline	1890	1899	Moved to North Carolina.
A. R. Beck	1892	1894	Moved to North Carolina.
	1904	1912	Moved to North Carolina.
A. L. Boliek	1894	1901	Moved to Indiana.
	1922		
F. C. Oberly	1894	1896	Moved to Pennsylvania.
J. K. Efird	1895	1912	Moved to New York.
E. K. Kohn	1897	1903	Moved to North Carolina.
M. L. Pence	1900	1908	Moved to North Carolina.
	1917	1924	Moved to North Carolina.
M. Grossman	1900	1904	Moved to Pennsylvania.
E. L. Wessinger	1903	1909	Moved to Pennsylvania.
J. L. Deaton	1903	1906	Health failed.
M. A. Ashby	1903	1922	Moved to Maryland
W. L. Darr	1907		
D. L. Miller	1907	1910	Moved to Pennsylvania.
O. W. Aderholt	1909	1916	Moved to North Carolina.
Enoch Hite	1910	1912	Moved to North Carolina.
P. L. Snapp	1911	1921	Transferred to Virginia Synod.
J. S. Wessinger	1911	1915	Moved to North Carolina.
C. K. Rhodes	1913	1920	Moved to North Carolina.
W. J. Finck, D. D.	1913		
L. L. Huffman	1916	1918	Deceased.
E. Z. Pence	1917	1924	Moved to South Carolina.
F. M. Speagle	1917	1924	Moved to North Carolina.
V. L. Fulmer	1921	1923	Moved to Pennsylvania.
D. H. Chapman	1921		
C. I. Morgan	1922		
L. L. Lohr, D. D.	1924		

THE LUTHERAN SYNOD OF VIRGINIA

NAME	Received Into Synod				Removed		REMARKS
	Date	Licensed	Ordained	Tr. From	Date	How	
R. Homer Anderson	1922			Va. Syd.			
R. H. Cline	1922			Va. Syd.			
C. W. Cassell	1922			Va. Syd.			
Norman E. Cooper	1922			Va. Syd.			
W. A. Craun	1922			Va. Syd.	1922	Tr.	Michigan Synod.
E. C. Cronk, D. D.	1922			Va. Syd.	1929	D'cd	New York, Feb. 26.
J. B. Derrick	1922			Va. Syd.	1922	D'cd	
D. S. Fox	1922			Va. Syd.			
D. W. Files	1922			Va. Syd.			
L. W. Gross	1922			Va. Syd.	1923	Tr.	W. Pa.
A. D. R. Hancher,D.D.	1922			Va. Syd.			
W. P. Huddle	1922			Va. Syd.			
J. A. Huffard, D. D.	1922			Va. Syd.	1927	D'cd	Kingsport, Tenn. Feb. 12.
G.C.H.Hasskarl,Ph.D.	1922			Va. Syd.	1929	D'cd	Brooklyn,N.Y.Aug. 9
C. W. Hepner	1922			Va. Syd.			
D. Honda	1922			Va. Syd.	1927	Tr.	Japan
S. W. Kuhns	1922			Va. Syd.	1928	D'cd	Frederick, Md. Feb. 6
T. O. Keister, D. D.	1922			Va. Syd.	1928	D'cd	Edinburg, Va. Jan.13
A. A. Kelly	1922			Va. Syd.	1925	Tr. E. Pa.	
J. W. Link	1922			Va. Syd.	1927	Tr. N. C.	
E. W. Leslie	1922			Va. Syd.	1927	Tr. S. C.	
C. A. Marks	1922			Va. Syd.	1926	D'cd	Tampa, Fla. Jan. 29
J. A. Morehead, D. D., LL. D.	1922			Va. Syd.			
E. R. McCauley, D. D.	1922			Va. Syd.	1924	Tr. N. C.	
J. A. L. Miller	1922			Va. Syd.			
L. S. G. Miller, D. D.	1922			Va. Syd.			
Grover Morgan	1922			Va. Syd.	1923	Tr. S. C.	
W. B. Oney	1922			Va. Syd.			
James Oosterling	1922			Va. Syd.	1923	Tr. Md.	
P. H. Pearson	1922			Va. Syd.	1928	Tr. E. Pa.	
Asa Richard	1922			Va. Syd.			
E. L. Ritchie	1922			Va. Syd.	1922	Tr. Pg.	
Paul L. Royer	1922			Va. Syd.			
W. W. J. Ritchie	1922			Va. Syd.			
H. E. H. Sloop	1922			Va. Syd.			
J. W. Shuey	1922			Va. Syd.			
J. J. Scherer, Jr., D.D.	1922			Va. Syd.			
P. L. Snapp	1922			Va. Syd.			
K. Y. Umberger	1922			Va. Syd.			
I. D. Worman	1922			Va. Syd.	1925	Tr. Md.	
N. Yamanouchi	1922			Va. Syd.	1925	Dm.	Japanese minister.
S. C. Ballentine	1922			Sw. Va.			
H. E. Bailey	1922			Sw. Va.	1923	D'cd	Eggleston,Va. Sept. 8
O. F. Blackwelder	1922			Sw. Va.	1926	Tr. Md.	
James A. Boord	1922			Sw. Va.	1928	Tr. Al.	Sometimes spelled Bourde.
W. R. Brown	1922			Sw. Va.			
E. A. Byers	1922			Sw. Va.	1926	Tr. N. Y.	
W. G. Cobb	1922			Sw. Va.	1923	Tr. N. C.	
E. H. Copenhaver	1922			Sw. Va.			
C. Brown Cox, D. D.	1922			Sw. Va.			
B. W. Cronk	1922			Sw. Va.			
L. A. Fox, D.D.,LL.D.	1922			Sw. Va.	1925	D'cd	Salem, Va. July 9.
C. K. Hunton	1922			Sw. Va.			
J. A. C. Hurt	1922			Sw. Va.	1922	D'cd	Wytheville, Va.
J. M. Killian	1922			Sw. Va.			
J. W. McCauley	1922			Sw. Va.	1922	Tr. Md.	
J. C. Rice	1922			Sw. Va.			
J. H. Richard	1922			Sw. Va.	1927	Tr. Ga. Syd.	
J. L. Sieber, D. D.	1922			Sw. Va.			
Paul Sieg	1922			Sw. Va.	1922	Tr. N. C.	Returned 1926.
J. L. Smith	1922			Sw. Va.	1923	Tr. S. C.	
G. W. Spiggle	1922			Sw. Va.	1925	D'cd	Wytheville,Va. Oct. 1

THE LUTHERAN SYNOD OF VIRGINIA
(Continued)

NAME	Date	Licensed	Ordained	Tr. From	Date	How	REMARKS
				Received Into Synod → / Removed →			
C. F. Steck, Jr.	1922			Sw. Va.			
J. M. Tise	1922			Sw. Va.			
A. F. Tobler	1922			Sw. Va.	1927	Tr. Md.	
J. D. Utt	1922			Sw. Va.			
Herman P. Wyrick	1922			Sw. Va.	1923	Tr. N. C.	
P. E. Shealy	1922			Sw. Va.			Tr. from S. C. before the merger.
F. M. Harr	1922			Hol.			Morristown, Tenn. May 9
J. G. Graichen	1922			Hol.	1929	D'cd	
B. S. Brown, Jr.	1922			Hol.	1924	Tr. N. C.	
E. B. Smith	1922			Hol.			
J. C. Miller	1922			Hol.	1926	Tr. Ga. Syd.	
George H. Rhodes	1922			Hol.	1927	Tr. N. C.	
W. H. Roof	1922			Hol.	1926	Tr. N. C.	
Chas. J. Smith, D. D.	1922			Tr. N. Y.			
Geo. S. Bearden	1922			Tr. S. C.	1925	Tr. Ind.	
H. E. Beatty	1922			S. C.	1927	Tr. Md.	
P. A. Atkins	1922		1922		1927	D'cd	Harrisonburg,July 13
C. E. Kepley	1922		1922				
E. L. Baker	1923			Tr. Pg.			
E. O. Graham	1923			Tr. Pg.	1928	Tr. Pg.	
C. F. Steck, D. D.	1923			Tr. Md.			
Geo. S. Bowden	1923			S. C.	1929	Tr. N. C.	
V. Y. Boozer	1924			S. C.	1927	Tr. N. C.	
L. Raymond Haus	1924			E. Pa.	1927	Tr. E. Pa.	
C. L. Hunt	1924			Pg.			
Joseph S. Kleckner	1924			Min. Pa.	1926	D'cd	Nazareth, Pa. Feb. 14
Fred J. Lottich	1924			Ind.	1928	Tr. Ill.	
P. E. Seidler	1924						Member Mo. Synod Received by vote.
J. A. Shealy	1924			S. C.			
A. L. Boliek	1925			N. C.			
H. D. Chapman	1925			N. C.	1926	Tr. Md.	
I. Conder	1925			N. C.	1928	D'cd	McGaheysville, August 31.
W. L. Darr	1925			N. C.			
W. J. Finck, D. D.	1925			N. C.			
L. L. Lohr, D. D.	1925			N. C.	1925	Tr. S. C.	
C. I. Morgan	1925			N. C.	1925	Tr. S. C.	
J. P. Stirewalt, D. D.	1925			N. C.			
W. C. Huddle	1925		1925				
T. A. Graves	1925		1925				
J. P. Derrick	1925			S. C.			
S. L. Nease	1925			N. C.			
Russell Snyder	1925			Min. Pa.	1927	Tr. Min. Pa.	
C. M. Teufel, D. D.	1925			Pg.			
Frederich Christ	1925			N. Y.	1927	Tr. Al.	
R. R. Sowers	1925			S. C.	1925	D'cd	
C. A. Freed, D. D.	1926			S. C.	1929	Tr. S. C.	
H. A. Jackson	1926		1926		1927	Tr. S. C.	
F. C. Longaker, Ph. D.	1926			N. C.			
Frank H. Miller	1926		1926		1927	Tr. Pg.	
Luther F. Miller	1926			Md.			
D. W. Zipperer	1926		1926				
J. H. Booher	1926	L					
Kenneth Killinger	1926	L					
B. D. Castor	1927		1927				
H. E. Henning	1927			Ga.			
James A. Lotz	1927			Ohio	1928	Withdrew	
T. G. Shuey	1927			Pg.			
L. W. Strickler	1927			Ga.			
C. K. Rhodes	1928			N. C.			
A. W. Ballentine	1928			S. C.			
P. J. Bame	1928			N. C.			

THE LUTHERAN SYNOD OF VIRGINIA
(Continued)

NAME	Received Into Synod				Removed		REMARKS
	Date	Licensed	Ordained	Tr. From	Date	How	
B. A. Barringer	1928			N. C.			
W. C. Buck	1928			N. C.			
C. M. Coffelt	1928			Ga.			
J. I. Coiner	1928			Miss.			
B. S. Dasher	1928			Ga.			
J. W. Groth	1928			W. Va.	1928	Tr. W. Va.	
M. J. Kluttz	1928			N. C.			
Russell P. Knoebel	1928			Sq.			
R. S. Poffenberger	1928			Min. Pa.			
Geo. S. Stoudemayer	1928			Ga.			
R. T. Troutman	1928			N. C.			
Snyder Alleman	1928			Al.			
H. Edgar Knies	1928			Pa.			
E. J. Lowe	1928			Md.			
R. L. Markley	1928			Al.			
J. P. Miller, D. D.	1928			Ind.			
Walter V. Simon	1928			Md.			
Lester A. Wertz	1928			S. C.			
A. K. Yount	1928			N. C.			
A. J. Shumate	1929		1929				
A. R. Shumate	1929		1929				
H. E. Poff	1929		1929				
M. L. Minnick	1929		1929				
A. L. Hahn	1929			N. C.			
Hugh J. Rhyne	1929			Md.			
Arthur M. Huffman	1929			N. C.			
W. H. Kibler	1929			Ohio			

ORGANIZATIONS AND CONVENTIONS

SPECIAL VIRGINIA CONFERENCE OF THE
MINISTERIUM OF PENNSYLVANIA

Date	Place of Meeting	President	Secretary	Ministers Present	Laymen Present
1793—Jan. 6,7	Winchester	Christian Streit	J. D. Young	4	7
1793—Oct. 6,7	Strasburg	Christian Streit	J. D. Young	4	9
1794—Oct. 12,13	Martinsburg	Christian Streit	J. D. Young	4	4
1795—Oct. 5	Staunton	Christian Streit	J. D. Young	4	7
1796—Oct. 3,4	Madison	Paul Henkel	V. G. C. Stork	5	4
1797—Oct. 1,2	Woodstock	Christian Streit	J. D. Young	6	7
1798—Oct. 7,8	Shepherdstown	Christian Streit	J. D. Young	8	
1799—No record of meeting.					
1800—No record of meeting.					
1801—No record of meeting.					
1802—Meeting held. Date and place not known. Minutes printed and sent to Ministerium.					
1803—Meeting held. Date and place not known. Minutes read to Ministerium.					
1804—Meeting held. Date and place not known. Minutes printed and sent to Ministerium.					
1805—Oct. 6,7	Woodstock	Christian Streit	Paul Henkel	5	5
1806—Oct. 5,6	Rader's	Paul Henkel	A. Spindler	5	10
1807—Oct. 4,5	New Market	Paul Henkel	Wm. Carpenter	7	4
1808—Oct. 2,3	Winchester	Paul Henkel	Christian Streit	3	3
1809—Oct. 1,2	Solomon's	Christian Streit	S. Henkel	4	5
1810—No record of meeting.					
1811—No record of meeting.					
1812—No record of meeting.					
1813—No record of meeting.					
1814—No record of meeting.					
1815—Mar. 19,20	Solomon's	Paul Henkel	J. P. Schmucker	5	7
1815—Mar. 19,20	Woodstock	Paul Henkel	F. Haas	7	6
1816—Appointed to meet at Strasburg 2nd Sunday in September. No known record.					
1817—Sept. 14,16	Madison	G. H. Riemenschneider	A. Reck	5	12
1818—*Appointed to meet at McGaheysville 1st Sunday in October. No known record.					

Academic titles are omitted in these tables.

*It is believed that meetings were held each year until 1820, but records are known only as of the above. Recently minutes of meetings not before known, were found at New Market by Dr. W. J. Finck.

THE SYNOD OF MARYLAND AND VIRGINIA, 1820–1828

Year	Date	Name of Synod	Place of Meeting	President	Secretary	Treasurer
1820	Oct. 11	Synod of Maryland and Virginia and so forth	Winchester, Va.	J. D. Kurtz	D. F. Schaeffer	A. Reck
1821	Sept. 2	Synod of Maryland and Virginia and so forth	Frederick, Md.	J. D. Kurtz	D. F. Schaeffer	A. Reck
1822	Aug. 31	Synod of Maryland and Virginia	Cumberland, Md.	J. D. Kurtz	D. F. Schaeffer	A. Reck
1823	Nov. 2	Synod of Maryland and Virginia	Shepherdstown, W. Va.	J. D. Kurtz	S. S. Schmucker	C. P. Krauth
1824	Oct. 17	Synod of Maryland and Virginia	Middletown, Md.	D. F. Schaeffer	S. S. Schmucker	C. P. Krauth
1825	Oct. 15	Synod of Maryland and Virginia	Hagerstown, Md.	C. P. Krauth	D. F. Schaeffer	F. Ruthrauff
1826	Oct. 15	Synod of Maryland and Virginia	Winchester, Va.	C. P. Krauth	D. F. Schaeffer	F. Ruthrauff
1827	Oct. 20	Synod of Maryland and Virginia	Frederick, Md.	J. D. Kurtz	D. F. Schaeffer	A. Reck
1828*	Oct. 18	Synod of Maryland and Virginia	Shepherdstown, W. Va.	J. D. Kurtz	D. F. Schaeffer	A. Reck

*In 1828 the Synod agreed for the Virginia pastors to organize a separate synod. Organization of the synod took place at Woodstock, August 10, 11, 1829. In 1829 the name "Virginia" was dropped from the title of the old synod. It was taken up again in 1831 and 1832, but dropped in 1833.

TIME, PLACE AND OFFICERS OF THE REGULAR CONVENTIONS OF THE MERGING SYNODS FROM THEIR ORGANIZATION UNTIL THE MERGER, 1922

Synod	No.	Date	Place of Meeting	President	Secretary	Treasurer
Virginia	1	1829—Aug. 10	Woodstock	Nicholas Schmucker	John Kehler	Dan J. Hauer
Virginia	2	1830—Oct. 10	Union Ch., Rockingham Co.	Michael Meyerhoeffer	John Kehler	J. P. Dagey
Virginia	3	1831—Oct. 15	Zion Ch., Botetourt Co.	Michael Meyerhoeffer	Dan. J. Hauer	J. P. Dagey
Virginia	4	1832—Oct. 20	St. John's Ch., Augusta Co.	Michael Meyerhoeffer	J. P. Cline	J. P. Cline
Virginia	5	1833—Oct. 15	New Market	J. P. Cline	Wm. Scull	S. Oswald
Virginia	6	1834—Oct. 11	Madison	Thos. Miller	Wm. Scull	S. Oswald
Virginia	7	1835—Oct. 8	Zion Ch., Augusta Co.	Thos. Miller	S. Oswald	A. Babb
Virginia		1836—No meeting. Adjourned 1835 to meet at Newtown on Thursday before 2nd Sunday in Oct., 1836.				
Virginia		1837—No meeting. A conference was held in Strasburg, November 1837.				
Virginia	8	1838—May 21	Madison	J. B. Davis	Theo. Stork	Thos. Miller
Virginia	9	1839—May 20	Zion Ch., Roanoke Co.	J. B. Davis	Theo. Stork	Thos. Miller
Virginia	10	1840—May 15	Mt. Tabor, Augusta Co.	J. B. Davis	Theo. Stork	Thos. Miller
Virginia	11	1841—May 22	Union Ch., Rockingham Co.	Lewis Eichelberger	D. F. Bittle	J. J. Reimensnyder
Virginia	12	1842—April 30	Newtown	Lewis Eichelberger	D. F. Bittle	Thos. Miller
Southwestern Va.	1	1842—Sept. 20	Zion Ch., Floyd Co.	Jacob Scherer	Elijah Hawkins	Mr. Joseph Brown
Virginia	13	1843—May 6	Woodstock	L. Eichelberger	S. Wagner	Thos. Miller
Southwestern Va.	2	1843—June 6	Burke's Garden	Jacob Scherer	Elijah Hawkins	Mr. Joseph Brown
Virginia	14	1844—May 11	Winchester	J. B. Davis	L. Eichelberger	Thos. Miller
Southwestern Va.	3	1844—May 25	Union Ch., Botetourt Co.	Jacob Scherer	Elijah Hawkins	Mr. Jonas Huddle
Virginia	15	1845—May 8	Shepherdstown	J. B. Davis	L. Eichelberger	Thos. Miller
Southwestern Va.	4	1845—June 7	St. John's Ch., Wythe Co.	Elijah Hawkins	J. A. Brown	G. Scherer
Virginia	16	1846—May 7	Strasburg	J. B. Davis	L. Eichelberger	Thos. Miller
Southwestern Va.	5	1846—May 16	Stony Creek, Giles Co.	J. J. Greever	J. A. Brown	G. Scherer
Virginia	17	1847—May 6	Churchville	S. Wagner	J. Few Smith	J. F. Campbell
Southwestern Va.	6	1847—Aug. 28	Chilhowie Ch., Smyth Co.	J. J. Greever	J. A. Brown	G. Scherer
Virginia	18	1848—May 5	New Market	J. P. Cline	A. P. Ludden	P. Shickle
Southwestern Va.	7	1848—Aug. 26	St. Peter's Ch., Wythe Co.	J. A. Brown	Elijah Hawkins	J. J. Greever
Virginia	19	1849—May 17	German Settlement, Preston Co.	J. P. Cline	A. P. Ludden	P. Shickle
Southwestern Va.	8	1849—Sept. 3	Pine Ch., Roanoke Co.	J. A. Brown	Elijah Hawkins	J. J. Greever
Virginia	20	1850—May 17	Madison	J. P. Cline	J. F. Campbell	Thos. Miller
Southwestern Va.	9	1850—Sept. 21	St. Peter's Ch., Montgomery Co.	Elijah Hawkins	G. Scherer	J. J. Greever
Virginia	21	1851—May 15	Newtown	J. F. Campbell	X. J. Richardson	Thos. Miller
Southwestern Va.	10	1851—Sept. 18	Luther Chapel, Wash. Co.	Elijah Hawkins	J. A. Brown	S. Rhudy
Virginia	22	1852—May 13	Harrisonburg	J. F. Campbell	X. J. Richardson	Thos. Miller
Virginia	23	1852—Oct. 17	Mt. Tabor, Augusta Co.	A. P. Ludden	X. J. Richardson	A. R. Rude
Southwestern Va.	11	1852—Sept. 2	Copp's Ch., Botetourt Co.	Elijah Hawkins	J. A. Brown	S. Schaeffer

TIME, PLACE AND OFFICERS OF THE REGULAR CONVENTIONS OF THE MERGING SYNODS FROM THEIR ORGANIZATION UNTIL THE MERGER, 1922

(Continued)

Synod	No.	Date	Place of Meeting	President	Secretary	Treasurer
Virginia	24	1853—Oct. 6	Smithfield, Jefferson Co.	A. P. Ludden	R. A. Fink	A. R. Rude
Southwestern Va.	12	1853—Sept. 22	St. Paul's Ch., Wythe Co.	J. J. Greever	Elijah Hawkins	S. Rhudy
Virginia	25	1854—Nov. 16	Martinsburg	C. P. Krauth	R. A. Fink	W. F. Greaver
Southwestern Va.	13	1854—Sept. 29	Zion Ch., Floyd Co.	Elijah Hawkins	J. A. Brown	S. Rhudy
Virginia	26	1855—Oct. 4	Zion Ch., Augusta Co.	J. B. Davis	A. R. Rude	W. F. Greaver
Southwestern Va.	14	1855—Sept. 21	Kimberlin Ch., Wythe Co.	Elijah Hawkins	J. A. Brown	S. Rhudy
Virginia	27	1856—Oct. 16	Woodstock	J. B. Davis	A. R. Rude	L. Keller
Southwestern Va.	15	1856—Aug. 21	Stony Creek, Giles Co.	D. H. Bittle	W. D. Reodel	S. Rhudy
Virginia	28	1857—Oct. 8	Staunton	X. J. Richardson	A. R. Rude	L. Keller
Southwestern Va.	16	1857—Aug. 27	St. John's Ch., Wythe Co.	D. H. Bittle	W. D. Reodel	S. Rhudy
Virginia	29	1858—Oct. 21	New Market	X. J. Richardson	Wm. Rusmiselle	L. Keller
Southwestern Va.	17	1858—Aug. 20	Salem	W. D. Reodel	J. A. Brown	S. Rhudy
Virginia	30	1859—Oct. 26	Shepherdstown	A. R. Rude	Wm. Rusmiselle	L. Keller
Southwestern Va.	18	1859—Aug. 18	St. James' Ch., Smyth Co.	Elijah Hawkins	J. A. Brown	S. Rhudy
Virginia	31	1860—Oct. 20	Bridgewater, Va.	J. P. Cline	W. M. Baum	C. Beard
Southwestern Va.	19	1860—Aug. 16	Sharon Ch., Wythe Co., Va.	Elijah Hawkins	J. A. Brown	S. Rhudy
Holston	1	1860—Jan. 2	Zion Ch., Sullivan Co., Tenn.	Wm. Hancher	A. J. Brown	
Virginia	32	1861—Oct. 18	Mt. Tabor Ch., Augusta Co., Va.	J. Summers	J. I. Miller	A. R. Rude
Southwestern Va.	20	1861—Sept. 7	St. John's Ch., Wythe Co., Va.	J. C. Repass	W. D. Reodel	S. Rhudy
Holston		1861—Meeting appointed for Monroe County, St. Paul's Church, October, 1861, but not held because of Civil War.				
Virginia	33	1862—Oct. 23	Lebanon Ch., Shen. Co., Va.	L. Keller	D. M. Gilbert	J. D. Shirey
Southwestern Va.	21	1862—Aug. 15	Newport, Giles Co., Va.	J. A. Brown	J. G. Frey	S. Rhudy
Holston	2	1862—Oct. 23	Miller's Ch., Knox Co., Tenn.	J. M. Shaeffer	J. C. Barb	J. K. Hancher
Virginia	34	1863—Oct. 22	Salem Ch., Augusta Co., Va.	C. Beard	J. D. Shirey	J. P. Cline
Southwestern Va.	22	1863—Aug. 13	St. Peter's, Mont. Co., Va.	P. Shickel	J. G. Frey	E. H. McDonald
Holston	3	1863—Sept. 1	Weaver's Ch., Sullivan Co., Tenn.	Wm. Hancher	A. J. Brown	Mr. Wm. Akard
Virginia	35	1864—Oct. 13	Churchville, Va.	Wm. Rusmiselle	W. S. McClanahan	Mr. Wm. A. Coiner
Southwestern Va.	23	1864—Aug. 18	Zion Ch., Wythe Co., Va.	P. Shickel	J. G. Frey	E. H. McDonald
Holston		1864—No meeting because of Civil War.				
Virginia	36	1865—Oct. 26	Bethany Ch., Rockbridge Co., Va.	T. W. Dosh	G. A. Long	C. Beard
Southwestern Va.	24	1865—Aug. 17	Pine Grove, Roanoke, Va.	J. C. Repass	L. A. Mann	E. H. McDonald
Holston	4	1865—Sept. 23	Union Ch., Sullivan Co., Tenn.	J. K. Hancher	A. J. Brown	Mr. Wm. Akard
Virginia	37	1866—Oct. 18	Winchester, Va.	J. I. Miller	T. W. Dosh	L. Keller
Southwestern Va.	25	1866—Aug. 16	Ebenezer Ch., Smyth Co., Va.	J. C. Repass	Alex. Phillippi	E. H. McDonald
Holston	5	1866—Sept. 20	St. Paul's Ch., Monroe Co., Tenn.	J. K. Hancher	J. C. Barb	Mr. John H. Houser

TIME, PLACE AND OFFICERS OF THE REGULAR CONVENTIONS OF THE MERGING SYNODS FROM THEIR ORGANIZATION UNTIL THE MERGER, 1922

(Continued)

Synod	No.	Date	Place of Meeting	President	Secretary	Treasurer
Virginia	38	1867—Aug. 8	New Market, Va.	H. Cupp	P. Miller	G. A. Long
Southwestern Va.	26	1867—Aug. 16	Stoney Creek, Giles Co., Va.	J. A. Brown	Alex. Phillippi	E. H. McDonald
Holston	6	1867—Aug. 1	Solomon's Ch., Greene Co., Tenn.	A. J. Brown	J. M. Wagner	Mr. John Kinser
Virginia	39	1868—Sept. 24	West Union, Preston Co., W. Va.	G. A. Long	J. A. Snyder	L. Keller
Southwestern Va.	27	1868—Aug. 13	Luther Chapel, Wash. Co., Va.	J. A. Brown	J. C. Repass	E. H. McDonald
Holston	7	1868—Sept. 26	Zion Ch., Sullivan Co., Tenn.	J. C. Barb	Andrew Rader	Mr. Adam Knipp
Virginia	40	1869—Oct. 14	Madison, Va.	J. A. Snyder	Webster Eichelberger	Mr. Henry S. Baker
Southwestern Va.	28	1869—Aug. 13	Zion Ch., Floyd Co., Va.	J. A. Brown	J. C. Repass	E. H. McDonald
Holston	8	1869—Sept. 4	Miller's Ch., Knox Co., Tenn.	A. J. Brown	J. C. Barb	Mr. J. H. Howser
Virginia	41	1870—Aug. 17	Shepherdstown, W. Va.	J. F. Campbell	R. C. Holland	Mr. Henry S. Baker
Southwestern Va.	29	1870—Aug. 25	Pleasant Hill, Smyth Co., Va.	W. B. Yonce	S. A. Repass	E. H. McDonald
Holston	9	1870—Aug. 27	Sinking Springs, Greene Co., Tenn.	J. M. Wagner	J. H. Turner	Mr. L. E. Williams
Virginia	42	1871—Aug. 24	Woodstock, Va.	P. Miller	G. A. Long	W. H. Baker
Southwestern Va.	30	1871—Aug. 24	Kimberlin, Wythe Co., Va.	J. J. Scherer	S. A. Repass	J. A. Brown
Holston	10	1871—Aug. 26	St. Paul's Ch., Monroe Co., Tenn.	J. K. Hancher	J. C. Barb	Mr. A. G. Easterly
Virginia	43	1872—Aug. 15	Harrisonburg, Va.	J. H. Cupp	J. M. Schreckhise	D. M. Gilbert
Southwestern Va.	31	1872—Aug. 15	St. Peter's Ch., Wythe Co., Va.	J. J. Scherer	J. B. Greiner	J. A. Brown
Holston	11	18?2—Sept. 21	Immanuel Ch., Sullivan Co., Tenn.	A. J. Brown	J. K. Hancher	Mr. J. A. Williams
Virginia	44	1873—Aug. 7	Mt. Tabor Ch., Aug. Co., Va.	R. C. Holland	D. M. Gilbert	C. Beard
Southwestern Va.	32	1873—Aug. 22	Cedar Grove Ch., Smyth Co. Va.	J. A. Brown	J. B. Greiner	Alex. Phillippi.
Holston	12	1873—Aug. 30	Blue Springs Ch., Greene Co. Tenn.	J. C. Barb	Geo. H. Cox	Mr. Wm. Burnett.
Virginia	45	1874—Aug. 27	Mt. Jackson, Va.	J. Hawkins	M. B. Minnich	J. Miller
Southwestern Va.	33	1874—Aug. 20	Brick Union, Botetourt Co., Va.	J. A. Brown	J. B. Greiner	Alex. Phillippi
Holston	13	1874—Sept. 26	Zion's Ch., Knox Co., Tenn.	Geo. H. Cox	J. C. Barb	J. M. Wagner
Virginia	46	1875—Aug. 13	Newtown, Va.	D. M. Gilbert	J. H. Barb	C. Beard
Southwestern Va.	34	1875—Aug. 19	St. John's Ch., Wythe Co., Va.	J. C. Repass	J. J. Scherer	Alex. Phillippi
Holston	14	1875—Sept. 5	Salem Ch., Cocke Co., Tenn.	J. K. Hancher	J. C. Miller	J. C. Barb
Virginia	47	1876—Aug. 8	Strasburg, Va.	Webster Eichelberger	J. P. Obenschain	D. M. Gilbert.
Southwestern Va.	35	1876—Aug. 24	Burke's Garden, Va.	J. C. Repass	J. J. Scherer	Alex. Phillippi.
Holston	15	1876—Sept. 31	Luther Chapel, Sul. Co., Tenn.	A. J. Brown	J. G. Schaidt	Geo. H. Cox
Virginia	48	1877—Aug. 22	Salem, Augusta Co., Va.	R. C. Holland	J. H. Barb	P. Miller.
Southwestern Va.	36	1877—Aug. 16	Stoney Cr., Giles Co., Va.	J. C. Repass	J. J. Scherer	J. B. Greiner
Holston	16	1877—Aug. 30	St. Paul's Ch., Monroe Co., Tenn.	A. J. Brown	J. G. Schaidt	Geo. H. Cox
Virginia	49	1878—Aug. 6	Winchester, Va.	R. C. Holland	J. H. Barb	D. M. Gilbert.
Southwestern Va.	37	1878—Aug. 22	Ebenezer, Smyth Co., Va.	J. B. Greiner	J. A. Brown	J. J. Scherer
Holston	17	1878—Sept. 19	Sinking Springs, Greene Co., Tenn.	J. M. Shaeffer	J. C. Barb	Mr. J. H. Howser.

TIME, PLACE, AND OFFICERS OF THE REGULAR CONVENTIONS OF THE MERGING SYNODS FROM THEIR ORGANIZATION UNTIL THE MERGER, 1922

(Continued)

Synod	No.	Date	Place of Meeting	President	Secretary	Treasurer
Virginia	50	1879—Aug. 26	Woodstock, Va.	J. F. Campbell	J. H. Barb	D. M. Gilbert
Southwestern Va.	38	1879—Aug. 21	Mt. Tabor, Mont. Co., Va.	J. B. Greiner	J. A. Brown	J. J. Scherer
Holston	18	1879—Sept. 25	New Haven Ch., Sul. Co., Tenn.	J. G. Schaidt	Geo. H. Cox	Mr. W. H. Burnett
Virginia	51	1880—Aug. 17	Mt. Jackson, Va.	J. F. Campbell	J. H. Barb	D. M. Gilbert
Southwestern Va.	39	1880—Aug. 25	Pine Grove, Roanoke Co., Va.	J. B. Greiner	W. E. Hubbert	J. J. Scherer
Holston	19	1880—Sept. 9	Bethel Ch., Knox Co., Tenn.	J. K. Hancher	J. C. Barb	Mr. Adam Knipp
Virginia	52	1881—Aug. 28	Shepherdstown, W. Va.	J. F. Campbell	J. H. Barb	D. M. Gilbert
Southwestern Va.	40	1881—Aug. 24	Burke's Garden, Va.	W. B. Yonce	W. E. Hubbert	Mr. T. J. Schickel
Holston	20	1881—Sept. 3	St. Mary's Ch., Monroe Co., Tenn.	Geo. H. Cox	J. H. Summitt	Mr. L. E. Williams
Virginia	53	1882—Sept. 26	New Market, Va.	D. M. Gilbert	J. H. Barb	D. M. Moser
Southwestern Va.	41	1882—Aug. 23	Clover Hollow, Giles Co., Va.	W. B. Yonce	W. E. Hubbert	Mr. T. J. Schickel
Holston	21	1882—Aug. 16	St. James Ch., Greene Co., Tenn.	A. J. Brown	J. C. Barb	Mr. Geo. Neas
Virginia	54	1883—Oct. 9	Zion Ch., Augusta Co., Va.	D. M. Gilbert	L. L. Smith	D. M. Moser
Southwestern Va.	42	1883—Aug. 17	Marion, Va.	J. J. Scherer	F. V. N. Painter	Mr. T. J. Schickel
Holston	22	1883—Aug. 16	Buehler's Ch., Sullivan Co., Tenn.	J. K. Hancher	J. G. Schaidt	Geo. O. Houser
Virginia	55	1884—Sept. 30	Stephens City, Va.	D. M. Gilbert	L. L. Smith	D. M. Moser
Southwestern Va.	43	1884—Aug. 1	Trinity Ch., Botetourt Co., Va.	J. J. Scherer	F. V. N. Painter	Mr. T. J. Schickel
Holston	23	1884—Aug. 15	Miller's Ch., Knox Co., Tenn.	A. J. Brown	J. B. Fox	Mr. W. R. Gibbs
Virginia	56	1885—Sept. 23	Carmel, W. Va.	D. M. Gilbert	L. L. Smith	J. H. Barb
Southwestern Va.	44	1885—Aug. 21	Salem, Va.	J. J. Scherer	J. B. Greiner	Mr. C. H. Coley
Holston	24	1885—Aug. 13	Solomon's Ch., Greene Co., Tenn.	A. J. Brown	Geo. H. Cox	Mr. H. J. Kinzel •
Virginia	57	1886—Oct. 12	New Haven, W. Va.	D. M. Gilbert	L. L. Smith	J. H. Barb
Southwestern Va.	45	1886—Aug. 20	Ebenezer, Smyth Co., Va.	L. G. M. Miller	J. B. Greiner	Mr. H. S. Trout
Holston	25	1886—Aug. 11	Immanuel's Ch., Sul. Co., Tenn.	J. K. Hancher	A. J. Brown	Mr. Wm. Akard
Virginia	58	1887—Oct. 2	Harrisonburg, Va.	J. A. Snyder	L. L. Smith	V. R. Stickley
Southwestern Va.	46	1887—Aug. 25	St. John's Ch., Wythe Co., Va.	L. G. M. Miller	J. E. Bushnell	Mr. H. S. Trout
Holston	26	1887—Aug. 18	Holy Trinity, Morristown, Tenn.	A. J. Brown	J. H. Summitt	Mr. T. F. Leach
Virginia	59	1888—Aug. 21	Madison, Va.	J. A. Snyder	L. L. Smith	V. R. Stickley
Southwestern Va.	47	1888—Aug. 10	Pembroke, Va.	W. B. Yonce	W. E. Hubbert	Mr. H. S. Trout
Holston	27	1888—Aug. 16	St. Peter's Ch., Monroe Co., Tenn.	W. G. Wolford	J. B. Rodgers	Mr. R. A. Cobble
Virginia	60	1889—Aug. 20	Woodstock, Va.	J. A. Snyder	L. L. Smith	V. R. Stickley
Southwestern Va.	48	1889—Aug. 21	Sharon Ch., Bland Co., Va.	J. B. Greiner	W. E. Hubbert	Mr. H. S. Trout
Holston	28	1889—Aug. 22	Sinking Springs, Greene Co., Tenn.	J. K. Hancher	J. B. Rodgers	Mr. J. L. Cobble
Virginia	61	1890—Aug. 19	Mt. Tabor, Augusta Co., Va.	D. M. Moser	L. L. Smith	V. R. Stickley
Southwestern Va.	49	1890—Aug. 13	Salem, Va.	J. C. Repass	W. E. Hubbert	Mr. H. S. Trout
Holston	29	1890—Aug. 28	Zion Ch., Sul. Co., Tenn.	A. J. Brown	J. B. Rogers	Mr. Andrew Bible

TIME, PLACE AND OFFICERS OF THE REGULAR CONVENTIONS OF THE MERGING SYNODS FROM THEIR ORGANIZATION UNTIL THE MERGER, 1922

(Continued)

Synod	No.	Date	Place of Meeting	President	Secretary	Treasurer
Virginia	62	1891—Aug. 10	Lebanon Ch., Shen. Co., Va.	D. M. Moser	L. L. Smith	V. R. Stickley
Southwestern Va.	50	1891—Aug. 12	St. John's Ch., Wythe Co., Va.	J. E. Bushnell	C. A. Miller	Mr. H. S. Trout
Holston	30	1891—Aug. 6	St. Paul's Ch., Monroe Co., Tenn.	J. K. Hancher	J. B. Rodgers	Mr. Wm. Knipp
Virginia	63	1892—Aug. 23	Meianchthon Chapel, Aug. Co., Va.	D. M. Moser	L. L. Smith	mr. L. S. walker
Southwestern Va.	51	1892—Aug. 24	Burke's Garden, Va.	J. B. Greiner	L. A. Fox	Mr. H. S. Trout
Holston	31	1892—Aug. 11	Salem Ch., Cocke Co., Tenn.	A. J. Brown	J. B. Rodgers	F. M. Harr
Virginia	64	1893—Sept. 5	Toms Brook, Va.	G. W. Spiggle	L. L. Smith	mr. L. S. walker
Southwestern Va.	52	1893—Aug. 16	Rural Retreat, Va.	J. B. Greiner	F. A. Fox	Mr. H. S. Trout
Holston	32	1893—Aug. 10	Luther Zion, Wash. Co., Tenn.	J. H. Summitt	J. B. Rodgers	F. M. Harr
Virginia	65	1894—Aug. 21	Strasburg, Va.	J. M. Shreckhise	L. L. Smith	Mr. L. S. Walker
Southwestern Va.	53	1894—Aug. 15	Blacksburg, Va.	J. B. Greiner	J. A. Huffard	Mr. H. S. Trout
Holston	33	1894—Aug. 8	Solomon's Ch., Greene Co., Tenn.	A. D. R. Hancher	J. B. Rodgers	F. M. Harr
Virginia	66	1895—Aug. 20	New Market, Va.	H. F. Shealy	L. L. Smith	Mr. L. S. Walker
Southwestern Va.	54	1895—Aug. 14	Graham, Va.	J. J. Scherer	J. A. Huffard	Mr. H. S. Trout
Holston	34	1895—July 31	Knoxville, Tenn.	A. D. R. Hancher	J. M. Moser	F. M. Harr
Virginia	67	1896—Aug. 18	Zion, Augusta Co., Va.	H. F. Shealy	L. L. Smith	Mr. L. S. Walker
Southwestern Va.	55	1896—Aug. 12	East Radford, Va.	J. J. Scherer	J. A. Huffard	Mr. E. L. Greever
Holston	35	1896—Aug. 6	Blue Springs Ch., Wash., Tenn.	J. C. Barb	H. E. Baily	F. M. Harr
Virginia	68	1897—Aug. 17	Winchester, Va.	H. F. Sheele	L. L. Smith	Mr. L. S. Walker
Southwestern Va.	56	1897—Aug. 11	Glade Creek Ch., Bot. Co., Va.	J. B. Greiner	W. H. Greever	Mr. E. L. Greever
Holston	36	1897—Aug. 5	Immanuel Ch., Sul. Co., Tenn.	J. C. Barb	H. E. Baily	F. M. Harr
Virginia	69	1898—Aug. 24	Madison, Va.	W. J. Smith	L. L. Smith	Mr. L. S. Walker
Southwestern Va.	57	1898—Aug. 17	Rural Retreat, Va.	J. B. Greiner	W. H. Greever	Mr. E. L. Greever
Holston	37	1898—Aug. 11	Zion Ch., Sul. Co., Tenn.	A. D. R. Hancher	H. E. Baily	F. M. Harr
Virginia	70	1899—Aug. 22	Winchester, Va.	W. J. Smith	L. L. Smith	Mr. L. S. Walker
Southwestern Va.	58	1899—Aug. 15	Bluefield, W. Va.	J. B. Greiner	W. H. Greever	Mr. E. L. Greever
Holston	38	1899—Aug. 10	Sinking Springs, Greene Co., Tenn.	J. C. Barb	H. E. Baily	F. M. Harr
Virginia	71	1900—Oct. 23	Norfolk, Va.	W. L. Seabrook	L. L. Smith	Mr. L. S. Walker
Southwestern Va.	59	1900—Aug. 17	Ebenezer Ch., Smyth Co., Va.	J. B. Greiner	W. H. Greever	Mr. E. L. Greever
Holston	39	1900—Aug. 9	St. Mary's Ch., Monroe Co., Tenn.	J. B. Greever	H. E. Baily	Mr. W. H. Greer
Virginia	72	1901—Oct. 22	Mt. Zion, Ch., Shen. Co., Va.	W. L. Seabrook	L. L. Smith	Mr. L. S. Walker
Southwestern Va.	60	1901—Aug. 14	Salem, Va.	J. B. Greiner	B. W. Cronk	Mr. E. L. Greever
Holston	40	1901—Aug. 8	St. James' Ch., Greene Co., Tenn.	F. M. Harr	C. Brown Cox	Mr. W. H. Greer
Virginia	73	1902—Oct. 21	Staunton, Va.	C. A. Freed	L. L. Smith	Mr. L. S. Walker
Southwestern Va.	61	1902—Aug. 13	St. Paul's Ch., Wythe Co., Va.	J. B. Greiner	C. W. Cassell	Mr. E. L. Greever
Holston	41	1902—Aug. 3	Zion Ch., Knox Co., Tenn.	J. C. Miller	C. Brown Cox	Mr. W. R. Neas

TIME, PLACE AND OFFICERS OF THE REGULAR CONVENTIONS OF THE MERGING SYNODS FROM THEIR ORGANIZATION UNTIL THE MERGER, 1922

(Continued)

Synod	No.	Date	Place of Meeting	President	Secretary	Treasurer
Virginia	74	1903—Aug. 18	Mt. Jackson, Va.	P. Miller	L. L. Smith	Mr. L. S. Walker
Southwestern Va.	62	1903—Aug. 12	Burke's Garden, Va.	J. B. Greiner	C. W. Cassell	Mr. A. S. Greever
Holston	42	1903—July 30	Soloman's Ch., Greene Co., Tenn.	F. M. Harr	D. S. Steffey	Mr. W. H. Greer
Virginia	75	1904—Aug. 23	Woodstock, Va.	L. L. Smith	A. D. R. Hancher	Mr. M. Coffman
Southwestern Va.	63	1904—Aug. 17	Damascus, Va.	J. B. Greiner	C. W. Cassell	Mr. A. S. Greever
Holston	43	1904—Aug. 4	Knoxville, Tenn.	M. M. Kinard	S. D. Steffey	Mr. W. H. Greer
Virginia	76	1905—Aug. 22	Toms Brook, Va.	L. L. Smith	A. D. R. Hancher	Mr. M. Coffman
Southwestern Va.	64	1905—Aug. 15	Zion Ch., Wythe Co., Va.	J. B. Greiner	Paul Sieg	Mr. A. S. Greever
Holston	44	1905—Aug. 3	Salem Ch., Cocke Co., Tenn.	M. M. Kinard	H. E. H. Sloop	Mr. J. M. Kinser
Virginia	77	1906—Aug. 22	Mt. Tabor, Aug. Co., Va.	L. L. Smith	A. D. R. Hancher	Mr. M. Coffman
Southwestern Va.	65	1906—Aug. 15	Wheatland, Botetourt Co., Va.	J. B. Greiner	Paul Sieg	Mr. A. S. Greever
Holston	45	1906—Aug. 2	Immanuel Ch., Sul. Co., Tenn.	H. E. H. Sloop	W. H. Roof	Mr. J. M. Kinser
Virginia	78	1907—Aug. 20	Stephens City, Va.	L. L. Smith	A. D. R. Hancher	Mr. M. Coffman
Southwestern Va.	66	1907—Aug. 14	Tazewell, Va.	J. B. Greiner	Paul Sieg	Rev. W. R. Brown
Holston	46	1907—Aug. 1	St. Paul's Ch., Monroe Co., Tenn.	W. H. Roof	W. C. Davis	Mr. J. M. Kinser
Virginia	79	1908—Aug. 25	Richmond, Va.	Geo. S. Bowers	A. D. R. Hancher	Mr. M. Coffman
Southwestern Va.	67	1908—Aug. 8	Corinth Ch., Wythe Co., Va.	W. R. Brown	Paul Sieg	A. B. Greiner, M. D.
Holston	47	1908—July 30	Sinking Sp gs Ch., Greene Co. Tenn.	W. H. Roof	W. C. Davis	Mr. J. M. Kinser
Virginia	80	1909—Aug. 17	Bethany, Rockbridge Co., Va.	Geo. S. Bowers	A. D. R. Hancher	Mr. M. Coffman
Southwestern Va.	68	1909—Aug. 11	Bristol, Tenn.	L. A. Fox	Paul Sieg	A. B. Greiner, M. D.
Holston	48	1909—Aug. 5	Immanuel Ch., Sul. Co., Tenn.	W. H. Roof	W. C. Davis	Mr. J. M. Kinser
Virginia	81	1910—Aug. 23	Shepherdstown, W. Va.	Geo. S. Bowers	A. D. R. Hancher	Mr. M. Coffman
Southwestern Va.	69	1910—Aug. 17	Roanoke, Va.	L. A. Fox	Paul Sieg	A. B. Greiner, M. D.
Holston	49	1910—Aug. 10	St. James' Ch., Greene Co., Tenn.	W. H. Roof	W. C. Davis	Mr. J. M. Kinser
Virginia	82	1911—Aug. 29	Salem Ch., Augusta Co., Va.	Geo. S. Bowers	A. D. R. Hancher	Mr. M. Coffman
Southwestern Va.	70	1911—Aug. 16	Radford, Va.	L. A. Fox	Paul Sieg	A. B. Greiner, M. D.
Holston	50	1911—Aug. 9	Salem Ch., Cocke Co., Tenn.	V. C. Ridenhour	H. G. Davis	Mr. J. M. Kinser
Virginia	83	1912—Aug. 29	St. James' Augusta Co., Va.	Geo. S. Bowers	A. D. R. Hancher	Mr. M. Coffman
Southwestern Va.	71	1912—Aug. 16	Graham, Va.	T. O. Keister	Geo. H. Rhodes	A. B. Greiner, M. D.
Holston	51	1912—Aug. 8	Immanuel Ch., Sul. Co., Tenn.	W. H. Roof	H. G. Davis	Mr. J. M. Kinser
Virginia	84	1913—Aug. 20	Norfolk, Va.	A. D. R. Hancher	E. A. Repass	Mr. M. Coffman
Southwestern Va.	72	1913—Aug. 13	Marion, Va.	C. K. Hunton	Geo. H. Rhodes	A. B. Greiner, M. D.
Holston	52	1913—Aug. 7	St. Paul's Ch., Monroe Co., Tenn.	W. H. Roof	H. G. Davis	Mr. J. M. Kinser
Virginia	85	1914—Aug. 19	Zion Ch., Shen Co., Va.	Geo. S. Bowers	E. A. Repass	Mr. M. Coffman
Southwestern Va.	73	1914—Aug. 12	Salem, Va.	C. K. Hunton	Geo. H. Rhodes	A. B. Greiner, M. D.
Holston	53	1914—Aug. 6	Solomon's Ch., Greene Co., Tenn.	W. H. Roof	W. G. Cobb	Mr. J. M. Kinser

TIME, PLACE AND OFFICERS OF THE REGULAR CONVENTIONS OF THE MERGING SYNODS FROM THEIR ORGANIZATION UNTIL THE MERGER, 1922

(Continued)

Synod	No.	Date	Place of Meeting	President	Secretary	Treasurer
Virginia	86	1915—Aug. 21	Lebanon Ch., Shen. Co., Va.	J. A. Huffard	E. A. Repass	Mr. M. Coffman
Southwestern Va.	74	1915—Aug. 11	Rural Retreat, Va.	J. L. Sieber	K. Y. Umberger	A. B. Greiner, M. D.
Holston	54	1915—Aug. 5	Immanuel Ch., Sul. Co., Tenn.	W. H. Roof	W. G. Cobb	Mr. J. M. Kinser
Virginia	87	1916—Aug. 23	Mt. Tabor, Augusta Co., Va.	J. A. Huffard	E. A. Repass	Mr. M. Coffman
Southwestern Va.	75	1916—Aug. 18	Bluefield, W. Va.	J. L. Sieber	K. Y. Umberger	A. B. Greiner, M. D.
Holston	55	1916—Aug. 10	Luther Memorial, Cocke Co., Tenn.	W. C. Davis	W. G. Cobb	Mr. J. M. Kinser
Virginia	88	1917—Aug. 21	Madison, Va.	J. A. Huffard	C. W. Cassell	Mr. N. I. Kagey
Southwestern Va.	76	1917—Sept. 3	Wytheville, Va.	J. L. Sieber	K. Y. Umberger	A. B. Greiner, M. D.
Holston	56	1917—Sept. 12	Knoxville, Tenn.	W. C. Davis	W. G. Cobb	Mr. J. M. Kinser
Virginia	89	1918—Aug. 20	Luray, Va.	J. A. Huffard	C. W. Cassell	Mr. N. I. Kagey
Southwestern Va.	77	1918—Sept. 3	Lynchburg, Va.	J. L. Sieber	K. Y. Umberger	Mr. G. D. Brown
Holston	57	1918—Aug. 8	Zion Ch., Sul. Co., Tenn.	W. C. Davis	E. B. Smith	Mr. J. M. Kinser
Virginia	90	1919—Aug. 18	New Market, Va.	J. A. Huffard	C. W. Cassell	Mr. N. I. Kagey
Southwestern Va.	78	1919—Sept. 2	Bristol, Tenn.	J. L. Sieber	K. Y. Umberger	Mr. G. D. Brown
Holston	58	1919—Aug. 7	St. James' Ch., Greene Co., Tenn.	W. C. Davis	E. B. Smith	Mr. J. M. Kinser
Virginia	91	1920—Aug. 16	Stephens City, Va.	J. J. Scherer	C. W. Cassell	Mr. N. I. Kagey
Southwestern Va.	79	1920—Aug. 10	St. Paul's Ch., Wythe Co., Va.	Geo. H. Rhodes	J. A. Brosius	Mr. G. D. Brown
Holston	59	1920—Aug. 6	Salem Ch., Cocke Co., Tenn.	B. S. Brown, Jr.	E. B. Smith	Mr. Junius A. Neas
Virginia	92	1921—Oct. 10	Richmond, Va.	J. J. Scherer	C. W. Cassell	Mr. N. I. Kagey
Southwestern Va.	80	1921—Aug. 10	Va. Hgts. Ch., Roanoke, Va.	E. H. Copenhaver	S. C. Ballentine	Mr. G. D. Brown
Holston	60	1921—Aug. 10	Immanuel Ch., Sul. Co., Tenn.	B. S. Brown, Jr.	E. B. Smith	Mr. J. A. Neas
Virginia	93	1922—Sept. 7	St. Mark's, Roanoke, Va.	J. J. Scherer	C. W. Cassell	Mr. N. I. Kagey
Southwestern Va.	81	1922—Sept. 7	St. Mark's, Roanoke, Va.	E. H. Copenhaver	S. C. Ballentine	Mr. Geo. D. Brown
Holston	61	1922—Aug. 10	Sinking Springs, Greene Co., Tenn.	B. S. Brown, Jr.	E. B. Smith	Mr. J. A. Neas.

THE VIRGINIA SPECIAL CONFERENCE OF THE TENNESSEE SYNOD

Organized in 1856, later the Virginia Conference of the North Carolina Synod, which in 1925 became the New Market Conference of the Lutheran Synod of Virginia. Because of the form of organization of the Tennessee Synod the Conference performed many of the functions of a Synod

Date	No.	Place	President	Secretary	Treasurer
1856—May 17	1	McGaheysville	Henry Wetzel	S. Henkel	
1857—Aug. 29	2	St. Paul's, Aug. Co.	Jacob Killian	Martin Sandhous	
1858—May 3d Sun.	3	Rader's	S. Henkel	Martin Sandhous	
1859—May 3d Sun.	4	Frieden's, Shen. Co.	S. Henkel	Jacob Killian	
1860—May 3d Sat.	5	Mt. Calvary, Page Co.	J. Killian	J. H. Hunton	
1861—May 6	6	Minutes lost. No other meeting during Civil War.			
1865—Oct. 3d Sun.	7	Rader's	J. Killian	J. E. Seneker	
1866—May 3d Sun.	8	McGaheysville	S. Henkel	J. E. Seneker	
1866—Nov. 24	9	Solomon's	J. Killian	S. Henkel	
1868—Oct. 17	Extra	Rader's	J. Killian	S. Henkel	
1869—May 15	10	McGaheysville	J. Killian	I. Conder	
1870—May 14	11	Mt. Calvary, Page Co.	S. Henkel	I. Conder	
1871—May 25	12	St. Paul's, Page Co.	S. Henkel	J. S. Bennick	J. N. Stirewalt
1872—May 11	13	Zion, Shen. Co.	S. Henkel	L. A. Fox	
1872—Nov. 9	14	Bethlehem, Aug. Co.	I. Conder	J. S. Bennick	
1873—May	15	Trinity, Rock. Co.	S. Henkel	I. Conder	
1873—Dec. 6	16	St. Mary's, Shen. Co.	T. Miller	J. N. Stirewalt	
1874—May 16	17	Mt. Calvary, Page Co.	J. N. Stirewalt	L. A. Fox	
1874—Oct. 31	18	St. Jacob's, Rock. Co.	S. Henkel	J. S. Bennick	
1875—Apr. 3	19	Mt. Zion, Shen. Co.	I. Conder	J. N. Stirewalt	
1875—Oct. 30	20	McGaheysville	S. Henkel	J. P. Stirewalt	
1876—May 20	21	St. Matthew's, Shen. Co.	I. Conder	J. N. Stirewalt	
1877—May 11	22	Solomon's, Shen. Co.	S. Henkel	J. P. Stirewalt	
1877—Sept. 11	23	St. Paul's, Aug. Co.	S. Henkel	J. P. Stirewalt	J. P. Stirewalt
1878—May 17	24	St. Paul's, Page Co.	S. Henkel	J. P. Stirewalt	
1879—June 3	25	St. Mary's, Shen. Co.	J. N. Stirewalt	J. P. Stirewalt	
1880—May 8	26	McGaheysville	S. Henkel	J. S. Bennick	
1880—Dec. 4	27	Mt. Zion, Shen. Co.	I. Conder	J. P. Stirewalt	
1881—June 30	28	St. Paul's, Shen. Co.	J. N. Stirewalt	I. Conder	J. P. Stirewalt
1882—Aug. 25	29	Mt. Nebo, Mad. Co.	J. N. Stirewalt	A. L. Crouse	J. N. Stirewalt
1883—Aug. 18	30	St. Stephen's, Shen. Co.	S. Henkel	A. L. Crouse	J. N. Stirewalt
1884—Oct. 2	31	Morning Star, Page Co.	I. Conder	A. L. Crouse	J. N. Stirewalt
1885—Aug. 15	32	Rader's	J. N. Stirewalt	J. P. Stirewalt	J. N. Stirewalt
1886—Aug. 28	33	St. Peter's, Page Co.	J. N. Stirewalt	I. Conder	J. N. Stirewalt
1887—July 29	34	Mt. Calvary, Shen. Co.	A. L. Crouse	J. N. Stirewalt	J. W. Hausenfluck
1888—Aug. 17	35	Trinity, Rock. Co.	A. L. Crouse	P. C. Wike	J. N. Stirewalt
1889—Aug. 9	36	St. David's, Shen. Co.	J. P. Stirewalt	I. Conder	J. N. Stirewalt
1890—Aug. 14	37	St. Paul's, Page Co.	I. Conder	P. C. Wike	J. N. Stirewalt

THE VIRGINIA SPECIAL CONFERENCE OF THE TENNESSEE SYNOD

Organized in 1856, later the Virginia Conference of the North Carolina Synod, which in 1925 became the New Market
Conference of the Lutheran Synod of Virginia. Because of the form of organization of the Tennessee
Synod the Conference performed many of the functions of a Synod

(Continued)

Date	No.	Place	President	Secretary	Treasurer
1891—Aug. 6	38	Solomon's, Shen. Co.	S. Henkel	J. P. Stirewalt	J. N. Stirewalt
1892—Aug. 25	39	St. Jacob's, Shen. Co.	R. H. Cline	J. P. Stirewalt	L. Conder
1893—Apr. 27	Extra	Powder Springs, Shen. Co.	R. H. Cline	J. P. Stirewalt	L. Conder
1893—Aug. 10	40	St. Peter's, Page Co.	J. P. Stirewalt	J. S. Koiner	L. Conder
1894—Aug. 25	41	Emmanuel	P. C. Wike	J. S. Koiner	L. Conder
1895—Aug. 22	42	St. Stephen's	J. N. Stirewalt	F. C. Oberly	L. Conder
1896—Aug. 15	43	Zion, Shen. Co.	J. P. Stirewalt	J. K. Efird	Silone Zirkle
1897—Aug. 6	44	St. David's	J. P. Stirewalt	J. K. Efird	Silone Zirkle
1898—Sept. 3	45	St. Mary's, Shen. Co.	J. P. Stirewalt	E. H. Kohn	Silone Zirkle
1899—Oct. 7	46	St. Paul's, Aug. Co.	J. N. Stirewalt	E. H. Kohn	Silone Zirkle
1900—Sept. 6	47	Morning Star, Page Co.	J. N. Stirewalt	L. Conder	Silone Zirkle
1901—Apr. 4	48	Morning Star, Shen. Co.	J. N. Stirewalt	L. Conder	Silone Zirkle
1901—Oct. 24	49	St. Paul's, Shen. Co.	J. P. Stirewalt	A. L. Boliek	Silone Zirkle
1902—Oct. 30	50	Mt. Zion, Shen. Co.	J. P. Stirewalt	J. W. Hausenfluck	Silone Zirkle
1903—Sept. 9	51	St. Paul's, Rock. Co.	J. P. Stirewalt	J. W. Hausenfluck	Silone Zirkle
1904—May 19	Extra	St. Peter's, Page Co.	J. P. Stirewalt	J. W. Hausenfluck	Silone Zirkle
1904—Sept. 7	52	St. Jacob's, Rock. Co.	E. L. Wessinger	M. A. Ashby	Silone Zirkle
1905—Aug. 31	53	St. Matthew's, Shen. Co.	E. L. Wessinger	M. A. Ashby	Silone Zirkle
1906—Sept. 6	54	Trinity, Rock. Co.	E. L. Wessinger	M. A. Ashby	Silone Zirkle
1907—Aug. 15	55	Rader's	A. R. Beck	M. A. Ashby	Silone Zirkle
1908—Aug. 27	56	Mt. Calvary, Page Co.	A. R. Beck	D. L. Miller	C. S. Kerlin
1909—Aug. 26	57	Morning Star, Shen. Co.	A. R. Beck	D. L. Miller	C. S. Kerlin
1910—Aug. 25	58	Solomon's, Shen. Co.	J. P. Stirewalt	M. A. Ashby	C. S. Kerlin
1911—Aug. 24	59	St. Stephen's, Shen. Co.	J. P. Stirewalt	J. K. Efird	C. S. Kerlin
1912—Sept. 5	60	St. Paul's, Rock. Co.	J. P. Stirewalt	W. L. Darr	C. S. Kerlin
1913—Aug. 28	61	St. James', Page Co.	P. L. Snapp	W. L. Darr	C. S. Kerlin
1914—Aug. 27	62	Bethel, Prince Wm. Co.	M. A. Ashby	J. S. Wessinger	C. S. Kerlin
1915—Aug. 19	63	St. David's	M. A. Ashby	W. L. Darr	C. S. Kerlin
1916—July 27	64	Mt. Calvary, Page Co.	M. A. Ashby	W. L. Darr	C. S. Kerlin
1917—July 26	65	St. Jacob's, Shen. Co.	W. J. Finck	C. K. Rhodes	C. S. Kerlin
1918—Aug. 15	66	St. Matthew's, Shen. Co.	M. L. Pence	C. K. Rhodes	C. S. Kerlin
1919—Aug. 14	67	St. Paul's, Shen. Co.	M. L. Pence	C. K. Rhodes	C. S. Kerlin
1920—July 29	68	Mt. Zion, Shen. Co.	M. L. Pence	F. M. Speagle	C. S. Kerlin
1921—July 28	69	St. Paul's, Page Co.	M. L. Pence	F. M. Speagle	C. S. Kerlin
1922—July 27	70	Mt. Nebo, Mad. Co.	M. L. Pence	F. M. Speagle	C. S. Kerlin
1923—July 26	71	Zion, Shen. Co.	M. L. Pence	F. M. Speagle	C. S. Kerlin
1924—July 24	72	St. Peter's, Page Co.	M. L. Pence	F. M. Speagle	C. S. Kerlin
1925—Jan. 27	Extra	Staunton	Consummation of merger with Virginia Synod.		

THE LUTHERAN SYNOD OF VIRGINIA*

Date	No.	Place	President	Secretary	Treasurer	Statistician
1922—Sept. 7-11	1	Roanoke	C. Brown Cox	C. W. Cassell	A. B. Greiner	H. E. Pugh
1923—Jan. 16-18	2	Lynchburg	C. Brown Cox	C. W. Cassell	A. B. Greiner	H. E. Pugh
1924—Jan. 15-18	3	Roanoke	C. Brown Cox	C. W. Cassell	A. B. Greiner	H. E. Pugh
1925—Jan. 27-30	4	Staunton	C. Brown Cox	C. W. Cassell	A. B. Greiner	H. E. Pugh
1926—Jan. 26-29	5	Knoxville	J. J. Scherer	C. W. Cassell	A. B. Greiner	H. E. Pugh
1927—Jan. 25-28	6	Roanoke	J. J. Scherer	C. W. Cassell	A. B. Greiner	H. E. Pugh
1928—Jan. 24-27	7	Roanoke	J. J. Scherer	C. W. Cassell	A. B. Greiner	H. E. Pugh
1929—Jan. 29-Feb. 1	8	Roanoke	J. J. Scherer	C. W. Cassell	A. B. Greiner	H. E. Pugh

*The Merger meeting held at Roanoke on March 17, 1922, effected a temporary organization under the name of the United Lutheran Synod of Virginia, electing as President the Rev. J. J. Scherer, as Secretary, the Rev. Geo. H. Rhodes, as Treasurer, A. B. Greiner, M. D. The organization was completed in Roanoke Sept. 6-7, 1922, when the permanent officers were elected and name selected as above.

The first convention of the Lutheran Synod of Virginia was the one hundred and second annual convention of a Lutheran synod including the name "Virginia" in its corporate title, and the ninety-third annual convention of a Lutheran synod bearing continuously no other geographical name.

INDEX

INDEX

For the sake of brevity, titles are omitted in 'this index, except that the "Rev." is used to distinguish the ministers and laymen.

PAGES

Abram's Creek _____ 265
Academy, New Market _____ 302
Aderholt, Rev. O. W. _____
    129, 175, 226, 232, 233, 234, 353
Adventist (Dunkers) Settlement __ 190
Ahl, Rev. Peter _____ 211
Ailshie, W. C. _____ 147
Ainsworth, Rev. J. A. _____ 242
Airheart, J. W. _____ 147
Akard, Miss Martha_143, 329, 331, 337
Albemarle County _____ 282
Albin _____ 180
Aldrich, Rev. N. _____ 184, 349
Alma _____ 200, 201
Alpine, L. L. _____ 145
Alt, Sarah _____ 10
Alther, J. W. _____ 200
Altrith, Christoph (Aldrich, El-
    dridge) _____ 5
Alleghany _____ 191
Allenbaugh, Rev. S. _____ 189, 200, 344
Alleman, Rev. Snyder __ 149, 180, 356
Amelia _____ 282
Anderson, Alexander _____ 9
Anderson, John _____ 9
Anderson, Rev. R. Homer 144, 170, 233,
    235, 238, 239, 347, 351, 354
Anderson, Robert _____ 9
Aoyama, Rev. T. _____ 347
Argenbrecht, August _____ 21, 91
Arlington _____ 261
Arends, J. G. _____ 44
Arndt, Rev. J. A. _____ 245, 249, 350
Armentrout's Church, Rockingham
    Co. (St. Philip's) _____ 213, 219
Armentrout, Philip _____ 27
Arehart, Mr. _____ 21
Arehart, D. C. _____ 161
Arehart, L. L. _____ 145
Artz, Rev. William _____ 248
Asbury, Bishop _____ 224
Ascension, Church of Chattanooga
    _____ 266, 267
Ascension, Church of Danville __ 203
Ashby, Rev. M. A. 129, 201, 202, 213,
    218, 226, 232, 234, 353
Atkins, Rev. P. A. 148, 195, 210, 218,
    253,355
Atkins, Smyth County _____ 237
Atonement, Church of _____ 237
Attoway _____ 236, 237
Augy, Abraham _____ 21

PAGES

Auge, Peter _____ 21
Augsburg Confession _____ 43, 86
Augusta County 15, 18, 21, 64, 91, 95,
    290
Augusta County Churches__155, 165, 208
Augusta County Parish _____ 161, 162
Aull, Rev. W. B. _____ 210, 347
Auxiliary Organizations _____ 317-338
Aylor, Anthony _____ 21
Babb, Rev. A. _____ 156, 343
Bachtell, Rev. M. M. _____ 344
Back Creek, Botetout Co. _____ 165
Back Creek Roanoke Co. ____ 165, 207
Bailey, Rev. H. E. 146, 156, 166, 238,
    262, 263, 346, 348, 352, 354
Bailey, L. G. _____ 26, 171
Baker, Abraham _____ 9
Baker, Rev. E. L. _____ 148, 239, 355
Baker, Rev. Isaac 106, 182, 217, 259, 343
Baker, Isaac _____ 233
Baker, Jerome _____ 4
Baker, John _____ 97
Baker, Hieronomous _____ 235
Baker, Joseph _____ 233
Baker, Miss Linda P. _____ 302
Baker (Becker), Peter Philip __ 4, 90
Baker, Rev. Robert _____ 182
Baker's Schoolhouse _____ 199
Bald, Hill _____ 253
Ballentine, Rev. A. W. 149, 216, 239,
    351, 355
Ballentine, Rev. S. C. 146, 191, 243, 246,
    350, 354
Baltheis, Leonhard _____ 4
Bame, Rev. P. J. _____ 149, 241, 355
Bame, Rev. R. L. _____ 173, 350
Baptist, Missionary _____ _____ 169
Barbe, Mr. _____ 9
Barb, Jacob _____ 10, 27
Barb, Rev. J. C. 79, 80, 135, 137, 269,
    271, 273, 278, 280, 301, 351
Barb, Rev. J. H. __ 160, 211, 215, 345
Barger, C. H. _____ 147
Barger, F. _____ 123
Barger, George _____ 27
Barger, Jacob, Sr. _____ 19
Barren Ridge _____ 160
Barr, Abraham _____ 26, 171
Barringer, Rev. B. A. 149, 245, 246,
    356 ·
Basil, Michael _____ 21

PAGES

Bauer, Rev. _____ 255
Bauer, G. _____ 91
Bauer (Bower), Henry _____ 27
Bauer, John _____ 27, 272
Bauer (Bower), Lewis _____ 11
Bauer, Louis _____ 91
Baughman, Rev. C. C. 107, 110, 205,
  291, 292, 344
Baughman, Jacob _____ 10
Baughman, Settlement _____ 259
Baum, Geo. C. _____ 307
Baum, Rev. W. M. _____ 178, 344
Bauman (Bowman), George _____ 4
Bauman, Johannes _____ 21
Bauman, John _____ 87, 91, 93
Baylor _____ 20
Baylor, Amanda _____ 110
Baylor, Geo. _____ 110, 159, 297
Baylor, Miss Mary Sue _____ 110
Beale, Taverner _____ 6
Beamer, S. A. _____ 169
Bear Creek _____ 237
Beard, Rev. C. 156, 157, 159, 160, 161,
  164, 200, 298, 344
Beard, Jacob _____ 21, 155
Bearden, Rev. Geo. S.__ 148, 233, 355
Beatty, Rev. H. E. _____ 148, 218
Beauchamp, Jean _____ 7
Beck, Rev. A. R. 129, 175, 201, 202,
  223, 226, 229, 353
Becker (Baker), Heinrich _____ 5
Becker, Philip Peter _____ 90
Beckford Parish _____ 45, 229
Beckley, Rev. G. H. _____ 189, 345
Bedford, Mission _____ 165
Bedford County _____ 165
Beerbower, Rev. W. P. _____ 345
Berry, Rev. W. H. _____ 165
Beile, John _____ 90
Beile, Henry _____ 90
Beisel, Jacob _____ 90
Bell, Rev. C. K. _____ 170, 206, 350
Bell, Rev. J. A. __ 243, 248, 272, 348
Bell, Rev. Joseph E. (1) ____ 78, 303
Bell, Rev. Joseph E. (2) 137, 272, 351
Bell, Rev. L. G. _____ 345
Beller, Matthias _____ 2
Bender, Adam _____ 10
Bender, Conrad _____ 18
Bender, Geo. P. _____ 10
Bender, Leonhard _____ 18
Bender, Philip _____ 91
Bender, John _____ 91
Benham's _____ 265
Bennick, Rev. J. S. 126, 128, 216, 218,
  223, 225, 227, 228, 353
Bennick, Mrs. C. W. _____ 302
Bens, John _____ 41

Bens, William _____ 91
Bentz (Pence), Conrad _____ 11
Bentz, Jacob _____ 21, 41
Bentz, John _____ 102, 103
Bentz (Pence), Wm. _____ 18
Bercke, Jacob _____ 41
Berea, Wythe Co. _____ 246
Bergton _____ 226, 281
Bergdoll, Nicodemus _____ 92
Bergman, Rev. Christian _____ 238
Berkeley County _____ 90, 254
Berkeley, Gov. Wm. _____ 1
Bernheim's German Settlement ____ 77
Berry, J. T. _____ 157
Berry, S. W. _____ 165
Berry, Rev. W. H. _____ 165, 346
Bethany, Rockbridge Co. _____ 209
Bethany, Rock'h. Co. (St. Jacob's)__ 213
Bethany, Shen. Co. _____ 213
Bethany, Waynesboro _____ 155, 282
Bethany, Wythe Co. _____ 247
Beth Eden, Page Co. __ 130, 195, 199
Bethel, Bland (Wythe) Co. _____ 166
Bethel, Brock's Gap ___ 129, 226, 228
Bethel, Craig Co. _____ 183, 184
Bethel, Fred. Co. _____ 180, 182
Bethel, Manassas _____ 129, 173, 175
Bethel, Rock'h. Co. _____ 226, 228
Bethel, Shen. Co. _____ 223, 224, 225
Bethel, Wythe (Bland) Co. __ 115, 166
Bethesda, Wash. Co., Tenn. _____ 278
Bethlehem Church, Augusta Co. __ 20,
  161, 162
Bethlehem, Page Co. _____ 195, 200
Bethlehem Church, Richmond _ 111, 282
Bible, Andrew _____ 27
Bible, Ezra _____ 27
Bible, John _____ 27
Bible, Isaac _____ 27
Bible, Miss Louie _____ 143
Bible, Rev. Noah _____ 278, 279, 280
Bickel, Rev. H. M. ____ 159, 160, 344
Biedefisch, Wm. _____ 200
Biederfisch _____ 201
Bierly, David _____ 22
Bierly, Jacob _____ 22, 168
Bisch, Friedrich _____ 94, 95
Bishop, Jacob _____ 90, 97
Bittle, C. C. _____ 175
Bittle, Rev. D. F. 106, 109, 205, 209,
  242, 292, 293, 343, 348
Bittle, Rev. D. H. ____ 256, 344, 348
Bittle, J. O. _____ 15
Black Lick _____ 250
Blacksburg Parish _____ 190, 322
Blackwelder, Rev. O. F. 146, 166, 297,
  351, 354
Bland County _____ 24

PAGES

Bland Parish ------------------ 165
Blank, Rev. Arthur ------------ 281
Blankenbeker, Balthaser --------- 2
Blankenbeker, Matthias --------- 2
Blankenbeker, Nicholas --------- 2
Blaum, Jacob ------------------ 92
Blount Co. -------------------- 78
Blountville Parish -------------- 261
Bluefield (Graham), Va. 238, 239, 261,
300
Bluefield, W. Va. ---------- 238, 239
Blue Ridge ------------------- 2, 15
Blue Ridge Springs ------------ 169
Blue Springs ------------------ 278
Blue Springs Church ------------ 278
Bluff City Parish -------------- 264
Boaker, Wm. ------------------ 110
Boessinger, Geo. --------------- 272
Borner, Henry ----------------- 91
Boland, Rev. M. Q. ------- 243, 350
Boliek, Rev. A. L. 129, 131, 148, 198,
201, 202, 205, 226, 228, 353, 355
Bolton, Rev. V. F. 159, 160, 168, 211,
217, 344, 348
Bonewitt, Jacob ---------------- 11
Bomberger -------------------- 201
Bonham, E. B. ---------------- 147
Bonham, H. L. ---------------- 242
Bonham, Rev. Nehemiah -------- 166
Boltz, Jacob ------------------- 90
Booher, Rev. J. A. 147, 275, 277, 355
Booher, Daniel ---------------- 27
Booher, James ----------------- 27
Booher, John ------------------ 28
Booher, Martin ---------------- 28
Booher, Rev. Sam ------------- 351
Book of Concord, published 312, 314
Book of Common Prayer -------- 188
Boone Co., Ky. --------------- 188
Boone, Rev. John -- 236, 243, 294, 348
Booze, A. T. ------------------ 168
Booze, R. L. ------------------ 169
Boozer, Rev. V. Y. ---- 148, 189, 355
Bowman, Abraham -------------- 57
Bowman, A. M., Sr. ----------- 205
Bowman, D. F. ---------------- 175
Bowman, Elias ----------------- 279
Bowman, Jacob ---------------- 21
Bowman, James ---------------- 159
Bowman, John ----------------- 10
Bowman, Rev. W. S. 8, 159, 160, 189,
200, 235, 344
Bourde (Boord), Rev. J. A. 146, 169,
205, 207, 226, 229, 263, 266, 347, 354
Borden, Joel ------------------ 9
Borden's Schoolhouse ----------- 232
Boscher, George --------------- 25
Boscher, Henry ---------------- 112

PAGES

Bostian, F. A. ---------------- 339
Botetourt Co. 22, 53, 74, 75, 167, 204
Botetourt Parish ----------- 165, 167
Bowden, Rev. G. S. --- 148, 235, 355
Bowers, Rev. A. J. ---- 173, 187, 349
Bowers, Rev. H. G. 118, 168, 182, 257,
344, 348
Bowers, Mary Lou -------------- 329
Bowers, Rev. Geo. S. 178, 187, 332,
333, 347
Bowman ---------------------- 8
Boyd, Rev. J. M. -------------- 352
Boyd, Robert ------------------ 27
Boyers ----------------------- 185
Boyer, Adam ------------------ 27
Boyer, Alwinus ---------------- 41
Boys School in Japan ---------- 328
Boys, W.-H. School for --------- 307
Brakebill, William ------------- 27
Brakebill, Mrs. W. L. ---------- 331
Branner, Casper --------------- 11
Bramwell -------------------- 261
Bramer, Harrison -------------- 216
Brandy Station ---------------- 177
Braun, Andreas ---------------- 23
Braun, Christopher --------- 23, 92
Braun, George --------------- 22, 91
Braun, Jacob ------------------ 5
Braun, Michael ---------------- 23
Brick Church, Wythe Co. -------- 250
Brick Union ------------------ 167
Bridgewater ------ 157, 211, 212, 297
Bridgewater, The Female Sem. 212, 297
Bringman, Mrs. J. G. -- 327, 335, 336
Bristol, Church at ---------- 140, 266
Bristol Parish ---------------- 266
Brock's Gap ------- 64, 96, 125, 281
Brock, John ------------------ 14
Brobst, George --------------- 92
Brobst, S. K., Dr. ------------- 113
Brodfuhrer, Rev. J. C. ----- 236, 349
Bromm, Lewis ----------------- 112
Brook Union ------------------ 233
Brosius, Rev. J. A. ---- 184, 191, 351
Brotherhood, The -------------- 291
Brotherhood, The Luther -------- 339
Brown ----------------------- 24
Brown, Rev. Abel J. 79, 134, 135, 138,
262, 264, 275, 279, 280, 289, 301, 351
Brown, Rev. B. S., Sr. 156, 189, 191,
262, 346, 350
Brown, Rev. B. S., Jr. 147, 268, 269,
352, 355
Brown, Rev. C. A. --------- 173, 349
Brown, Christopher ------------ 117
Brown, Rev. C. L. 121, 187, 239, 324,
350

PAGES

Brown, Rev. J. A. 117, 119, 121, 166, 242, 244, 247, 251, 253, 292, 294, 296, 348
Brown, Mrs. J. A. (1) _____ 118
Brown, Mrs. J. A. (2) _____ 321, 322
Brown (Braun), Rev. John 87, 201, 211 212
Brown, Joseph _____ 115, 116
Brown, Miss Mary _____ 331
Brown, Michael _____ 114
Brown, Rev. W. R. 146, 162, 164, 244, 249, 253, 346, 349, 354
Brown, Mrs. W. R. _____ 327, 335
Brown, Rev. T. S. _____ 208, 253, 349
Browntown _____ 240
Brown Memorial Church _____ 213
Broyles (Prial), John _____ 2
Brubeck, Rev. J. J. _____ 165
Bruch, Rev. J. F. __ 156, 164, 210, 347
Brubaker, Abraham _____ 6
Bruegmann, Rev. C. A. _____ 352
Brugell, Rev. P. M. _____ 76, 190
Brunnerer, John _____ 92
Brunnholtz, Rev. _____ 39
Bucher (See Booher)
Bucher, David _____ 110
Bucher, John _____ 110
Bucher (Booher), John _____ 28
Bucher (Booher), Martin _____ 28
Buck, Rev. J. L. 205, 211, 215, 253, 261, 346, 349
Buck, Rev. W. C. 149, 173, 191, 238, 243, 350, 356
Buchanan _____ 168
Buchanan, H. C. _____ 147
Buchanan, J. R. _____ 161
Buehler's Church _____ 79, 140, 264
Buena Vista _____ 164, 210, 298
Büffel, Adam _____ 52
Buger (Bucher), Immanuel _____ 5
Buhrman, Rev. A. _____ 180, 345
Bunyons _____ 160
Burchard, W. A. _____ 146
Burke's Fork, Floyd Co. _____ 172
Burke's Garden Parish __ 115, 117, 238
Burket, M. _____ 90
Burwell, Nathaniel _____ 292
Busby, Rev. L. E. _____ 348
Bush, Martin _____ 19
Bush, Nicholas _____ 19
Bushong, Rev. A. A. J. 7, 156, 165, 207, 229, 232, 233, 345, 348
Bushong, Barbara Lohr _____ 7
Bushong, David _____ 27
Bushong, Henry _____ 7
Bushong, John _____ 8
Bushong, Peter _____ 7

PAGES

Bushnell, Rev. J. E. 180, 183, 191, 199, 201, 207, 229, 345, 349
Butler, Rev. John Geo. 73, 75, 86, 93, 167, 168, 204, 211, 261, 263
Butler, Rev. J. W. 173, 184, 205, 349
Byrd, Andrew _____ 14
Byrd, William _____ 14
Byers, Rev. E. A. _____ 144, 351, 354

Cabin Creek _____ 237
Cadwallader, James K. _____ 183
Cahoon, M. C. _____ 168
Cahoon, N. S. _____ 169
Cain, Leonhard _____ 27
Cale, Mrs. Margaret _____ 21, 156
Caldwell, Mrs. W. J. _____ 331
Cammann, Rev. D. P. _____ 348
Campbell _____ 20
Campbell County _____ 170
Campbell, Rev. J. F. 159, 160, 180, 200, 228, 231, 233, 235, 256, 344
Campbell, Rev. W. G. 189, 211, 215, 225, 345, 348
Cany Branch _____ 270
Cannaday, Rev. Isaac _____ 172, 173
Canup, Rev. M. L. _____ 233, 347
Capon _____ 60
Capon Bridge, W. Va. _____ 258
Capon Church _____ 258
Capon-North River Parish _____ 257
Capp, Mr. _____ 84
Carpenter, Virginia Lohr _____ 15
Carpenter, A. Rebecca Lohr _____ 15
Carpenter (Zimmerman), Christopher 91
Carpenter, Rev. L. J. S. _____ 281
Carpenter, Cornelius _____ 91
Carpenter, Samuel _____ 91, 95
Carpenter, Rev. William 58, 59, 61, 63, 82, 83, 86, 88, 90, 93, 188, 189, 213
Carroll Co. _____ 26, 171
Cassell Family _____ 24
Cassell, Rev. C. Willis 24, 130, 133, 144, 159, 166, 199, 210, 239, 253 261, 347, 350, 354
Cassell, Jacob _____ 296
Cassell, James _____ 26, 171
Cassell, James L. _____ 26
Cassell, Rev. Joseph B. __ 24, 181, 183
Cassell, Thomas _____ 26
Cassell, David _____ 26
Cassell, Michael, Sr. _____ 23, 24
Cassell, Michael, Jr. _____ 250
Cassell, Dr. Nellie __167, 121, 327, 334
Castor, Rev. B. D. 149, 268, 269, 355
Catalpa _____ 15, 175
Catawba River _____ 52
Catechisms Published _____ 312
Cave Creek _____ 271

PAGES

Cave Springs, Roanoke Co. _____ 204
Cedar Grove Church, Smyth Co.,
_____ 237, 248
Cedar Grove Church, Sul. Co. __ 264
Cedar Creek _____ 178, 181
Cedar Point _____ 202
Central Church, Taz. Co. _____ 238
Central Parish _____ 247, 252
Centennial Celebration of Lutheran
Church in America _____ 107
Centennial of 1922 _____ 149
Ceres _____ 166
Chapman, Rev. H. D. 129, 131, 148,
213, 214, 260, 263, 266, 353, 355
Chapman, William _____ 199
Charleston, S. C. _____ 57
Chattanooga Parish _____ 266
Chattanooga Mission _____ 140, 142
Cherokee River _____ 27
Childs, J. H. _____ 148
Chilhowie _____ 115, 242
Chilhowie Church _____ 236
Chimes, Glaize Memorial _____ 178
Christ's Church, Radford ____ 192, 193
Christ's Church, Staunton _____ 162
Christ, Rev. Frederick __ 148, 194, 355
Christler, George _____ 84
Christiansburg _____ 190
Christman, Jacob _____ 4
Churchville _____ 21
Churchville, Parish _____ 156
Civil War Interference 111, 126, 135,
160, 178, 180, 217, 220, 235, 292,
293, 294, 297
Clemens, Messrs. _____ 19
Clemmer, Jacob _____ 27
Cline, Rev. John Philip 9, 65, 99, 102,
103, 104, 108, 201, 221, 222, 223,
225, 231, 343
Cline, Rev. R. H. 129, 144, 180, 201,
202, 209, 210, 213, 225, 226, 228, 232,
303, 347, 353
Cline, W. H. _____ 297
Cline, Rev. W. P., Jr. 193, 204, 351
Cline, Rev. W. Y. 168, 169, 187, 345
349
Cloninger, Rev. Jacob 135, 138, 276,
280, 351
Clore, Michael _____ 2
Clover Hollow _____ 183, 184
Clowser, J. _____ 182
Cloyd, Mrs. John R. _____ 331
Coalfields, Flat Top _____ 261
Cobb, Rev. W. G. 143, 146, 204, 243,
249, 262, 273, 351, 352
Cobble, John _____ 27
Cocke County Parish _____ 268
Co-educational Schools _____ 299-303

PAGES

Coffelt, Christian _____ _____ 10
Coffelt, Rev. C. M. 149, 218, 235, 356
Coffelt, George _____ 10
Coffelt, Rev. H. F. _____ 235
Coffman, Augustine _____ 10
Coffman, Milton _____ 9, 159, 231
Coffman, Obed _____ 9
Coffman, George _____ 9
Coffman, William _____ 9
Coffman, Jacob _____ 9
Coiner, Rev. J. I. 20, 165, 209, 347,
350, 356
Coleman, L. A. _____ 146
Coley, C. K. _____ 296
College Church _____ 205, 206, 208
Collins, James _____ 21
Columbus, Texas _____ 294
Common Service Book A. _____ 325
Compton, Rev. G. A. _____ 345
Cone, Rev. W. H. 201, 224, 345, 348
Concord _____ 238
Concordia Synod _____ 127
Conder, Rev. I. 127, 128, 148, 189, 201,
213, 214, 353, 355
Confirmation, Certificate _____ 190
Conferences in Va. Synod (Evan.
Luth.) _____ 107
Conference, New Market 132, 133, 210,
212, 218
Conference, Northern Va. Synod __ 233
Conference, Potomac _____ 219
Conference, Special Va. (Pa. Syn.) 81-97
Constitution _____ 96
Conference, Staunton _____ 210
Conference, Va. Special of Tenn.
Synod:
Organized _____ 122, 124
Div. in _____ 126-128
Ed. in _____ 129, 288, 301
Mergers _____ 130-133
Miss. Soc. _____ 132
Luther League _____ 132
S. S. Convention _____ 132
Conference, W. of Ohio _____ 96
Conference, Winchester _____ 219
Congregational Sketches _____ 153-281
Coniceville _____ 224
Conrad, Rev. F. W. _____ 162
Constitution of Cong. 42, 73, 74, 167,
190, 211, 248
Constitution Synod, Va. _____ 101-104
Constitution, Synod of Pa. _____ 81
Constitution, Synod of S. W. Va. 115,
116
Constitution, Synod of Holston __ 136
Constitution of W. M. Society 321, 333
Conventions and Officers, Va. Conf.
of Pa. Minn. _____ 357

PAGES

Conventions and Officers of Synod
of Md. and Va. _____ 358
Conventions and Officers, Lutheran
Evan. Synod of Va.' _____ 359-365
Conventions and Officers, Synod of
S. W. Va. _____ 359, 365
Conventions and Officers, Va. Conf.
Tenn. Synod _____ 366, 367
Conventions and Officers, Hol. Syn.
_____ 360-365
Conventions and Officers of Luth-
eran Synod of Va. _____ 368
Cook, David _____ 21, 156
Cook, John P. _____ 21, 209
Cook, Rev. Samuel _____ 159, 185, 348
Cook, Michael _____ 2
Coopers _____ 110
Cooper, Rev. E. C. _____ 170, 350
Cooper, Rev. E. R. _____ 183
Cooper, Thomas _____ 6
Cooper, Edward _____ 6
Cooper, Rev. J. E. _____ 178, 195, 345
Cooper, Rev. G. _____184
Cooper, Rev. N. E. 144, 183, 212, 261,
  347
Copenhaver _____ 236
Copenhaver, Rev. A. 253, 257, 344, 348
Copenhaver, Rev. B. A. 223, 237, 347
Copenhaver, Mrs. Ella _____ 322
Copenhaver, Rev. E. H. 146, 236, 238
  243, 296, 350
Copenhaver, Mrs. E. H.__325, 335, 336
Copenhaver, John _____ 296
Copenhaver, John S. _____ 296
Copenhaver, James _____ 296
Copenhaver, John _____ 115
Copenhaver, (Mrs. B. E.) Laura
  Scherer _____ 72, 326, 327
Cops (Copps), Botetourt Co. 115, 168
Corney's Schoolhouse _____ 165
Corinth _____ 249, 250
Costler, Matthias _____ 2
Costner, Jacob _____ 78
Counts, Rev. H. P. _____ 249, 350
County Line Church _____ 222
Cove, The _____ 253
Cover, F. P. _____ 240
Cox, Rev. George H. 28, 79, 80, 137
  241, 262, 275, 277, 280, 351
Cox, Rev. C. Brown 149, 194, 204, 270,
  273, 278, 279, 296, 347, 351, 352
Coyner, Miss Effie _____ 20
Coyner, Martin _____ 125
Crabtree, C. A. _____ 147
Crabtree, Prof. J. T. __ 142, 254, 306
Crabill, David _____ 10
Crabill, George _____ 10
Crabill, Harry S. _____ 146

PAGES

Craig County _____ 183
Craig Creek _____ 183
Craun, Rev. W. A. 144, 165, 195, 210
  347, 354
Crickenberger, Dr. W. P. _____ 302
Crickenberger, Rev. D. P. T. 149, 160,
  169, 184, 199, 201, 346, 349
Crigler, Aaron _____ 88, 91
Crigler, Jacob _____ 2
Crigler, Rev. J. F. _____ 189
Crigler, Rev. Jacob _____ 96, 189
Crigler, W. H. _____ 145
Cripple Creek Parish _____ 246, 248
Crimora _____ 154
Crockett _____ 247
Craft, Amanda E. _____ 168
Craft, David G. _____ 168
Craft, Jacob M. _____ 168
Craft, Jacob _____ 169
Croft, Lewis _____ 21
Croll, Rev. J. P. _____ 163, 345
Cronk, Rev. B. W. 146, 169, 173, 184
  205, 243, 264-266, 306, 349, 354
Cronk, Eli _____ 26
Cronk, Rev. E. C. 113, 143, 144, 160,
  164, 173, 236, 237, 239, 346, 350
Cronk, Henry _____ 102
Cronk (Mrs. E. C.) Katherine Scherer
  72, 143, 327, 329, 330, 333, 335
Cronk, Miss Jessie _____ 208, 334
Cronk, Miss Vivian _____ 339
Cronise, Jacob _____ 22
Cronise, William H. _____ 22
Cronise, J. L. _____ 168
Cronise, W. R. _____ 168
Cross Roads-Hudson's _____ 224
Cross Roads (N. M.) _____ 13, 219
Cross Road Schoolhouse _____ 228
Cross Keys _____ 212
Crouse, Rev. A. L. 129, 162, 225, 228
  353
Crum, Frank _____ 147
Crum, Jacob _____ 21
Crum, William _____ 27
Crumley, George _____ 27
Cullers, Henry _____ 8
Cullop's Church _____ 237, 248
Culpeper _____ 173
Cummings, J. L. _____ 168
Cumberland Valley _____ 3
Cumberland _____ 282
Cupp, Rev. Alexander _____ 165
Cupp, Alexander _____ 21
Cupp, Frederick _____ 21
Cupp, Rev. J. H. _____ 165, 344
Cupp, J. H. _____ 21
Curran Valley _____ 237

PAGES

Dagey, Rev. John _____ 104, 343
Daggy, W. S. _____ 131
Dahl, Oscar _____ 113
Danville _____ 203
Damascus _____ 242
Dapper, Rev. R. A. _____ 281
Darr, Rev. W. L. 129, 131, 148, 175,
    225, 226, 228, 309, 353, 355
Daser, Rev. W. F. A. ____ 77, 190, 243
Dasher, Rev. B. S. 100, 149, 271, 272,
    273, 347, 356
Davidson, Mrs. _____ 306
Davidsburg Church (St. Matthew's) 14,
    17, 54, 64, 218, 220
Davis, Elvira _____ 110
Davis, Rev. H. G. 79, 143, 268, 271,
    272, 273, 276, 352
Davis, Rev. J. B. 106, 110, 156, 162,
    179, 181, 292, 343
Davis, Rev. W. C. 79, 140, 265, 269,
    271, 272, 276, 278, 330, 352
Davoult, Michael _____ 26
Day, Rev. C. H. _____ 159, 347
Day, Rev. D. A. _____ 322
Dayton, Rock'h. Co. _____ 212
Deal, Rev. J. F. _____ 166, 350
Deaton, Rev. J. L. 129, 166, 225, 226,
    228, 353
Declaration of Principles _____ 114
Deck, Abraham _____ 28
Deck, Adam _____ 28
Deck, Rev. J. P. 28, 80, 137, 263, 352
Deck, Jacob _____ 28
Deck, Rev. J. E. _____ 28
Deck, Michael _____ 28
Deck, Rev. William H. _____ 28
Deck, Rev. L. B. _____ 28, 80
Deford, B. F. _____ 199
Definite Syn. Platform _____ 124
Degen (Daggy), Johannes _____ 21
Degen _____ 214
Deiner, Caspar _____ 84
Dellinger, Emanuel _____ 10
Dellinger, George _____ 10
Denton _____ 171
Denton, Margaret _____ 26
Detrick, Rev. _____ 232
Derrick, H. D. _____ 147
Derrick, Rev. J. B. _ 145, 221, 347, 354
Derrick, Rev. J. P. 148, 193, 232, 355
Derrick, Rev. P. H. E. 162, 166, 347,
    350
Deschler, Rev. Gottlieb Abraham 211,
    213, 225
Devil's Hole _____ 258
Dieters, The _____ 12, 13, 41
Dieters, Barbara _____ 12
Diehl, Rev. Geo. _____ 343

Dieterich, David _____ 5
Diffenderfer, Rev. G. M. _____ 240
Dill, John _____ 168
Dingel, Daniel _____ 18
Dingledine, Peter _____ 159
Dingledine, Miss _____ 15
Dinkle, Rev. W. H. 212, 218, 297, 345
Dinkle, Sam _____ 212
Dinkel, Daniel _____ 87
Disciple Church _____ 226
Diller, Margaret _____ 18
Diven, Rev. Geo. S. _____ 191, 350
Dobler, Mr. _____ 52
Dobler, Jacob _____ 23
Domer, Hon. H. Tennyson _____ 150
Donalds Schoolhouse _____ 210
Dorsey, Rev. E. _____ 344
Dorpat, Rev. L. G. _____ 282
Dosh, John _____ 9
Dosh, Rev. T. W. 159, 178, 258, 293,
    303, 344
Dougens, M. _____ 52
Dreher, Prof. J. D. _____ 293
Dreyer, Rev. F. _____ 282
Dry Run _____ 181
Droke, Jacob _____ 27
Dull, George _____ 21, 155
Dunbar, A. P. _____ 168
Dutch Meeting House _____ 265
Dutch Mess, The _____ 5
Dutch Calvinist _____ 167
Dutch Hollow _____ 259
Dutton, Adam _____ 248
Dutton, Rev. W. A. ___ 191, 253, 349
Dusinger, Nicolas _____ 11

Early, John _____ 211
Easterly, Rev. Geo. _ 78, 271, 272, 280
Easterly, Philip _____ 272
Ebberle, Jacob _____ 25
Ebberle, Christian _____ 25
Ebeling, Rev. H. E. _____ 218, 346
Ebenezer, Rio, W. Va. _____ 258
Ebenezer, Warren Co. _____ 240
Ebenezer, Smyth Co. _____ 236, 237
Eberhard, Doring _____ 5
Eberly, George _____ 25, 92
Ebert, Philip _____ 272
Eccord, Jacob _____ 156
Eckman _____ 261
Educational Activities _____ 287-308
Ed. in Virginia Conf. __ 288, 301-303
Ed. Tenn. Synod _____ 288, 301-303
Ed. in Synod of S. W. Va. 288, 293-296
Ed. in Synod of Va. 288, 293, 296-298
Ed. in Holston Synod _____ 289, 301
Ed. & Miss. Soc., Va. Synod _____ 319
Ed. & Miss. Soc., S. W. Va. Syn. 118, 320

PAGES

Education, Female __ 59 109, 293, 297
Edinburg Parish _____ 224
Efird, Rev. J. K.   129, 175, 177, 259
  346, 353
Egel, Peter _____ 91
Eggleston _____ 183, 184
Ehrhard (Arehart), Christian ____ 11
Eichelberger, Rev. Lewis F. 99, 102,
  103, 104, 105, 178, 179, 181, 182,
  259, 297, 343
Eichelberger, Rev. W.   181, 257, 259,
  345
Eisenberg, Rev. W. E. _____ 165
Eisenberg, Mrs. W. F. C. _____ 332
Eley, Nicholas _____ 272
Elizabeth College 120, 288, 298, 299,
  307
Elk Creek _____ 184
Elkhorn _____ 261
Elkton _____ 3, 195
Elkwood _____ 15, 173, 177
Emmanuel, Augusta Co. _____ 165, 214
Emanuel Church, New Market 123, 218
Emanuel Roanoke _____ 204, 207
Emanuel, Woodstock 103, 229, 230, 231,
  232
Emmert, Rev. J. B. _____ 135, 351
Emporia _____ 282
Engelman, Philip _____ 21, 209
Ergebrecht, Jacob E. _____ 41
Ergebrecht, Jacob _____ 41
Erman, John _____ 91
Ermantraut Neighborhood _____ 18
Ermentraut, Christopher _____ 41
Ermentraut, Frederick _____ 41
Ermentraut, Philip _____ 41
Ermentraut, Henry _____ 18, 41, 91
Ermentraut, John _____ 41
Ermentraut, Peter _____ 18, 41, 91
Estes, Mary Ann Kipps _____ 15
Essick, Rev. Abraham _____ 178, 344
Euler, Peter _____ 41
Etter, J. S. _____ 147, 246
Etter, Mrs. J. S. _____ 246
Evans, Mrs. M. S. _____ 325
Evans, Fighting Bob _____ 173
Eyster, Rev. David 102, 103, 104, 257,
  343

Fahs, Rev. J. F. _____ 179, 180, 344
Fairfax, Lord, Land given by 4, 177,
  224, 226, 235
Fairview, Page Co. _____ 202
Fairview, Wash. Co. _____ 237
Fairview, Fred. Co. ___ 257, 258, 259
Fairview, Wythe Co. _____ 246
Farensworth, Benjamin _____ 27
Farmville _____ 282

PAGES

Fawcett's Gap _____ 180
Federation of Y. P. Societies _____ 338
Feitig, Carl _____ 282
Felkner, Henry _____ 4, 235
Fernsler, Henry _____ 11
Feuerbach, Philip (Firebaugh) ____ 22
Fied, Mr. _____ 21
Files, Rev. D. W. 145, 156, 159, 259,
  346, 354
Filler, Rev. S. 208, 209, 212, 217, 218,
  343
Fincastle _____ 168
Finck, Rev. W. J. 129, 131, 148, 219,
  353, 355
Fink, Rev. R. A. _____ 179, 344
Fink, Rev. S. P. _____ 344
Fischer, John _____ 90
Fisher, Sister Alice _____ 327
Firebaugh, C. M. _____ 168
Firebaugh, P. M. _____ 168
Firebaugh, Philip _____ 102
First Luth. Pastor in Va. _____ 36
Fitzer, Rev. S. J. _____ 201
Flatwoods Church _____ 195, 201
Fleenor, Rev. Adam 135, 272, 278, 351
Fleenor, Rev. James _____ 135, 351
Fleischman, Samuel _____ 92
Flemming _____ 214
Flenor, James _____ 26
Flenor, Henry _____ 26
Fleshman, Zerichias _____ 2
Flickinger, Rev. J. A. _____ 189, 346
Flohr, Rev. Geo. D. 73-90, 98, 166,
  190, 236, 238, 244, 249, 251, 252
Flook _____ 169
Floyd County _____ 25, 167, 171, 204
Folk, Rev. E. L. 160, 169, 218, 223,
  257, 346, 349
Folk, Mrs. E. L. _____ 332
Foltz, D. B. _____ 145, 210
Foltz, Jacob _____ 91, 93
Foltz, George _____ 86-91
Foltz, Rev. John 64, 84, 86, 88, 90, 93,
  220-223, 225, 281, 283
Foltz, John W. _____ 131
Foltz, Joseph _____ 10
Foltz, Peter _____ 10
Foreign Missions, begun _____ 109
Foreign Missionary Society __ 106, 111
Forest, The _____ 221
Forestville, Shen. Co. _____ 219
Forestville Parish _____ 221, 222
Forster, William (Wilheim) 64, 84, 86
Forthham, Rev. John _____ 344
Fort McDonald _____ 190
Fort Run _____ 39
Fort Sumter _____ 224
Fort Valley _____ 224, 281

PAGES

Fox, Ambrose _____ 199
Fox, Miss Alice V. _____ 325
Fox, Rev. A. J. __ 269, 272, 278, 280
Fox, Rev. C. M. 169, 184, 208, 247, 252,
  259, 279, 280, 349, 352
Fox, Rev. D. S. 145, 162, 193, 204, 228,
  243, 244, 247, 249, 250, 252, 253,
  347, 349, 354
Fox, Rev. J. B. 80, 137, 163, 269, 271,
  272, 278, 280, 346, 352
Fox, Rev. L. A. 129, 146, 161, 169, 170,
  189, 199, 204, 206, 208, 314, 348,
  353, 354
Fox, Mrs. L. A. _____ 322, 326
Fraenckel, Stephen _____ 5
Francis, Jas. H. _____ 296
Franck, Ernest _____ 282
Frank, Rev. Anthony _____ 246
Frank, Rev. Jacob 34, 42, 61, 188, 213
Franklin Co. _____ 177
Franklin, Master Michael _____ 7
Frantz _____ 8
Frantz, Rev. J. Luther 278, 350, 352
Fravel, Henry _____ 6
Fray, John H. _____ 189
Frazier, Rev. Jacob _____ 257, 345
Freed Family _____ 21
Freed, Rev. C. A. 148, 160, 165, 178,
  346, 355
Freemont Church, Fred. Co. 180, 182
Frederick, Rev. E. J. _____ 283
Frederick, Md. _____ 98
Frederick Co. 22, 38, 79, 90, 197, 257
Fredericksburg _____ 187
French, Mr. _____ 27
Frenckerer, George _____ 91
Frey, Henry _____ 11
Frey, Rev. J. G. _____ 348
Frey, Rev. W. W. _____ 241, 347
Frieden's, Shen. Co. _____ 9, 233
Frieden's Church, Rockingham Co. 21,
  65, 77, 211
Friedly, Andreas _____ 5
Friermood, Matthias _____ 201
Fries, G. Casper _____ 178
Frowman (Froman), Paul _____ 4
Frondt, H. W. _____ 113
Front Royal _____ 1, 240
Froschauer (Freshour), John __ 27, 272
Fry, Mrs. C. L. _____ 329
Fry, R. E. _____ 147
Frye, Jacob _____ 10
Frye, Moses _____ 10
Frye, Ben _____ 180
Fuchs, Christian _____ 92
Fudge, Nelson _____ 296
Fulk, George _____ 112
Funkhouser, Abraham _____ 10

PAGES

Funkhouser, Christian _____ 10
Funkhouser, Mary A. _____ 228
Fulmer, Rev. V. L. ____ 129, 216, 353
Fultz, John _____ 20
Funerals & Communion Service ___ 88
Funeral Service, Forms for _____ 88
Furnace Church (Taylor) _____ 181
Furnace Hill _____ 237

Gabel, Peter _____ 272
Gaesdorf, Geo. _____ 112
Gantz _____ 182
Garr, Adam _____ 2
Garr, Andrew _____ 2
Gausle, G. _____ 90
Geary, Geo. R. _____ 145
Gearhart, Rev. A. C. 137, 139, 157, 159,
  280, 301, 345, 352
Gebert, Jacob _____ 21, 91
Geckle, Christian _____ 92
Geiger, Christian _____ 41
Geisler's Chapel _____ 242
Geisler, Rev. H. D. _____ 135, 351
Gerberding, Rev. W. P. _____ 184
Germanna _____ 187
German Chapel _____ 187
German Regiment (Eight Va. Reg.) 47
Germany Valley _____ 13
Gerrardstown _____ 257
Gettysburg Seminary _____ 111
Gibbs, Mrs. L. R. _____ 275
Gibbs, Nicolas _____ 27, 275
Gibbs, U. S. _____ 189
Gibbs, Mrs. U. S. _____ 189
Gilbert, Rev. D. M. 69, 82, 108, 163,
  178, 345
Gilbert, Rev. Frank _____ 181, 347
Giffin, Thomas _____ 198
Giles County _____ 183
Giles-Craig Parish _____ 183, 184
Giles Mission _____ 184
Gilmore, Jas. H. _____ 296
Glade, The _____ 246
Gladesboro _____ 26, 171
Glade Creek _____ 22, 115, 169, 207
Glaize, David Brevitt _____ 178
Glaize, M. S. _____ 145
Glenn, Rev. Peter _____ 343
Glen Wilton _____ 167
Gluck, Michael _____ 5
Gooch, Gov. _____ 188
Godshall, Frederick _____ 271, 272
Goertner, Rev. N. W. _____ 178
Goette, Rev. C. J. _____ 282
Gohn, Michael, Jr. _____ 92
Golden Horseshoe, Knights of __ 1, 2
Golden Springs _____ 278
Goldman, Jacob _____ 25

PAGES

Golladay, George E. _____ 8
Golladay, Jacob _____ 8
Golladay, Geo. R. _____ 131
Golladay, Rev. R. E. _____ 236
Gomer's (Comer's) Church _____ 198
Good, _____ 202
Goodman, Rev. R. A. _____ 172, 173
Gore, Isaac _____ 14
Goring, Pastor _____ 44
Gossner, Missionary _____ 111
Gottingen _____ 95
Gottschall (Cutshall), Frederick ___ 27
Gotz, Bernhard _____ 91, 93
Gotz, Baltzer _____ 11
Gowl, C. L. _____ 146
Graber, Rev. Henry _____ 244, 248
Grabill (Graybill), Rev. J. M. 169, 211,
   217, 344
Grace Page Co. _____ 129, 195, 198
Grace Church Ref., Shen. Co. ____ 211
Grace Church, Waynesboro __ 163, 164
Grace Church, Winchester 116, 117, 178
Grace Church, Wythe Co. _____ 243
Graham, (Bluefield W. Va.) 239, 260,
   261   .
Graham, Rev. E. O. ___ 148, 180, 355
Graichen, Rev. J. G. 147, 164, 183, 210,
   273, 347, 352, 355
Graph of Organizations ____ 341, 342
Graves, Miss Bell _____ 110
Graves, Rev. T. A. 148, 189, 221, 307,
   355
Gravel Hill, Bland Co. _____ 166
Gravel Springs Parish _____ 180
Gravel Springs, Shen. Co. __ 180, 181
Gray, Rev. G. T. _____ 172, 349
Grayson County _____ 184, 237
Grayson Mission _____ 185
Greaver, Rev. W. F. __ 179, 344, 348
Grebil _____ 8
Gregory, Mrs. J. C. _____ 175
Greenbrier Co. _____ 92
Green Valley, Giles Co. _____ 184
Greene County Parish _____ 269
Greene Memorial, Roanoke _____ 207
Greene County _____ 26, 27, 78
Greeneville, Tenn. _____ 141, 272
Greever, Rev. J. B. 139, 239, 245, 246,
   260, 261, 264, 266, 300, 301, 348, 352
Greever, Rev. John J. 114-116, 166,
   237, 238, 252, 348
Greever, Rev. W. H. 118, 150, 239, 261,
   315, 350
Greer, Rev. G. J. _____ 351
Grim _____ 214
Grim, Charles _____ 5
Greiner, Rev. J. B. 168, 184, 236, 243,
   245, 246, 250, 296, 348

PAGES

Griffith, David _____ 15
Griffith, D. F. _____ 199
Griffith, David H. _____ 199
Griffith, Mary B. _____ 199
Griffin, John H. _____ 292
Grob, John _____ 97
Groseclose, Rev. A. L. _____ 167
Groseclose, Rev. D. B. 166, 167, 191,
   192, 349
Groseclose, Jacob _____ 166
Groseclose, J. A. _____ 147
Groseclose, John _____ 114, 115
Groseclose, John _____ 296
Groseclose, Joseph _____ 296
Groseclose, Rev. Levi _____ 238, 348
Groseclose, Stephen _____ 296
Gross, Rev. Carl _____ 282
Gross, Rev. L. W. _____ 145, 228, 347
Grossman, Rev. M. ____ 129, 175, 353
Groth, Rev. J. W. _____ 149, 160, 356
Grove, Alexander _____ 110
Grove, G. M. _____ 146
Grove Hill _____ 200
Gruber, John _____ 85, 309, 310
Grummet, Friedrich _____ 92
Guard, Rev. John _____ 183
Gudheim, Prof. H. _____ 147
Gurtherie _____ 172
Guthrie, Prof. W. T. _____ 301

Haar (Harr), Simon _____ 27
Haar (Harr), John _____ 27
Haas, Rev. Friedrich __ 88, 94, 95, 98
Haas, Michael _____ 91, 94
Habron _____ 8
Haeger, Rev. John _____ 188
Haenli, Johann Sigmond _____ 5
Hafer _____ 8
Hagerstown _____ 96, 97, 309
Hagerstown Female Seminary ____ 292
Hahn _____ 8
Hahn, Heinrich (Henry) _____ 89, 90
Hahn, Rev. A. L. _____ 243, 356
Hahn, Rev. S. W. _____ 239, 249, 351
Haigler, Rev. J. B. ____ 169, 205, 351
Hailman, B. F. _____ 291, 292
Haines, Rev. G. _____ 344
Haithcox, Rev. H. C. _____ 256, 347
Hale, Amanda Kipps _____ 15
Haller, Miss Kate _____ 321, 327
Hamburg _____ 223, 224
Hamer, F. C. _____ 339
Hamilton, Rev. John 106, 225, 258, 259,
   343
Hamman, Mr. _____ 9
Hamman, A. J. _____ 113
Hammond, Lawrence _____ 233
Hampshire Co. _____ 12, 48, 92, 257

PAGES

Hancher, Rev. A. D. R. 80, 140, 145, 163, 210, 278, 337, 347, 352
Hancher, Mrs. A. D. R. 330, 332, 334
Hancher, Rev. G. B. ___ 137, 262, 352
Hancher, Rev. J. K. 79, 135, 138, 262, 265, 272, 278, 289, 351, 354
Hancher, Rev. William 27, 79, 135, 151, 262, 264, 279
Hancock, Esq. L. D. _____ 294
Hankley, Miss Rose _____ 325
Happes, Heinrich (Henry) ____ 23, 92
Harbein (Harpine), Philip _____ 11
Hardy Co. __ 12, 66, 92, 94, 125, 258
Harless, Adam _____ 192
Harless, Elizabeth _____ 190
Harless, John Philip, Sr. _____ 25
Harless, John Philip, Jr. _____ 25
Harkins, A. P. _____ 147
Harkins, Peter _____ 27
Harman, Adam _____ 190
Harman, Jacob _____ 27
Harmon, John _____ 27
Harner, Henry _____ 159
Harner, Jacob _____ 21
Harnsburger, John _____ 2
Haroff, Lewis _____ 21, 156
Harper, S. B. _____ 145
Harpers Ferry _____ 3, 49
Harpine, Geo. M. _____ 131
Harr, A. Lee _____ 147
Harr, Rev. F. M. 79, 140, 147, 150, 247, 269, 275, 280, 352, 355
Harr, John _____ 27
Harr, J. Edgar _____ 147
Harr, Rev. Joseph _____ 262
Harr, Simon _____ 27
Harrison, Burr _____ 6
Harrisonburg _____ 13, 107, 110, 216
Hartman, John H. _____ 115
Hartwick, Rev. J. C. _____ 43, 177
Hartwig Seminary _____ 43
Haskell, Rev. J. B. _____ 163, 345
Hassinger, Mr. and Mrs. L. C. __ 305
Hasskarl, Rev. G. C. H. 145, 160, 347
Hau, Christopher _____ 41
Hauer, Rev. D. J. 69, 76, 99, 102, 104, 168, 173, 191, 204, 343 .
Hauf (Huff), Joseph _____ 27
Hauk, John _____ 27
Haus, Rev. L. R. __ 148, 159, 223, 355
Haus, Michael _____ 95
Haus, Matthias _____ 91
Hauser, Geo. _____ 27
Hauser, John _____ 27
Hausenfluck, Rev. J. W. 29, 201, 202, 210, 213, 214, 226, 353
Hausman, John _____ 41
Havler, Rev. M. _____ 282

PAGES

Hawksbill, (Hoxbeihl) ____ 91, 94, 198
Hawkins, Rev. Elijah 114-117, 236, 237, 244, 245, 247, 250, 292, 348
Hawkins, Rev. I. P. 172, 211, 215, 236, 346, 349
Hawkins, Rev. J. _____ 256, 345
Hayes, Rev. J. M. _____ 352
Hayfield _____ 182
Haymaker, Geo. _____ 168
Hebron Church Colony __ 2, 18, 61, 74
Hebron, Hampshire Co., W. Va. __ 258
Hebron, Madison Co. _ 37, 186-189, 200
Hebron Church School _____ 287
Hedings Chapel _____ 183
Hedrick, Rev. J. M. 156, 160, 172, 345, 349
Heigel, Dewald _____ 5
Heise, Mr. _____ 91, 214
Heiskell, Adam _____ 5
Heist, John _____ 90
Heintz, Christoph _____ 5
Hefner, Michael _____ 21
Hefner, O. V. _____ 147
Helfenstein, Peter _____ 5
Helms, Rev. R. A. ____ 165, 210, 346
Helsley, Jacob _____ 10
Helsley, Philip _____ 10
Helton _____ 237
Helmuth, Dr. _____ 75
Henderlight _____ 169
Henger, Friedrich _____ 91
Hengerer, Friedrich _____ 7, 21
Hengerer, Eva Margaretha _____ 7
Henkel, A. D. _____ 9, 146
Henkel, Rev. Ambrose 14, 51, 53, 93, 94, 95, 122, 128, 195, 198, 213-216, 219, 222, 225, 226, 281, 283, 310, 311, 314, 353
Henkel, Rev. Andrew _____ 55, 93
Henkel, Anthony _____ 53
Henkel, Rev. Anthony Jacob __ 12, 37
Henkel, Rev. Benjamin ____ 55, 66, 67
Henkel, Rev. Casper G. _____ 303
Henkel, Rev. Charles _____ 55
Henkel, Rev. David _ 55, 272, 276, 311
Henkel, Rev. D. M. _____ 187, 345
Henkel, David S. _____ 303
Henkel, Elon O. _____ 150, 314
Henkel, Rev. Isaac _____ 55, 67
Henkel, Rev. Jacob _____12, 41
Henkel, Rev. John _____ 55, 67
Henkel, Rev. Joseph _____ 55, 67
Henkel, Justus _____ 12, 13, 41
Henkel, Julia Virginia _____ 6
Henkel, Mary M. _____ 15
Henkel, Rev. Moses _____ 13, 84
Henkel, Noah I. _____ 14, 303

PAGES

Henkel, Rev. Paul 4, 13, 24, 59, 65, 71, 73, 93, 222, 229, 309-311
Life Sketch _____ 48-55
Missionary, in Ky. 55; N. C. 53; Ohio 54; S. W. Va. 52, 54, 69, 166, 168, 243; Tenn. 55, 261, 263
Ordained _____ 37, 50
Pastor 188, 216, 218, 220, 222, 223, 225, 283
Five Sons _____ 66
Synods _____ 122
Henkel, Rev. Philip 55, 78, 88, 271, 272, 280, 303
Henkel, Dr. Samuel G. _____ 303, 312
Henkel, Dr. Siram P. ___ 20, 125, 312
Henkel, Rev. Socrates 122-129, 198, 202, 214, 218, 219, 222, 232-234, 281, 287, 303, 314
Henkel, Solomon 6, 14, 86-94, 184, 214, 222, 303, 309, 311
Henkel, Solon P. C. _____ 6, 312
Henkel Family _____ 66
Henkel Fort _____ 13
Henkel Press _____ 87
Henkel Publication House ____ 309-314
Henning, Rev. H. E. __ 149, 266, 355
Henrickson, G. C. _____ 339
Henrico County _____ 185
Heusckel (Heiskel), Christoph ____ 5
Henson, Mr. J. A. ____ 141, 277, 279
Henson, Mrs. Martha __ 141, 277, 279
Hepners _____ 11, 226
Hepner Brothers _____ 11
Hepner, Rev. C. W. 110, 145, 335, 347, 354
Hepner, S. B. _____ 146
Herbst, John E. _____ 291
Herche, Samuel _____ 97
Herchelroth, Henry _____ 272
Hercherother, Jacob _____ 23
Hercheröther, John _____ 92
Herchelroth (Harkleroad), Henry 27, 272
Herman, Adam _____ 25, 41
Herman, Henry _____ 91
Herman, John _____ 91
Herrmann, Jacob _____ 25, 272
Hershberger, Rev. C. E. 202, 211, 215, 276, 352
Hess, Abraham _____ 10
Hess, S. Frank _____ 219
Hessian Soldiers _____ 34
Hetrich, Adam _____ 41
Hetrick, John _____ 41
Hettinger, John _____ 15
Hickerson, Rev. Festus 183, 185, 243, 348
Hill, Dr. _____ 59

PAGES

Hinke, W. J. _____ 40
Hinderlicht, John _____ 22
Hite, Rev. Enoch _____ 129, 219, 353
Hite, Joist (Justus Heid) _____ 4, 178
Hoak, Gideon _____ 198
Hoak, D. A. _____ 198
Hoak, John _____ 198
Hoak, J. L. _____ 131
Hockman, Anthony _____ 110
Hockman, I. S. _____ 124
Hoffart _____ 214
Hoffert, Heinrich _____ 21
Hoffman _____ 214
Hoffman, Philip _____ 6
Hogshead, Rev. Luther _____ 165
Holt, Michael _____ 188
Holland, Rev. R. C. 142, 187, 189, 200, 256, 269, 277, 330, 333, 337, 345
Holland, Robert H. _____ 110
Holland, Rev. Geo. W. 165, 211, 212, 215, 218, 297, 302, 304, 345
Holman's Creek _____ 11, 17
Holy Advent, Wythe Co. __ 252, 253
Holy Trinity, Aug. Co. _____ 160, 161
Holy Trinity, Kingsport _ 143, 273, 374
Holy Trinity, Lynchburg _____ 170
Holy Trinity, Wytheville _____ 251
Holston Grove, Sul. Co. _____ 264
Holston River _____ 26, 52, 166
Holston River, S. Fork _____ 242
Holston Synod, (See Synods)
Holston Synod and Union _____ 143
Holston Synod Mission _____ 137
Holston Synodical College _____ 139
Holt, James _____ 27
Holt, Michael _____ 2, 36
Holtzle, Jacob _____ 91
Holtzman, Jacob _____ 6
Home Missions _____ 324
Home Mission News _____ 326
Home Missionary Society _____ 320
Honda (Hunda), Rev. D. ____ 347, 354
Hone Meeting House _____ 65
Hontz, A. H. _____ 169
Hoover, C. N. _____ 145
Hoover, Rev. Jesse ____ 159, 211, 343
Hopeful _____ 188
Hopewell, Va. _____ 282
Horine, Rev. M. C. _____ 241
Horn, Benjamin _____ 27
Horn, Rev. _____ 336
Hoshour, Rev. S. K. __ 65, 98, 221, 223
Hostler, J. _____ 123
Hottel, David _____ 9
Hottel, Heinrich (Huddle) _____ 23
Hottel, John (Huddle) _____ 23
Hottle's Schoolhouse _____ 232
Houff _____ 157

PAGES

Houff, W. L. _____ 157
Houser, Elmer _____ 148
Houser, Rev. Joseph _____ 351
Houseman, J. P. _____ 209
Housman, Christian _____ 167, 168
Housman, Eva _____ 167
Houserman, Jno. G. _____ 21
Howberts _____ 119, 206
Howison, Mrs. A. M. _____ 332
Howrytown _____ 167
Hoxar, Prof. Henri G. Von _____ 292
Hoxbiehl (Hawksbill) Church ____ 198
Huber, Philip _____ 90
Hubbert, Rev. W. E. 191, 193, 203,
   236, 248, 314, 321
Hubbert, Mrs. W. E. _____ 322
Huddle, C. Max _____ 189
Huddle, Eve _____ 246
Huddle, Jonas _____ 185, 248
Huddle, Rev. J. T. _____ 254
Huddle, Rev. M. D. __ 166, 253, 350
Huddle, Rev. W. C. 148, 189, 208, 233,
   234, 355
Huddle, Rev. W. P. 37, 62, 145, 156,
   189, 236, 244, 246, 253, 346, 349,
   354
Hudson Cross Roads ____ 223, 224, 227
Huffard, Rev. J. A. 131, 141, 145, 162,
   193, 199, 204, 207, 253, 273, 347,
   349, 354
Huffard, W. R. _____ 147
Huffman, Rev. A. M. _____ 278, 356
Huffman (Hoffman), Rev. Dan 221, 222
Huffman (Hoffman), Jacob _____ 222
Huffman, Rev. L. L. 129, 202, 226, 232,
   233, 234, 238, 353
Hughs, Rev. S. P. _____ 173
Humiliation and Fasting, Day of __ 83
Hunda (Honda), Rev. D. 145, 347, 354
Hunt, Rev. C. L. 148, 201, 202, 278,
   279, 280, 355
Hunt, Pemberton _____ 27
Hunton, Rev. C. K. 146, 206, 350, 354
Hunton, Rev. J. H. 123-126, 225, 233,
   353
Hupp, Abraham _____ 292
Hurt, Rev. J. A. C. 146, 169, 254, 350,
   354
Hutsell, James _____ 171
Hymn Book, Published _____ 311
Hymnal, Res. to introduce ____ 93, 94

Ide, Julius _____ 112
Indian Fort Farm _____ 11
Indiana _____ 28
Intelligencer (Lutheran) _____ 101
Institute, The Virginia Collegiate 290, 291

PAGES

Immanuel, Alexandria _____ 282
Immanuel, Bluefield, W. Va. ____ 260
Immanuel, Charlottesville _____ 282
Immanuel, Church Sul. Co. 79, 261, 262
Immanuel Church, Wash. Co., Tenn. 278

Jackson's Church _____ 168
Jackson, M. _____ 296
Jackson, Rev. H. A. 148, 165, 184, 355
Jager, Simon _____ 18, 84
Jager, John _____ 84
James River _____ 21, 97, 117
James River Parish _____ 167
James, Thomas _____ 21
Janice James School _____ 331
Japan _____ 109
Jasinski, Rev. F. W. _____ 255, 257
Jefferson County _____ 26, 90, 257
Jefferson Co. Ministers _____ 257
Jeffersonville _____ 239
Jerome _____ 226
Jeter's Chapel _____ 165
Jewish Synagogue _____ 203
Joint Literature Committee _____ 329
Jones, Rev. E. H. 168, 181, 257, 345,
   348
Julian, Rev. W. A. _____ 252
Jurie _____ 201

Kagey, N. I. _____ 146
Kagley, Mr. _____ 23
Kaifer, Michael _____ 2
Kapp, Michael _____ 272
Karkau, Rev. A. C. _____ 241, 347
Keahler, Rev. John _____ 255
Keezletown _____ 18
Keezletown, Pike _____ 162
Kegley, Rev. C. R. W. 239, 253, 261,
   350
Keicher, Conrad _____ 27, 272
Keicher, John _____ 272
Keifer, Frederick _____ 97
Kehler, Rev. J. 99, 100, 101, 104, 189,
   343
Keil, Rev. W. G. 181, 235, 258, 259
Keiner, Casper _____ 91
Keiner, George _____ 91
Keinardt, Michael (Koiner) _____ 18
Keiser Brothers _____ 15
Keiser, E. L. _____ 146
Keiser, Daniel _____ 19, 159
Keiser, Rev. L. R. 20, 178, 257, 343
Keister, Adam _____ 4
Keister, Amos _____ 4
Keister, Henry _____ 4
Keister, Rev. T. O. 163, 207, 208, 218,
   346, 350, 354
Keller, Abraham _____ 6

PAGES

Keller, Catherine _____ 228
Keller, George _____ 6
Keller, Rev. H. _____ 344
Keller, Jacob _____ 10
Keller, Rev. Levi 180, 189, 200, 224,
    225, 228, 231, 233, 235, 344
Keller, Philip _____ 91
Keller, Rev. S. L. ____ 160, 235, 346
Kelly, Rev. A. A. _____ 145, 178, 347
Kelly, J. A. _____ 296
Kepley, Rev. C. E. ____ 148, 193, 355
Keplinger, Mr. _____ 27
Kenney, Chesley _____ 110
Kenzie, William _____ 147
Kerlin, Samuel _____ 11
Kerlin, Chas. S. _____ 131
Kerker, Andrew _____ 2
Kern, Adam _____ 4
Kern, Rev. R. E. _____ 236, 350
Kessler, Benjamin _____ 22, 169
Kessler, Daniel _____ 22
Kessler, George W. _____ 22
Kessler, Isaac _____ 22
Kessler, Jacob _____ 25
Kessel, Henry _____ 91
Keystone _____ 261
Keyler, John _____ 97, 99, 104
Kibler _____ 8
Kibler, Rev. J. A. ____ 200, 201, 344
Kibler, J. A. _____ 177
Kibler, J. L. _____ 175
Kibler, Rev. Harry _____ 235
Kibler, J. Luther _____ 113
Kibler, Martin _____ 97
Kibler, Rev. W. H. ___ 184, 236, 356
Kieselstadt _____ 53
Kiefer, John _____ 90
Killian, Rev. Jacob 20, 122-124, 128,
    213, 214, 283, 353
Killian, Rev. J. M. ____ 146, 191, 350
Killian, Rev. Philip _____ 161, 162
Killinger, Mr. _____ 23
Killinger, G. H. D. _____ 296
Killinger, Rev. Kenneth 119, 185, 237,
    355
Kilterman, Johannes _____ 26
Kimberlin Church __ 74, 92, 115, 243,
    248, 250, 253
Kimberlin Parish _____ 248
Kimberlin, Jacob _____ 166
Kimmerling, John _____ 92
Kimberlin, Martin _____ 248
Kime, R. W. _____ 307
Kinard, Rev. M. M. __ 140, 278, 352
Kinard, J. C. _____ 151
King, Mary _____ 157
King, Samuel _____ 157
King, Rev. C. B. _____ 253, 349

PAGES

Kingsport _____ 273
Kingsport Mission _____ 141
Kinser, John _____ 27
Kinser, Miss Dora E. _____ 143, 330
Kinzel, Henry _____ 27
Kinzer, J. W. _____ 26
Kinzer, W. R. _____ 26, 171
Kinzer, E. H. _____ 148
Kiplinger, Mr. _____ 27
Kipps, Rev. Casper _____ 190
Kipps, Geo. W. _____ 15
Kipps, Henry _____ 15
Kipps, Rev. M. M. _____ 129, 190
Kipps, Mary _____ 14
Kipps Schoolhouse _____ 219
Kirchhof _____ 214
Kirchhof, Mr. _____ 91
Kirchhof, Wilhelm (Caricofe, Kira-
    cofe) _____ 21
Kirchner, Rev. Johann Casper __ 5, 177
Kirkpatrick, Charles P. _____ 21
Kiser, Rev. J. F. _____ 169, 348
Kishi, Rev. _____ 334
Kisling, Mrs. Sallie _____ 110
Kister (Kuster), Adam __ 95, 102, 103
Kistler, Rev. H. A. ____ 263, 266, 352
Kissling, Jacob _____ 41
Kites _____ 3
Kite, H. J. _____ 177
Kittel, Rev. Frederick _____ 281
Kittingers _____ 207
Kitzmeyer, Rev. J. F. W. __ 232, 347
Kizer, Mrs. John A. _____ 322
Kizer, John P. _____ 292
Kleckner, Rev. J. S. _____ 148, 355
Klein, Andreas _____ 27
Klein, Anton _____ 90, 95
Klein, Jacob _____ 49
Klein, Henry _____ 8
Klein, Philip _____ 92
Klein, John P. _____ 9
Klein (Cline), Rev. John Philip __ 9
Klug, Rev. C. S. _____ 166
Klug, Rev. Geo. S. __ 36, 38, 188, 195
Kluttz, Rev. M. J. ____ 149, 162, 356
Knies, Rev. H. Edgar __ 149, 207, 356
Kneisley, Reuben _____ 9
Kneisley, Lewis _____ 9
Kneisley, J. Grove _____ 9
Knipp, Adam _____ 27
Knoebel, Rev. R. P. ___ 149, 226, 356
Knop, Valentine _____ 90
Knox, County _____ 26-27, 78
Knoxville Parish _____ 277
Knox-Monroe Parish _____ 273
Kock, John _____ 272
Kohler, Rev. _____ 257

PAGES

Koiner's Church 54, 55, 122, 127, 128, 155, 214, 282
Koiner Family _____ 18
Koiner, Absolom _____ 162
Koiner, A. Z. _____ 20
Koiner, Conrad _____ 18
Koiner, Casper _____ 18
Koiner, Catherine _____ 18
Koiner, Christian _____ 18
Koiner, Elizabeth _____ 18
Koiner, Frederick _____ 19
Koiner, George A. _____ 18
Koiner, George M. _____ 18
Koiner, Gideon _____ 302
Koiner, Jacob _____ 18
Koiner, John _____ 18
Koiner, Rev. Junius S. 20, 129, 175, 189, 353
Koiner, Margaret _____ 20
Koiner, Martin _____ 18
Koiner, Mary _____ 18
Koiner (Keinadt), Michael _____ 18
Koiner, Philip _____ 18
Koiner, Susan _____ 20
Kohler, Henry _____ 41
Kohler, Rev. _____ 257
Kohn, Rev. E. H. 129, 214, 219, 238, 350, 353
Konnarock Training School _____ 305
Konrad, Christian _____ 200
Koon, Rev. S. P. _____ 261, 350
Koontz, Charles _____ 131
Kopenhafer, Thomas _____ 23
Kopp, Rev. W. _____ 344
Koppenhäfer, Jacob (Copenhaver)_ 5
Kraft, Philip _____ 90
Kramer, John F. _____ 339
Krank, Henry _____ 92
Krause, Mrs. Louis _____ 335
Krauth, Rev. Charles Philip, Sr. 59, 69, 97, 107, 254, 255, 257, 313
Krauth, Rev. Charles Porterfield 60, 69, 178, 255, 344
Krauth, Rev. G. E. _____ 183, 218, 346
Kregger, Mrs. _____ 243
Kregger (Cregar), Michael _____ 23
Kreps, Irma, Fund _____ 334
Kreps, Rev. M. O. J. 184, 191, 333, 349
Kreps, Mrs. M. O. J. 326, 327, 330, 333
Krigler, Aaron _____ 95
Krohne, Theodore _____ 112
Kropf, Daniel _____ 41
Kropf, Jacob _____ 41
Kronk, Heinrich _____ 25
Koyte _____ 201
Koyte, Gerhard _____ 200
Kublinger, Jacob _____ 18
Kuegele, Rev. F. _____ 283

PAGES

Kuder, Mrs. C. F. _____ 333
Kuhns, Rev. S. W. 145, 199, 232, 347
Kuhn, Rev. Daniel _____ 56
Kuhn, Rev. D. A. _____ 257
Kummerling, Martin (Kimberlin) _ 23
Kuntzes _____ 3
Kurtz, John Adam _____ 5
Kurtz, Anna Maria (Miller) ____ 6
Kurtz, Rev. Benjamin _____ 97
Kurtz, Rev. Daniel _____ 97
Kurtz, John Adam _____ 5
Kuster, Adam _____ 95
Kyle, Rev. _____ 249
Kyle, Rev. H. D. _____ 65
Kyle, Noah _____ 202
Kyushu Gakuin _____ 328

Ladd _____ 161
Ladies' Cooperative Association _ 321
Lambert, Christopher _____ 5
Lambert, James _____ 166
Lambert, Henry _____ 23
Lancaster Co., Pa. _____ 2
Landis, Rev. B. F. ____ 165, 191, 350
Lang, George _____ 2
Lang (Long), Philip _____ 3
Larrick, A. _____ 182
Larrick, D. W. _____ 182
Larrick, J. H. _____ 182
Laubinger, Geo. Michael _____ 5
Lauck, Abraham _____ 89, 90
Lauck, Peter _____ 5, 90
Laudy, J. M. _____ 147
Laurel Chapel _____ 259
Lay-Reader _____ 89
Lay-Services _____ 89, 90
Layman, Joseph _____ 168
Layman, Lydia _____ 168
Lebanon Church, Shen. Co. _____ 228
Lebanon, Wythe Co. _____ 252
Lechleiter, Adam _____ 91
Lechleiter, Joseph _____ 91
Lechleiter, N. N. _____ 90
Lederer, John _____ 1
Ledden, Rev. P. D. ____ 191, 243, 350
Lee, Rev. Geo. A. ____ 156, 161, 345
Lee Highway _____ 200, 248, 252
Lehman's Schoolhouse _____ 49
Lehman, Rev. W. F. _____ 313
Leidy, Rev. Geo. _____ 198
Leinenweber, Johannes _____ 21
Lemley, Johannes _____ 5
Lenoir College _____ 129, 288
Lentz, Johannes _____ 5
Lentz, Rev. H. Max _____ 256, 347
Leonard, Jacob _____ 90
Leondardt, G. C. L. _____ 212

PAGES

Leslie, Rev. E. W. 145, 169, 208, 218, 306, 347, 350, 354
Lexington, Va. _____ 21
Lexington, S. C. _____ 117
Liberty Church _____ 265
Lick Creek Church _____ 278
Lichtenwanger, J. M. _____ 147
Lichtlighter, Jacob _____ 8
Lideck, Jacob _____ 27
Lideke, George _____ 263
Light Brigade _____ 327
Limeston _____ 279
Lindamood, Andrew _____ 10
Lindamood, Christopher _____ 10
Lindamood, Geo. Henry _____ 10
Lindamood, John _____ 10
Lindamood, Michael _____ 10
Lingle, Jacob _____ 41
Link, Abraham _____ 125
Link, Adam _____ 90
Link, G. V. _____ 145
Link, Rev. J. W. 145, 203, 221, 233, 235, 259, 264-266, 347, 350
Link, Matthias _____ 91, 157
Link, Peter _____ 91
Linn, John _____ 90
Linn, Rev. J. A. __ 269, 271, 272, 352
Lintz, Mrs. W. J. _____ 331
Lintz, William I. _____ 27
Lippard, Rev. C. O. __ 207, 208, 351
Literature, Miss. Society _____ 325
Littleford, J. W. _____ 147
Lits, Catherine _____ 246
Livingstone, Rev. R. E. _____ 187
Lochner, Rev. L. _____ 282
Locust Bottom _____ 167
Logan, B. I. _____ 292
Lohr, Catherine _____ 15
Lohr, Frederick _____ 97
Lohr, George (1) _____ 11
Lohr, George (2) _____ 219
Lohr, Michael _____ 11
Lohr, Philip _____ 11
Lohr, Rev. L. L. 129, 131, 132, 148, 216, 353, 355
Lohr, Luther A. _____ 131
Lohr, Mary C. _____ 15
Lohr, Philip _____ 14
Lonas Church _____ 273
Lonas, George _____ 10
Lonas, Henry _____ 27, 275
Lonas Hollow _____ 11
Lonas, Leonard _____ 10
Long, Rev. Geo. A. 159, 179, 180, 183, 235, 257, 344
Long, William _____ 41
Longaker, Rev. F. C. _____ 148, 355
Longanecker, Rev. R. A. _____ 229

PAGES

Look, N. L. _____ 296
Lord, Fairfax __ 4, 177, 224, 226, 235
Loretz, Andrew _____ 52
Lose, Rev. G. W. _____ 226
Lottich, Rev. F. J. ____ 148, 251, 355
Lotz, Rev. J. A. _____ 149, 207, 355
Lovenstein, Conrad _____ 41
Lovettsville _____ 76
Lowe, Rev. J. E., Jr. __ 149, 181, 356
Lowry, Benjamin _____ 14
Lowry, Daniel _____ 15
Lowry's Chapel, Roanoke Co. _____ 204
Lubkert, Rev. E. _____ 344
Ludden, Rev. A. P. 146, 183, 189, 200, 292, 344
Ludi, Anthony _____ 34, 177
Ludwicks _____ 160
Luger, Walter _____ 169
Luther Brotherhood _____ 339
Luther League, Synod _____ 315, 338
Luther League, N. M. Con. _____ 132
Luther's Church Postils _____ 313
Lutheran Chapel, Aug. Co. _____ 214
Luther Chapel, Bot. Co. _____ 168
Luther Chapel, Sul. Co. _____ 265
Luther Chapel, Wash. Co. _____ 242
Luther Zion, Wash. Co. _____ 279
Luther Mem., Cocke Co., Tenn. 268, 269
Luther Mem., Portsmouth _____ 195
Luther Mem., Blacksburg ___ 190, 191
Luther Pl. Mem., Wash. D. C. __ 20
Lutheran Pioneer Pastors _____ 33
Lutheran Periodicals 98, 314, 315, 326, 327
Lutheran Home, The _____ 326
Lutheran Messenger _____ 315
Lutheran Observer _____ 162
Lutheran Visitor _____ 326
Lutheran, Virginia _____ 314
Lutheran Woman's Work _____ 326
Lutheran Settlers:
In Madison, 2, In Shen. Valley, 20-22, In S. W. Va. 22-26, In Tenn. 26-29, In Towns, 29-30
Lutherville, Female Seminary ____ 80
Luray _____ 15, 195, 199, 240, 298
Lutz, Henry _____ 11
Lutz, Rev. J. H. _____ 281
Lynchburg _____ 119, 170

Madison County 2, 62, 74, 91, 95, 106
Madison Parish _____ 187
Madisonville _____ 275
Mahood, Rev. J. A. 166, 191, 238, 348
Maichel, Wilhelm _____ 25
Maichel, Jacob _____ 25
Mallo, George, Sr. _____ 41
Mallo, George, Jr. _____ 41

PAGES

Mallo, Henry _____ 92
Mallo, Michael _____ 41
Manassas _____ 15
Manassas Parish _____ 173, 174
Mann, John _____ 41
Mann, Rev. L. A. 223, 236, 243, 244, 245, 345, 348
Marckert, Rev. Louis _____ 88
Marion Parish _____ 322
Marion Male & Female High School 294
Marion Female (Junior) College 72, 120, 236, 288, 294-296
Marion Female (Junior) College, First Trustees _____296
Markley, Mary (Dr.) _____ 240
Markley, Mary _____ 208
Markley, Rev. R. L. ___ 149, 170, 356
Marker, Wm. F. _____ 182
Marks, Rev. C. A. 145, 156, 160, 168, 169, 172, 173, 183, 187, 346, 348, 354
Marks, Mrs. C. A. _____ 321
Marshall, Aylette _____ 189
Marsteller, J. H. _____ 147
Martinsburg _____ 63, 254
Martin, Rev. Charles _____ 255, 345
Martin, Miss Hattie E. _____ 321
Martin's Tank _____ 203
Mason Co. _____ 92
Massanutten _____ 195, 201
Massanutten Mountains _____ 3
Matthias, Rev. H. J. ___ 278-280, 352
Matter, John _____ 90
Mau, Rev. Samuel _____ 83, 84
Mauck, Henry _____ 27, 275
Mauney, Rev. J. D. _____ 170
Maures Mill, Shen. Co. _____ 22, 219
Maurer, John _____ 27
Maurer, Johannes _____ 25
Maus, Daniel _____ 87
May, William R. _____ 15, 175
Maybeury _____ 261
Mayer, Rev. C. C. _____ 348
Mayer, George _____ 2
Mayer, Johannes _____ 25, 172
Mayer, Jacob 22, 35, 48, 49, 51, 52, 167
Mayer, Sarah _____ 167
McCall, John _____ 27
McCauley _____ 20
McCauley, Rev. E. R. 15, 145, 191, 194, 208, 347, 350
McCauley, Mrs. W. J. _____ 322
McCauley, Rev. J. W. 15, 146, 169, 205, 207, 208, 351, 354
McCauley, John _____ 15, 205, 292
McCauley, Wm. _____ 205, 296
McCauley, Rev. Victor _____ 15, 208
McClanahan _____ _____ 20
McClanahan, Rev. Geo. W. _____ 208

PAGES

McClanahan, Rev. W. S. 120, 156, 160, 209, 218, 257, 305, 306, 345, 348
McClelland _____ 20
McConoughty _____ 20
McComb _____ 20
McComb, William Alexander 21, 145, 156
McComb, Wm. A., Jr. _____ 145, 156
McCron _____ 20
McCune, T. C. _____ 157
McCune, C. M. _____ 157
McDaniel, Rev. R. E. _____ 345
McDonald, Rev. E. H. 172, 236, 245, 247, 252, 294, 348
McGaheysville 18, 39, 126, 211, 212
McGaughey, Rev. J. C. _____ 159, 346
McHenry _____ 20
McIntyre, Dr. J. H. _____ 208
McKee _____ 20
McMullen Hall _____ 295
McMullen, Fayette, Hon. _____ 296
McReynalds _____ 20
Meadow View _____ 242
Medtart, Rev. Jacob 99-104, 254, 255, 257, 343
Meherrin _____ 282
Melanchthon Chapel 157, 158, 162, 165
Melsheimer, Rev. _____ 257
Mercer County _____ 260
Meigel, Petrus _____ 25
Merger of Synods _____ 121, 144
Merger _____ 114
Mess, Johannes _____ 84
Messerschmidt _____ 214
Metz, Rev. Geo. A. _____ 239
Meuschke, Rev. F. H. _____ 282
Meyer, John William (Teacher) 35, 69, 88
Meyer, J. A. _____ 35, 69, 88
Meyer, Henry _____ 27
Meyer, William _____ 112
Meyerhoeffer, Rev. M. 95, 97, 99, 102, 104, 156, 159, 160, 189, 213, 343,
Michael, Rev. D. W. _____ 259, 346
Michael, George _____ 18
Michel, William _____ 41
Middlebrook _____ 156
Middlebrook Parish _____ 160
Midway _____ 279
Mildeberger, John _____ 41
Mildeberger, Nicholas _____ 41
Mill Creek, Grayson Co. _____ 237
Mill Creek, Shen. Co. _____ 16
Miller _____ 202
Miller, Abraham _____ 6
Miller, Abraham Schultz _____ 6
Miller, Adam (1) (Müller) 2, 3, 18, 38, 195

PAGES

Miller, Adam (2) _____ 27
Miller (Müller), Adam (3) _____ 202
Miller, Rev. Adam, Sr. 262, 272, 275, 277
Miller, Rev. C. Armand 21, 165, 206, 349
Miller, Rev. C. B. _____ 160, 189, 346
Miller, Rev. C. L. ____ 147, 268, 355
Miller, Rev. D. L. 129, 198, 202, 222, 223, 253, 302
Miller, E. Clarence _____ 339
Miller, Rev. Frank H. __ 148, 249, 355
Miller, George _____ 10
Miller, Godfrey (1) _____ 6
Miller, Godfrey (2) _____ 227
Miller, Henry _____ 125, 126
Miller, Rev. H. N. 236, 251, 296, 350
Miller, Jacob (1) _____ 227
Miller, Jacob (2) _____ 6, 22, 92
Miller, Jacob (3) _____ 275
Miller, Rev. J. A. L. 145, 160, 172, 173, 212, 215, 347
Miller, Rev. J. C. 147, 269, 271, 272, 275-277, 278, 280, 351
Miller, J. D. _____ 177
Miller, Rev. J. H. _____ 282
Miller, Joseph (1) _____ 27
Miller, Joseph (2) _____ 21
Miller, Rev. J. I. 21, 129, 156, 199, 200, 210, 218, 240, 256, 297, 298, 345, 350, 353
Miller, Rev. J. P. 149, 238, 251, 296, 350, 356
Miller, Rev. J. W. _____ 344
Miller, John (1) _____ 10
Miller, John (2) _____ 15
Miller, Julius _____ 15
Miller, Lafayette _____ 227
Miller, Rev. Luther F. 133, 148, 175, 355
Miller, Rev. L. G. M. 178, 183, 204, 206, 320, 321, 346, 348
Miller, Rev. L. S. G. 110, 145, 183, 347, 354
Miller, Michael (1) _____ 102
Miller, Michael (2) _____ 292
Miller, Nicholas _____ 125
Miller, Rev. O. C. ____ 207, 302, 349
Miller, P. _____ 123
Miller, Paul _____ 198
Miller, Peter _____ 22, 52, 53
Miller, Rev. Peter 21, 156, 173, 210, 218, 224, 227, 229, 231, 233, 258-260, 344, 349
Miller, Rev. P. H. _____ 345
Miller, Rev. P. L. ____ 180, 235, 346
Miller, Rev. R. J. 69, 71, 167, 168, 172

PAGES

Miller, Rev. Thomas 106, 125, 126, 168, 173, 189, 191, 205, 225 343, 353
Miller's Church, Knox Co. _____ 273
Millerstadt _____ 6
Mills, J. D. _____ 216
Milnes _____ 200
Ministers of the Luth. Synod of Va. _____ 355, 356
Ministers of the Ev. Luth. Synod of S. W. Va. _____ 348-351
Ministers of the Virginia Special Conference _____ 353
Ministers of the Ev. Luth. Hol. Synod _____ 351-352
Ministers of the Ev. Luth. Synod of Virginia _____ 343-347
Ministers from Aug. Co. _____ 165
Ministers from Bland Co. _____ 167
Ministers from Bot. Co. _____ 169
Ministers from Carroll and Floyd Counties _____ 173
Ministers from Fred. Co. _____ 183
Ministers from Jefferson County __ 257
Ministers from Madison County __ 189
Ministers from Page County ____ 202
Ministers from Prince Wm. Co. __ 177
Ministers from Roanoke Co. ____ 208
Ministers from Rockingham Co. __ 218
Ministers from Shenandoah Co. __ 235
Ministers from Smyth Co. _____ 238
Ministers from Tazewell Co. ____ 239
Ministers from Wythe Co. ___ 253-254
Ministerium of New York ____ 32, 105
Ministerium of Penn. 34, 94, 105, 106, 112
Mink Creek _____ 279
Minnich, Rev. M. R. __ 156, 163, 345
Minnick, E. M. _____ 131, 302
Minnick, George W. _____ 226
Minnick, Matthias _____ 11
Minnick, Rev. M. L. __ 149, 275, 356
Missionary Journal _____ 326
Missions of Woman's Missionary Society of Synod _____ 336
Missionary Pastors _____ 33
Missionaries sent to India _____ 109
Missionaries sent to Japan _____ 109
Missionary Tours ___ 69-71, 167, 172
Missionary of The W. Soc. of S. W. Virginia Synod _____ 324
Mitchell Creek _____ 237
Mock's Chapel _____ 242
Mohler, Friedrich _____ 91
Moller, Rev. Henry _____ 43, 177
Mottern, Henry _____ 26
Monger's Church _____ 201
Monongahela County _____ 95
Monroe County _____ 27

PAGES

Monroe, Rev. P. E. ____ 193, 204, 350
Montgomery County 22, 76, 92, 167,
  183, 204
Montgomery County Churches ____ 190
Moomaw, William _____ 131
Moomaw, John _____ 131
Moose, Rev. J. B. 204, 239, 261, 351
Mordath _____ 8
Morehead, Rev. J. A. 142, 145, 150,
  208, 210, 238, 253, 262, 293, 333,
  346, 349
Morehead, Mrs. W. F. 326, 327, 330,
  331, 333, 335, 336
Moretz, Christian _____ 78
Morgan, General _____ 5
Morgan, Rev. J. L. _____ 150-151
Morgan, Rev. F. G. __ 145, 189, 347
Morgan, Rev. C. I. 129, 130-132, 148,
  353, 355
Morning Star, Page Co. _ 129, 195, 198
Morning Star, Shen. Co. 129, 226, 228
Morris, Rev. J. G. ____ 65, 223, 313
Morristown _____ 141
Moser, Rev. D. H. _____ 256, 345
Moser, John _____ 27
Moser, Rev. J. M. 205, 208, 269, 271,
  275, 277, 350, 352
Moser, Rev. J. S. 187, 189, 200, 218,
  223, 345, 348
Mosheim Academy _____ 137
Mosheim Institute _____ 301
Mosheim Parish _____ 278
Mosheim Synodical College _____ 301
Motz, John _____ 2
Mountain Mission ____ 119, 185, 237
Mt. Airy Parish 243, 244, 245, 246, 248
Mt. Carmel, Craig _____ 183, 184
Mt. Calvary, Mt. Jackson _____ 223
Mt. Calvary, Page Co. 38-39, 125, 195,
  198, 199
Mt. Calvary, Shen. Co. __ 132, 222, 281
Mt. Herman _____ 160, 161
Mt. Jackson Parish _____ 223
Mt. Nebo, Madison Co. _____ 189
Mt. Nebo, Shenandoah Co. _____ 129
Mt. Moriah, Bot. Co. _____ 169
Mt. Moriah, Hardy Co. _____ 259
Mt. Olive, (New) Rockbridge Co. _ 210
Mt. Olive, Shenandoah Co. _____ 233
Mt. Pisgah _____ 189
Mt. Sidney _____ 157, 211
Mt. Solon _____ 20, 21, 165, 214
Mt. Tabor, Augusta Co. 21, 65, 107, 155,
  160, 164, 165, 290
Mt. Tabor, Montgomery Co. 190, 191
Mt. Vernon, Hardy Co. _____ 258
Mt. Zion, Augusta Co. __ 15, 103, 160
Mt. Zion, Fort Valley _____ 218

PAGES

Mt. Zion, Hampshire Co. _____ 258
Mt. Zion, Mont. Co. _____ 192
Mt. Zion, Prince Wm. Co. 130, 173, 175
Mt. Zion, Shen. Co. (Ohio) 225, 281
Mt. Zion Church, Shen. Co. near
  Woodstock _____ 228, 229
Mt. Zion, Shen. Co., N. M. Conf. 219
Mt. Zion, Smyth Co. _____ 236
Muhlenberg Church _____ 216, 217
Muhlenberg, Rev. (Gen.) J. P. G.
  Student _____ 45, 56
  Became Minister _____ 45, 56
  Labors at Woodstock__ 7, 44-48, 229
  Pastoral Services 46, 108, 198, 225,
    231, 235, 258
  Military Service _____ 47-61
  Service as Layman _____ 48
Muhlenberg, Rev. H. M. 39, 44, 56,
  58, 74
Mueller, John _____ 200
Mueller, Christian _____ 200
Mueller, Rev. Gerhard ____:____ 200
Müller, Peter _____ 41
Mumpower Church ___:_____ 265
Mumpower, Isaac _____ 26
Munch, Daniel _____ 8
Murphy, Rev. J. L. 80, 203, 264, 266,
  272, 273, 352
Murphy, Mr. _____ 113
Murry _____ 169
Murray, Frederick _____ 22
Musser, M. M. _____ 237

Nägley, Balthaser _____ 41
Nägley _____ 13
Naiman, Rev. E. G. _____ 283
Naked Creek, Aug. Co. _____ 157
Naked Creek, Page Co. ____ 195, 200
National Luth. Council _____ 240
Nauman, John _____ 91
Neas, A. H. _____ 147
Nease, Rev. S. L. 148, 160, 172, 173,
  243, 355
Nees, J. _____ 84, 86, 88, 93
Negley, George _____ 92
Nehs (Neas), Joseph _____ 27
Nehs, Jacob _____ 86
Nehs (Neas), John _____ 27, 272
Nehs (Neese), Michael _____ 11, 49
Neibert (Newbert), Frederick ____ 27
Neice Michael _____ 215
Neiffer, Rev. J. G. 112, 185, 187, 343
Nelson, Henry _____ 6
New Amsterdam Parish _____ 167
New Haven Church, Sul. Co. ____ 263
New Holland _____ 18
New Market (settled) _____ 13

PAGES

New Market 54, 218, 219, 287, 297, 301, 302, 309, 314
New Market Weekly _____ 311
New Market Parish, Winchester Conference _____ 219
New River Parish _____ 191
New River Settlement _____ 190
Newberry, S. C. _____ 303
Newport, Augusta Co. _____ 160
Newport Parish _____ 184, 322
Newport News ____ 112, 113, 240, 241
Newtown, see Stephens City
Neubert's Springs _____ 276
Neuman _____ 200
Nicodemus, Rev. _____ 255
Niclas, Peter _____ 41
Niclas, Jacob _____ 41
Ninevah _____ 177
Nixdorff, Rev. G. A. _____ 344
Nokesville _____ 15, 173, 175
Nolting, O. _____ 282
Norfolk _____ 112, 113, 193, 194
North Carolina _____ 220
North Fork _____ 261
North River, Aug. Co. _____ 162
North River Meeting House _____ 259
North River Mills _____ 258
North River Parish _____ 257
North River of Shenandoah _____ 235
North Tazewell _____ 239
Nowman, John _____ 201
Nussmann, Rev. Adolph _____ 44

Oak Grove, Washington Co. ____ 265
Oak Grove Schoolhouse _____ 245
Oak Shade Schoolhouse _____ 221
Obenchain, Mr. _____ 21
Obenchain, Rev. A. B. _____ 210
Obenchain, Rev. J. P. 173, 209, 345, 348
Obenchain, Lucy _____ 168
Obenchain, Samuel _____ 25, 168
Oberly, Rev. F. C. ____ 129, 199, 353
Oehl, Valentine _____ 90
Oehler, Anthony _____ 41
Oehlschlaeger, Rev. C. _____ 282
Oesterly (Easterly), Ambrose _____ 27
Offman, Rev. D. I. _____ 236
O'Hara, Theodora _____ 30
Old Bell Tavern _____ 162
Old Furnace _____ 60
Old Hickory Church _____ 168
Old Pine Church _____ 182
Olivet, Craig Co. _____ 183, 184
Olive, Olive Hill _____ 172
Olinger, P. C. _____ 175
Olinger, Jacob _____ 11
Oneil, John _____ 14

PAGES

Oney, Rev. W. B. 145, 150, 159, 160, 162, 173, 209, 211, 215, 228, 242, 243, 346, 349
Oosterling, Rev. J. ____ 145, 347, 354
Orebaugh, G. A. _____ 123
Organizations _____ 81
Orkney Springs Parish _____ 226
Orndorff, Isaac _____ 182
Orohrbach, Wilhelm (Orebaugh) __ 21
Orphan Home 120, 205, 254, 305-307
Oswald, Rev. Sam 106, 201, 221, 223
Oswald, Rev. Solomon _____ 343
Ott, George _____ 102
Ott, Sarah _____ 110
Ott, Jacob _____ 9, 94, 95, 97, 100
Ottinger, Rev. F. M. _____ 352
Ottinger, Jacob _____ 27
Ottinger, John _____ 27, 272
Ottinger, Matthias _____ 147
Ottinger, Michael _____ 269
Otto, Catherine _____ 5
Otto, John Tobias _____ 5
Our Church Paper _____ 313, 314
Oven Creek _____ 268
Ovenschein, Samuel _____ 92

Page Co. _____ 15, 18, 38, 195, 210
Page County Churches _____ 196-197
Page County, Luth. Ministers from 202
Painter (Bender), George _____ 11
Painter (Bender), John _____ 10
Painter, Peter _____ 198
Painter, Alexander _____ 215
Painter, Rev. F. V. N. 169, 206, 306, 348
Palsel, Peter _____ 13
Parent Mission and Ed. Soc. ____ 118
Parker, Rev. T. C. 146, 169, 173, 184, 191, 205, 208, 350, 354
Park, Rev. J. N. C. _____ 253
Parman, David _____ 27
Parrottsville _____ 268, 269
Pass Run _____ 200
Pastures _____ 160
Pastors in Eastern Tenn. _____ 77-80
Patmos Church _____ 218, 232, 281
Patterson's Creek _____ 3
Patterson Church _____ 278
Patterson, Rev. R. S. __ 142, 266, 337
Patton, James _____ 190
Pearson, Rev. P. H. 145, 241, 347, 354
Peaked Mountain _____ 39, 212
Peaked Mountain Church ____ 38, 96
Peer, Philip _____ 9
Peery _____ 24
Peery, Dr. E. W. _____ 147
Peery, Rev. J. C. 166, 170, 239, 296, 299, 350

PAGES

Peery, Rev. R. B. 109, 121, 178, 239, 324, 346, 349
Peiss, Jacob _____ 23
Pembroke _____ 183, 184
Pembroke Parish _____ 184
Pence, C. A. _____ 302
Pence, Rev. M. L. 129, 130, 218, 226, 227, 232, 233, 234, 353
Pence, Rev. E. Z. ____ 129, 175, 353
Pence, Rev. A. M. _____ 218
Pence, Rev. C. H. _____ 218
Pence, Rev. L. P. ____ 199, 201, 236
Pendleton Co., 12, 66, 92, 94, 95, 125
Pennywitt, John _____ 221
Pens, Wilhelm _____ 3
Pens, William _____ 87
Perkey, Daniel _____ 166
Perst, John _____ 91
Peter's Creek _____ 208
Peters, Daniel _____ 27
Peterson, Rev. O. C. 278, 279, 350, 352
Petrea, Rev. B. E. _____ 252, 350
Petrea, Rev. H. M. _____ 187
Pfleiffer _____ 214
Pflieger, Geo. R. _____ 172
Pflum, Rev. H. J. _____ 191, 351
Pfluger, Abraham _____ 25
Pfluger, Geo. F. _____ 25
Pfluger, Michael _____ 25
Phanuel Church _____ 228, 281
Philadelphia _____ 220
Philippi, Henry _____ 23
Phillippi, Rev. A. 251, 252, 253, 266, 300, 348
Phillips, Rev. C. A. _____ 268, 352
Phlegar, Benjamin _____ 296
Piedefish, John _____ 18
Pifer, George _____ 297
Pilgrimage, made by Jacob Scherer and Robert J. Miller _____ 71
Pickering, Miss Carrie _____ 110
Pine Grove, Roanoke Co. 204, 206, 320
Pine Church, Shen. Co. 10, 11, 16, 17, 46, 49, 221, 222
Piney Grove _____ 191
Pine Hill _____ 49
Pine Hills _____ 60
Pioneers, The Old (Poem) _____ 31
Pittman, Lawrence _____ 100
Pittsylvania County _____ 203
Pleasant Hill, Smyth Co. 115, 236, 238, 243, 244, 246, 250
Plehn, Rev. H. E. _____ 283
Pleasant View _____ 157, 158
Po, Balthaser _____·___ 5
Pocahontas _____ 261
Poff, Rev. H. E. 149, 173, 193, 356
Poffenbarger, Rev. R. S. 149, 221, 356

PAGES

Point Pleasant _____ 16, 54, 93, 220
Points, James _____ 110
Polig, August _____ 112
Polytechnic Institute, N. M. __ 129, 303
Poor Valley _____ 167
Poor Valley, Tazewell Co. _____ 238
Poplar Grove _____ 253
Portsmouth, First Church 112, 113, 194
Potomac River _____ 98, 99, 254
Powder Springs, Shen. Co. 129, 226, 227
Powell's Fort _____ 8, 64, 225
Powlas, Miss Maude _____ 329
Prayer, Week of _____ 326
Preisch, Conrad _____ 41
Preisch, Augustine _____ 41
Preisch, Heinrich _____ 25
Presbyterian _____ 201
Prial (Broyles), John _____ 2
Price, Jacob _____ 92
Price's Fork, Parish _____ 190, 191
Prince William County _____ 68, 173
Printz, Church _____·____ 198
Prinz, George _____ 3, 84, 87, 91
Probst, Adam _____ 27
Probst, Rev. L. K. 277, 278, 336, 337
Probst, W. J. _____ 147
Proctor, Rev. E. G. ____ 182, 257, 344
Protzman, Miss Sallie _____ 329
Prufer, Frank _____ 110
Publications _____ 309
Publication, Religious, Considered _ 98
Puffenberger, Rev. S. H. _____ 281
Pulaski _____ 193, 203
Pugh, Joseph _____·___ 6

Quaker Church _____ 248

Rader _____ 214, 215
Rader's Church 125, 126, 128, 215, 218
Rader's Church, Founders of _____ 11
Rader's Church (Old Röders) 49, 52, 64
Rader, Rev. A. 137, 269, 271, 272, 279, 280, 351
Rader, Rev. D. M. K. _____ 173
Rader, G. E. _____ 168
Rader, Geo. W. _____ 22, 168, 292
Rader, Isaac _____ 27
Rader, Rev. J. K. ____ 236, 243, 348
Radford _____ 193
Radford Parish _____ 190, 193
Rahn, Rev. S. S. ____ 193, 252, 349
Raymey, P. _____ 182
Raymey, J. _____ 182
Ramsey, Mrs. Sarah _____ 21
Rapidan _____ 187
Rausch, Daniel _____ 92
Rausch, Jacob _____ 16, 84, 86, 89
Rausch, John (John Adam) __ 10, 16

PAGES

Rausch, Johannes _____ 84
Rausch, Henry _____ 16, 222
Rebenach, Rev. J. C. 89, 90, 255, 257
Reck, Rev. Abraham 69, 94-97, 178,
   179, 235, 258
Reck, John _____ 65
Redeemer, Church of Bristol _____ 266
Redemptioners, Lutheran _____ 2
Red Oak, Bland Co. _____ 167
Reed Creek _____ 52, 246
Reedy Creek _____ 261
Reformed Church 4, 24, 40, 52, 86, 87,
   156-159, 167, 185, 188, 189, 201,
   211-214, 221-226, 233, 235, 246, 252,
   258, 261, 272
Register of Congregations and Officers
   as of 1809 _____ 90-92
Rehoboth Schoolhouse _____ 209
Reider, Adam _____ 11
Reil, Peter _____ 90
Reimensnyder, Rev. G. H. 95, 98, 102-
   104, 159, 213, 283, 343
Reimensnyder, Rev. J. B. _____ 105
Reimensnyder, Rev. J. G. 159, 160, 343
Reimenschneider, Rev. J. J. 104, 106, 211
Reinhart, Michael _____ 21, 91
Reisch, John _____ 41
Reitenauer _____ 8
Renner, John _____ 272
Repass Family _____ 24
Repass (Rabatz), Rev. Daniel 23, 24, 52,
   246
Repass, Daniel, Jr. _____ 24
Repass, Rev. E. A. 156, 162, 218, 221,
   253, 302, 346
Repass, Mrs. E. A. _____ 332
Repass, Frederick _____ 24
Repass, John _____ 24
Repass, Rev. J. C. 118, 171, 172, 173,
   184, 243-249, 252, 253, 348
Repass, Rev. S. A. 119, 120, 163, 205,
   253, 303, 346, 348
Repass, Samuel _____ 24
Repass, Rufus _____ 24
Repentance and Thanksgiving, Day
Repentance and Prayer, Day of __ 89
   of _____ 94
Reuss, C. F. _____ 282
Rex, E. _____ 112
Rexrode, J. H. _____ 175
Rhodes, Frank _____ 15
Rhodes, Rev. C. K. 129, 149, 189, 213,
   214, 302, 353, 355
Rhodes, Rev. Geo. H. 113, 147, 193,
   204, 245, 246, 250, 278, 280, 350
Rhudy, Rev. Stephen 115, 116, 121, 166,
   239, 348
Rhyne, Rev. Hugh J. _____ 236, 356

PAGES

Rice, F. E. _____ 303
Rice, Rev. C. J. 146, 204, 223, 252,
   351, 354
Rich Valley Church, Wash. Co., Va. 265
Richard, Rev. Asa 145, 150, 159, 180,
   183, 229, 345
Richard, Rev. H. F. _____ 169, 281
Richard, Henry P. _____ 181, 182
Richard, Rev. J. J. 181, 228, 258, 259,
   344
Richard, Rev. J. W. _____ 183
Richard, Rev. J. H. 146, 183, 245, 246,
   351, 354
Richard, Rev. M. G. _____ 183
Richard, Rev. R. R. _____ 183
Richardson, Rev. X. J. 156, 159, 200,
   210, 258, 259, 297, 344, 346
Richter, Peter _____ 271
Richmond _____ 29, 110, 119
Richmond, 1st Lutheran Ch. _____ 185
Richmond, Mission Established 110, 112
Ridenour, Rev. W. L. _____ 281
Ridenhour, Rev. V. C. _____ 278, 352
Ridninger, Samuel _____ 25
Riede, Jacob _____ 23
Riede, John _____ 92, 184
Rieder, Adam _____ 215
Riley, James _____ 27
Rileyville _____ 200
Rinker _____ 8
Rinker, Jacob _____ 226
Rio, W. Va. _____ 258
Riser, Rev. M. C. _____ 352
Riser, Rev. G. A. _____ 159, 346
Riser, Rev. S. T. _____ 163, 346
Riser, Rev. Y. von A. _____ 164, 347
Riser, Rev. W. H. 170, 194, 195, 229,
   259, 346, 351
Risch, Charles _____ 41
Risch, Col. _____ 84
Risch, Jacob _____ 41
Risch, John _____ 18, 41, 84, 95
Ritenour, John _____ 8
Ritenour, E. H. _____ 113
Ritchie, Rev. E. L. 145, 160, 164, 238,
   266, 347, 350
Ritchie, Mrs. E. L. _____ 334
Ritchie, Rev. W. W. J. 145, 156, 159,
   160, 162, 215, 249, 347, 350
Rixey, Samuel _____ 175
Roanoke _____ 119, 206
Roanoke College 106, 109, 120, 155,
   169, 288, 289, 291, 292
Roanoke County _____ 167, 204
Roanoke County Churches _____ 169
Roanoke County Parish _____ 204
Roanoke Women's College _____ 298
Robinson River _____ 2, 187

PAGES

Rochelle, Madison Co. _____ 14, 189
Rockbridge Co. _____ 21, 91, 208
Rockey, Rev. C. H. _____ 256, 346
Rockingham Co. 13, 15, 20, 22, 38, 91,
  101, 107
Rockingham Parish _____ 210, 212
Roder's Church, see Rader
Rodeffer, George (Rodeheaver) __ 27
Rodgers, Rev. J. B. 137, 269, 271, 272,
  275, 280, 352
Roedel, Rev. W. D. 237, 252, 294, 348
Roehm, Rev. L. J. _____ 282
Roger, Michael _____ 5
Rohr, Johannes _____ 84
Roler's Church, Sul. Co. _____ 263
Roler, Martin _____ 27,·263
Roller, Mr. _____ 84
Roller, Johannes _____ 21
Roller, Gen. J. E. _____ 195, 200
Roller, Martin _____ 4, 235
Roller, John _____ 11, 86, 87, 89, 91
Roof, Rev. W. H. 140, 147, 262, 272,
  352
Rotenhaffer, Samuel _____ 91
Rother, Casper _____ 23, 92
Rose, Rev. C. A. _____ 172, 173, 349
Rosenbaum's Chapel _____ 247
Rosenbaum _____ 236
Rosenbaum, M. _____ 237
Rosenbaum, John _____ 185
Rosenbaum, Stephen _____ 247
Rosenbaum, Rev. R. G. 238, 345, 349
Rosenberger _____ 180
Rosenberger, Paul _____ 233
Rosenberg, Rev. J. S. _____ 344
Royer, Rev. P. L. 145, 223, 261, 347,
  354
Rubberd, Johannes _____ 11
Rubbert, John _____ 93
Rude, Rev. Anders Rudolph 107, 200,
  223, 225, 292, 297, 344
Rude's Hill _____ 107, 221
Rudebush, Rev. Emanuel _____ 200
Rudibush, Emanuel _____ 21, 156
Rudolph, Elijah _____ 180
Ruhlman, Christian _____ 92
Ruhlman, Christian, Jr. _____ 92
Runkle, Jeremiah _____ 156
Runkle, Jacob _____ 161
Runyon, I. Sears _____ 308
Ruppert, Henry _____ 91
Rural Retreat _____ 295, 322
Rural Retreat Parish _____ 243
Rural Male and Female Academy 245,
  300
Rusmiselle, Rev. W. 164, 179, 180, 228,
  235, 259, 344
Rusmiselle, David _____ 21

PAGES

Russell, William _____ 3
Ruth, Madison Co. _____ 189
Ruth, Jacob _____ 51, 53
Ruthrauf, Johannes _____ 26
Ruthrauf, Wilhelm _____ 25

Sackman, Martin _____ 97
Sadtler, Rev. W. A. _____ 350
Salem _____ 15, 109, 119, 291
Salem Church, Aug. Co. _____ 158
Salem Church, Cocke Co. ____ 269, 270
Salem, Parish, Aug. Co. _____ 157
Salem, Shen. Co. _____ 226
Salyards, Joseph _____ 303
Santmires, Geo. F. _____ 307
Sauer, Balthaser _____ 3, 86, 198
Sauer, Frederich _____ 91, 95
Sauer, Geo. _____ 25
Sauer, Heinrich _____ 25
Sauer, Rev. O. A. _____ 282
Saumsville _____ 232
Savage, Abraham _____ 13
Sayford, Rev. Sam 106, 115, 117, 118,
  168, 173, 205, 343, 347
Schaeffer, Rev. C. F. _____ 313
Schäfer, Daniel (f) _____ 21, 91
Schaeffer, Rev. D. F. _____ 95, 96, 97
Schaeffer, Frederick _____ 27
Schäfer, George _____ 11
Schaeffer, Rev. H. B. __ 141, 267, 352
Schaeffer, John _____ 23
Schaeffer, Peter _____ 296
Schaeffer, Rev. J. M. _____ 79
Schaeffer, Rev. Solomon 118, 173, 183,
  184, 190, 191, 192, 343, 348
Schaeffer, Rev. W. C., Sr. 79, 140, 141,
  266, 273, 275, 277, 345, 352
Schaeffer, Mrs. W. C. __ 143, 331, 333
Schaeffer, Rev. W. C., Jr. _____ 266
Schaidt, Rev. J. G. _____ 137, 352
Sheets, Jacob _____ 94
Scheible, George _____ 2, 36
Schenk, John _____ 91
Schenk, Jacob _____ 91
Scherers _____ 25
Scherer Family _____ 70-73
Scherer, Rev. Daniel 25, 70, 73, 93, 168,
  204, 244
Scherer, Frederick _____ 70
Scherer, Rev. Gideon 25, 72, 114-119,
  168, 205, 247, 253, 348
Scherer, Rev. J. A. B. 109, 121, 166,
  324, 349
Scherer, Rev. Jacob D. ____ ____ 70
Scherer, Rev. Jacob 25, 70, 71, 72, 114,
  116, 167, 168, 172, 236, 244, 247,
  249, 252, 347

PAGES

Scherer, Rev. J. J., Sr. 25, 72, 120, 121, 142, 236, 237, 253, 294, 296, 320, 321, 323, 348
Scherer, Mrs. J. J., Sr. _____ 322
Scherer, Rev. J. J., Jr. 72, 145, 187, 238, 347, 354
Scherer, Rev. L. P. _____ 349
Scherer, Miss May _____ 72, 325, 327
Scherer, Rev. M. G. G. 72, 211, 215, 224, 345
Scherer, Rev. W. J. D. _____ 232, 347
Scherer, Rev. Simeon 25, 72, 118, 120, 183, 253, 348
Scherretz, C. M. _____ 26
Scheuerer, Martin _____ 92
Schierman, Mr. _____ 91
Schillinger, George _____ 41
Schirmer, Gotwald _____ 84
Schlatter, Rev. Michael _____ 235
Schlosser, Christopher _____ 26
Schmal, Jacob _____ 90
Schmitt _____ 8
Schmidt, Louis _____ 91
Schmidt, Thomas _____ 5
Schmidt, Rev. _____ 213
Schmidt, Rev. C. Z. H. 77, 263, 270, 271, 272, 275, 278, 279, 280
Schmogrow, Rev. W. (J. W. S.) 111, 282, 344
Schmucker Family _____ 65
Schmucker, Rev. B. M. 69, 254, 255, 344
Schmucker, Rev. George 125, 126, 127, 128, 281
Schmucker, Ferdinand _____ 10
Schmucker, Rev. J. Nic. 8, 66, 89, 90-97, 99, 100, 101, 103, 104, 105, 125, 220, 223, 225, 226, 227, 231, 232, 281, 343
Schmucker, John Christopher ____ 7, 8
Schmucker, Rev. John Geo. 8, 65, 84, 88
Schmucker, Rev. John Peter 8, 66, 93, 94, 95, 96, 231, 281
Schmucker, Jacob _____ 91, 94
Schmucker, Rev. S. S. 65, 98, 220, 221, 223
Schnaudigel, Peter _____ 90
Schnebely, Jacob _____ 23
Schnebely, Johannes _____ 23
Schneble, John _____ 92
Schneider, John _____ 92
Schneider, Martin _____ 41
Schnell, Rev. Leonard _____ 190
School Buildings _____ 291, 293
School Teachers, Conduct Funerals 88
School, 1st to be established _____ 38
Schools, Private _____ 289
Schools for Young Women _____ 293
Schoenberg, Rev. J. A. C. _____ 249

PAGES

Scholl, Nicolas _____ 90
Schott, Philip _____ 90
Schrack, Nicolaus _____ 5
Schramm, Mr. _____ 18
Schreckhise, Rev. J. M. _____ 20
Schreiber, Rev. O. L. _____ 170, 351
Schroder, Rev. H. A. _____ 203
Schuler, Michael _____ 21
Schultz, John _____ 5
Schulz, Rev. John Christian _____ 36
Schumacker, Christian _____ 5
Schwarbach, Rev. John (Johanas) 34, 39, 41, 188, 195, 212, 213, 258, 283
Scotch-Irish __ 19-20, 21, 22, 23, 208
Scottsville _____ 282
Scott Co. _____ 26
Scull, Rev. Wm. _____ 160, 189, 343
Seabrook, Rev. W. L. _____ 178, 346
Seagle, Rev. H. L. _ 275, 276, 277, 352
Seawright Springs _____ 157
Seay, Henry L. _____ 302
Seckinger, Rev. E. K. _____ 166
Sechrist, Mr. _____ 92
Secrist, Rev. Andrew _____ 236
Seegers, Rev. J. C. 187, 210, 346, 352
Seibert _____ 8
Seibert, Henry _____ 90
Seidel, Rev. W. C. _____ 261
Seidler, Rev. P. E. ____ 148, 243, 355
Seiss, Rev. J. A. 69, 107, 108, 162, 216, 217, 255, 343
Self Denial, Week of _____ 326
Selzer, Matthias _____ 3
Senaker, John _____ 27
Sendmeier, John _____ 92
Seneker, Rev. Joseph _____ 263
Seneker, Rev. J. A. 135, 263, 272, 351
Seneker, Rev. J. E. 126, 127, 189, 213, 232, 283, 353
Settlemeyer, Rev. W. H. __ 163, 345
Seventh Day Adventists _____ 25, 190
Sevier, John _____ 13
Shaeffer, Frederick _____ 272
Shaffer, Catherine _____ 198
Shaffer, Edgar _____ 175
Shaffer, F. P. _____ 175
Shaffer, Henry (1) _____ 175
Shaffer, Henry (2) _____ 198
Shaffer, Jacob (1) _____ 27
Shaffer, Jacob (2) _____ 198
Shaffer, Rev. Jacob M. 135, 263, 275, 277, 351
Shaner, Geo. B. _____ 21, 209
Shank, Jacob _____ 125
Shantz, Rev. E. _____ 210
Sharon, Bland Co. (Wythe) ____ 115
Sharon Church _____ 165
Sharon Springs _____ 167

PAGES

Shaver, Peter _____ 22
Shealey, Rev. J. A. 148, 210, 239, 241, 271, 272, 347, 355
Shealey (Sheele), Rev. H. F. 163, 346
Shealy, Rev. P. E. 146, 228, 249, 355
Shelly, Isaac _____ 26
Sheetz, Marshall _____ 157
Sheetz, G. _____ 123
Sheetz, Mill _____ 232
Sheffey, J. W. _____ 296
Shenandoah Caverns _____ 151
Shenandoah Co., 38, 90, 99, 104, 107, 218
Shenandoah Lutheran Institute ___ 301
Shenandoah National Park _____ 198
Shenandoah Parish _____ 200
Shenandoah County Parish _____ 228
Shenandoah Publishing House, Inc. 315
Shenandoah Valley _____ 3, 43
Shenk, Rev. E. A. 162, 164, 169, 202, 240, 241, 346
Shenk, Rev. J. E. 20, 162, 163, 164, 193, 194, 202, 240, 346
Shenk, Wm. J. _____ 199
Shenk, John _____ 199
Shepherd, Rev. J. W. S. 160, 210, 246, 345, 349
Shepherdstown _____ 63, 90, 254
Shepperson, Rev. Wm. __ 181, 259, 343
Shepperson, Rev. C. M. _____ 344
Shickel, Rev. Peter 156, 159, 168, 205, 211, 212, 343, 348
Shiloh _____ 191
Shipp, Phoebe _____ 110
Shirey, George _____ 159
Shirey, Rev. J. D. 20, 156, 165, 173, 345, 348
Showalter, Rev. Daniel _____ 20
Showalter, Wm. J. _____ 20
Shreckhise, Rev. J. M. 156, 159, 160, 165, 200, 209, 210, 344
Shryock, George _____ 97
Shuey, Rev. Geo. E. 156, 165, 187, 211, 215, 218, 345, 349
Shuey, George 21, 110, 155, 291, 292
Shuey, Rev. J. W. 130, 145, 160, 165, 194, 195, 209, 273, 346, 354
Shuey, Rev. Theo. Geo. ____ 149, 355
Shugart, Michael _____ 14
Shuler, Michael _____ 91
Shulers _____ 3
Shumate, Rev. A. J. 149, 156, 165, 356
Shumate, Rev. A. R. 149, 160, 165, 356
Shutz, Dora _____ 157
Shutz, Josiah _____ 157
Shutters, Jonathan _____ 125
Sibold, Miss Chloe _____ 327
Sibole, Rev. E. E. _____ 205, 235, 348

PAGES

Sibole, Rev. J. L. _____ 235
Sibole, Rev. L. M. 180, 228, 235, 257, 259, 345
Sibert, Daniel _____ 125
Sibert, Rev. W. M. _____ 281
Sieber, Casper _____ 49
Sieber, Rev. J. Luther 146, 207, 307, 350, 354
Sieg, Paul, Sr. _____ 21, 110
Sieg, Rev. Paul 149, 156, 165, 193, 203, 210, 252, 266, 299, 307, 346, 349, 354
Sigmon, Rev. P. C. _____ 166
Sizer, D. L. T. _____ 169
Silver Grove Church, Sul. Co. ___ 264
Sinking Springs Church _____ 279
Sinking Creek _____ 183
Simon, John _____ 92
Simmons, S. F. _____ 306
Simon, Rev. W. V. ___ 149, 256, 356
Skyles, Henry _____ 102
Slaves _____ 159, 161, 188
Slemp's Creek _____ 237
Sloop, Rev. H. E. H. 18, 133, 140, 143, 145, 169, 181, 213, 214, 215, 259, 269, 271, 272, 347, 352, 354
Sloop, Rev. Wm. G. ____ 236, 243, 348
Slovak, Lutheran Church _____ 282
Sluss, D. _____ 123
Sluss Massacre _____ 166
Slusser, Mrs. Virginia _____ 322
Smelser, John _____ 27
Smeltzer, Rev. J. P. 205, 256, 257, 344, 348
Smith, A. D. _____ 146
Smith, Rev. A. M. ____ 229, 259, 345
Smith, Rev. C. J. 148, 149, 235, 293, 355
Smith, Rev. E. B. 147, 169, 183, 266, 271, 272, 352, 355
Smith, Rev. Frisby D. _____ 110, 183
Smith, Rev. G. M. _____ 235
Smith, John (Greene Co.) _____ 27
Smith, John (Washington Co.) __ 27
Smith, J. E. B. _____ 190
Smith, Rev. J. Few ____ 178, 182, 344
Smith, Mrs. J. L. _____ 334
Smith, Rev. J. L. 146, 166, 218, 249, 266, 347, 350, 354
Smith, Rev. J. W. _____ 173, 346
Smith, Rev. L. L. 156, 180, 233, 240, 257, 345
Smith, Miss Mary P. _____ 305
Smith, Michael _____ 2, 36, 188
Smith, Uncle Sammy _____ 192
Smith, Rev. S. R. _____ 191, 243, 348
Smith, Rev. W. J. 181, 207, 257, 346, 349
Smith Creek _____ 17

PAGES

Smithfield _____ 257
Smyth Co. _____ 74, 185, 236, 237
Snarr, John _____ 9
Snapp, C. W. _____ 146
Snapp, Rev. D. E. _____ 232
Snapp, Laurence _____ 4, 6, 235
Snapp, Martin _____ 180
Snapp, Rev. P. L. 129, 145, 156, 160,
  198, 249, 281, 349, 353, 354
Snyder, Rev. C. C. _____ 212
Snyder, Daniel _____ 201
Snyder, Henry _____ 2
Snyder, H. L. _____ 146
Snyder, Rev. J. A. 165, 221, 223, 224,
  231, 233, 235, 345
Snyder, J. O. _____ 146
Snyder, Rev. R. D. 148, 150, 159, 162,
  193, 256, 355
Soloman's Ch., Shen. Co. 11, 16, 91, 93,
  127, 221-223
Solomon's Church, Tenn. _____ 271
Solomon's Schoolhouse _____ 219
Solomon's Temple _____ 184
Somers, Geo. A. _____ 15
Sommer, Peter _____ 11
Sommers, Rebecca C. _____ 14
Sondhaus, Rev. Martin 124, 281, 353
Souders, Josiah _____ 125
Souder, Philip _____ 11
Souer, Balthaser _____ 86
Sours _____ 202
Sours, George _____ 198
Sours, John _____ 198
Sours, Simon _____ 198
Sours, William _____ 15
South Fork _____ 265
Southview (Roanoke Co.) _____ 204
Southern Lutheran Seminary __ 117, 120
South View Home _____ 120
Sowers, Philip _____ 115
Sowers, Rev. R. R. 148, 166, 172, 173,
  191, 280, 350, 352, 355
Sox, Rev. C. J. _____ 172, 350
Spader's Church _____ 213
Spangler, Jacob _____ 166
Spangler, Mr. _____ 23
Spangler, Peter _____ 246
Spangler, Solomon _____ 27
Spanish American War _____ 240
Speagle, Rev. F. M. 129, 131, 132, 222,
  223, 353
Speedwell _____ 248
Sperry, Jacob _____ 5
Spicard, Henry _____ 169
Spickert, Henry _____ 22
Spickert, Julius _____ 5
Spickert, Philip _____ ____ 22, 53
Spiegel, Lawrence _____ 87-88, 91

PAGES

Spiggle, Rev. G. W. 146, 156, 184, 224,
  251, 346, 349, 354
Spiggle, J. L. _____ 168
Spiggle, Philip _____ 22
Spindler, Rev. Adolph 64, 84, 86, 90,
  155, 156
Spitler, George _____ 161
Spott, Albert _____ 282
Spott, Carl _____ 282
Spottswood, Governor A. ___ 1, 2, 187
Spracher (Spraker), Christopher 23, 246
Spracher, Rev. L. B. 172, 184, 239, 266,
  350, 352
Sprecher, Christophel _____ 92
Sprecher, Stephen _____ 114
Sprecher, Rev. Samuel _____ 255
Spring Valley, Rockbridge Co. ____ 210
St. Andrew's, Wythe Co. _____ 248
St. David's, Shen. Co. _____ 224, 225
St. Jacob's, Bot. Co. _____ 168
St. Jacob's (Bethany, Spader's)
  Rockingham Co. _____ 213
St. Jacob's, Shen. Co. _____ 224, 226
St. James', Augusta Co. 157, 158, 159,
  211, 212
St. James' (Zion)—St. James', Au-
  gusta Co. _____ 160
St. James' Church, Greene Co.,
  Tennessee _____ 269, 270
St. James', Hardy Co. _____ 259
St. James', Jefferson Co. ___ 256, 257
St. James', Page Co. 129, 195, 200, 202
St. James' (Cedar Creek), Shen. Co. 180,
  181
St. James' (Mt. Jackson), Shen. Co. 223,
  224
St. James', Smyth Co. _____ 236, 242
St. James', Vinton _____ 207, 208
St. John's, Augusta Co. (Luth. and
  Ref.) _____ 65, 155
St. John's, Fred. Co. __ 180, 181, 183
St. John's, Luth. and Ref., Gray-
  son County _____ 185
St. John's Ev. Luth. Ch., Phila., Pa. 48
St. John's, Knoxville _____ 141, 277
St. John's, Rock'h. Co. _____ 214
St. John's (Timberville), Rocking-
  ham Co. _____ 129, 216
St. John's, Wythe Co. 23, 74, 114, 115,
  171, 251
St. Joseph's, Fred. Co. _____ 182
St. Luke's Ch., Culp. Co. 15, 130, 173,
  175
St. Luke's Ch. (St. William's), Page
  County _____ 200, 201, 202
St. Luke's Church, Shen. Co. __ 228, 229
St. Luke's Church, Wythe Co. 252, 253
St. Mark's, Augusta Co. ____ 160, 161

PAGES

St. Mark's, Botetourt Co. ___ ___ 168
St. Mark's, Mont. Co. _____ 191, 192
St. Mark's, Luray, Va. 133, 195, 199, 298
St. Mark's, Richmond _____ 112
St. Mark's, Roanoke 144, 204, 206, 207
St. Mark's, Shen. Co. _____ 219, 221
St. Mark's (Cullop's, St. Matthew's) Smyth Co. _____ _____ 74, 248
St. Mark's, Wythe Co. _____ 252
St. Mary's Church, Monroe Co., Tennessee _____ 275
St. Mary's Church, Shen. Co. ____ 221
St. Martin's Church, Shen. Co. 219, 221
St. Matthew's, Bland Co. _____ 166
St. Matthew's (Toms Brook), Shen. County _____ 233
St. Matthew's (Davidsburg), New Market _____ 17, 218, 219, 333
St. Matthew's, Smyth Co. _____ 237, 248
St. Michael's, Bridgewater ___ 67, 157
St. Michael's, Mont. Co. _____ 190
St. Michael's, N. C. _____ 114
St. Paul's (Mt. Solon), Augusta Co. 124, 165, 212, 214
St. Paul's, Fred. Co. _____ 180
St. Paul's, Giles Co. _____ 183, 184
St. Paul's, Greensburg _____ 254
St. Paul's Church, Monroe Co. __ 276
St. Paul's, Page Co. _____ 200, 201
St. Paul's, Roanoke Co. _____ 208
St. Paul's, Rock'h. Co. _____ 216
St. Paul's (Jerome), Shen. Co. 226, 227
St. Paul's, Strasburg _____ 235
St. Paul's, Wythe Co. 23, 74, 115, 166, 243, 244, 248, 253
St. Peter's (Churchville) _____ 156
St. Peter's, Hardy Co., W. Va. 258, 259
St. Peter's, Mont. Co. (old, new) 76, 77, 190, 204
St. Peter's, Page Co. _____ 200
St. Peter's, Rock'h Co. (old) 39, 64, 200
St. Peter's, Shen. Co. _____ 200, 232
St. Peter's, Shepherdstown __ 254, 255
St. Peter's, Wythe Co. __ 115, 247, 253
St. Stephen's, Shen. Co. ____ 132, 233
St. William's, Page Co. (St. Luke) 201
Staehlin, Rev. G. F. 106, 201, 225, 226, 343
Stahler, Rev. W. E. 194, 223, 243, 343
Staley's Creek _____ 237
Stanley _____ 200
Stanley Hall _____ 303
Stanger, Rev. John _____ 77, 190, 247
Star, Henry _____ 167
Statler, Jacob _____ 22
Stattler, Jacob _____ 91

Staubus, Christian _____ 21
Stauffer, Jacob _____ 4
Stauffer, W. T. _____ 113, 146, 241
Staufferstadt _____ 4
Staunton _____ 21, 91, 107, 110, 220
Staunton Female Sem. _____ 297, 298
Staunton Parish _____ 162, 163
Stautemeier, Johannes _____ 21
Steck, Rev. C. F., Sr. 130, 148, 164, 355
Steck, Rev. C. F., Jr., 146, 235, 261, 278, 308, 351
Steffey, Rev. S. D. 169, 243, 253, 262, 265, 349, 352
Steffey, S. D. _____ 147
Steffy, Michael _____ 23
Steigle, Jacob _____ 14
Stephan, Peter _____ 4
Stephensburg _____ 4
Stephens City 4, 60, 95, 178, 179, 240
Stephenson, Miss Maggie M. ____ 9
Stevens, H. C. _____ 296
Stickley, Daniel _____ 10
Stickley, Rev. V. R. 160, 184, 210, 228, 345, 348
Stigelman, Philip _____ 25
Stirewalt, Prof. W. J. _____ 68, 302
Stirewalt, Rev. Quintus Spener 68, 125
Stirewalt, Rev. Paul J. _____ 67
Stirewalt, Rev. M. L. ___+_____ 68
Stirewalt, Rev. Julius L. 67, 123, 124, 126, 303, 353
Stirewalt, Rev. John N., Sr. ____ 67
Stirewalt, Rev. John N., Jr. 68, 128, 189, 198-202, 232, 233, 353
Stirewalt, Capt. John _____ 67, 68
Stirewalt, Rev. J. P. 68, 128, 131, 175, 216, 218, 222, 223, 225, 226, 227, 228, 233, 353, 355
Stirewalt, Rev. Jacob 68, 122, 124, 125, 128, 198, 201, 202, 211, 219, 222, 223, 225, 226, 353
Stirewalt, Rev. A. J. 68, 129, 202, 333
Stock (Stockus), Rev. V. G. C. 84, 213
Stoever, Rev. Christian _____ 200
Stoever, Rev. John Casper, Sr. ____ 36
Stoever, Rev. John Casper, Jr. 36, 188
Stoltz, John Michael _____ 2
Stomback, David _____ 199
Stomback, George _____ 198
Stoneberger Church _____ 201
Stoneberger, Frederick _____ 201
Stone's Chapel _____ 60, 257
Stony Creek, Craig Co. ____ 183, 184
Stony Man Parish _____ 195
Stony Run, Page Co. _____ 201
Stony Creek, Shen. Co. __ 11, 48, 224
Stork, Rev. Theo. 106, 178, 257, 343
Stoudemayer, Rev. G. A. 149, 260, 356

PAGES

Stoudemire, G. W. _____ 147
Stoudemire, Rev. Wm. _____ 184, 349
Stover, Frederick _____ 6
Streit, Christian, Sr. _____ 56
Streit, Rev. Christian:
  Army Service _____ 57
  School _____ 59
  Monument _____ _____ 61
  Life Sketch ____ _____ 56-61
  Va. Conference _____ 82, 93
  Pastor 178, 179, 181, 212, 213, 235,
    257, 258
Streit, John Leonhard _____ 56
Strickler, Rev. J. W. 160, 162, 166, 172,
  180, 189, 211, 215, 243, 257, 346, 349
Strickler, Rev. L. W. __ 149, 194, 355
Strole, O. S. _____ 210
Strouse, Peter _____ 21, 155
Studebaker, Rev. E. 166, 244, 246, 249,
  349
Styne, G. W. _____ 168
Styne, C. L. _____ _____ 168
Sugar Grove Schoolhouse __ _____ 265
Sullivan Co., Tenn. 26, 27, 28, 78, 261-
  264
Suman, Rev. J. J. 159, 160, 162, 165,
  211, 217, 257, 344
Summers, David _____ _____ 21
Summers, Rev. J. _____ 181, 224, 344
Summitt, Eusebius _____ 27
Summitt, Rev. J. H. 137, 269, 276, 352
Surface, Michael _____ _____ 190
Swank, Mr. _____ 20
Swaney, Rev. Dennis _____ 202
Swaney, Rev. W. H. 126, 128, 202, 226,
  227, 303, 353
Swartz, David _____ 10
Swartz, George _____ 9
Swartz, Rev. Joel 122, 123, 124, 125,
  233, 234, 353
Swartz, Rev. W. P. _____ 322, 333
Swinehardt, Rev. T. S. _____ 283
Swope, Peter _____ 20
Synod, Concordia of Va. ____ 128, 216
Synod, General 97, 100, 101, 103, 104,
  106, 109, 254
Synod, Holston, Organized 133-135, 342
  Constitution _____ 136
  Doctrinal Basis _____ 136
  Educational 137, 139, 288, 289, 301,
    303
  Missions _____ 137, 140, 142
Synod, Joint Ohio 128, 218, 228, 232,
  281
Synod, Maryland 97, 98, 108, 254, 299,
  342, 358
Synod, Md. and Va. Organized 96, 97
  Gen. Synod _____ 98

PAGES

Southern Boundary _____ 97
Sent out Missionary _____ 76
Synod Merger _____ 144
Synod, Missouri 111, 128, 139, 155, 279,
  282, 283
Synod (Min.) of N. C. 35, 44, 66, 69,
  70, 73, 76, 78, 96, 115, 198, 201, 204,
  216, 247, 264, 342
Synod, United Evan. Luth. Syn. of
  N. C. _____ 130, 132, 342
Synod, United South 109, 121, 141, 187,
  193, 195, 204, 240
Synod (Min.) of New York _____ 105
Synod, E. Penna. _____ 104
Synod (Min. of Penna.) 34, 35, 38, 39,
  42, 44, 46, 49, 54, 56, 63, 66, 70, 74,
  75, 81, 85, 105, 188, 198
Synod, Evan. Luth. of Va.:
  Boundary Line _____ 117
  Centennial _____ 150, 151
  Church Publications _____ 101
  Conference Organized __ _____ 107
  Discouragements _____ 107
  Doctrinal Basis _____ 101
  Education in 108, 109, 288, 290, 297,
    298
  General Synod _____ 105, 106
  Mergers _____ 114
  Missions _____ 109, 113
  Organized _____ 99-104, 342
  Superintendent _____ 113
Synod, Evan. Luth. of S. W. Va.:
  Boundary _____ 117
  Constitution _____ 116
  Education in _____ 120, 288, 291-300
  General Bodies _____ 120, 121
  Mergers _____ 121
  Missions _____ 119, 121
  Organized _____ 114-117, 172, 342
  Orphanage _____ 120
  Semi-Centennial _____ 121
Synod, Evan. Luth. of Tenn. 96, 122,
  130, 133, 134, 342
Synod, Luth. of Va. _____ 144-149
  Organized _____ 144
  Centennial _____ 149-151, 342
Synod, S. C. _____ 303
Synodical Lay Reader _____ 208
Synodical Monitor _____ 314

Tabler, Rev. J. T. 173, 179, 181, 191,
  252, 259, 343
Tanner, John _____ 2
Tanner, Michael _____ 2
Tayloe, George P. _____ 292
Taylor, Bayard _____ 63
Tazewell County _____ 238, 239
Teaford, Elijah _____ 21

PAGES

Teaford, Henry _____ 21, 209
Teaford, J. H. _____ 21, 209
Teaford, Thomas _____ 21
Tennessee Congregations _____ 261-280
Tenth Legion _____ 11
Terrys _____ 119, 206
Teufel, Rev. C. M. 113, 148, 163, 268, 355
Theiss, Jacob _____ 25
Theological Seminaries _____ 303
Theological Seminary in Tenn. ___ 78
Thom's Creek _____ 190
Thornburg, Rev. M. L. __ 137, 280, 351
Thomas, Henry _____ 27
Tidings _____ 327
Timber Ridge, Botetourt Co. ____ 168
Timber Ridge, Frederick Co. ____ 257
Timber Ridge, Tenn. _____ 279
Timberville Parish _____ 215
Tipton, John _____ 6
Tise, Rev. J. M. 146, 156, 169, 173, 205, 208, 228, 347, 350
Tolbert, Rev. _____ 238
Tobler, Mr. _____ 26
Tobler, Rev. A. F. 146, 172, 173, 181, 247, 351
Toms Brook _____ 233
Toms Brook Parish _____ 232
Tracey _____ 182
Trails, Indian _____ 3, 4
Trambauer, Andrew _____ 11
Tranbarger, Jacob _____ 26
Trautwein, Jacob _____ 5
Traut, Jacob _____ 41
Tressler, Rev. J. W. _____ 345
Trinity, Aug. Co. _____ 155, 282
Trinity, Buena Vista _____ 210
Trinity, Bridgewater _____ 211
Trinity, Botetourt County _____ 168
Trinity, Culpeper Co. 15, 130, 173, 177
Trinity Hall _____ 251, 300
Trinity, Hardy Co. _____ 259
Trinity, Norfolk _____ 282
Trinity, Newport News _____ 240
Trinity, Richmond _____ 187
Trinity, Rockingham Co. _____ 212
Trinity, Shenandoah Co. _____ 213
Trinity, Stephens City 178, 179, 182, 183
Trinity Church, Wytheville 250, 251, 253
Troutman, Rev. R. T. __ 149, 206, 356
Trout, Samuel _____ 21
Trout, Hon. John _____ 119, 206
Trout Run _____ 258
Tusing, Johannes _____ 11
Tusing, Mary M. _____ 15
Tussing, Michael _____ 15
Tussing, Moses _____ 125
Tussing, Philip _____ 11

PAGES

Tussing, Samuel _____ 14
Turner, Rev. J. H. 80, 137, 208, 348, 351
Tutwiler, Adley _____ 15
Tyler, Gov. Hoge _____ 193

Ulrich, Rev. J. _____ 231, 343
Umberger, Alex _____ 166
Umberger, Mrs. Catherine Cox __ 305
Umberger, Rev. J. B. _____ 253, 349
Umberger, Rev. K. Y. 145, 160, 239, 247, 252, 253, 261, 263, 266, 347, 350, 354
Umlauf, Jacob _____ 113
Umstadt, Peter _____ 92
Unaca Mountains _____ 269
Union Church _____ 65, 202
Union, Botetourt Co. _____ 115, 118
Union Church, Rock'h. Co. __ 212, 216
Union Church, Wash. Co., Tenn __ 279
Union Church, Sul. Co. _____ 261
Utt, W. L. _____ 26, 171
Utt, Rev. J. D. 146, 169, 172, 173, 207, 208, 350
Utz, Anna Sybella _____ 5
Utz, Daniel _____ 91, 95
Utz, George _____ 2
Utz, J. _____ 189
Uvilla _____ 257

Van Meter, John _____ 4
Van Meter, Isaac _____ 4
Vance, Samuel _____ 27
Vauhuss, Valentine _____ 296
Vasdesslord, Rev. F. W. _____ 201
Vaught, Henry _____ 246
Venerable, Abraham _____ 110
Vicars _____ 192
Villa Heights _____ 119, 207
Virginia (Classical) Collegiate Institute _____ 108, 109, 119, 120, 155
Virginia Heights, Roanoke __ 119, 207
Virginia Lutheran _____ 314
Virginia, Synod (See Synod)
Vivian _____ 261
Von Bora College _____ 199, 298

Wachter, Michael _____ 97
Wacker, Elias _____ 27, 52
Wade, Rev. P. J. 172, 173, 259, 346, 349
Wade, Rev. W. A. _____ 172, 173
Wahl, John _____ 25, 190
Wall's Schoolhouse _____ 191
Wagner, Rev. J. M. 79, 137, 275, 278, 351
Wagner, Rev. L. M. 80, 137, 279, 351
Wagner, Rev. Samuel __ 159, 160, 343

PAGES

Walker, J. F. _____ 184
Walker, Luther S. _____ 15
Walker, Robert J. _____ 15
Walker, R. S. _____ 273
Walker, S. T. _____ 15
Walters, Frank _____ 147, 339
Walther, Rev. C. F. W. _____ 282
Walther, Henry _____ 891
Walther, Rev. Martin 8, 75, 93, 94, 99,
  102, 168, 173, 204, 235, 343
Wampler, Michael _____ 23
War Interference, 1812 _____ 9?
Wardensville, W. Va. _____ 258
Ware, Mrs. Mary _____ 9
Warm Springs (Pembroke Springs) 60
Waring, Michael _____ 5
Warren County _____ 240
Wartburg Church _____ 238, 239
Wartburg Seminary _____ 239, 300
Wartman, John _____ 311
Warwick County _____ 240
Washington County, Va. 26, 236, 237,
  242
Washington County, Tenn. ____ 26, 78
Washington Declaration _____ 114
Washington, George _____ 8
Waynesboro _____ 18, 19
Waynesboro Parish _____ 163
Wayland, Adam _____ ?
Wayland, John W. (Ph.D.) _____ 40
Wayman, Mr. _____ 2
Wayman, Rev. B. C. 160, 161, 189, 345
Weakhouse, Edward _____ 175
Weaver, David _____ 15
Weaver, George _____ 248
Weaver, John _____ 2
Weaver, Rev. J. L. _____ 348
Weaver, Moses _____ 102, 103
Weber, Johannes _____ 25
Weber, Moses _____ 91
Weber, Peter _____ 35
Weddle _____ 171
Wehn, Henry _____ 110
Weiser, Conrad _____ 45
Weiser, Rev. Reuben __ 254, 255, 257
Weisgerber, Jacob _____ 26
Weiss, G. _____ 90
Weissling, Rev. G. F. _____ 239
Welch _____ 261
Weller, Heinrich _____ 5
Wells, S. C. _____ 179, 292
Welz, Daniel _____ 25
Wendel, Samuel _____ 5
Wenrich, Harrison D. _____ 15
Wentz, A. R. _____ 63, 98
Wertz, Rev. L. A. 149, 278, 280, 356
Wessinger, Rev. E. L. __ 129, 219, 353
Wessinger, Rev. J. C. __ 175, 275, 277

PAGES

Wessinger, Rev. J. S. 129, 226, 232,
  233, 234, 353
West Virginia Churches _____ 254-261
Wetzel, Christoph _____ 5
Wetzel, George _____ 124
Wetzel, Rev. Henry 120, 124, 126, 127,
  128, 175, 213, 214, 216, 225, 226,
  232, 233, 253, 281, 353
Wetzel, M. L. _____ 126
Weyman, Rev. _____ 255
Wheatland Church _____ 168
White, Jacob _____ 258
White Oak Run _____ 2, 187
White, Top _____ 237
Whitman, Rev. N. A. 173, 247, 252,
  349
Whiteman, Samuel _____ 27
Whitmer, J. C. _____ 175
Whitmer, Suffary _____ 15, 175
Wiegel, Carl H. _____ 240
Wike, Rev. P. C. 129, 175, 214, 225,
  226, 227, 232, 233, 234, 353
Wildbahn, Rev. Carl Friedrich 34, 43,
  177, 255
Wile, Rev. H. B. _____ 163
Wilhoit, Immanuel _____ 27
Wilhoit, J. H. _____ 147
Wilkins, R. A. _____ 175
William's Church _____ 201
Williams-Henson Home 280, 307, 308
Williams, L. E. _____ 280, 308
Williams, Rev. P. H. _____ 183
Williamson, L. B. _____ 169, 184
Williamson, T. L. _____ 303
Willis _____ 172
Willis, Rev. Jas. 163, 173, 180, 235,
  298, 345
Willey, Rev. Bernhard _____ 225
Willy, Rev. Leonard 52, 73, 244, 248
Wilson Aaron _____ 110
Wilson, Rev. J. H. _____ 306
Wilson, William _____ 110
Witt, Rev. E. C. _____ 278, 352
Winchester _____ 4, 5, 8, 60, 95, 177
Winchester, Church founded __ 4, 5, 58
Winchester, founders of Church __ 5
Windle, Catherine _____ 228
Windle, Jacob _____ 228
Wine, Daniel _____ 177
Winecoff, Rev. J. _____ 345
Winter, Rev. J. _____ 257
Wittig, Isaac _____ 15
Wittig, I. P. _____ 131
Wittig, Ulrich _____ 11
Wolford, George _____ 27
Wolford, Houston _____ 147
Wolford, Rev. W. G. 79, 265, 275,
  279, 351

PAGES

Wolfersberger, Rev. S. _____ 200, 344
Women and Mission Boards _____ 336
Women's Miss. Conf. U. S. S. 328, 330
Women's Miss. Soc., Sketch __ 317-338
Women's Miss. Soc., Evan. Luth.
  Syd., Va. _____ 331-334
Women's Miss. Society, Hol. Syd. 143,
  330
Women's Miss. Society, S. W. Va.
  Synod _____ 320-330
Women's Miss. Society, Luth. Synod
  of Va. _____ 331
Women's Miss. So. of U. L. C. A. 334
Women's Miss. Society of U. S. S.
  328-330
Woodroof, George _____ 2
Woodstock, 6, 9, 65, 66, 91, 93, 94, 99,
  107
Woodstock, Luth. Ch. and founders 6, 9
Woodstock Church Unfinished ____ 86
Woodstock Parish _____ 229
Worman, Rev. I. D. 145, 241, 256, 347,
  354
Worman, Mrs. I. D. _____ 334, 335
Wrangel, Dr. _____ 45, 56
Wyant, M. R. _____ 177
Wyrick, Rev. H. P. 146, 169, 191, 254,
  351, 355
Wyse, Rev. J. H. 156, 238, 347, 350
Wytheville _____ 24, 119, 120
Wytheville Female Seminary 286, 294
Wytheville Parish _____ 251
Wythe Co. _____ 22, 74, 92, 243
Wythe Courthouse _____ 23
Wythe County Parish _____ 252

Yager, Nicholas _____ 2
Yamanouchi, Rev. R. _____ 347
Yamanouchi, Rev. N. _____ 145, 347
Yeakley, Rev. Luther _____ 183
Yeakley, Rev. T. B. _____ 183, 199
Young, Rev. David _____ 83
Young Women's Work _____ 325
Yonce, Miss Ella _____ 322
Yonce, Miss Fannie __ 321, 322, 325
Yonce, Rev. C. N. A. 156, 191, 208,
  218, 346, 349
Yonce, Rev. W. B. ___ 203, 253, 348
Yost, Rev. J. L. _____ 266, 351
Young, Adam _____ 90
Young, John David 15, 63, 82, 84, 93
Young, Nicholas _____ 92

PAGES

Young, Jacob _____ 92
Young, Rev. J. G. _____ 255
Young, Rev. J. D. _____ 255, 257
Young, Rev. H. J. _____ 177
Young, R. F. _____ 275
Young, W. J. _____ 175
Yount, Rev. N. D. _____ 273
Yount, Rev. A. K. ____ 149, 203, 356
Yuenling, David G. _____ 112

Zanger, Jacob _____ 84, 211
Zehring, Matthias _____ 48
Zentmeyer, Johannes _____ 25
Zerfass, George _____ 92
Zerfass, Jacob _____ 11, 91
Zerfass, Michael _____ 25
Ziegler, Frederick _____ 200
Ziegler, Rev. Godfrey _____ 200
Ziegler, John _____ 200
Zink, Jacob ___ 48, 77, 264, 265, 272
Zink, Peter _____ 48
Zimmerman, Christopher (Carpen-
  ter) _____ 2
Zimmerman (See Carpenter) ___ 2, 61
Zimmerman, William (Carpenter) _ 2
Zimmerman, George _____ 41
Zimmerman, Joshua _____ 95
Zion Church _____ 25
Zion, Augusta Co. _____ 159
Zion, Botetourt Co. _____ 167
Zion's Hill _____ 169
Zion, Floyd Co. _____ 115, 172
Zion Church, Knox Co. _____ 276
Zion Roanoke _____ 115
Zion (New), Roanoke Co. _____ 204
Zion-St. James', Parish _____ 159
Zion, Shenandoah Co. _____ 223, 224
Zion, Sul. Co. _____ 135, 263
Zion, Wythe Co. _____ 115, 243, 246
Zipperer, Rev. D. W. 133, 149, 223, 355
Zirkle, Andrew _____ 11, 17, 49, 87
Zirkel Family _____ 17
Zirkel, George Adam (Zirkle) ___ 17
Zirkle, George _____ 95
Zirkle, John _____ 17, 102
Zirkle, J. D. _____ 303
Zirkle, Ludwig _____ 17
Zirkle, Lewis _____ 14, 17, 220
Zirkle, Louis _____ 91
Zirkle, Michael _____ 11, 17
Zirkle, Peter _____ 17
Zirkle Schoolhouse _____ 221

www.ingramcontent.com/pod-product-compliance
Lightning Source LLC
Chambersburg PA
CBHW072042020426
42334CB00017B/1362

* 9 7 8 0 8 0 6 3 5 4 4 4 6 *